Banks in Distress:
Lessons from the American Experience of the 1980s

International Banking, Finance and Economic Law

VOLUME 17

The titles published in this series are listed at the end of this volume.

SMU Institute of International Banking and Finance, Dallas, Texas

Centre for Commercial Law Studies University of London

Institute of International Banking, Finance and Development Law, London

Asian Institute of International Financial Law, University of Hong Kong

Banks in Distress: Lessons from the American Experience of the 1980s

by

G. N. Olson

KLUWER LAW INTERNATIONAL

THE HAGUE – LONDON – BOSTON

Published by
Kluwer Law International Ltd
Sterling House
66 Wilton Road
London SW1V 1DE
United Kingdom

Sold and distributed in
the USA and Canada by
Kluwer Law International
675 Massachusetts Avenue
Cambridge MA 02139
USA

Kluwer Law International incorporates
the publishing programmes of
Graham & Trotman Ltd,
Kluwer Law & Taxation Publishers
and Martinus Nijhoff Publishers

In all other countries, sold and distributed by
Kluwer Law International
PO Box 322
3300 AH Dordrecht
The Netherlands

ISBN 90-411-9787-7
CIP 00-039091

First published 2000

Library of Congress Cataloging-in-Publication Data
Olson, G.N.
Banks in distress : lessons from the American experience of the 1980s / by G.N. Olson.
p. cm. -- (International banking, finance, and economic law ; v. 17)
Includes bibliographical references and index.
ISBN 9041197877 (alk. paper)
1. Bank failures--United States--History. 2. Banks and banking--United States--State supervision--History. 3. Banking law--United States. 4. Monetary policy--United States--History. I. Title. II. Series

HG2491 .O47 2000
332.1'0973'09048--dc21

00-039091

Typeset in Palatino 10/11pt by The Midlands Book Typesetting Company, Leicestershire.
Printed and bound by CPI Antony Rowe, Eastbourne

Sponsoring Organisations

Centre for Commercial Law Studies
The Centre was established in 1980 as a distinct department within the Faculty of Laws of Queen Mary College, University of London. The primary objectives of the Centre are to promote systematic study and research in national and international commercial law and its social and economic implications, and to develop a body of knowledge, information and skills that can be placed at the service of government, public bodies, overseas institutions, the legal profession, industry and commerce. The International Financial Law Unit is one of the four internationally-renowned post-graduate research and teaching units at the CCLS.

London Institute of International Banking, Finance and Development Law
The London Institute is a privately incorporated educational institution. Among other functions, the Institute assists the International Financial Law Unit at the Centre for Commercial Law Studies at Queen Mary and Westfield College, University of London, in directing research seminars, professional conferences, executive training sessions, law reform and consulting projects, and the publication of major journals and book series. This legal think-tank is also responsible for conducting research and publishing articles and essays on an array of important legal issues concerning banking, finance and development.

SMU Institute of International Banking and Finance
The Southern Methodist University Law School in Dallas, Texas has one of the oldest and most comprehensive international law programmes in the United States. Its Institute of International Banking and Finance was established in 1982. The Institute serves as an interdisciplinary forum for research, publications, conferences and research seminars in the area of international finance, with input from SMU's Law School, Political Science and Economic Departments, and the Edwin L. Cox School of Business. The Institute conducts major international conferences, is actively involved in economic law reform projects in relating to emerging economies, and regularly produces books and other scholarly articles and papers.

Asian Institute of International Financial Law, University of Hong Kong Chinese Law Group and Centre for Comparative and Public Law

The University of Hong Kong Law Faculty is the oldest and most respected law faculty in Hong Kong. Its Asian Institute (AIIFL) was established in 1999 in cooperation with HKU's School of Business and Management and Department of Economics and is committed to postgraduate programmes, research, publications, conferences, short courses and seminars in the international financial law area, with emphasis on the East Asian and Greater China Areas. The AIIFL works closely with the Law Faculty's Chinese Law Group, one of the few such groups outside of Mainland China, and the Centre for Comparative and Public Law, which was founded by the Law Faculty in 1996.

TABLE OF CONTENTS

Preface .... *xv*

Acknowledgement .... *xix*

PART I ASSET VALUE INFLATION AND US GOVERNMENT INTERVENTION

Introductory Note 3

1. Legislative Deregulation and Tax Revision and their Policy and Economic Implications 11

I. Introduction 11
II. DIDMCA 11
  A. Reserve Requirements 12
  B. Removal of Regulation Q Interest Rate Ceilings 13
  C. NOW Accounts and Deposit Insurance Coverage 15
  D. Expansion of Thrift Powers and Permissible Activities 16
  E. Pre-emption of State Usury Laws 17
  F. The Effect of DIDMCA on Monetary Policy Operations 20
III. The Reagan Administration 22
IV. Policy Conflicts Between the Fed and the Reagan Program 25
V. Monetary Conditions Following DIDMCA 28
VI. ERTA 29
  A. Provisions Affecting Real Estate 29
  B. Impact of Reagan Administration Package and ERTA 30
VII. Monetary and Exchange Rate Conditions Following ERTA 31
  A. Beginnings of the Superdollar 32
  B. Recession 33
  C. Fed Monetary Policy Errors 34

2. **Cracks in the Banking and Financial System** 37

I. Introduction 37
II. LDC Debt Crisis (February 1982) 37
III. Drysdale Securities (May 1982) 42
IV. May 1982 FOMC Meeting 43
V. Penn Square Bank (June 1982) 44
VI. June 1982 FOMC Meeting 46
VII. Abandonment of the Monetarist Operating Technique 46
VIII. Continental Illinois Bank Crisis (July 1982) 47
IX. Mexico Defaults (August 1982) 48

3. **The Garn-St. Germain Act of 1982: A Final Deregulatory 'Push'** 51

I. Introduction 51
II. The Backdrop 51
III. Diversification of Asset Holdings 53
IV. FDIC and FSLIC Powers to Assist Distressed Institutions 54
  A. Open Bank Assistance 55
  B. Emergency Acquisitions 55
  C. Net Worth Certificates 57
V. Real Estate Lending Provisions for National Banks and Thrift Institutions 59
  A. National Banks 59
  B. Thrift Institutions 60
    1. Aggregate Lending Limits and LTV Ratios 60
    2. Appraisals 61
    3. Loan Charges and Repayment 61
    4. Home Loans 61
    5. Home Improvement Loans 62
    6. Loans to Acquire or Improve Real Estate 62
    7. Combination Loans and Other Real Estate Loans 63
VI. Concluding Observations: Drawing Together the Effects of Legislative Deregulation and Tax Revision and their Policy and Economic Implications 63

PART II ASSET VALUE INFLATION: SUPERVISORY DEREGULATION AND REGULATORY FORBEARANCE – THE US THRIFT INDUSTRY AND BANKING EXPERIENCE

Introductory Note 71

4. **US Thrift Industry: FHLBB Deregulation** 73

I. Introduction 73

II. Regulatory Structure and Supervisory Environment 74
III. Capital Requirements 75
IV. Accounting Standards 77
A. Regulatory Accounting Principles 77
B. Inflation of Reported Capital 79
1. Deferral of Losses on the Sale of Assets 79
2. Loan Origination Fees 81
3. Appraised Equity Capital 82
V. Accounting Interpretations 83
A. Purchase and Goodwill Accounting 83
B. FSLIC Acquisitions Programs: Supervisory Goodwill 85
1. Capital Credits 87
2. FHLBB-Industry Agreements 88
C. Effects of Accounting Deviations 89
D. SFAS No. 72 Interpretations 89
VI. Acquisition, Development and Construction (AD&C) Loans 91
VII. FHLBB Deregulatory Permissiveness: 1980–1983 92
A. May–December 1980 92
B. Calendar Year 1981 93
C. Calendar Year 1982 94
D. Calendar Year 1983 95
VIII. Conclusions and Summary Observations 96

5. Banking Agency Deregulation and Forbearance 99

I. Introduction 99
II. Bank Entry and the Chartering Process 99
III. Penn Square Bank Failure and Brokered Deposits as Sources of Funding 101
IV. The Expansion of Bank Powers 103
V. Capital Requirements and Forbearance 107
A. Evolution of Bank Capital Requirements 107
B. LDC Debt Crisis 109
C. Risk-Based Capital Requirements 115
D. Differences in Bank-Thrift Capital Requirements 117
VI. Concluding Note: State Banking Agency Deregulation 118

6. Commercial Real Estate and the Thrift and Banking Crises 121

I. Introduction 121
II. The Real Estate Boom (Revisited) 121
III. US Real Estate Values, 1980s and 1990s 123
IV. Real Estate Appraisals 127
V. Appraisal Methods and Standards 130
VI. Appraisals Affecting Appraisals 130
VII. Concluding Note: The Practice of Nonrecourse Financing 131

PART III ASSET VALUE DEFLATION: SUPERVISORY AND LEGISLATIVE REREGULATION

Introductory Note 135

7. The Immediate Post-Deregulatory Years (with summary observations) 143

I. Introduction 143
II. Monetary Policy and the End of Inflation 143
III. Monetary and Fiscal Policy Conflict 145
IV. The Real Interest Rate Dilemma 147
V. Beginnings of Dollar Appreciation 148
VI. Collision of Monetary, Fiscal and Benign Exchange Rate Policies 149
VII. Continental Illinois National Bank Debacle 150
VIII. Economic Fragility and Government Forbearance 154
IX. Exchange Rate and Monetary Policy in 1985 158
X. Concluding Observations: The End of the Deregulation Era and Asset Value Inflation 159
  A. Thrift Industry Crisis 160
  B. Consensus Points on the Thrift Industry Crisis 161
  C. The Trigger Points of Insolvency and the Onset of Policy Reversal 162
  D. Banking Crises 164
  E. Banking and Monetary Priorities and Regulatory Capture 164
  F. Legislative Gridlock 166
  G. The Beginnings of Reregulation 167

8. Supervisory and Legislative Reregulation in the Thrift Industry 169

I. Introduction: The Stage for Disaster 169
II. FHLBB Reregulation 170
  A. Calendar Year 1985 170
  B. Calendar Year 1986 171
  C. Calendar Year 1987 172
  D. Reregulation and Asset Value Deflation 172
III. Legislative Reregulation – The Beginnings 173
  A. The Tax Reform Act of 1986 173
  B. The Competitive Equality Banking Act of 1987 176
    1. FSLIC Recapitalization 178
    2. Distressed and Failed Banking Organizations and Thrift Institutions 181
    3. Post-CEBA: The Thrift Crisis Unfolds 181
IV. Concluding Note: The FHLBB's Southwest Plan 182
  A. Rationale for Transactions 183
  B. Structure of Transactions 184
  C. Effects and Implications 187

9. The 1989 FIRREA Legislation: The Culmination of Legislative Reregulation in the 1980s 191

I. Introduction 191
II. Review of FIRREA Objectives 192
 A. In General 192
 B. Capital Requirements and Accounting Compliance 194
 C. Qualified Thrift Lender Test 199
 D. Deposit Insurance Reorganization 200
III. Resolution Trust Corporation 201
IV. The Enforcement Superpowers 204
 A. The Concept of 'Institution-Affiliated Party' 204
 B. Cease and Desist Orders and Affirmative Corrective Actions 205
 C. Burden of Proof for Temporary Cease and Desist Orders 205
 D. Suspension, Removal, or Prohibition Orders 206
 E. Civil Money Penalties 207
 F. Personal Liability of Directors and Officers 208
 G. FDIC Enforcement Provisions 208
V. Certain FIRREA Restrictions 209
 A. Restrictions on Thrift Activities 209
 B. Restrictions on Thrift Subsidiaries, Affiliates and Insiders 211
 C. LTV Ratios and Real Estate Appraisal Standards 212
VI. FIRREA: Impact on the Thrift Industry 213
VII. Concluding Note: Move to Further Criminalization – The Crime Control Act of 1990 215

10. Effect of Supervisory and Legislative Reregulation on the Thrift and Banking Industries and Real Estate Lending Markets 219

I. Introduction 219
II. Impact on Thrift Financial Operations 219
III. Impact on Real Estate Lending Practices 222
 A. Thrift Industry and Texas Banks 223
 B. National Banks 224
  1. Project Information Files 224
  2. Data Base Problems 224
  3. Real Property Accounting Systems 225
  4. Value Enhancement 225
  5. Real Estate Marketing and Sales 225
  6. Appraisal Systems 225
IV. Recharacterization of Real Estate Lending Transactions 226
 A. In Substance Foreclosure 226
 B. Interest Capitalization 228
 C. Troubled Debt Restructurings 229
V. Real Estate Appraisals 231
 A. Effect of Tightening of Appraisal Standards 231
 B. Problematic Definitions: Market Value, FMV and Fair Value 232
VI. Cost of Funds and Restrictions on Growth 234

VII. 'Mark to Market' Asset Value 235
VIII. Decreased Leverage 236
IX. Concluding Note: Shifts in Monetary Policy and Political Accountability 237

11. Further Deregulation: The 1991 FDICIA Legislation 241

I. Introduction 241
II. Rationale for FDICIA 242
III. FDICIA and Capital Adequacy 243
A. FDICIA Classifications 244
B. PCA Intervention Mandates 245
1. Operation Restrictions 246
2. Affirmative Actions 246
3. Appointment of Receiver 247
C. Problematic Aspects of PCA 247
IV. Bank Capital and Prompt Corrective Action 249
V. FDICIA and Bank Reregulation 251
A. Examinations 251
B. Safety and Soundness Standards 251
C. Uniform Standards for Real Estate Lending 252
D. State-Chartered vs. Federally Chartered Banks 252
E. Brokered Deposits 252
F. Deposit Insurance Reform 252
G. 'Too Big To Fail' Policy 252
VI. Concluding Observations 253

PART IV CONCLUDING OBSERVATIONS

12. Concluding Observations 261

I. Introduction 261
II. Lessons to be Learned from the US Thrift Industry and Banking Crises of the 1980s 262
A. Monetary and Fiscal Policies and Exchange Rate Neutrality 262
B. The Coordination and Sequencing of Legislative, Regulatory, Monetary and Fiscal Policies 263
C. 'Special Relationship' Between Government and Banking Systems and 'Political Goodwill' 264
D. Legislation, Deregulation and Asset Value Inflation 264
E. Legislative, Regulatory and Exchange Rate Forbearance, Permissiveness and Nontransparency 265
F. Legislation, Reregulation, Reactive Policy Reversals and Asset Value Deflation 266

G. Government Accountability and Loss Allocation 268
H. The Recognition of Linkage Between Government Intervention, Asset Valuation and Bank Capital 270
III. Critique of External Evaluations 271
A. FDIC Report on the US Banking Crisis of the 1980s and 1990s 271
B. G-10 Report of the Working Party on Financial Stability 274
IV. A Final Reflection: Future Change is Possible and Critical in Developing and Transition Economies 275

Selected Bibliography 279

Index 329

Preface

Today, as we enter the 21st century, developed, transitioning and emerging economies alike are struggling to deal with the consequences of this ongoing financial tragedy, without coming to grips with its precipitating causes. Perhaps the analyses presented here will enable those concerned by this tragedy to better cope with future crises of bank distress and insolvency through more appropriate and transparent public policies and appropriate laws to recognize and implement those policies.

The Message. The close of the 20th century is witness to a worldwide phenomenon of banks in distress and bank insolvencies. Although bank insolvencies are not unknown historically, the current phenomenon is extraordinary by any standard. What has become largely forgotten is the fact that the US experienced a major financial system crisis in the 1980s. This work analyses the legal and policy implications of this crisis and attempts to draw lessons for the future.

This work is an effort to reconcile the causes and effects of and the role of governmental intervention in the increasing incidence of credit crises and bank distress which have proliferated worldwide, beginning in the United States in the 1980s.

The primary message of this volume is that the origins of the extraordinary numbers of American banking institution insolvencies during the 1980s and early 1990s were not simply the result of well-publicized individual incidents of fraud or malfeasance, but were largely precipitated and exacerbated by uncoordinated and dysfunctional acts and policies of government intervention. These interventions were played out against a backdrop of an American fiscal policy of deficit finance, exacerbated by reactive and opaque monetary policy. The connections between the causes and effects of this profound financial distress are not readily apparent, and therefore government policies and attempts to resolve this distress, including the enactment of intrusive and manipulative banking and tax laws, disjointed policies of regulation, supervision and enforcement, bank closures and well-publicized programs of retribution and recrimination became misdirected. A well-developed legal infrastructure for a viable and stable financial system requires transparent, coordinated and proactive (not simply reactive) governmental policies in the banking, fiscal and monetary, and national economic areas.

The Approach. In presenting this message, this volume reviews the evolution of the US banking system and the significant legislative, regulatory, and monetary policies of the 1980s and sets the stage for thrift industry and banking crises. This volume also examines what is perhaps the fundamental precondition to a system of coherent bank regulation and supervision: a critical understanding of the importance of asset valuation, asset value inflation and deflation, and capital adequacy for banking organizations and thrift institutions. The volume also examines the US legislative, monetary, fiscal, and regulatory and supervisory policies over 1980–1982, primarily from the thrift industry perspective, which generated asset value inflation and paved the way for distress, crisis, and failure in that industry as well as in the US banking system in the 1980s and early 1990s. Finally, this volume considers important 'lessons learned' from the US experience for future study in developed, transitioning and developing economy banking regimes.

The Setting. In the early 1980s, US property values nationwide skyrocketed as lenders from newly deregulated savings and loan associations to prominent money center banks pumped money into the US economy. It appeared by the mid-1980s that pressures for bank reregulation were increasing, reversing the deregulation of the early 1980s. Sources for financings and refinancings were drying up. The lenders were on the run.

Regulatory authorities attacked the lenders' portfolios with reregulatory fervor. Appraisal requirements changed daily. The Tax Reform Act of 1986 virtually abolished the primary source of project purchasers, tax shelter syndications. All of a sudden, no one knew what a real estate project was worth. There was no equity capital available for purchases and there were no loans available to prospective purchasers or to owners for refinancing.

The only apparent hope for debtors at that time was to shrink their asset base, extend loan maturities where possible, negotiate foreclosures and repossession of untenable collateral with a minimum of loss, and to attempt to preserve apparent equities until assets could be sold, capturing the proceeds to satisfy unsecured creditors, and with any luck, to retain some equity. But it was early in the cycle. As the downward spiral of asset values continued, the wholesale default of debt in America reached epidemic proportions. As creditors were forced to recognize the underlying losses in collateral asset values and as the proportion of bank assets classified as nonperforming became larger, the financial institutions themselves became insolvent and were closed by the score, resulting in the insolvency of America's deposit insurers, the Federal Savings and Loan Insurance Corporation and the Federal Deposit Insurance Corporation.

In recent years there has been increasing pressure on asset values and banking systems worldwide, as well as increasing financial volatility and the increasing incidence of business and bank distress and insolvency. For example, the collapse of the former Soviet Union as well as other totalitarian systems with centrally-planned economies, the ongoing reform transformation and modernization of the Chinese economy, and their moves to free-market systems through massive asset privatization and enterprise restructuring efforts, is introducing into the global economy an enormous body of investment and lending opportunities under circumstances where the vast majority of the owners, investors and lenders have little experience with 'free-market' economic activity; and where there are little to no legal or regulatory systems in place to establish property rights, provide for lending security or to govern investment and lending activity. All this is occurring in a global economic environment which links and interrelates the respective domestic credit, asset valuation and liquidity volatility concerns faced by so-called 'developed economies'.

In filling out this approach, this volume examines the role of uncoordinated government intervention in the American domestic economy as a fundamental precipitating and aggravating cause of US, and to some degree, worldwide financial dysfunction. In doing so, this study traces the development of the economic and legal policies underlying the systemic crisis of capital inadequacy in the US, and some of the connections between the US crisis and current global financial pressures. Recognition of the context of worldwide financial dysfunction and the US's role in its expansion calls for significant changes in the policies and laws of most developed economies and emerging economies relating to the resolution of bank distress and insolvency.

When beginning this study several years ago, this author intended to focus to a significant degree on the nexus between expansionary fiscal and monetary policy in America and other economies and the effects of policies of reactive government intervention in precipitating bank insolvencies. First, that task proved to be far beyond the scope of this study. Second, during this time there has developed a considerable body of research and writing confirming the deleterious effects of expansionary fiscal and monetary policy in America, accompanied by the effects of these policies on the US dollar as the world's reserve currency in other economies. These effects have been compounded by similar expansionary policies in those economies, resulting in global financial dysfunction. The author, therefore, has concentrated on the recent American policy, legislative and regulatory responses to this financial dysfunction with some reference to, and commentary on, the underlying 'macroeconomic' context, international implications, and trends.

The financial relations of debtors and creditors, as well as the financial relations of nations are now subjected to awesome forces which the participants little understand. An examination of these forces and the ways in which they emerged in the US financial crisis, as filtered through government policies of expediency and intervention, should shape the participants' relationships to one another and should serve us in coping with epidemic global and domestic financial dislocations with the minimum degree of appropriate retribution and recrimination (which, in the larger context, has become increasingly irrelevant) with the focus on the minimization of loss and the rational allocation of that loss among the participants.

Public interest in the stability of a market economy's banking system is generally accepted as paramount. The maintenance of depositor confidence is generally thought to avoid deposit runs and resulting 'systemic' threats to banking systems and to permit banks the latitude to make prudent loans and investments which have less liquidity than their deposit base. Stable banks in a stable banking system are thought to be integral to an effective market economic system. These conditions are also thought to be vital to the conversion of formerly centrally planned economic systems to functioning market economies. It is not at all clear, however, that systems in the so-called 'developed economies' whether the predominant 'mixed economies' of Europe or US 'regulatory capitalism,' actually function properly in this regard or are suitable examples for the emerging economies. The American failure has affected economies worldwide, and has been magnified by special fiscal, monetary and bank regulatory policies in those economies. These economies have also, to a greater or lesser degree, adopted opaque and misdirected efforts to resolve or remediate bank distress and inappropriate and diversionary programs to recriminate the private sector participants, while rationalizing the culpability of government responsibility. Existing market economic systems and reforms are doomed to failure unless political leadership is given to understand the origins of the recent phenomenon of bank distress and financial disruption.

This is not a study in economics; and it is not a study of the role of fraud and crime which is an unfortunate by-product of bank distress and failure. It is a study of the origins of bank distress and failure, beginning with an examination of non-performing assets where asset value inflation and deflation are reflected, recognition of the manifestations of 'lost value' and the dominant role of government intervention in and manipulation of the US financial system in prompting both domestic and international financial dysfunction.

Acknowledgement

I am most grateful to certain of my former professional colleagues in law practice and bank consulting; Bill Sechrest and John Walker for their support and collaboration in the early iterations of my analyses.

I also express my gratitude to my academic colleague, Professor Joseph J. Norton at the Centre for Commercial Law Studies, Queen Mary and Westfield College, University of London, for his encouragement and support in bringing productive order and academic assistance and direction out of my prior 'hands-on' experiences and for introducing me to the academic world of international banking and financial law at the CCLS, as well as to my other colleagues at the CCLS and London Institute, including Dr Christos Hadjiemmanuil, George Walker and Doug Arner for their critical comments and editorial interest. I wish especially to thank Chris Olive of the CCLS for his tremendous contributions in the unraveling of the complexity of US monetary and fiscal policy, as well as incisive critical comments. I further thank the staff of the Centre and its Director, Ian Fletcher, for their personal and financial support as a Visiting Senior Fellow at the Centre.

I also wish to thank Dean Paul Rogers of the Southern Methodist University School of Law for appointment as a Visiting Scholar to facilitate my continuing research while in the US. I am indebted to Dee McKnight at Southern Methodist University, and Helen Brownstone at the Centre, and I am especially grateful to Barbara Springfield, WordScribe, Inc., Dallas, Texas, for their respective attention to my secretarial and word processing needs.

Naturally, I could not produce this manuscript without the support of my wife, Trish, in this significant departure in pursuit of an academic interest, ranging far from my hectic professional and business career.

I thank the National Council of Real Estate Investment Fiduciaries for their permission to publish private compilations of real estate values for the relevant periods, previously available only to members of that association.

Part I
Asset Value Inflation and US Government Intervention

Introductory Note

One of the apparent roots of the US thrift industry and banking crises was generated in the 1970s by abrupt policy reversals concerning US exchange rate and monetary policies and other destabilizing constraints and trends within these industries.[1] The period was characterized by the following:[2]

- The breakdown of the Bretton Woods system of fixed exchange rates, beginning in 1971 and with ensuing periods of severe exchange rate instability and depreciation in the dollar by 1979;
- The onset of several 'oil price shocks' in the early 1970s, in direct response to the devaluation of the dollar following the breakdown of Bretton Woods, which accelerated inflation in all commodities, assets, and services, and continued deficit financing in the US generating domestic inflation and inflationary expectations, particularly in areas sensitive to banking and inflation, such as financial assets and real estate;
- The *de facto* policy reversal resulting from the shift of dominant focus on domestic and international exchange rate policy to anti-inflationary monetary policy as the US Federal Reserve Board of Governors (Fed) abruptly initiated the campaign against inflation and tightened the money supply, resulting in abrupt increases in interest rates, with the prime lending rate eventually exceeding 20 per cent;
- The thrift industry became subject to the 'interest rate mismatch dilemma' through legal and regulatory constraints imposed on the industry since its origin and the widely fluctuating US short-term (deposit) and long-term (mortgage lending) interest rates through the late 1970s;
- Competition between the banking and thrift industries and between these industries and securities firms and government-sponsored enterprises to attract and maintain deposits and mortgages; and

1 See, inter alia, C.K. Olive, 'US Monetary Polity Framework – A Primer', *Research Series on International Financial and Economic Law,* (London Institute of International Banking, Finance and Development Law, 1999).

2 C.K. Olive and G. N. Olson, 'Exchange Rate and Monetary Policy Reversals and Interest Rate Deregulation – Setting the Stage for Financial System Crises, Lessons Respecting the US Crisis of the 1980s' (1999) (on file with SMU Institute of International Banking and Finance)

- Significant demand for investments in real estate and energy as hedges against inflation.

The unfortunate truth was that the US savings and loan (S&L) industry was losing its historical social and economic function.[3] The loss of social function occurred primarily through competition for their depositor bases. Banks were offering savings accounts, and mutual funds were offering various high-yielding uninsured alternatives for S&L customers.[4] The loss of social function also occurred partly as a result of the proliferation of Government Sponsored Enterprises (GSEs) involved in mortgage origination and secondary market trading.[5] In short, in the economic environment entering the 1980s, the S&L industry was coming under significant competition in its primary business activity.

The significant problems experienced by financial institutions, particularly thrift institutions, flowed from several variables. First, was the emergence of significant undercapitalization and excessive leverage in S&L institutions. The early 1970s represented a period of growth, particularly in residential mortgage lending, during which the FHLBB consistently reduced capital requirements, rather than holding the line in requiring a relatively high ratio of capital to liabilities. This retreat occurred during a time when thrift institutions had sufficient earnings to develop an adequate capital base. Second, were the statutory and regulatory limitations with respect to the interest rates banks and thrifts could pay for small deposits imposed through federal statute[6] and the Federal Reserve Board's (Fed's) Regulation Q.[7] At the time, thrift institutions were permitted to charge depository interest rates one-half of one percentage point higher than commercial banks under Regulation Q, and financial institutions such as securities firms were not limited by Regulation Q.

---

3 i.e., providing home mortgages and serving as a community depository institution.

4 See, inter alia, L. Goldberg and L. White (eds), *The Deregulation of the Banking and Securities Industries* (1979).

5 As part of the 1930s New Deal legislation, the Federal National Mortgage Association (FNMA) was established to sell bonds and use the proceeds to purchase mortgages to create a secondary market for mortgages. Investors largely failed to purchase the bonds, so the government started FNMA as a customer for the mortgages insured by the Federal Housing Administration. In the 1960s, new federal budget rules inadvertently placed FNMA 'on budget', the result of which was that its mortgage purchases would increase the federal deficit. The US Congress thereafter privatized FNMA, keeping its social purposes, but subsidized its lending through the newly formed Government National Mortgage Association (GNMA).

The FNMA and GNMA institutions primarily related to a secular group of mortgage bankers as their agents, and S&Ls were the lenders that held mortgages they originated. In 1970, the FHLBB formed the Federal National Mortgage Corporation, which offered the public 'pass through securities' – bonds which passed through to their holders each month the payments made by homeowners on their mortgages – so that S&Ls could improve their liquidity by 'securitizing' and selling some of the mortgages otherwise held in portfolio. The GSEs had various privileges with their quasi-government status, and by 1980 were enormous holders of mortgages in the US.

6 Deposit rate limitations were imposed on financial institutions prior to legislation in 1980. See 12 U.S.C. § 371a (1979).

7 See 12 C.F.R. § 217 (1979).

Deposit disintermediation was the logical result, as small depositors sought to minimize the ravages of high inflation by taking advantage of the interest rates offered by money market funds and cash management accounts. Throughout 1979–1980, securities firms took advantage of the environment of high market interest rates and invaded the markets for deposits by introducing the money market mutual fund. The money market mutual fund quickly became the most prevalent financial innovation and money substitute by offering many of the deposit services of banks and thrifts without imposing the costs of deposit rate limitations, reserve requirements and federal deposit insurance.[8]

Banks and thrifts were unable to offer market interest rates to depositors, and found themselves at a severe competitive disadvantage. As interest rates increased into the double digits by early 1980, money market mutual funds quickly attracted away billions of dollars of deposits from banks and thrift institutions. Congress held hearings on the matter but ultimately refused to bring the money market mutual funds under the authority of Regulation Q.[9]

Banks and thrift institutions were forced to replace small depositors with large certificates of deposit at competitive rates as sources of funding. This had a particularly devastating effect on thrift institutions, whose assets consisted primarily of lower fixed-rate residential mortgages, and the resulting negative spread caused thrift institutions to rapidly lose capital.

Rising market interest rates fueled significant political opposition to Regulation Q. In late 1979, President Carter's Interagency Task Force on Regulation Q reported its recommendation that the depository interest rate ceilings be removed.[10]

The special interest groups representing the S&L industry accumulated significant political power through monetary contributions to key politicians over the 1970s and gained direct access to define the national interest for the thrift industry, largely without limitations. The special interest groups were unduly influential and generally crossed the line between sound advocacy and improper influence and played a large part in facilitating the legislation and deregulatory initiatives which actually accelerated the demise of the thrift industry.[11]

---

8 See Michael Mussa, 'Competition, Efficiency, and Fairness in the Financial Services Industry', in *Deregulating Financial Services: Public Policy in Flux* (George G. Kaufman and Roger C. Kormedi (eds), 1986), pp.121, 142–143.

9 See 'Money Market Mutual Funds: Hearings on Oversight on the Supervision and Regulation of Money Market Mutual Funds and the Effects of the Funds in Financial Markets', before the Subcommittee on Financial Institutions of the Senate Committee on Banking, Housing, and Urban Affairs, 96th Cong., 2d Sess. (1980).

10 See President's Interagency Task Force on Regulation Q, 'The Report of the President's Inter-Agency Task Force on Regulation Q'(1979) (on file with author). The task force members included the federal banking agencies and FHLBB. Within months of the release of this Report, President Carter signed into law the first legislative initiative which, among other things, liberalized depository interest rate ceilings, preempted state usury ceilings on mortgage loans, and allowed depository institutions to offer negotiable order of withdrawal (NOW) accounts. See Depository Institutions Deregulation and Monetary Control Act of 1980, Pub. L. No. 96-221, 94 Stat. 132 (1980).

11 See Stanley I. Langbein, 'The Thrift Crisis and the Constitution' 53 Wash. & Lee L. Rev. 159, 175 (1996).

By late 1979, thrift institution industry groups argued that they could not compete against money market interest rates, and proposed two primary legislative solutions. First, in late 1979, a proposal was made to render interest on thrift deposits exempt from taxation, justified on grounds that it directed funds to the mortgage market. Second, a proposal was made to have the federal government purchase low-rate fixed mortgages held on thrift institution balance sheets at face value, which in effect would have compensated the thrift institutions for interest rate-related losses on their lending portfolios.[12] These proposals were not enacted, but certainly facilitated legislative action regarding the thrift industry crisis in 1980.

This combination of factors resulted in a series of reactive legislation and deregulatory initiatives in the early 1980s. The legislation and deregulatory initiatives, coupled with sustained increasing inflation and monetary policy actions designed to combat inflation through increasing interest rates, resulted in an upward 'finance/tax push' on real estate and other financial assets. This upward 'finance/tax push' may be generally recognized as 'asset value inflation'.

The elements contributing to asset value inflation and particularly the upward surge of real property values in the US during the early 1980s included, as will be discussed in Part One, legislation and deregulation which significantly liberalized legal parameters governing thrifts and commercial banks, coupled with a continuation of significant monetary policy operations by the Fed in its attempt to combat inflation and mitigate inflationary expectations. The legislative, deregulatory, and monetary policy actions were equivalent to an overall major policy shift in the initial conditions upon which the US thrift and banking systems relied.

The most significant legislative and monetary policy actions occurred between 1980 and 1982, and Part One reviews those actions and their relation to, and connection with asset value inflation. Thus, each policy action must each be considered in conjunction with its inflationary effect on real property values and other inflation sensitive assets and how those inflationary effects impacted bank and S&L balance sheets income statements, and capital adequacy.

This Part also examines the legislation enacted during 1980–1982 as well as the monetary and fiscal policies implemented during this period, and attempts to weave these analyses together to present a coherent framework of how these policies developed but were connected and conflicted, and therefore exacerbated the thrift industry and banking crises and asset value inflation into the mid-1980s. The primary legislative actions which precipitated asset value inflation and magnified the thrift industry and banking crises in the US in the early 1980s include: (1) the Depository Institutions Deregulation and Monetary Control Act of 1980 (hereinafter 'DIDMCA')[13]

---

12 *Ibid.*

13 Pub. L. No. 96-221, 94 Stat. 132 (1980). § 202 indicates that DIDMCA was promulgated as an attempt at an orderly phase-out and, ultimately, an elimination of limitations on the maximum rates of interest and dividends which could be paid on deposits and accounts by depository institutions. Congress determined that all depositors were entitled to receive a market rate of return on their savings as soon as it was economically feasible for depository institutions to pay such a rate.

enacted in March 1980; (2) the Economic Recovery Tax Act of 1981 (hereinafter 'ERTA')[14] enacted in August 1981; and (3) the Garn-St. Germain Depository Institutions Act of 1982 (hereinafter 'Garn-St. Germain Act')[15] enacted in December 1982, respectively.[16]

During the early 1980s, legislation and monetary (and fiscal) policy actions interacted dynamically with one another, and when coupled with the factors of leverage, momentum, reactive thinking and inflationary expectations, stimulated uncontrollable upward surges in financial asset prices, particularly real estate asset values. The asset value inflation generated significant price bubbles in the real estate sector, the collapse of which unquestionably contributed to the magnitude of the crises in the mid- to late-1980s.[17]

In order to understand the dynamics of these variables collectively, it is necessary to consider each of these changes individually and sequentially, change by change and then dynamically, through their connections and interrelationships. The dynamics of these connections and interrelationships were in all likelihood not readily apparent to Congress, the US banking and thrift industries, and their respective regulatory agencies in the early 1980s.[18]

The non-transparency arose in large part from the preoccupation of Congress, the Executive branch (including the Department of the Treasury), and the Fed in cracking down on inflation and dealing with the political fallout therefrom, and with the banking agencies in dealing with other immediate and potentially systemic events as part of the anti-inflation fallout which cracked the US banking system between 1980 and 1982. If the dynamics of connections and interrelationships between legislation, monetary and fiscal policies were readily apparent to Congress, the industries, and their regulatory agencies, then the thrift industry and banking 'capital adequacy' crises of the 1980s, with their global implications, would likely not have occurred to such a significant extent and would not have cost US taxpayers hundreds of billions of dollars to resolve.[19]

Part One initially examines the DIDMCA legislation, enacted under the Carter Administration and aimed at removing many of the distinctions between thrift and banking industries to enhance competitiveness and eliminate interest rate ceilings on deposit accounts. DIDMCA opened the door to

---

[14] Pub. L. No. 97-34, 95 Stat. 172 (1981). § 212 of ERTA amended §§ 46 and 48 of the Internal Revenue Code (Title 26, US Code) and increased the investment tax credit for rehabilitation expenditures to 15 per cent for non-residential 30-year-old buildings; 20 per cent for non-residential 40-year-old buildings; 25 per cent for residential and non-residential certified historic structures; and repealed the accelerated cost recovery and demolition disincentives for certified historic structures.

[15] Pub. L. No. 97-97-320, 96 Stat. 1469 (1982).

[16] The primary deregulatory and market actions which precipitated asset value inflation and magnified the thrift industry crisis in the early 1980s include: (1) deregulatory initiatives by the FHLBB and banking agencies; (2) general regulatory forbearance and permissiveness as crisis set into these industries; and (3) resultant questionable practices by market professionals, particularly with respect to real estate appraisals and application of accounting standards and interpretations permitted and encouraged by the FHLBB. These items are examined in detail in Chapter Three.

[17] See Part Two, *infra*.

[18] See, e.g., Chapters 1–3 of Part One, *infra*.

[19] *Ibid*.

uncontrolled expansion and competition in the banking and thrift industries and seriously exacerbated the thrift industry crisis. This legislation resulted presumably from good intentions but was enacted at the wrong time and for the wrong reasons.

The Carter Administration, in a continuation of the oft adopted policy of 'benign neglect', often directed at the complexities of monetary policy and finance, likely did not comprehend the full magnitude of the thrift industry crisis and the perverse incentives that DIDMCA introduced to exacerbate the crisis, as well as the economic conditions existing at that time which would lead the US money center banks into increasingly speculative activities and exposure to circumstances generated by the anti-inflationary monetary policies. In addition, the DIDMCA legislation caused significant confusion and misalignment in monetary policy operations and ultimately caused the Fed to misinterpret monetary signals and guide the economy into recession in 1981.

This Part then provides brief overviews of the political agendas of President Ronald Reagan, elected in November 1980, and the Reagan Administration. The Reagan agendas included the introduction of 'deregulation' and 'supply side economics', and initial support of the abrupt monetary policy initiatives adopted by the Federal Reserve to combat inflation.

Part One also briefly underscores inherent conflicts between Fed monetary policy, and the 'deregulation' and 'supply side economics' programs introduced by the Reagan Administration. These conflicts predictably resulted in the expansion of US budget deficits and massive asset value inflation. The political avoidance of these conflicts resulted in the enactment of ERTA in August 1981, which significantly accelerated asset value inflation in the real estate sector, facilitated increasing interest rates by the Fed due to conflicts with monetary policy, and set the stage for long-term appreciation of the dollar in global currency markets.

Part One next reviews the dynamic monetary conditions which facilitated a series of closely related events during 1982 which cracked the US banking system and preoccupied the primary authorities, permitting the thrift industry crisis to magnify significantly over this period without being addressed.

Finally, this Part reviews the abrupt policy reversals inherent in the abandonment of the monetarist operating technique by the Federal Reserve in late 1982, and the adoption of the Garn-St. Germain Act legislation in December 1982. The Garn-St. Germain Act was designed to complete the process of giving expanded powers to the thrift industry and enabled them to diversify their activities with the view of expanding growth and increasing profits, particularly in real estate lending activities, earning their way out of difficulty. The implementation of this Act significantly enhanced asset value inflation by stimulating the demand for real estate investments and development, particularly in connection with the tax incentives provided under ERTA for real estate activities. The totality of the legislative deregulation and policies introduced during this period significantly exacerbated the thrift industry crisis and the fragility of the banking system, and set the stage for abrupt policy reversals which would threaten the very survival of the thrift industry, many local and regional banks, as well as certain money center banking institutions.

Notably, the legislation and policies examined in this Part One were significantly complemented and augmented by the primary deregulatory initiatives introduced by the thrift industry and banking regulatory agencies, and actions engaged in by real estate market professionals which contributed significantly to, and otherwise precipitated, asset value inflation and magnified the thrift industry crisis in the early 1980s. These initiatives and actions included: (1) deregulatory initiatives by the FHLBB and banking agencies; (2) general patterns of intentional regulatory forbearance and permissiveness as crisis set into these industries; and (3) questionable practices by market professionals, particularly with respect to real estate appraisals, and application of accounting standards and interpretations permitted and encouraged by the FHLBB. These items supplement the issues examined in Part One and are further explored in detail in Part Two.

1. Legislative Deregulation and Tax Revision and their Policy and Economic Implications: 1980–1982

I. INTRODUCTION

The US Congress enacted significant banking and thrift legislation in 1980 and 1982, designed to 'deregulate' the US banking and thrift industries and prevent them from continuing their slide into distress and failure under the prevailing monetary conditions.[1] The legislation consisted of deregulatory statutes, 1980 Depository Institutions Deregulation and Monetary Control Act (DIDMCA) legislation,[2] and the 1982 Garn-St. Germain Act.[3] Also of interconnected significance was the 1981 Economic Recovery Tax Act (ERTA), the tax revision statute.[4] This chapter analyses these three pieces of legislation, their interconnections, and their policy and economic implications.

II. DIDMCA

The problems with the thrift industry and competitive trends within the banking industry were manifest by 1980 and certain provisions of the DIDMCA were designed to address them. In particular, the entire thrift industry had become generally unprofitable due largely to the interest rate and asset-liability mismatch dilemma. The vast number of distressed or failed thrift institutions that occurred in the early 1980s was entirely predictable, purportedly due to their inability to diversify activities or sources of funding under the current legal framework to mitigate the dilemma. The swift enactment of DIDMCA was for all practical purposes the legislative

1 See generally, Joseph J. Norton, 'The 1982 Banking Act and the Deregulation Scheme', 38 Bus. Law. 1627 (1983).

2 Depository Institutions Deregulation and Monetary Control Pub. L. No. 96–221, Act of 1980, 94 Stat. 132 (1980).

3 Pub. L. No. 97–320, 96 Stat. 1469 (1982).

4 Economic Recovery Tax Act of 1981, Pub. L. No. 97–34, 95 Stat. 172 (1981).

response to the environment of high interest rates and inflationary expectations and evolution of the financial services industry over 1979–1980. Its success depended on continuing inflation and inflationary expectations. DIDMCA was enacted just as the Fed's anti-inflation monetary policy measures were driving interest rates to historic levels.

DIDMCA provisions were largely anticipated and debated during the 1970s. DIDMCA had five key provisions that unfortunately accelerated asset value inflation and magnified the thrift industry crisis:

1 the elimination of differential reserve requirements for various types of financial institutions;
2 the removal of interest rate ceilings on time and savings accounts;
3 the introduction of NOW accounts and amendments to the deposit insurance scheme;
4 the addition of new powers for banking organizations and thrift institutions; and
5 the pre-emption of State usury laws.[5]

A. Reserve Requirements

In 1978, the FRB paid no interest on reserve balances of commercial banks held at the 12 Federal Reserve Banks. The FRB understood that federal reserve system membership was declining as dozens of banks withdrew from the system and placed themselves under State regulation and lower reserve requirements that could otherwise be invested. The banking community argued that the maintenance of idle reserve requirements was unfair, notwithstanding their ability to access the 'safety net' of discount window borrowings and the free services of check-clearing and payments and settlements available through federal reserve system membership. In addition to the banking community arguments, the Fed sought to exert control over the Eurodollar markets. The Eurodollar markets were firmly established by the late 1970s, and such offshore dollar holdings were technically not subject to reserve requirements. The absence of complete reserve requirements had dire consequences for the Fed's ability to conduct monetary policy and further, to maintain controls on Eurodollar activities. Congress sought to reach a compromise between the interests of the banking community and Fed under DIDMCA.[6]

Title I of DIDMCA, the *Monetary Control Act of 1980*, imposed uniform FRB reserve requirements on all depository institutions.[7] The Act further required that all depository institutions report their assets and liabilities to the Federal

---

5 See 'The Report of the President's Commission on Financial Structure and Regulation' (1971) (Hunt Commission Report); U.S. House Committee on Banking, Currency, and Housing, Subcommittee on Financial Institutions Supervision, 'Regulation, and Insurance, Financial Institutions in the Nation's Economy (FINE),' 'Discussion Principles', Hearings, 94th Cong., 1st Sess., 1975 ('FINE Study').

6 See Steven Greider, *Secrets of the Temple: How the Federal Reserve Runs the Country,* (Touchstone Books, 1988) at pp.154–155.

7 See Charles McNeill, 'The Depository Institutions Deregulation and Monetary Control Act of 1980', Fed. Res. Bulletin 66, No. 6 (June 1980), pp.444–453.

Reserve Board (FRB). Congress attempted to provide the Fed with improved monetary control by expanding the scope of liabilities and institutions subject to reserve requirements under DIDMCA. Prior to DIDMCA, only deposits of FRS member banks were subject to reserve requirements, but following the passage of Title I thereof all depository institutions offering transaction accounts or non-personal time deposits, including savings deposits and most importantly the Eurodollar market transactions, became subject to reserve requirements.[8]

Title I further established phased-in uniform reserve requirements for all depository institutions for the purposes of enhancing the FRB's ability to conduct monetary policy, to mitigate industry withdrawals of member banks from the Federal Reserve System, and to equalize the capital positions of commercial banks and thrift institutions.[9]

The imposition of universal reserve requirements could be viewed as an indirect covert means by which to protect the Fed's political base for independence in the face of attacking inflation, and not simply as a means for Fed to control effectively the money supply.

Thus, Title I both broadened the base of Fed reserves while simultaneously lowering that amount for all member institutions, and the impact of the change was similar to a multibillion dollar tax cut for the largest banks. The impact of this 'tax cut' was offset to some extent under Title I through requirements that the FRB establish a pricing schedule for Federal Reserve Bank services, including fee-based access to the discount window, for all depository institutions.[10]

B. Removal of Regulation Q Interest Rate Ceilings

In DIDMCA, Congress enacted a virtual repeal of the Regulation Q interest rate ceilings that restricted depository interest rates. The notion of substantive changes in US banking and thrift laws in early 1980 was politically impossible as President Carter was running for re-election, but the US House of Representatives Banking Committee decided that government-regulated interest rates under Regulation Q should be eliminated. Regulation Q, the interest rate control regulation, had supporters in Congress who declared that for the thrift industry to continue functioning it was necessary to guarantee the long term extension of Regulation Q with an interest rate differential. The smaller banking institutions and the thrift industry believed, however, that if interest rate controls were removed the large money center banks would pay higher interest rates and capture their depositor bases. The House Banking Committee agreed to permit a six-year phase-out of interest rate controls under DIDMCA.[11]

---

8 See Pub. L. No. 96–221, 94 Stat. 133 (1980); 12 U.S.C. §§ 461(a), (b); 12 C.F.R. § 204.

9 Moreover, under § 411 of the Garn-St. Germain Depository Institutions Act of 1982, reservable liabilities up to USD2 million are not subject to reserve requirements, and the FRS is to adjust the amount of the exemption based on the total reservable liabilities of all depository institutions. See David M. Jones, *The Politics of Money* (NYIF, 1991), at p.266 (App. F).

10 See 46 Fed. Reg. 1338 (6 January 1981).

11 See R. Alton Gilbert, 'Requiem for Regulation Q: What It Did and Why It Passed Away', *Federal Reserve Bank of St. Louis Review* 68, No. 2 (February 1986), at pp.22–37.

Title II of DIDMCA, the *Depository Institution Deregulation Act of 1980*, therefore deregulated the liability side of bank and S&L balance sheets and provided for the gradual removal of interest rate ceilings on deposit accounts. In particular, Title II of DIDMCA provided for the orderly phase-out of interest ceilings under FRB Regulation Q over a six-year period,[12] and established the Depository Institutions Deregulation Committee[13] to implement this aspect of 'deregulation'. The statutory requirements and Regulation Q that previously had set ceilings on the rates of interest financial institutions could pay on demand and time deposits were therefore removed through a 'phasing out' process.

As interest rates on certificates of deposits of USD100,000 or more were negotiable under Title II, a depositor or agent thereof could freely negotiate not only the term of the certificate of deposit, but also its interest rate. Title II further authorized banks and thrift institutions to pay any interest rate it chose on deposits, particularly if the deposits were in USD100,000 increments represented by certificates of deposit. This provision was a response to the massive deposit account disintermediation caused by the combination of deposit interest-rate ceilings and increasing interest rates generated by Fed monetary policy operations over 1979–1980.[14]

The removal of Regulation Q interest-rate ceilings was particularly designed to increase the ability of depository institutions to compete with money market mutual funds that could establish accounts paying market interest rates, and to liberate the small depositors from captive low-yielding deposit accounts. In other words, the purported intent of Title II was to alleviate the effects of deposit disintermediation which characterized the 1970s. The express notion was that thrift institutions were reasonably categorized within depository institutions in this respect, and that the removal of interest rate ceilings was designed in part to revive this failing industry.[15]

In reality, the protected status and implicit subsidy enjoyed by the thrift industry was unraveled with the elimination of Regulation Q. The depository institutions were nonetheless presently limited in the interest rates they could pay depositors in 1980, and when short-term rates increased higher than long-term rates (resulting in an inverted yield curve) under Fed monetary policy in 1980–1981, money market funds could easily construct AAA rated short-term debt portfolios of Treasury bills and commercial paper to yield a higher return than the federal laws then permitted banks and S&Ls to pay, and therefore capture the thrift industry depositor bases.[16]

---

12 The DIDC consisted of all federal banking agencies represented by the FFIEC and the Secretary of the Treasury. The purpose of DIDC was to phase out over a six-year period all interest rate ceilings on all types of deposits and accounts, and its power terminated in 1986. See 51 Fed. Reg. 9767 (1986). See DIDMCA, note 1, *supra*, at § 204(a), 94 Stat. at 143 (codified at 12 U.S.C. § 3502).

13 See DIDMCA, *supra*, note 1, at § 203(a), 94 Stat. at 142 (codified at 12 U.S.C. § 3502).

14 *Ibid.*

15 See generally, Weaver and O'Malley, 'The Depository Institutions Deregulation and Monetary Control Act of 1980: An Overview', 98 Banking L. J. 100 (1981).

16 *Ibid.*

In addition, the removal of interest rate ceilings impacted upon the effectiveness of Fed monetary policy during the early 1980s. As the Fed increased interest rates to attack inflation, the impact on the banking and thrift industries was no longer inherently predictable as the supply of funds could continue uninterrupted so long as the larger banking institutions could obtain funds for their clients through the Eurodollar markets or otherwise.[17] In short, in the inflationary environment, borrowers deviated from the traditional assumptions as to the interest rates they would be willing to pay for borrowed funds, and continued to borrow at ever increasing interest rates that would have been impermissible under Regulation Q.[18]

C. NOW Accounts and Deposit Insurance Coverage

Title III of DIDMCA authorized all depository institutions to offer negotiable order of withdrawal (NOW) accounts and raised the level of deposit insurance coverage for accounts from USD40,000 per account to USD100,000 per account.[19] NOW accounts were essentially interest-bearing checking accounts, and remained subject to interest rate ceilings for several years while the Depository Institutions Deregulation Committee (DIDC) phased out these and other existing limitations on depository interest rates.[20] The authorization of NOW accounts had a significant if not devastating impact on Fed monetary policy operations by obscuring the meaning and content of the most important monetary aggregate for purposes of imposing monetary policy to combat inflation, the M-1 aggregate.

The US League of Savings Associations, a savings and loans (S&L) industry special interest organization, and several other powerful S&L organizations based in California were the principal advocates for amending the deposit insurance scheme under DIDMCA. The deposit insurance provisions of DIDMCA were, ironically, among the least debated provisions in the legislation. These provisions would soon come to be perceived as having played a leading role in exacerbating the S&L crisis. The increase in the level of deposit insurance coverage effectively guaranteed the liabilities of distressed or insolvent thrift institutions and enabled thrift management to gamble with depositor funds knowing that the US Government would bear any losses. The increased deposit insurance coverage also undoubtedly limited incentives for depositors to investigate the activities or solvency of their thrift institutions.[21] Finally, and perhaps most importantly, the increased deposit insurance

---

17 See 'Regulation Q and Related Matters: Hearings', before the US House Committee on Banking, Finance and Urban Affairs, Subcommittee on Financial Institutions Supervision, Regulation and Insurance, 96th Cong., 2d Sess. (1980).

18 See Greider, note 6, *supra*, at pp.177–179.

19 See DIDMCA, note 1, *supra*, at §§ 308(a)-(c), 94 Stat. at 147–148 (codified as amended in various sections of 12 U.S.C.). See also 'Hearings on Deposit Insurance Reform and Related Supervisory Issues', before the US Senate Committee on Banking, Housing and Urban Affairs, 99th Cong., 1st Sess. (1984).

20 See Edward L. Symons and James White, *Banking Law*, at pp.45–46 (2nd edn, 1984).

21 See L. William Seidman, *Full Faith and Credit: The Great S&L Debacle and Other Washington Sagas*, (Times Books, 1993), at pp.178–179.

coverage was also not premised upon any risk-based assessment of the institution in question. The premiums paid by thrift institutions to the Federal Savings and Loan Insurance Corporation (FSLIC) for deposit insurance were established by statute and applied the same premium rate for all insured depository institutions, regardless of the riskiness of their assets, the size of their equity capital, or the capability of their management. The increase of deposit insurance for thrift institutions to USD100,000 under DIDMCA occurred at the behest of S&L special interest groups and, coupled with the advent of brokered deposits and multiple deposit schemes, facilitating reckless investment activities, created a real 'moral hazard', under the protection of the federal deposit insurance guarantee.[22]

In addition, in implementing Title III of DIDMCA, the Federal Home Loan Bank Board (FHLBB) allowed the term 'depositor' to be construed broadly allowing imaginative, multiple extensions of deposit insurance to attract new funds to distressed thrift institutions, particularly through 'brokered deposits' and 'multiple deposit' schemes. 'Brokered deposits' were deposit transactions conducted by 'money brokers' where funds were deposited in banks and S&Ls in multi-million dollar blocks of separate USD100,000 certificates of deposit with each certificate being owned by a separate depositor.[23]

Prior to 1981, as thrift institutions lost their depositor bases to financial service competitors, their ability to purchase brokered deposits were limited to a mere total of 5 per cent of all deposits. The brokered deposit ceiling was removed by the FHLBB in 1981, however, and a vast number of brokered deposits filled S&Ls which required payment of high interest rates on the deposits. Although S&Ls were successful in raising more funds through brokered deposits and the high interest rates paid on such deposits, given the Fed's monetary policy operations over 1980–1981, the increase in brokered deposits further augmented the asset-liability mismatch dilemma for the thrift industry.[24]

D. Expansion of Thrift Powers and Permissible Activities

Title IV of DIDMCA removed the 'one product' limitation from the thrift industry and authorized federally-chartered thrift institutions to expand and

---

22 *Ibid.*

23 For example, a securities brokerage firm ('money broker') representing fifty customers would raise USD100,000 from each customer. With a total of USD5,000,000 to place, the money broker could 'shop' for the best yields without concern for risk. There were always banks or S&Ls that were seeking funds and 'bidding up' interest rates on deposit transactions in order to attract large deposits. There was no risk to the money broker since each of the fifty customers would have his or her USD100,000 subject to protection by the newly augmented deposit insurance scheme.

24 'Multiple Deposits' schemes were deposits made in multiple banks all under one umbrella of deposit ownership. For example, a single depositor with USD1 million could arrange through a holding company owning 10 banks, to make USD100,000 deposits in each of those banks through the coordinating efforts of the holding company, and each deposit was subject to deposit insurance. These arrangements allowed a small number of individuals to control large amounts of deposits in both banks and S&Ls. The result was that the focus of deposit insurance shifted from the need to protect small depositors from losing their deposits to the need to protect the overall banking and thrift systems from losing their deposits.

diversify into various new activities.[25] These deregulatory measures were designed to diversify sources of revenue for thrift institutions. For instance, DIDMCA authorized thrift institutions to invest up to 20 per cent of their assets in short-term market investments, such as consumer loans, commercial paper, and corporate debt securities.[26] DIDMCA further authorized all depository institutions to provide checking account services and NOW accounts,[27] trust services,[28] and credit card services[29] for their customers.

More importantly, DIDMCA removed the USD75,000 limit on real estate loans and authorized loans by thrift institutions of up to 80 per cent of the value of real estate (and greater if covered by mortgage insurance), and further liberalized the ability to make acquisition, development and construction (AD&C) loans.[30] The authorization of commercial real estate loans, similarly to the deposit insurance provisions, was largely uncontested prior to enactment, but was later perceived as one of the primary catalysts of the thrift industry crisis. Notably, commercial banks and insurance companies were already aggressively offering commercial real estate loans, and pension funds were aggressively purchasing commercial real estate.[31]

E. Pre-emption of State Usury Laws

Title V of DIDMCA pre-empted State usury laws that had previously restricted interest rates on certain types of loans, particularly residential real estate mortgages, in order to assist in curing the interest rate mismatch dilemma[32] for the benefit of certain lenders.[33] Title V further pre-empted

---

25 § 401 of DIDMCA generally authorized S&Ls to lend and invest in many new areas. § 402 of DIDMCA authorized S&Ls to engage in credit card activities. § 403 authorized S&Ls to engage in trust banking activities. § 501 of DIDMCA removed state usury law limitations on residential real estate mortgage lending activities. Thus, S&Ls could increase earnings by continuing to engage in mortgage lending without state law usury limitations, and could expand into new areas to generate additional earnings.

26 See DIDMCA, *supra* note 1, at § 401(c)(2), 94 Stat. at 153 (codified in various sections of 12 U.S.C.).

27 *Id.* at 12 U.S.C. § 1832(a).

28 *Id.* at § 403, 94 Stat. at 156–158 (codified as amended at 12 U.S.C. § 1464).

29 *Id.* at § 402, 94 Stat. at 155–156 (codified as amended at 12 U.S.C. § 1464(b)).

30 See J. J. Norton and S.C. Whitley, *Banking Law Manual* (1984, as annually suppl.), Ch. 9.

31 Interestingly, the authorization of thrifts to engage in commercial real estate lending did little to solve their basic maturity mismatch dilemma, and thrift institutions had no experience in this highly competitive and risky sector of lending activities. The apparent hope was that the troubled thrifts could invest in ADC loans, made profitable by continued inflation in real estate prices. The S&Ls, however, were basically left to finance projects that were deemed to be too speculative by money center banks and insurance companies.

32 *Ibid.* at § 501(a)(1), 94 Stat. at. 161 (codified at 12 U.S.C. § 1735f–7).

33 *Ibid.* at § 501(a)(1). State usury laws were another method by which interest rate ceilings had historically been controlled in America. These state laws were in addition to the federal legislation that placed ceilings on the rate of interest banks and savings and loans could pay on their deposits. The state usury laws applied to all lenders under their jurisdiction. DIDMCA pre-empted state usury laws but only as to federally regulated lenders including banks and savings and loans. In essence, through DIDMCA, federally insured banks and savings and loans obtained a competitive advantage over other types of lenders by reason of the flexibility in the rate of interest they could charge on loans.

State usury laws to permit insured State banks and S&Ls to charge interest on loans at the rate of 1 per cent above the FRB discount rate. Thus, Congress dictated under DIDMCA that in the area of mortgage usury there would be no effective standard, as interest rates would be dictated by neither federal law nor the laws of State jurisdictions, but by the markets themselves.[34]

The pre-emption of State usury laws provided for unlimited interest rates on first lien loans on residential property (houses, condominiums, apartments, townhouses) and permitted interest rates on business and agricultural loans of USD25,000 or more to equal 5 percentage points above the discount rate.[35] The States were given three years to 'opt out' of this pre-emption,[36] but few of the States opted out.[37] The two pre-emptive measures possessed the following significant aspects. The first pre-emption measure permitted any federally regulated lender (including banks and S&Ls) to charge any interest rate it could negotiate on first lien loans on residential property.

In other words, all usury limitations on these loans were removed. Ultimately, 'first lien loans' were construed to include not only typical mortgages or deeds of trust having first lien priority, but also so-called 'wrap around' mortgages, or mortgages or deeds of trust of any lien priority as long as they secured loans including within their principal balance amounts remaining

---

34 See generally, 'To Authorize a National Usury Ceiling: Hearing', before the Subcommittee on Domestic Monetary Policy of the House Committee on Banking, Finance, and Urban Affairs, 97th Cong., 2d Sess. (1982).

35 See DIDMCA, note 1, *supra*, at §§ 501, 511. In April 1981, the FHLBB adopted regulations to authorize federal thrift institutions to issue Adjustable Rate Mortgages (ARMs). The ARM authorization came too late, however, as by mid-1981 many thrift institutions were severely distressed or insolvent and could not dedicate the funds to originating new ARM mortgages.

36 *Ibid.* at § 501. States were permitted to override the federal pre-emption of state usury limits on home mortgage loans within the period after 1 April 1980, and prior to 1 April 1983. The override could consist of the adoption of a law or a vote by voters in favor of any provision, constitutional or otherwise, which stated explicitly that the state did not want the federal pre-emption to apply to loans made in that state. At this time, interest rates were still at an historic high and the Fed discount rate regularly exceeded 14 per cent to 15 per cent.

37 Actually, most states were questioning their existing usury legislation at the time. Usury ceilings varied from state to state and caused pressures on certain states (and their financial institutions) that had (and were subject to) legislation setting forth (relative to other states) low usury ceilings. For example, some states had no usury ceiling on certain types of commercial loans while other states had very strict usury laws (in many cases lower than 10 per cent) on the same types of loans. Hence, the DIDMCA provisions were not resisted; but were in fact generally welcomed. Nevertheless, the provisions did 'knock down another pillar' of interest rate control that had served the states and their communities well. With the pre-emption, every homeowner and most businesses became vulnerable to free floating interest rates without limits.

available to repay the outstanding principal balance(s) of any prior loan(s) secured by any prior mortgage.[38]

The term 'residential property' was construed to include not only single family residential housing, but also apartment developments, condominium developments, development and construction loans made for such purpose, and land zoned for such purpose. The second pre-emption measure permitted any federally regulated lender (including banks and S&Ls) to charge interest on 'commercial loans' at a rate equal to 5 per cent above the per annum discount rate established by the Federal Reserve System. The term 'commercial' did not include consumer and personal loans for personal use, yet the term was construed broadly to include virtually every other type of loan. The banks and S&Ls (otherwise free of the restraints of State usury laws) in turn increased interest rates on all loans subject to the pre-emption features of DIDMCA.[39]

The increased interest rates on commercial loans were naturally passed along to consumers by commercial borrowers through price increases. In addition, increased interest rate costs on newly originated first lien loans on residential property were passed along to home buyers through higher mortgage interest rates and new loan instruments called Negotiated Rate Mortgages, Adjustable Rate Mortgages, Renegotiable Rate Mortgages, Graduated Equity Mortgages, and the like. Notably, the FHLBB adopted regulations to authorize federally-chartered thrift institutions to issue Adjustable Rate Mortgages (ARMs).[40]

The ARM authorization came far too late, however, as by mid-1981 many thrift institutions were severely distressed or insolvent and could not dedicate the funds to originating new ARM mortgages. The increased prices necessarily resulted in inflation and higher interest rates that in the short-term started and repeated the asset value inflation cycle.

DIDMCA may have temporarily alleviated the focus of the thrift disintermediation problem, but it certainly did not stop the huge losses suffered by thrift institutions which continued to carry lower fixed-rate assets in the

---

[38] The following represents a *'wrap-around' mortgage* which was deemed to be a first lien for purposes of the DIDMCA pre-emption:

> Assume the developer of a 200-unit apartment complex financed the complex for USD2,000,000 with an insurance company secured by a first mortgage. Assume the developer subsequently sells the complex for USD3,500,000 to a buyer who pays USD1,500,000 in cash to the developer and takes the ownership of the complex subject to the first mortgage of USD2,000,000. Assume that the buyer intends to finance his acquisition with a new loan from a savings and loan association for USD1,000,000 with the buyer providing USD500,000 of his own cash. Because of state usury laws, assume the savings and loan association is restricted to a 10 per cent rate of interest on second mortgage loans. The savings and loan association could avoid the 10 per cent usury ceiling by instead making a 3 million dollar all-inclusive wrap-around loan. The 3 million dollar loan would include the USD1,000,000 the buyer is borrowing plus a reserve of USD2,000,000 to pay the first mortgage. Under DIDMCA, the USD3,000,000 wrap-around loan, although secured by a mortgage second in priority to the USD2,000,0000 first mortgage, was deemed a first mortgage and hence, satisfied the pre-emption requirement of being a first lien loan residential real property.

[39] See, inter alia, J. Norton and S. Whitley, *supra*, note 30, Ch. 9 (1984 version)

[40] *Ibid.*

asset-liability mismatch dilemma. Not long after the DIDMCA was enacted, the thrift industry was immersed in terminal crisis and the only intermediate solution was to create the incentives for healthy thrift institutions to acquire the less healthy institutions.

F. The Effect of DIDMCA on Monetary Policy Operations

While DIDMCA legislation was a significant victory for private US banking interests, it had an appreciable and negative impact on Fed monetary policy operations going into 1981. The sharp interest rate increases in 1980 induced a brief recession in early 1980 followed by a weak recovery. Interest rates declined after the recession, but not to their pre-1980 levels. The federal funds rate, which had been 11.9 per cent on average during 1979 and 7.93 per cent on average in 1978, peaked at 19.08 per cent in January 1981 and then declined to 16.28 per cent by April 1981.[41]

In the May 1981 Federal Open Market Committee (FOMC) meeting, debate focused on what the confusing monetary data represented. The bottom line was that the M-1 aggregate was distorted by the innovations authorized by Congress under DIDMCA, particularly with respect to the establishment of NOW accounts (checking accounts that paid interest) which altered the economic meaning of M-1. Title III of DIDMCA resulted in billions of dollars from M-1 demand deposits and M-2 savings accounts flowing into NOW accounts, which contained characteristics of both M-1 and M-2 type accounts. The Title III provisions caused the traditional definitions of liquid money to erode, and the distinctions generally relied upon to decide money supply questions were being eliminated in unpredictable ways. The economic relevance of M-1, the focus of monetarist doctrine, was thereafter uncertain.[42]

In other words, the Fed attempted to manage the economy using an inherently unstable and uncertain monetary aggregate in M-1, an economic number that had largely lost its meaning. Following DIDMCA, M-1 was 'contaminated' by idle 'savings account' money commingled with active 'checking account' money, and therefore appeared larger than it really was (in terms of what level of economic activity it would permit). Therefore, the M-1 statistics were dangerously misleading if FOMC continued to act upon M-1 without further consideration under the pretext of the monetarist doctrine: by holding M-1 down, the Fed could be squeezing the economy tighter than it had intended.[43]

The FRB nonetheless derived that the M-1 expansion was excessive, and after much debate over the meaning of M-1 and M-2 the FOMC accepted this interpretation at the March 1981 meeting, basing policy on monetary

---

[41] See 67 Federal Reserve Bulletin (May 1981), at A25. The M-1 aggregate surged abruptly by April 1981, however, and the FOMC agreed to let the Federal Funds rate move above the target range, on the premise that uncontrolled expansion of money and credit would be dampened by rendering money more expensive. By April 1981, inflation declined to 7.2 per cent, but by the second week of May 1981 the Federal Funds rate increased by 260 basis points and exceeded 18 per cent. Notwithstanding the surge in M-1, all other economic signals indicated that money and credit were tightening, not easing.

[42] See Greider, *supra*, note 6, at pp.383–384.

[43] See note 6, *supra*, at pp.384–385.

aggregates instead of interest rates. The Fed adopted a directive that ordered a 'substantial deceleration' of money supply growth. The results were dramatic, as the one-year economic expansion ceased and the economy plunged into recession, the second contraction in two years.[44] Thus, a short time after the March 1981 FOMC meeting it became clear that the FOMC reading of M-1 was incorrect. The error in judgment resulted in painful consequences for the nation and extreme criticism of the Fed's policies going into 1981–1982.[45]

---

44 In this author's view, the Fed, at this time, either did not fully understand, or would not admit, that modern recessions did not flow naturally from forces of the business cycle, but were instead induced in large part by the federal government. In the seven recessions since World War II, the same phenomena had preceded each contraction: the Fed's decision to force up interest rates to an abnormal level. Notably, it was not price inflation that broke economic expansions, but high interest rates engineered by the Fed to pre-empt inflation. Thus, to pre-empt inflationary expectations, there is always the risk of recession induced by increasing interest rates, and the Fed never declared its expectations in advance. Although policymakers may agree informally that their policy was steering the economy into recession, they never informed the public about the connection between higher interest rates and the likelihood of a consequent recession or depression. If the public understood the connection, the Fed would find it much more difficult to discreetly conduct monetary policy operations, as secrecy and evasion were essential components to the task. The other branches of government also possessed an interest in obscuring reality. If the public understood that the government itself generally induced recession, the President and Congress would be in an awkward position, having to answer questions about why the Fed was permitted to induce recession. The continued independence of the Fed was a means for elected politicians to evade responsibility for these events. If the situation worsened, they could blame the Fed and the Fed would retain its role as the public scapegoat. This arrangement was essential to the US Federal Reserve and political systems. The government's silence on this question and the absence of fair warning and debate pre-empted all reasonable questions that might have been asked about whether the Fed was 'doing the right thing'. The foregoing process of secrecy and evasion of responsibility for government policies and their predictable consequences enables the respective governmental authorities to 'purchase' political advantages with the price paid by inflation, high rates of interest and ultimately exchange rate and balance of payments distortions, currency devaluation, asset value deflation and recession or depression. With the elimination of the mandatory fiscal and monetary policy discipline imposed under the Bretton Woods fixed exchange rate system, the responsibility for voluntary, informed, coordinated enforcement of financial discipline and maintenance of a sound currency fell to the US Government, in particular, to the Treasury Department, Congress and the Fed. The government had failed in its responsibility. The general public undoubtedly agreed that inflation should be limited or stabilized, but it was not clear that inducing recession was the best way to address inflationary expectations. For instance, in 1981, inflation was driven by increasing prices in oil and agriculture, both of which might have been contained by direct price controls and other aggressive government policies, and the parties that were harmed by such policies could have been compensated in other ways. Thus, by evading the question, the political community did not have to examine the alternatives or which interests would be most injured by the Fed's chosen method. All solutions had their respective costs, but the political debate never compared them and was in any event not in a position to choose which solution might do the least damage to the largest number of people or to the economy or sectors thereof. The Fed therefore imposed its decisions on the national and global economies, and at times the particular cures were actually worse than the afflictions.

45 Although the general consensus was that the Fed's policy decisions were incorrect from the economic perspective, the decisions only made sense in the political context of the time. The Fed was subjected to pressure on several grounds at the same time, and did not want to repeat the same mistakes of 1980. The cumulative perspective of the outside pressures (White House, bond markets, commercial banks) guided the Fed in the same direction, towards greater tightening and maintaining credibility.

III. THE REAGAN ADMINISTRATION

In November 1980, Ronald Reagan was elected President of the United States. President Jimmy Carter and his Administration lost the November 1980 election largely as a result of the economic fallout of exchange rate volatility over the late 1970s and the massive policy reversal in 1979 from focusing on the inability to stabilize exchange rates to the Federal Reserve's abrupt implementation of anti-inflationary monetary policy. The Reagan Administration inherited perhaps the most volatile economic conditions of all time in November 1980, coupled with the DIDMCA legislation enacted under President Carter in March 1980.[46]

The economic disorder that helped to elect President Reagan continued onward with inflation in the double digits, and interest rates rising to unprecedented levels (up to 21 per cent by late 1980). In the Presidential campaign, President Reagan declared that in the present crisis, government intervention was the cause, and not the solution, and blamed the Carter Administration and 'government intervention' in general for the existing economic disorder. According to President Reagan, the problem started with burdensome federal taxes that depressed initiative and capitalism, and continued with fiscal deficit spending, and he promised to deliver a new program for economic recovery that would overcome the 'negative economic forces' and reverse the damage caused by the Carter Administration.[47]

The details of the Reagan Program focused on tax and regulatory relief for individuals and corporations, and formulated 'supply side economics' as the underpinning of the Program. The 'supply side economics' concept was actually an intent to reduce the progressive income tax, with the underlying assumption being that tax reductions would place more money in private control which would flow into capital investments, and augment the 'supply side' of the economy with new factories and technologies, thus establishing a larger base of productive capacity.[48]

The tax cuts would reduce government revenues by at least USD500 billion over five years, which necessarily implicated the issue of fiscal deficit spending. President Reagan promised to simultaneously reduce the size and influence of federal government and reduce government spending over the same period to avoid fiscal deficits. President Reagan ultimately promised

---

[46] The US Congress, the thrift industry and the FHLBB apparently did not understand the magnitude of the thrift industry crisis unfolding before them. The period before the election was dominated by abrupt monetary policy shifts and volatile interest rates, with uncertain consequences for the domestic economy. The initial federal response to the increasing number of thrift failures was deregulation on an extensive scale in the scope of permissible thrift investment powers and a similar expansion in a thrift institution's ability to compete for funds with other financial service providers.

[47] See generally Rowland Evans and Robert Novak, *The Reagan Revolution* (E.P. Dutton, 1981). Reagan ignored the sources of 'negative economic forces' unleashed by the abandonment of Bretton Woods and governments' subsequent failure to impose voluntary coordinated fisccal and monetary policy discipline. See note 44, *supra*.

[48] See generally Paul C. Roberts, *The Supply-Side Revolution: An Insider's Account of Policymaking in Washington* (Harvard University Press, 1984).

that in several years of cumulative budget cuts and revived economic prosperity, his Program would produce a balanced federal budget by 1984. The promise appeared to lack credibility in part, however, as the inevitable federal deficits would likely increase in the near future if the Program was enacted. The Reagan agenda included a massive increase in defense spending that would largely offset the savings envisioned from budget cuts for domestic programs, and the tax reductions would lose at least USD100 billion per year in government revenue. In short, the Reagan Program would more likely produce the opposite effect of what he promised – much larger federal deficits and a predicate for continued inflation.[49]

The Reagan Administration made fairly clear from the outset that it had little interest in the thrift industry crisis, however. The response to the crisis was aggravated by the relative secrecy of the bank and thrift examination processes, which implied that little information was available to the public, or to Congress, concerning the developing crisis within the thrift industry.[50] The immediate concern was to preclude an earnings crisis from becoming a liquidity crisis, which could have occurred if public confidence in the thrift institutions eroded. Thus, regulators and Congress were generally reluctant to disclose the mounting information to the public.[51]

The regulatory agencies themselves, including the FHLBB, FDIC and Federal Reserve, actually devised legislation in the spring of 1981, known as the 'regulators' bill', which was ultimately adopted into law as part of the banking legislation enacted in December 1982, discussed later in this chapter. The regulators' bill provided for the expansion of the regulatory agencies' powers to assist institutions by keeping them open.[52] The most significant elements of the bill were the proposals for merging distressed institutions into healthy institutions, including 'interindustry' mergers (i.e., between thrifts and banks or bank holding companies) and 'interstate' mergers.[53] In addition, the bill expanded regulatory authority to assist institutions without closing them through 'open bank assistance', which involved various transactions designed to provide government assistance through favorable transaction terms and assisted acquisitions by healthy institutions.[54]

These proposals were significant because they were related to initiatives to deregulate and strengthen the depository institutions that were advanced prior to and apart from the thrift industry crisis. These initiatives addressed

---

49 See Greider, *supra* note 6, at pp.352–353.

50 Bank and thrift examinations are generally protected from public disclosure by exemption (8) of the Freedom of Information Act. See 5 U.S.C. § 552(b)(8) (1998), and in the civil discovery process by a vaguely defined 'bank examination' privilege mandated by agency regulation, although the privilege has recently been questioned by federal courts. See, e.g., 12 C.F.R. § 261.2(b) (1998) (national banks); *Schreiber v. Society for Sav. Bancorp, Inc.*, 11 F.3d 217, 220–221 (D.C.Cir. 1993) (applying bank examination privilege); cf. *In re Bankers Trust Co.*, 61 F.3d 465, 471–472 (6th Cir. 1995) (refusing to apply bank examination privilege).

51 See, e.g., Richard Pratt, 'No S&L Liquidity Crisis', Am. Banker, 20 May 1981, at p.3 (reporting speech of FHLBB Chairman Richard Pratt).

52 See, e.g., Jay Rothstein,'Regulators Revise Crisis Merger Legislation', Am. Banker, 27 May 1981, at p.36.

53 *Ibid.* at p.36.

54 *Ibid.* at p.36.

three sets of reforms. First, the elimination of legal barriers under the Glass-Steagall Act to the affiliation of banking entities with entities providing other forms of financial services, primarily investment banking, securities advisory, and brokerage services. Second, the removal of barriers to interstate expansion by depository institutions. Third, the elimination of differences between different types of depository institutions, which implied that thrift institutions had to limit their activities to residential real estate lending.[55]

The regulators' bill provided the impetus for general deregulation of the financial services industry under banking legislation enacted in 1982. The Reagan Administration was generally preoccupied with its tax program progressing through Congress, however, and showed little interest in the regulators' bill and refused to support it.[56] The thrift industry, which was generally hostile to the emergency acquisition provisions in the regulators' bill that would likely lead to commercial bank acquisition of thrift institutions, opposed the bill and continued to press for more direct relief efforts through the FHLBB.[57] The commercial banking industry engaged in efforts during the summer of 1981 to restore the interest rate differential of 0.25 per cent that thrift institutions were permitted to pay on deposits before the DIDC.[58]

The accelerating rate of distressed and failed institutions continued, however, and by late summer 1981, after passage of the Reagan Administration tax program, discussed later, the regulatory agencies, together with Representative Germain, the House Banking Committee Chairman, revived momentum for the regulators' bill.[59] In order to satisfy the thrift industry, however, a third component was added to the regulators' bill in late summer and early fall of 1981, to significantly expand the authority of thrift institutions to engage in investment activities and thereby make them more like commercial banks, and to otherwise grant new powers beyond those already granted to commercial banks. The proposal was sponsored by the FHLBB, apparently without support of the other banking regulatory agencies. The Reagan Administration, following the policy of benign neglect, remained neutral and refused to oppose the regulators' bill throughout late 1981.[60]

---

55 See Stanley L. Langbein, 'The Thrift Crises and the Constitution', 53 Washington & Lee L. Rev. (1996), at p.179.

56 See, e.g., Joseph D. Hutnyan, 'Desertions on Rescue Bill Question Validity of Thrift Crisis', Am. Banker, 5 June 1981, at p.4.

57 The US League of Savings Associations, the largest thrift industry trade group, denounced the bill as a ploy to encourage commercial banks to acquire thrift institutions. See Hutnyan, *supra* note 57, at p.4.

58 See, e.g., Karen Slater, 'U.S. Savings League Threatens to Sue Over Deregulation Actions; Charges Decisions Exceeded Congressional Mandate', Am. Banker, 29 June 1981, at pp.1, 16; Jay Rothstein, 'Garn Tells Commercial Banks to Quit Griping About Thrifts', Am. Banker, 21 October 1981, at p.1 (reviewing commentary by Senator Garn, Chairman of the Senate Banking Committee).

59 See Jay Rothstein, 'Move is on to Revive Bank and Thrift Aid', Am. Banker, 3 August 1981, at p.6; Joseph D. Hutnyan, 'Congressional Support Seems to Grow for Crisis Mergers', Am. Banker, 1 October 1981, at p.1.

60 See Joseph D. Hutnyan, 'Two "Thrift" Bills Likely to Dominate Washington', Am. Banker, 28 August 1981, at p.4.

The following examination of the Reagan Administration fiscal policies and banking legislation enacted during this tenure reveals that the Administration's policies in banking and finance did not, in this author's view, represent any dramatic change in direction from those under the Carter Administration but directly conflicted with Fed monetary policy. The Reagan Program only represented a change of pace and degree, except that monetary policy became the most important policy instrument and remained beyond the control of the Administration. As President Reagan assumed office, the stage had already been set for a decisive assault on the banking and thrift framework, and financial 'speculation' became the norm of market participants.

IV. POLICY CONFLICTS BETWEEN THE FED AND THE REAGAN PROGRAM

President Reagan was the first President that could easily be labeled as a 'monetarist' and proponent of Milton Friedman, and he fully endorsed the Fed's adoption of monetarist operating techniques in October 1979 to reduce inflation by controlling money supply growth. The Reagan Administration generally endorsed the 'independence' of the Federal Reserve System, and stated that the government would not interfere with such independence but would consult with the Fed on all aspects of the economic program and purportedly pursue budget policies that would complement and support Fed policies in reducing money supply growth. When President Reagan took office in January 1981, the Fed was fully engaged in monetary restraint. The money supply targets had been reduced and commercial bank interest rates exceeded 21 per cent. The Reagan Administration was generally preoccupied with monetary policy, and literally filled with monetarist economists. The Reagan Administration generally supported the Fed's efforts to restrain money supply growth into 1981, even at the expense of high interest rates. The expected outcome from the Reagan Administration's economic program, however, was lower inflation, lower interest rates, and renewed vigor for financial markets and the economy.[61]

Fed Chairman Volcker reiterated publicly that the Reagan Administration policies were actually contradictory and conflicted with the proposition of reducing inflation. The Fed was engaged in restraining the economy to break inflation while the Reagan Administration promised to stimulate the economy under 'supply side economics'.[62] The Fed understood that the inherent conflict in policies, if sustained, would result in an economic 'squeeze'. As the Fed applied restraint on the money supply, it in essence set an upper limit on how much growth would be possible for nominal GNP (US economic output measured in dollars). The Fed could not control in the short term how much of the nominal GNP would simply reflect price inflation, and how much of it would

---

61 See Greider, *supra* note 6, at p.354.

62 See generally John T. Woolley, *Monetary Politics: The Federal Reserve and the Politics of Monetary Policy* (Cambridge University Press, 1984).

represent real growth in economic output. Either price inflation or the real output would have to worsen at the expense of improving the other.[63]

If inflation continued in double digits and the Fed kept its promise on limiting nominal GNP, there was no impetus for any sustained real growth, and in fact real growth would likely be negative, placing the US economy back into contraction or recession. The real economy would likely decline first, followed by declining inflation, not the other way around. Inflation would not decline first in light of increased growth in nominal GNP.[64]

The confusion generated throughout the Reagan Administration over conflicting economic policies coupled with the Fed's war against inflation resulted in the bond market becoming increasingly skeptical about the Administration's promises for the future.[65] The bond market clearly reflected inflationary expectations by increasing long-term interest rates.[66] As the

---

63 At the time, inflation was at 10–11 per cent; the economic growth would add another 3–5 per cent on top of the inflation in real growth; requiring a total of 13–15 per cent in nominal GNP. The FOMC, however, established a much lower growth target for the money supply in 1981, targets that would hold nominal GNP between 9—12 per cent. The 'squeeze' was derived from the gap in these numbers, and the discrepancy was suggestive of the problem.

64 In short, the Fed was attacking inflation with tight money and high interest rates by late 1980, and the Reagan Administration promised to take the opposite direction and stimulate the economy with tax reductions while the Fed was attempting to restrain it. The prospect of much larger fiscal deficits would encourage inflationary expectations in the bond markets, just as the Fed was attempting to persuade the bond markets of the opposite. If fiscal policy was stimulative, then monetary policy would singularly carry the burden of enforcing restraint and therefore needed to overcompensate to achieve the desired results. Therefore, the potential mismatch of government policies – President and Congress attempting to stimulate economic growth while the Fed simultaneously attempted to mitigate it by attacking inflation – could severely damage the economy.

65 The President and Fed were not obligated by law to confront the differences in their economic policies, and given the independence of the central bank, there was no forum in government that compelled them to formally resolve their differences. The Fed's control over money supply and the President's control over government spending and fiscal policy were each powerful factors in manipulating the economy, yet they could theoretically push in opposite and uncoordinated directions, regardless of the unintended side effects for the public. Thus, the Fed's arguments were easily evaded by the Reagan Administration. Congress declined to choose between the contradictory policies of stimulus and restraint, but instead accepted both and acknowledged that the political momentum was running clearly in favor of the Administration.

66 The Fed paid close attention to bond market activity as it was long-term interest rates that the Fed could not directly control and that was most significant to the implementation of monetary policy. The inflation forecasts were an implicit judgment on how well the Fed conducted monetary policy. The bond market participants wanted the Fed to protect the value of their assets, as inflation eroded the value of the dollar and the value of long-term financial assets. The issue of Fed credibility was directly reflected through bond market activity. Bond market participants did not necessarily want the same monetary policies that other sectors of the economy wanted. See also generally, David M. Jones, *Fed Watching and Interest Rate Projections* (2nd edn, NYIF, 1989). The bond market functioned like any other political interest group, although not formally organized as such, actively seeking to influence government policy that would benefit their interests, in particular the money regulation by the Fed. The bond market participants had many channels of influence, but the bond market itself was the primary channel by which they influenced public policy most directly. Fed officials listened to the bond market closely. Since 1979, when the Fed initiated the monetarist approach, the financial markets tracked M-1 closely, taking positions in anticipation of effects from money supply expansion or contraction. The most important group of investors in the bond markets, particularly long-term US government bonds, were the commercial banks, the Fed's primary constituency.

Reagan Program advanced through Congress and the bond market became extremely skeptical, inflationary expectations surged. Long-term interest rates began rising even as short-term rates continued falling, given the Fed's monetary policy operations in late 1980, and the money supply continued to expand rapidly.[67]

In effect, the financial markets were skeptical that the Fed could (or would) continue to maintain a steady but restrained growth in the money supply, and the Federal Advisory Council of commercial bank representatives warned the Fed to avoid explosive growth in the money supply as in 1980. In the meantime, it became apparent to the Reagan Administration that the financial markets were not assured by their promises and scenarios.[68]

The monetarists in the Reagan Administration believed that interest rates were determined by market forces, not Fed manipulation. The focus of monetary policy must be exclusively on M-1 and the money supply, and any attempts to bring down interest rates by injecting more money into the banking system would be canceled out by the market's fear of inflation and upward pressure on interest rates.[69]

Although the economic and monetary history in 1979–1980 suggested that the monetarist position was incorrect, the monetarist logic nonetheless conveniently guided the Reagan Administration to blame the Fed for the inflationary expectations evident in the bond market (and the inflationary stimulus generated by its own legislative Program) by focusing on the monthly control of M-1, which appeared to be growing explosively again. The bottom line argument of the Reagan Administration was that the Fed was deliberately undermining the President, and although certain members attempted to unduly influence the Fed, it gave no commitment to cooperate with Administration economic policy.[70]

---

67 See, e.g., Federal Reserve Board, 'Monetary Policy Report to Congress', in *Annual Report* (Washington, D.C., 1981).

68 The deeper problem was the Fed's perceived lack of credibility, the skepticism about future monetary policy in the face of impending budget deficits. Many years of experience instructed financial markets not to count on the Fed to hold the line against aggressive fiscal policy. The Reagan Administration braced itself for rigorous stance on monetary policy.

69 See generally Michael G. Hadjimichalakis, *The Federal Reserve, Money, and Interest Rates: The Volcker Years and Beyond* (Praeger, 1984) (reviewing monetarist proposals).

70 The Fed subsequently indicated that the near-term monetary policy objective was to reduce money supply growth rates on an annual basis until inflation was squeezed from the economy, and this approach would presumably avoid outright shocks to different economic sectors as people would be given time to adjust. Unfortunately, the Fed did not keep this promise, and tightened the money supply in line with the interests of the Reagan Administration, the bond market, and the commercial banking industry. Chairman Volcker indicated that monetary policy mistakes had been made in the recent past on the side of excessive monetary easing, but in the future, the Fed would strive to err only on the side of excessive monetary restraint. The direct policy conflict between the Fed's anti-inflationary monetary policy and Reagan Administration's fiscal policy, although not necessarily transparent, soon had an enormous impact on the economy and further exacerbated the thrift industry and banking crises.

V. MONETARY CONDITIONS FOLLOWING DIDMCA

The Reagan Administration soon understood that the 'rosy scenarios' (fiscal stimulus, economic expansion, and limited budget deficits) predicted under the massive deregulatory 'supply side economics' package with respect to monetary policy would fail to materialize. The substance of this recognition was debated between the Reagan Administration and Treasury Department as the Economic Recovery Tax Act of 1981 (ERTA)[71] was being reviewed by Congress (which included the massive deregulatory tax cuts promised by President Reagan during the election campaign). The ERTA was the centerpiece of the Reagan Administration's 'supply side' economics program, and disproportionately rewarded the highest income tax brackets. Internal debate ensued over whether the President should disclose the more credible expectation of the Administration (massive budget deficits and shrinking economy) or maintain the public fiction of 'rosy scenarios' until Congress passed the ERTA. The President's senior policy advisors decided not to disclose the new deficit forecasts, and to maintain the 'rosy scenarios' forecast as the official version of what the Reagan Program would do for the economy, at least until after the ERTA was enacted.

Although passage of the tax bill was at the time uncertain, the political decision was made to maintain the old 'rosy scenarios' forecast even though it was clearly incorrect.[72] This decision represented a pivotal point in US economics and politics. If accurate disclosures of the inherent conflicts and likely outcome of the Reagan Program were made public, then (1) Congress might not have passed the ERTA; (2) the ensuing federal deficits might not have soared to USD200 billion per year, doubling the national debt in five years; and (3) the ensuing recession would still have occurred, but interest rates would probably have been far lower and caused much less damage to various economic sectors as the Fed attacked inflation.[73] The ERTA turned out to initiate a process of much larger tax cuts and budget deficits than the Reagan Administration originally intended, however, and those tax cuts were not matched by reductions in fiscal expenditures.[74]

As the Reagan Program advanced through Congress, the original package of budget cuts decreased as members of Congress compromised and rejected many of the reductions, but the proposal for tax cuts under ERTA increased. The final tax measures enacted under ERTA would result in a loss of federal revenue of approximately USD750 billion. The net effect, greater loss of federal revenue combined with smaller savings on the spending side of the budget, implied that the Reagan Administration economic policy advisors'

---

[71] See Economic Recovery Tax Act of 1981, *supra* note 4.

[72] President Reagan himself was apparently not consulted by the senior policy advisors on the decision or informally advised by his own economic policy advisors that they now realized that the Reagan Program would produce disastrous fiscal consequences.

[73] See Greider, *supra* note 6, at p.397.

[74] See P. Volcker and T. Ghoyten, *Changing Fortunes: The World's Money and the Threat to American Leadership* (1992).

forecasts of fiscal deficit estimates were far too low.[75] In essence, the loss of federal revenue under ERTA implied far larger fiscal deficits, which placed enormous pressure on the Fed to tighten monetary policy and ultimately pushed in favor of higher interest rates.[76]

In the ensuing debate over the impact of the phased-in ERTA tax cuts on the economy, and how the Fed would or should react to them, the Fed position supported the tax cuts, but disfavored the budget cuts as grossly inadequate. On the evening before the Congressional vote on the Reagan Program, President Reagan made a public statement and explicitly noted that the program would generate smaller deficits and the budget would be balanced within a few years, promises that his own economic policy advisors knew to be without merit. The program passed Congress, with an income tax program under the ERTA that was regressive and generally favored the wealthy taxpayers and corporations.[77]

VI. ERTA

A. Provisions Affecting Real Estate

The ERTA represented the reaction of Congress to the sluggish economy resulting from the high interest rate environment of the late 1970s and the early 1980s, imposed by the Fed to combat inflation. Inflation in real estate prices continued, however, even as the general rate of inflation abated somewhat in 1981. Real property inflation was fueled by the acceleration of the tax shelter business, which received a large push from the real estate provisions of ERTA. The ERTA improved tax shelter opportunities in real estate principally by reducing the depreciable life of improvements to 15 years from 35 years,[78] thus permitting accelerated recognition of depreciable costs. In addition to this new incentive, real estate investors could already deduct investment interest, paid

---

[75] The Fed 'officially' supported the Reagan Administration program, but began discreetly lobbying Congress against voting for such a massive loss of federal revenue. The warnings were not made 'public' however, and later certain members of Congress conveniently criticized the Fed for failure to make such warnings public.

[76] In fact, the enactment actually created a 'structural' budget deficit. The 'structural' deficit is contrasted to the Keynesian 'full employment' deficit, which is defined as the difference between government revenues actually collected and those that would be collected if the economy were operating at 'full employment'. The full employment deficit purportedly measured the appropriate amount of fiscal stimulus necessary to move the economy from underemployment to full employment. The deficits implemented by the Democratic administrations and Congress from the early 1960s through the early 1980s were generally limited to full employment deficits. The larger deficits incurred after the passage of ERTA generally exceeded the measured full employment deficit in fiscal years since 1982, the first following the passage of ERTA. See generally Joseph Pechman, *Federal Tax Policy* (5th edn, 1987).

[77] See Greider, *supra* note 6, at p.400.

[78] See ERTA, *supra* note 4, at § 201; I.R.C. § 168 (the recovery period was subsequently extended to 18 years by the Deficit Reduction Act of 1984 and then to 19 years in 1985). The taxpayer was given the option to elect to use the straight-line depreciation method over 15 years, 35 years or 45 years for 15-year public utility property.

or accrued, and could take advantage of non-recourse mortgage financing for purposes of deducting losses.[79] If the property was held for longer than one year, investors were entitled to the 60 per cent long-term capital gains exclusion,[80] thus ensuring a maximum tax of 20 per cent on disposition.[81]

ERTA also provided for an increase in the investment tax credit for rehabilitation expenditures to 15 per cent for non-residential 30-year-old buildings; 20 per cent for non-residential 40-year-old buildings; and 25 per cent for residential and non-residential certified historic structures. Before long, limited partnerships and real estate syndications became an attractive way to invest in real estate because they generated enormous tax savings and profits that passed through to investors.[82]

ERTA established the age of tax shelters and syndications, and allowed accelerated depreciation on certain real estate assets, investment tax credits, deductions for all interest and multiple tax benefits for low income housing. The ERTA provided investors with tax incentives to invest in all types of real estate investments which generated deductions and other tax savings for investors.[83] This was the era of the tax shelter, some abusive, many legitimate. The result was tax push pricing causing real estate values to increase dramatically because of the tax benefits then attributable to real estate ownership.

B. Impact of Reagan Administration Package and ERTA

The immediate impact of the enacted Reagan Administration program and ERTA legislation contained therein was higher interest rates, as the Federal Funds rate was permitted to increase one full point. The bond market tightened as well, and long-term interest rates moved up as much as 200 basis points in two months' time. Although long-term rates should have declined as the economy's demand for investment funds subsided given the new-found capital flows from ERTA tax cuts, investors were actually demanding extra protection against future inflation.[84]

---

79 See I.R.C. § 163.

80 See I.R.C. § 1201(a).

81 In 1984, the holding period was shortened to six months. See Tax Reform Act of 1984, Pub. L. No. 98–369, 98 Stat. 494 (1984), at § 1001(a)(1).

82 The broadening of investor participation in the apparently highly profitable real estate business was viewed as a panacea for thrift institutions desiring to utilize their newly expanded powers under DIDMCA to engage in real estate lending activities. The opportunities for syndicating tax shelters flourished and real estate market values escalated. And, if the property were held for longer than one year, the owner was entitled to the 60 per cent long-term capital gains exclusion, thus insuring a maximum tax of 20 per cent on dispositions (in 1984, the holding period was shortened to six months).

83 Notably, cash investment of USD1 could create as little as USD2 and as much as USD10 of tax savings, depending on the structure of the tax shelter limited partnership or tax syndicate.

84 See Greider, *supra* note 6, at pp.400–402. The direct cause of the higher long-term rates was the Fed and bond market reacting together in fear of the inflationary potential of the budget deficits and moving protectively in anticipation of such potential. The logical explanation was that the tax cuts and budget deficits were not necessarily the direct cause of higher interest rates, however, as the deficits emerged gradually over a period of years. The Fed refused to accept responsibility for high interest rates, instead claiming to be reacting to conditions as it found them.

The financial institutions were well compensated for their inflationary expectations, as the real interest rate on bank loans (difference between prime rate and rate of inflation) generally soared from 3–4 per cent (normal spread) to 8–9 per cent in 1981. The US banking industry, notably excluding the S&L industry, therefore entered the most profitable cycle of the century,[85] but the high interest rates created additional distress on bank customers, including a significant increase in bankruptcy filings, and significant deterioration in the quality of existing loan portfolios.[86]

VII. MONETARY AND EXCHANGE RATE CONDITIONS FOLLOWING ERTA

The Fed's high interest rates in 1981 forced significant burdens on the US economy, but even greater shifts in commerce and finance upon the entire world. When the US economy declined, the world's exporters lost their best

---

85 The striking change in financial industry, particularly banking, income was reflected in the Fed's reporting on BHCs. For the previous decade, the banks' ROE averaged slightly more than 11 per cent, but by 1979 it increased to a new record of 13.9 per cent. The profit rate for banks remained at that rate or higher through the next three years while the economy struggled with failure and retrenched. In other words, bank profits increased by more than 25 per cent while the returns on other economic enterprises headed in the opposite direction. The mechanics of recession guaranteed this outcome, particularly for larger banks that depended on the managed liabilities strategy, borrowing from the money market to lend them out to customers. On the upside, as interest rates increased, banks increased their interest rate spreads. The real profits came on the downside, however, when the economy was subsiding and interest rates were declining. Banks would still collect interest payments on old loans made when interest rates were at their peak, but they could raise funds in the money market at lower interest rates available as demand declined. Thus, income remained high while operating costs declined, widening the spread that translated into greater profits. The banks attempted to maintain the mismatch as long as possible by decreasing their loan rates as the economy headed into recession, but more slowly than the decline of money market rates on which banks themselves borrowed. In short, as the recession gathered momentum, banks lent expensive money and funded the loans with cheaper money. As the recession continued and business failures spread too widely, however, eventually the banks would suffer when their long-term customers could no longer pay their debts and banks would be forced to write down more loans at a loss. The economic reality of banks profiting in recessions, however, surely cast a different light on the confidential advice that the Fed received regularly from the banks themselves. The 12 commercial bankers of the Federal Advisory Council, who met privately with the Fed four times per year, were not necessarily disinterested consultants devoted to the goal of sound economics. When these bankers urged the Fed to tighten its money control, to tolerate high interest rates and recession, and to ignore the inevitable political complaints from other interests, they were arguing for the policy that would enhance their own profits. As the recession bloomed in the third quarter of 1981, the Fed asked the Federal Advisory Council (FAC) to evaluate the present condition of financial institutions under stresses they were encountering as a result of Fed policies. The FAC failed to mention the 'stress' of record profits, but modestly allowed that they were holding up, and were able to cope with uncomfortably high interest rates. According to Fed statistics, the larger banks 'coped' with higher interest rates in 1981 by earning a ROE of 13.66 per cent.

86 See Greider, *supra* note 6, at pp.412–413.

and biggest customer, and the world economy headed towards recession. The central banks of other nations raised their interest rates, supporting the Fed's initiative against inflation and depressing their own economies.[87] As the Fed's monetary policy actions pulled the global economy in one direction, the US dollar appreciated dramatically against other currencies as interest rates increased during 1980–1981.[88]

The appreciating dollar that accompanied high interest rates was initially welcomed given the currency market crises of the 1970s, but in time the high interest rates attracted enormous amounts of foreign capital to finance the Reagan Administration budget deficits.[89] The adverse repercussions of this policy mix on international markets soon became obvious, except to those members of the Administration who viewed the appreciating dollar as a vote of confidence in US policy.[90]

A. Beginnings of the Superdollar

The allied governments in Europe urged the Treasury Department and FRB to moderate policies to reduce the value of the dollar with some success, but the lesser developed country (LDC) nations whose economies depended largely on sales of commodities to the developed nations came under tremendous pressure from the increasing interest rates and appreciating US dollar. The US recession would result in financial catastrophe in Africa, Latin America, and Asia, as their economic outputs and real incomes decreased dramatically, resulting in falling export markets and commodity prices.[91] The stronger dollar also represented another channel through which the Fed's monetary policy depressed the US economy as domestic exports became far more expensive and foreign imports became far less expensive on a relative basis. By the fourth quarter of 1981, the damage was considerable and obvious to the domestic economy, as US businesses lost both export markets and domestic market share.[92]

In the interests of halting inflation, the Fed monetary policy actions strained exports, but what damaged US production interests inherently

---

87 See generally Michael Moffit, *The World's Money: International Banking from Bretton Woods to the Brink of Insolvency* (Simon and Schuster, New York, 1983).

88 The higher interest rates in the US attracted more and more foreign capital into dollar-denominated financial assets, including foreign wealth held overseas by US multinational corporations. The worldwide demand for dollars was increasing, but the Fed tightened the money supply (of dollars), causing substantial appreciation of the dollar versus other currencies. Thus, the price of the dollar, represented by the foreign exchange rate at which other currencies were converted into the dollar, increased significantly during 1980–1981.

89 See generally Martin Mayer, *The Fate of the Dollar* (Times Books, New York, 1980).

90 See Volcker, *supra* note 75, at p.178.

91 The debt burdens of the lesser developed nations expanded dangerously. The worldwide increase in interest rates raised the cost of dollar-denominated debt in outstanding bank loans. Governments and businesses borrowed heavily just to keep up the payments on old loans at the time their economies were contracting sharply. See generally Darrell Delamaide, *Debt Shock: The Full Story of the World Credit Crisis* (Doubleday Books, 1984).

92 See generally *Group of Thirty, The Problem of Exchange Rates, A Policy Statement* (New York, 1982).

rewarded financial institutions, especially the major international banks active in international finance. The appreciating dollar meant that the value of their overseas dollar assets were also increasing, and that market demand was growing for US dollar-denominated financial assets.[93] As long as US interest rates remained at high levels, global capital flows sought out the higher returns in US financial instruments, and as the demand for dollars increased, the value of the dollar in foreign exchange markets would similarly increase.[94]

Interestingly, even as the high interest rates and value of the dollar were crippling major sectors of the US economy, the Reagan Administration had the legal authority to intervene on Fed monetary policy operations to adjust exchange rate policy, but did not use this authority as such direct government intervention flew in the face of the Reagan Administration policies of reduced government intervention and deregulation.[95]

B. Recession

On 18 October 1981, President Reagan formally announced the onset of recession.[96] The Reagan Program enacted by Congress resulted in short-term budget imbalances on a massive scale and enormous fiscal deficits.[97] The results of the fiscal-monetary mismatch effectively muted political pressure against the Fed, and actually enhanced the Fed's position of power. By enacting huge fiscal deficits, the Reagan Administration and Congress had effectively limited their political options against the Fed, and they were now confronted with the single dilemma of how to reduce the fiscal deficits over the next five years.[98] In periods of recession, the Fed normally injected more liquidity into the banking system and pulled interest rates down. In October and November 1981, the FOMC held its anti-inflationary course. The monetarist persuasion appears to have thoroughly dominated the Reagan

---

93 See generally William R. Cline, *International Debt and the Stability of the World Economy* (Institute of International Economics, September 1983).

94 See generally John S. Odell, *U.S. International Monetary Policy: Markets, Power, and Ideas as Sources of Change* (Princeton University Press, 1982).

95 The international value of the dollar was one of the few areas of monetary policy where both law and tradition gave the Executive Branch higher authority than the Federal Reserve. The Treasury Secretary was responsible for US dollar policy and he could ultimately advise the Fed to adjust its domestic interest rates accordingly. The Treasury could also coordinate interventions in foreign exchange markets by buying and selling dollars through both the Treasury and Fed to push the price of the dollar up or down. The Reagan Administration failed to take advantage of this leverage. If the Treasury Department wanted a monetary policy that favored a stronger or weaker dollar, then the Fed had to listen to that policy. *Ibid.* at p.419.

96 See *Greider, supra* note 6, at p.418.

97 See generally Thomas B. Edsall, *The New Politics of Inequality* (W.W. Norton, New York, 1984).

98 The political fixation with respect to the Fed rested on interest rates, as members of Congress decided they would attempt to instruct the Fed to reduce interest rates or threaten the Fed with loss of political independence.

Administration, and maintained pressure on the Fed for a gradual reduction in the money supply.[99]

C. Fed Monetary Policy Errors

The Fed questioned whether to remove itself from the 'monetarist box' resulting from the self-imposed pursuit of M-1, which surged in growth in 1981 notwithstanding the suspected reason for the surge was that the definition of M-1 had changed in fact because of the NOW account legislation enacted under DIDMCA. Nonetheless, the Fed maintained the monetarist operating technique well into 1982, and the February 1982 FOMC Directive represented perhaps the largest policy error ever made by the Fed. Notwithstanding suspicions about the credibility of M-1, the Fed understood that M-1 was continuing to surge explosively in early 1982, and that monetary tightening was necessary to mitigate it. As the money supply (M-1) aggregate appeared to increase, the FOMC tightened and pushed short-term interest rates higher, even though there was a recession.[100]

In the face of increasing interest rates during a continued recession, Congress increased pressure on the Fed in public debates and hearings, and the Fed countered that it was powerless to reduce interest rates by increasing growth of the money supply.[101] The Fed argued that if it increased M-1, the financial markets would react by bidding up interest rates on their own and cancel out the intended results. The Fed declined to state that this scenario would occur because the Fed's adherence to the monetarist operating technique and market credibility told markets to react in this manner. The Fed absolved itself of any responsibility for the recession by declaring itself subject to the circular realities between M-1 and market psychology.[102] Despite rigorous pressure from certain members of Congress, the Fed did not yield on its monetary policy stance and made no deals to ensure its continued independence.

---

99 See S. Solomon, *Confidence Game: How Unelected Central Bankers Are Governing the Changed World Economy* (Simon & Schuster, 1995), at p.155.

100 The Fed permitted the Federal Funds Rate to increase from 12.5 per cent to 15.6 per cent in just a couple of weeks. The sudden jump and continued increase in interest rates sustained the recession for many months longer than expected, multiplying the S&L and banking crises and failures. The Fed officials claimed that they had not decided to tighten, but merely declined to ease monetary policy. Although M-1 growth ceased abruptly as a result of this action, interest rates responded accordingly by rising, and discount window borrowing surged as liquidity in the money market tightened.

101 See *Confidence Game*, *supra* note 100, at p.156.

102 When M-1 rose above its target, financial markets scrambled for funds and bid up interest rates, anticipating that the Fed would react by tightening the money supply. The Fed witnessed market rates rising in response to M-1, and in order to maintain credibility with the financial markets, the Fed did indeed tighten, thus ratifying their expectations. The circular logic was a game of illusions that the Fed had the power to break. Thus, if the Fed pumped enough new money into the banking system, supply and demand would require short-term interest rates to fall over time. Neither investor psychology nor the monetarist operating technique could repeal the laws of supply and demand. See Greider, *supra* note 6, at pp.472–473.

By March 1982, the Fed understood that the assumptions leading the FOMC to tighten the money supply in February 1982 were clearly incorrect, however. The surge in M-1 in December 1981–January 1982 did not serve as a predicate for increased economic activity.[103] The quantity of money supplied by the Fed to the banking system should have been enough to stimulate economic recovery, but it clearly did not have that effect. The US economy continued to spiral downward, and the foundations of the monetarist operating technique largely dissolved at this time. The slowing money velocity (money slowing down in circulation) disrupted all standard monetary analysis. The money supply was actually far tighter than the Fed had intended, as a given quantity of M-1 could not guarantee a level of economic activity expected from it in the highly volatile economic environment.[104] When money velocity departed from normal expectations, the Fed's basic calculations by which it determined the pace for the economy were rendered inoperable.[105] M-1 was a reliable measure only if money velocity followed the predicted trend line. If the public began changing their borrowing and spending habits, for whatever reasons, then velocity changed unexpectedly and M-1 became grossly misleading.[106] Nonetheless, the Fed was unwilling to totally abandon the monetarist operating technique by March 1982.[107]

As market interest rates, the inflation rate, and yields on government securities exceeded the Regulation Q depository interest rate ceilings, the regulatory agencies were faced with the same pressures that existed late in the Carter Administration: to abolish the depository interest rate ceilings or extend Regulation Q to cover mutual funds and other innovative money substitutes.

More importantly, the policy conflicts, growing fiscal deficits, anti-inflation monetary policy, high interest rates, appreciating dollar, and

---

[103] See generally Hadjimichalakis, *supra* note 70 (stating that May 1981 FOMC meeting involved an error in judgment regarding the M-1 aggregate leading FOMC to a series of inaccurate predictions and miscalculations, which were compounded as FOMC continued to adjust its own operating premises, and struggled to defend the logical appearance of their decisions).

[104] See Federal Reserve Bank of New York, 'Monetary Policy and Open Market Operations in 1982', *New York Federal Reserve Quarterly* (Spring 1983) (reviewing March 1982 FOMC meeting and the inoperability of the monetarist operating technique).

[105] See generally William C. Melton, *Inside the Fed: Making Monetary Policy* (Dow Jones – Irwin, New York, 1985).

[106] Neither the US Government nor the Fed could do anything to directly affect the velocity of money, and the uncertainty of the variables following DIDMCA poisoned the monetarist operating technique. The theoretical underpinnings of monetarism were a series of constant money relationships that did not necessarily exist. If M-1 increased in size but decreased in velocity, the effects would offset each other. M-1 velocity continued to decline from the last quarter in 1981 for the next 18 months. There was no means available to monitor the changing velocity of money and adjust the supply accordingly. Velocity was a derived statistic, one that would only be known after the fact by dividing the money supply growth into the economic growth that had already occurred.

[107] The Fed officials feared that if they abandoned M-1, the banks and bond market and money market would understand that the Fed would focus attention on interest rates again, and the Fed would lose credibility as it attempted to maintain control over the informal program of national liquidation to eliminate price inflation and stabilize the money supply. See *Greider, supra* note 6, at pp.482–483.

mounting erosion of capital from bank and thrift balance sheets finally reflected more transparent effects through a series of 'cracks' in the banking and financial systems which appeared through continued LDC lending activities and first appeared in a public sense in March 1982. These 'cracks in the system', as discussed in Chapter Two *infra*, appear to have caused the Fed to shape monetary policy around these separate but interrelated events. Once again, the focus was on selected problems within the banking industry, which further redirected attention and focus away from the blooming thrift industry crisis. These 'cracks in the system', again paradoxically, resulted in omnibus legislation in 1982 that continued to accelerate the deregulation process for the banking and thrift industries.

2. Cracks in the Banking and Financial System

I. INTRODUCTION

During 1982, just as the deregulatory process was under 'full steam', a series of 'cracks' began to appear in, and to adversely impact on the US financial system. This chapter addresses these 'cracks'.

II. LDC DEBT CRISIS (FEBRUARY 1982)

As alluded to in Chapter One, the oil price shocks of the early 1970s resulted in a massive influx of deposits to the international banking system from OPEC nations. The systemic flow of deposits from OPEC nations to international banks resulted in the phenomena of 'recycling petrodollars' to lesser developed country (LDC) nation borrowers over the late 1970s and early 1980s.[1] The global phenomena of petrodollar recycling all but guaranteed that LDC economies in which such funds were recycled would enjoy initial prosperity and high growth rates for a sustained period of time. As long as LDC nations expanded their exporting capacities as quickly as their foreign borrowings, their capacity to increase borrowings was generally undiminished.[2] The developed nations, primarily the United States, encouraged international banks to facilitate the recycling process and reaped the international political benefits thereof, but maintained a discreet distance from the actual decision making process of where to invest or lend the

1 See generally William R. Cline, *International Debt and the Stability of the World Economy* (Institute of International Economics, September 1983). The oil price shocks were the direct result of abandonment of the Bretton Woods system, devalutaion of the US dollar, and US abandonment of financial discipline.

2 The foreign aid provided by the United States and other developed nations paled in comparison to the vast capital flows directed to the development of LDC nations through international banks, particularly US based money center banks. The recycling phenomena was a vast program of foreign aid that effectively transferred wealth from rich nations to poorer nations with no political consequences.

funds.[3] The pace and priorities of LDC lending activities were maintained by the banking institutions and supported by their respective governments.[4]

By early 1980, the financial condition of many LDC borrowing nations had visibly deteriorated, and the US banking institutions generally concentrated their LDC loans in too few nations. The LDC borrowings were generally dollar-denominated and largely short-term and variable-rate in nature. The LDC borrower nations were therefore compelled to pay the higher real interest rates that occurred given the Fed's monetary policy operations and to continuously roll-over the short-term loans at higher and higher interest rates and dollar values as the Fed continuously tightened monetary policy.[5]

The LDC nations kept going deeper into debt just to maintain timely interest payments. By the early 1980s, most of the LDC economies were simultaneously not expanding as robustly as they were in the 1970s, but were instead declining, especially as US economic growth all but ceased and approached recession. The US bank LDC lending through syndicated lending and floating rate interest loans therefore continued to be highly profitable, notwithstanding the obvious pressure on LDC economies.[6]

The Fed itself induced the foundations for a global financial crisis through its campaign against inflation. The fundamentals of credit were reversed for LDC nations, in a manner similar to the situation for domestic borrowers in the US, as the real value of their dollar-denominated loans increased with the increasing interest rates and appreciation of the dollar. The Fed in effect risked global economic disorder hoping the conflicting forces would 'de-conflict' without collision. The LDC debt crisis and implications thereof were undoubtedly quite clear to the Fed by 1979–1980.[7]

As the Fed eliminated inflation, imports that the US absorbed from those nations would be reduced while interest rates simultaneously increased and LDC exports declined. The result was a squeeze for the LDC borrower nations, a deadly side effect of the Fed's campaign against inflation and fiscal policy battle with the Reagan Administration.[8] The Fed could have prevented the rapid expansion of LDC debt by restraining US banks from aggressive lending activities as their bank capital levels declined or by enforcing regulations designed to limit excessive single-borrower exposures. Instead, the Fed was unwilling to permit

---

[3] The Reagan Administration generally urged large banks to recycle petrodollars to developing nation borrowers. The loans were generally not invested in productive projects but instead were used to cover shortfalls caused by declining export and oil prices in the late 1970s. See L. William Seidman, *Full Faith and Credit: The Great S&L Debacle and Other Washington Sagas* (Times Books, 1993), at p.36.

[4] The money center banks lost many of their large corporate customers to the commercial paper market which was dominated by securities firms, so the recycling of petrodollars was the first big 'replacement activity' to recover lost profits from securities firms, followed by real estate development in late 1980s. See Seidman, *supra* note 3, at p.39.

[5] See P. Volcker and T. Ghoyten, *Changing Fortunes: The World's Money and the Threat to American Leadership* (1992), at p.179.

[6] See S. Solomon, *The Confidence Game: How Unelected Central Bankers are Governing the Changed World Economy* (Simon & Schuster, 1995), at p.196.

[7] See Volcker, *supra* note 5, at p.179.

[8] See *Confidence Game*, *supra* note 6, at p.197.

continued increases in domestic inflation in order to ease the debt burdens of foreign nations, and whether such efforts would actually mitigate the burdens on LDC nations was questionable at best. By late 1981 the LDC debt crisis was rolling ahead, and there were essentially no viable policy options to stop the crisis from manifesting in a public sense in the near future.[9]

By 1981, the 70 largest banks on the average maintained a 4.5 per cent capital-to-assets ratio, and some of the largest banks were well below that average.[10] The money center banks were apparently not embarrassed or alarmed by their aggressive lending positions in the LDC markets, however, and the Fed did little to provide guidance or impose prudential directives to improve capital adequacy of these institutions.[11]

When the Fed initiated its aggressive campaign against inflation in 1979 by tightening the money supply and imposing strict discipline on the world economy, these processes conflicted with any means to cease expansion of LDC nation borrowings. In theory, the debt crisis might have been averted or postponed if the Fed had not chosen such an abrupt approach to reducing price inflation. The banks certainly should have foreseen (and probably did in fact understand) the collision and prepared for it by limiting their LDC lending activities, but instead the banks urged the Fed through the Federal Advisory Council to continue tightening the money supply and ignored warnings of their overconcentration of lending to LDC nations.[12]

As banking institutions expanded their lending aggressively and inflation depreciated the value of their capital, the ratio of bank capital to outstanding loans (particularly LDC nation loans) declined steadily, particularly at the largest banks, which were operating with a declining safety net. In December 1981, the Fed and Office of the Comptroller of the Currency (OCC) introduced higher capital standards, and required the banking industry to maintain a minimum ratio between capital and assets of 5 per cent for larger banks and 6 per cent for smaller banks. If an aggressive bank management expanded a bank's lending portfolio, it would have to raise more capital by selling equity to maintain the

---

9 See Volcker, *supra* note 5, at p.179.

10 See Federal Reserve Board, 'Financial Developments of Bank Holding Companies in 1984', Fed. Res. Bulletin (December 1985) (reviewing capital adequacy data for banks and bank holding companies in 1981).

11 FRB officials generally understood that the situation was unsustainable, that LDC defaults would likely occur in the near future, and that the capital levels of the largest money center banks were stretched to their limits. The roots of the LDC debt crisis were fundamentally in the collision of purposes within the Fed itself. In the 1970s and early 1980s, the Fed and OCC simply failed to impose prudential limitations on money center banks and their LDC lending activities.

12 See Steven Greider, *Secrets of the Temple: How the Federal Reserve Runs the Country,* (Touchstone Books, 1988), at p.519.

ratios.[13] The new capital requirements introduced in December 1981 came much too late to make any significant difference, however, as the Fed yielded to the ambitions of the industry it regulated instead of enforcing the larger public interest.[14]

If inflation abated and the Fed restarted the economy by easing monetary policy, the LDC debt crisis could likely have been mitigated, but if the Fed tightened the money supply long enough, major LDC borrowers and their money center banks would be in great trouble. Nonetheless, the Fed approach failed to provide financial institutions with time to adjust to the monetary policies designed to combat inflation. The Fed abruptly halted runaway inflation instead of gradually mitigating inflation over time, and thereby forced the LDC nations to the brink of insolvency for nearly the same reasons it forced thousands of US businesses into insolvency. The LDC nations and US businesses were all heavily dependent on credit, but the Fed monetary policy actions simultaneously increased the cost of borrowing and depressed their sales and incomes. The LDC nations had no time to adjust and no alternative but to continue borrowing, however, just as US businesses borrowed more to survive the recession. The Fed's narrow and (ultimately) successful campaign against inflation was purchased at the price of bursting the bubble of global debt and shaking the very foundations of the international banking system.[15] There was no viable solution with respect to the LDC borrower nations, given the economic conditions existing at the time. The dilemma would preoccupy the Fed for several years to come.

---

13 The Fed regulations temporarily exempted the 17 largest international banking institutions from these new capital requirements, however, as these institutions could not possibly meet the new capital standards. The largest single factor responsible for their weakened capital status of money center banks was their aggressive LDC lending activities. The loans to LDC nations were largely concentrated among a few US money center banks, as more than 80 per cent of the US lending was conducted by 24 banks. If the LDC nations defaulted for any reason, the capital bases of these institutions would be eliminated. The medium- and smaller-sized banks were generally in compliance with the Fed's new capital requirements. The FAC noted the deteriorating financial conditions of their customers, but nonetheless confidently advised the Fed that no general cause for alarm was in order from weakened capital positions.

14 The Fed (admittedly) lacked the will to discipline its primary constituency of money center banks although they were pursuing a dangerous course that potentially jeopardized the entire US banking system. The question is whether the Fed could have actually forced these banks to change course. When Fed officials warned the banks about their growing exposures on LDC lending activities, they were generally ignored, brushed aside, or stifled by follow-up political influence generated by the banks. This observation represents a damaging admission, that the commercial banks did not tremble at the slightest frown of the Fed and dared not to offend it. The reality for the largest commercial banks was quite the opposite. The Fed was simply too weak to handle the largest money center banks. Although the Fed was empowered by Congress to attend to these issues, in practice it failed to do so. The defensive explanations offered by the Fed were even more symptomatic. The Fed's regulation of commercial banks was conditioned and restrained by politics and political influence. The inhibition of political pressures had enormous impact on the Fed's ability to enforce tough regulations against the larger banks, particularly the top fifty institutions. Bank regulation cannot be maintained independently from the political climate, from the banks and the congressmen who get their contributions, and others sold on deregulation. Thus, the Fed would get tougher against these institutions only if the 'general political climate' would support the movement. The Fed responded to the political influence of bankers, similarly to other federal agencies and their constituents.

15 See Greider, *supra* note 12, at pp.519–520.

Mexico began to seriously concern the Fed and Treasury Department in February 1982 when enormous capital flight caused the peso to fall by 60 per cent and all but evaporated its foreign exchange reserves.[16] The imminent threat posed by Mexico to the global financial system was nontransparent, as dollar-denominated debt obligations were held by many banks spread across the world. The dilemma erupted in April 1982 with the official recognition by the Fed and Treasury Department of financial distress in Mexico and its need to build dollar reserves. The Fed issued the first of a series of short-term 'loans' to Mexico to keep the nation current on interest payments to money center banks and prevent formal negotiations with the International Monetary Fund (IMF) for borrowing facilities until after the Mexican presidential election.[17] The new Mexican president would then approach the IMF and private banks for new loans, and confront the citizens with new terms for economic austerity required for the new loans.[18]

The Fed's discreet supervision of international solvency is perhaps its highest unstated function. The Federal Reserve Banks, through discount window lending, protected the domestic banks against liquidity crises that could lead to failure.[19] The Fed, working with the IMF and other international lending organizations, however, played the same role for selected nations. The foreign assistance was provided to Mexico as discreetly as possible to avoid initiating a panic, but also to avoid US political controversy.[20] The bottom line is that the potential for global crisis in the international financial system was the top priority and placed above all other considerations, including the dedication to controlling domestic money supply in the 1980s and dealing with the blossoming thrift industry crisis. The Fed's monetary policy actions directly strained the international financial system, first by inducing global recession which made it difficult for borrowers to repay, and then by creating the same

---

16 See *Confidence Game, supra* note 6, at p.199.

17 The Fed was independently capable of arranging enormous international credit transactions and prevailing on other central banks to support them. The IMF acted like an international bankruptcy court judge, supervising the affairs of debtor nations on behalf of the lenders from developed nations. The IMF would issue loans to financially distressed nations, and set the terms on which those nations would address their balance sheets, thus forcing the governments to impose conditions of austerity on their own citizens in order to preserve their status as creditworthy borrowers. The IMF 'workout' agreements usually implied that debtor governments had to reduce imports, public spending and wages, and increase prices.

18 The 'loans' brokered by the Fed were technically currency swaps but recognized politically as 'bridging loans.' The Fed deposited the funds in Mexico's account with the NY Fed and Mexico would return to the Fed an equivalent amount of pesos at the going exchange rate, promising to redeem them with US dollars when the swap expired. The advantage of structuring currency swaps in this respect was secrecy. The Fed discreetly informed the Executive Branch and key congressional chairmen of the currency swap arrangements, and none objected. The public reporting of currency swaps in this respect was required only once per quarter, so the emergency loan from the Fed would not be disclosed for several months (those initiated in April 1982 would not be reported until October 1982). By that time, the prevailing expectation was that Mexico would obtain new financing from the IMF and the Fed could cease the temporary.

19 See generally General Accounting Office, 'Financial Crisis Management: Four Financial Crises in the 1980s,' GAO/GGD-97-96 (May 1997), at pp.19–32 (Mexican Debt Crisis of 1982).

20 See generally Joseph Kraft, *The Mexican Rescue* (New York, Group of Thirty, 1984).

liquidity squeeze that existed in the US economy, on a worldwide basis. Mexico was the first of several 'cracks' in the US banking system.[21]

III. DRYSDALE SECURITIES (MAY 1982)

The second crack in the US banking system occurred in May 1982 when a bond dealer, Drysdale Government Securities, failed to pay USD160 million owed in interest due on government securities subject to repurchase agreements with Chase Manhattan and other money center banks.[22] Drysdale became insolvent and threatened the liquidity and solvency of some of the largest US banking institutions. The bond dealer was trading government securities on leverage with funds borrowed from major banks, using short-term repurchase agreements on US government securities to speculate on future bond prices.[23]

The money center banks and investment banks disclaimed any responsibility for the losses other traders sustained on the repurchase agreement transactions with Drysdale.[24] The long-term bond market prices fell sharply, and rumors spread that other investment banks could be pulled down with the failed bond dealer. Similarly to the Hunt Brothers fiasco in 1980, the US banking institutions were clearly not subjected to strict bank supervision with respect to providing loans to bond dealers to support leveraged speculative trading activities.[25] The bottom line was that the Fed had de facto

---

[21] See Greider, *supra* note 12, at pp.486–487.

[22] See *Confidence Game*, *supra* note 6, at p.158.

[23] The Drysdale Securities Corporation and its subsidiary, Drysdale Government Securities, Inc., utilized a 'Ponzi' scheme that profited from the use of coupon interest on securities sold to other investors. The essence of the scheme was Drysdale's exploitation of an important difference between government securities transactions in (1) the 'securities' or 'cash' market, in which securities were purchased and sold at market prices; and (2) the repurchase market, in which government securities were purchased and sold pursuant to repurchase or reverse repurchase agreements. In the securities market, the price of a government security, such as a US Treasury note, includes the market price of a particular issue and the accrued 'coupon interest' on the security (the value of government payments due on the security at the time of sale). In the repurchase market, the accrued coupon interest is paid only on the repurchase (or resale) transaction, and the initial loan of the security is made at a price that includes only the market value of the security. Before the security is repurchased, its price will be 'marked to market' periodically to reflect changes in value. In borrowing increasing volumes of government bonds through reverse repurchase agreements, selling them in the cash market and utilizing the cash and temporarily obtained accrued interest to meet obligations on previously borrowed bonds to conduct trades, Drysdale managed to remain solvent between February-May 1982 until its collapse, and investors lost approximately USD300 million. The Drysdale debacle eventually resulted in significant litigation. See, e.g., *SEC v. Drysdale Securities Corp. et al.*, 785 F.2d 38 (2d Cir. 1986); *Manufacturers Hanover Trust Co. v. Drysdale Securities Corp. et al.*, 801 F.2d 13 (2d Cir. 1986).

[24] See, e.g., Chris Welles, 'Drysdale: What Really Happened', *Institutional Investor*, September 1982.

[25] The US government securities market, the largest financial market in the entire world, was largely unregulated by the federal government at the time, except for Fed supervision over the 36 major dealers authorized to trade with the Fed's Open Market Desk. See A. Meulendyke, 'Monetary Rules and Contracts: Why Theory Loses to Practice', Bus. Rev. (Fed. Res.Phila., March-April 1985), at p.97 ('*Meulendyke*').

obligated itself to step forward to stabilize markets caught in panic or crisis following its actions in the Hunt Brothers debacle, however, and the Fed provided stability through various approaches to mitigate the systemic risk arising from the Drysdale failure.[26]

IV. MAY 1982 FOMC MEETING

The day after Drysdale Government Securities disclosed its insolvent positions, the Federal Open Market Committee (FOMC) convened for its May 1982 meeting. The Fed was now caught in a web of conflicting pressures, the opposing demands of the financial community and the political community, pushing the Fed in opposite directions. By April 1982, the M-1 growth was running at about 9 per cent, far above the FOMC target range of 2.5–5.5 per cent. The Reagan Administration began to question the monetarist foundations of their deregulatory platform and generally concluded that interest rates needed to be reduced as the economic fallout from high interest rates continued to devastate the economy. The Treasury Department and certain members of Congress reviewed the independence of the Fed, principally under the view that the Fed should reduce interest rates.[27]

Nonetheless, the money market activities pressured the Fed to maintain rates and not ease prematurely to pre-empt inflation from returning. M-1 continued to be an elusive monetary aggregate, and many economists were urging the Fed to abandon M-1 and ease monetary policy. The Fed decided to follow the guidance of banks and financial markets and declined to ease interest rates, however, in order to prevent the revival of inflationary expectations. The decision to rely on the financial markets for the FOMC meeting directive issued in May 1982 was later viewed as a mistake, however, as the decision to decline to ease interest rates was devastating for the economy.[28]

---

26 See Greider, *supra* note 12, at pp.487–488. The Fed convinced the major banks to absorb some of the trading losses suffered by the firm, and underscored that discount window lending facilities would be available to cover liquidity shortfalls in banks related to the bond market panic. The Federal Reserve Bank of New York also provided several billion dollars in bonds from its own portfolio as credit to dealer firms to ensure that the market remained liquid in bonds of various maturities while the problems with Drysdale were resolved. The Open Market Desk also purchased bonds in order to provide bank reserves immediately to mitigate any undesired financial pressures. The best way to mitigate panic was to ensure that enough funds were available for borrowers in the money market so no one firm would be subject to liquidity pressures. This produced temporary increases in the money supply, but could be corrected by withdrawing reserves later when panic was mitigated. The Fed swift action resulted in the quick containment of the Drysdale crisis.

27 See Greider, *supra* note 12, at pp.489–490.

28 *Ibid.* at pp.491–492.

V. PENN SQUARE BANK (JUNE 1982)

The third crack in the banking system occurred in June 1982, however, as the Fed investigated Penn Square Bank (PSB), a small bank in Oklahoma City, Oklahoma that, following requests by its management to provide emergency discount window lending to maintain short-term liquidity, had made energy exploration loans to many companies that had failed to locate oil and gas and otherwise faced sharp declines in energy prices.[29]

For PSB to qualify for continued discount window access, the Fed examiners had to ensure that the bank maintained sufficient collateral to qualify for discount lending in the form of bonds or commercial paper the Fed could obtain as security for the discount lending facility. The OCC had purportedly been alarmed at PSB's condition in the months prior to June 1982, as loans made for oil and gas development in the 1970s (a time at which oil prices soared) became worthless following the subsequent collapse of oil prices. The collapse of oil and gas prices meant that the value of oil and loan collateral also collapsed. PSB's capital nearly evaporated, and the bank was for all practical purposes insolvent. The ultimate concern was that PSB had sold approximately USD2 billion in loan participations to other larger banking institutions, and that its failure could spread to those banks.[30] The Fed examiners uncovered many instances of reckless and even fraudulent lending in the PSB portfolio, but other 'upstream' banking institutions purchased many of these loan participations, providing PSB with the ability to make the loans and thereby absorb greater risks in the first place.[31]

The Fed agreed to provide emergency funds to keep PSB temporarily solvent, but the Fed, OCC and the Federal Deposit Insurance Corporation (FDIC) fundamentally disagreed over how the situation should be resolved. The Fed and OCC wanted PSB to be kept open until another institution could purchase it, while the FDIC wanted PSB to be closed down and pay off insured depositors up to USD100,000, while all other deposit holders would lose their funds.[32]

---

29 See generally Phillip L. Zweig, *Belly Up: The Collapse of the Penn Square Bank* (New York, Crown Publishers, 1985).

30 The primary banks with loan participation exposures to Penn Square Bank were Continental Illinois National Bank, with over USD1 billion in exposures; Seattle First National Bank with USD400 million in exposures; and Chase Manhattan Bank with USD212 million in exposures, respectively.

31 Notably, Continental Illinois Bank, the largest bank in the midwest and the seventh largest bank in the United States, purchased more than USD1 billion in loan participations from PSB. In short, PSB acted as a 'scout' for other larger banking institutions which desired to become engaged in oil and gas lending projects, and collected 'finders fees' in the process. As the price of oil increased following the OPEC price shocks in the 1970s, all of these institutions profited enormously, and the overconcentration risks were simply overlooked. See generally 'Essay, The Aftermath of Penn Square Bank: Protecting Loan Participants from Setoffs', (1982) 18 Tulsa L.J. 261.

32 See Greider, *supra* note 12, at pp.497–498.

Under the FDIC plan, the major banks that shared in the loan participations issued by PSB would lose their investments.[33] The Fed asserted that if the government agencies refused to intervene and assume the burden of loss in PSB, general panic among large investors regarding Continental Illinois Bank would necessarily follow and the bank would suffer a huge loss of liquidity that would extend to other banks involved with PSB. The only issue of real concern to the Fed and OCC was the effect that PSB would have on the money center banks. The Fed's position was that a deposit payoff contemplated by FDIC would be catastrophic and that the FDIC had to find another solution.[34] In short, the Fed wanted to avoid another disturbance to the banking system primarily because a liquidity crisis would force it to alter monetary policy by pumping up the money supply to avert a banking liquidity crisis.[35]

The FDIC solution was rejected in part as the upstream banks themselves all refused to risk any of their own funds to save the situation and refused to take responsibility for injecting new capital into PSB. The banking agencies suggested that the banks should waive their claims against PSB, which would make it easier and cheaper for the FDIC to assume responsibility and keep PSB open, but the banks rejected this proposal.[36] On 5 July 1982, the banking agencies and Treasury met to resolve the question; Treasury sided with FDIC, the next day PSB was closed. The OCC declared PSB insolvent, and the FDIC seized PSB assets and placed it into receivership. The insured depositors were reimbursed and other creditors and claimants received a share of the failed bank's diminished assets. The financial system reacted defensively but did not unravel into chaos in the short term (as the Fed and OCC had conveniently predicted). In the longer term, however, there were 'severe consequences', as within one year various other banks involved with PSB failed, and two years later the Continental Illinois Bank failed and the government was forced to de facto nationalize the bank. The PSB failure

---

33 These banks offered many different schemes designed to keep PSB open under new ownership to prevent the liquidation of the problematic loans. PSB had accumulated nearly USD3 billion in off-balance sheet commitments, including letters of credit and loan participations. The FDIC refused to take over an entire bailout beyond insured deposits, given the costs to the insurance fund, and strongly desired to bring discipline to the markets.

34 Continental Illinois Bank could not function if it could not obtain borrowed funds from the money markets, as it followed the 'managed liabilities' strategy that enabled it to grow aggressively (in effect booking the loans first and then borrowing the money to fund them).

35 Of course, if the worst scenario occurred, definite questions would be raised about the viability of the Fed and OCC in conducting banking regulation and supervision, in terms of how the reckless pyramid of lending occur in the first place. These questions would accompany those questions already raised concerning the Fed and OCC with respect to the LDC exposures and the Drysdale failure that were currently ongoing.

36 Many of these banks had recently incurred losses related to the Drysdale failure, and if they assumed responsibility for PSB then they could not sue their own insurance companies, alleging negligence against their own management officers who purchased the loan participations from PSB. In other words, the banks wanted the government to take the losses while the banks remained free to cover their own mistakes. See *Seattle-First Nat'l Bank v. FDIC*, 619 F.Supp. 1351 (W.D.Okla. 1985); *Chase Manhattan Bank, N.A. v. FDIC*, 554 F.Supp. 251 (W.D.Okla. 1983).

produced the third crack in the banking system, and the FOMC reacted to force Fed Chairman Volcker to yield on easing monetary policy.[37]

VI. JUNE 1982 FOMC MEETING

The FOMC convened an emergency meeting in the middle of the PSB crisis on 30 June 1982. As the Fed and OCC argued with FDIC over strategy for handling the PSB situation, the FOMC debated over M-1, interest rates, and the meeting was definitively influenced by the potential crisis facing the US banking system. The cumulative analysis of the 'random' isolated crises (Mexico in financial distress, the Drysdale and PSB failures, soon to be followed by the actual default of Mexico) placed great pressure on the FOMC to ease monetary policy.[38]

In the larger picture, it is clear that the instability of the domestic banking system, the LDC debt crisis, and the downward slide of the US economy were all related and all interacted with one another to present a sustained argument for easing monetary policy, regardless of what M-1 or other monetary aggregates suggested. If economic activity continued to decline, then the failure of banks, thrifts, and other institutions would substantially worsen and spread unpredictably. If the US economy did not begin to expand, the LDC debt crisis would dramatically worsen.[39] There was no way to resolve the LDC crisis unless US monetary policy permitted those nations to sell exports again. Thus, the Fed came to a critical point, and a new consensus developed in the FOMC to ease monetary policy and ignore contrary statistical signals generated by activity in the M-1 aggregate.[40]

VII. ABANDONMENT OF THE MONETARIST OPERATING TECHNIQUE

As M-1 growth accelerated in June 1982, the market interest rates were pushed higher in anticipation of further tightening of monetary policy. The FOMC adopted a policy directive, however, which presented a dramatic

---

37 See Greider, *supra* note 12, at p.501.

38 See Volcker, *supra* note 5, at p.180.

39 The US was the major market that purchased exports from the LDC nations, but if the US remained in economic contraction, export purchases would similarly contract. If the US did not begin purchasing exports from LDC nations, there would be no way for the LDC nations to find income to keep up with the mounting debt payments to US and other international banking institutions. In short, the LDC crisis would become the US crisis, and the situation threatened to collapse the US banking system from the money center banks downward. The LDC debt crisis also posed a serious threat to the international financial system, and the concern was to provide enough stimulus through monetary policy to turn the US economy and the world economy around and promote business activity again.

40 See Greider, *supra* note 12, at pp.504–505.

reversal in monetary policy: the effective abandonment of monetarist operations. This was a defining moment, notwithstanding attempts by the FRB to downplay the significance of the policy reversal. For over 33 months, the Fed engaged in a monetarist experiment and imposed the most severe monetary policy discipline on the US economy and, by implication, the world economies, in modern history. The Fed's monetary policy pushed interest rates to record levels. The interest rate levels would have been impossible to sustain before the deregulation of financial markets under DIDMCA.[41]

In October 1982, the Fed formally abandoned the monetarist operating technique.[42] The evidence clearly indicated that the relatively close linkage between M-1 and economic activity had broken down, and that the demand for M-1 strengthened relative to income more than had been anticipated due in large part to the proliferation of NOW accounts under DIDMCA.[43]

VIII. CONTINENTAL ILLINOIS BANK CRISIS (JULY 1982)

In July 1982, Continental Illinois Bank and other banks involved in the PSB debacle faced an immediate liquidity crisis as money markets refused to rollover their cash deposits and insisted on shorter maturities and higher interest rates. The spread between short-term commercial bank CDs and Treasury bills widened substantially, and the larger banks (particularly Continental Illinois Bank) encountered strained access to the overnight Federal Funds market. The Fed reactions resulted in a policy sequence of downward adjustments in the discount rate and Federal Funds rate, respectively.[44]

The Fed continued to ease in the face of receptive money markets, but claimed that it was merely following the decline in interest rates generated by money markets psychology. The bond markets supported these movements and long-term rates declined approximately in step with short-term rates. By August 1982, the equity markets and bond market rallied. Thus, as the financial markets celebrated the Fed's adjustments in monetary policy, the development could be attributed to a sudden and unpredictable change in market sentiment, a new confidence about inflation that developed in July 1982.[45] The July 1982 FOMC Directive was premised on potential financial

---

41 *Ibid.* at pp.506–507.

42 See *Confidence Game*, *supra* note 6, at p.162.

43 See Meulendyke, *supra* note 25, at p.52.

44 From July-December 1982, the Fed executed seven reductions in the discount rate alone, and the cumulative effect of this sequence was to reduce short-term interest rates by more than 40 per cent.

45 The more plausible explanation, however, was that the Fed was simply incorrect, and that the Fed had tightened the money supply excessively and kept interest rates high based on a false premise. The misperception had large consequences for the nation as the economy was driven deep into contraction. In other words, the Fed was being steered by the opinions of the bond market and their representatives, and those opinions were simply wrong.

chaos from the PSB debacle, the collapse of foreign debtors, and deepening strains on the banking system as the economy failed to recover.[46]

IX. MEXICO DEFAULTS (AUGUST 1982)

The unsustainable LDC debt situation came to a head in August 1982, when Mexico formally announced that it would default on its dollar denominated borrowings. On 13 August 1982, Mexico contacted the Treasury and Fed to declare that the game was over, and default was imminent. The declaration formalized the fourth crack in the banking system during a several month span in 1982.[47]

In theory, the Fed and other central banks could rescue banks with massive loans to those institutions losing their liquidity, in effect pumping up the money supply to save the banking system, but the more convenient and immediate solution was for the US to inject money into Mexico over the weekend. The Fed and Treasury arranged an unprecedented bailout in three days of meetings, of nearly USD3.5 billion in new loans to Mexico.[48] The new 'loan facilities' were designed to keep Mexico from declaring default until a more permanent solution could be worked out.

Mexico was thereafter effectively in 'financial receivership' of the developed nation central banks and governments. The survival of the largest money center banks and other international banks literally depended on Mexico remaining solvent.[49] The implicit recognition of this fact necessitated continuous lending facilities from the International Monetary Fund (IMF), the World Bank, and other similar institutions over time. This was the beginning of the

---

46 In August 1982, Senator Byrd introduced the Balanced Monetary Policy Act of 1982 in order to command the Fed by act of Congress to reduce interest rates to normal levels. The congressional action was too late to be effective, introduced after the battle had already been decided. Congress had no direct way of knowing this, as the July FOMC Directive was not publicly released. The strongest notice of the Fed's shift in policy was through mid-year testimony to the House Banking Committee, couched in vague language. The Fed lobbied furiously to maintain independence, and falling interest rates and the stock market rally collapsed any urgency in Congress to pass the bill. In August 1982, Senator Byrd conceded that as long as interest rates were coming down, he would not push the bill.

47 Two weeks prior to the declaration, the Fed provided USD700 million to Mexico in a dollar-peso swap facility, and the dollars evaporated. The nation's liquid dollar reserves dropped to less than USD200 million, and in several days the nation would be insolvent. The Fed and Treasury would not allow that to happen, as the largest money center banks and European banks would become subject to panic, and other nations would likely follow Mexico's lead and declare default. See General Accounting Office, 'Mexican Debt Crisis of 1982', *supra* note 19, at pp.25–26.

48 The DOE agreed to purchase USD1 billion of oil from Mexico and to pay in advance immediately, instead of paying on delivery. The Department of Agriculture provided another $1 billion line of credit for the future purchase of US grain and other food products. The Fed organized another USD1.85 billion loan pool among the developed nation central banks, with half of that money contributed by the Fed itself.

49 See generally E. Gerald Corrigan, *The Financial Disruptions of the 1980s: A Central Banker Looks Back* (Washington, D.C., Group of Thirty, 1993); Charles P. Kindleberger, *Manias, Panics and Crashes: A History of Financial Crises* (New York, Basic Books, 1989).

formal international LDC Debt Crisis, a continuing series of crisis points as one nation after another approached insolvency and appealed for relief from the Fed, Treasury, IMF, World Bank, and the private international banks.[50] The LDC Debt Crisis and the dangers it posed to the US banking system presented an opportunity for the Fed to expand its influence in the international financial markets in direct support of the IMF in dealing with the crisis.

Therefore, the underlying cracks in the US banking system over mid-1982 directly influenced Fed monetary policy operations and forced recognition of the thrift industry crisis to become a secondary priority. Meanwhile, the S&L industry remained fully engaged in crisis, the extent of which was generally known only to the federal regulatory agencies.[51] The volatile interest rates induced by Fed monetary policy and new-found powers under the DIDMCA undoubtedly set the stage for current and future havoc regarding the financial condition of the thrift industry.

The Federal Home Loan Bank Board (FHLBB), through various deregulatory measures[52] induced Congress to address the regulators' bill pending before the House and Senate Banking Committees, particularly with respect to the emergency acquisition provisions so heavily opposed by the thrift industry. The impetus for acceptance of these provisions accelerated following the Federal Reserve Board's (FRB) approval of an acquisition by a prominent bank holding company of a solvent California thrift institution on grounds that the operation of the thrift institution was 'closely related to banking' and thereby permissible under the Bank Holding Company Act.[53] The thrift industry and House Banking Committee advanced proposals for thrift 'subsidy borrowings' from the government to recapitalize balance sheets,[54]

---

50 Within the next year, 14 other nations entered the same dilemma faced by Mexico in 1982, accepting new conditions of economic austerity in exchange for new credits from the IMF and the international banks. The Fed played crisis manager throughout the LDC Debt Crisis.

51 See Jay Rothstein, 'House Committee Delays Vote on Thrift Emergency Bill, Skeptical Members Say Regulators Have Yet to Make Their Case For It', Am. Banker, 3 October 1981, at p.3 (reviewing political exchanges implying that limited information was made available to Congress by regulatory agencies).

52 The FHLBB adopted various deregulatory measures during 1980–1982 which effectively forced mergers through creative adjustments to regulatory capital and accounting principles, deemed 'supervisory mergers', to find ways to address the record number of troubled thrift institutions. The FHLBB frequently effected 'phoenix' transactions, where multiple troubled institutions would be combined into a single institution.

53 See 12 U.S.C. § 1843(c)(8) (authorizing activities that are 'closely related to banking so as to be a proper incident thereto); 'Citicorp', (1982) 68 Federal Reserve Bulletin 656 (approving Citicorp proposal to acquire Fidelity Savings & Loan Association of San Francisco). The FRB approval was invalidated by a federal district court, but was reinstated on appeal. See *Fidelity Sav. & Loan Ass'n v. FHLBB*, 540 F.Supp. 1374 (N.D.Cal.), rev'd, 689 F.2d 803 (9th Cir. 1982), cert. denied, 461 US 914 (1983).

54 See Joseph D. Hutnyan, 'Thrift Rescue Plans Getting Serious', Am. Banker, 12 February 1982, at p.1. The thrift assistance plans were purportedly inspired by the Democratic Party to use the crisis to embarrass the Reagan Administration. See Joseph D. Hutnyan, 'Rescue the Thrifts and You Question Reaganomics', Am. Banker, 26 February 1982, at p.4. The rescue plans were supported by the thrift industry and FHLBB, but the FRB remained critical. See Linda W. McCormick, 'Volcker Says No to Thrift Bailout', Am. Banker, 2 March 1982, at p.3.

and the Reagan Administration finally abandoned neutrality in April 1982 and supported the regulators' bill but opposed direct bailout.[55] Congress nonetheless pressed emergency legislation forward that would purportedly restore the appearance of solvency for thousands of S&L institutions. The next legislative solution introduced by Congress to address the thrift industry crisis was the enactment of the Garn-St. Germain Depository Institutions Act of 1982 ('Garn-St. Germain Act')[56] in October 1982.

---

55 See Linda W. McCormick, 'Reagan Council Endorses Aids to Thrifts but Bars Direct Bailout', Am. Banker, 27 April 1982, at p.1.

56 See Pub. L. No. 97–320, 96 Stat. 1469 (15 October 1982).

3. The Garn-St. Germain Act of 1982: A Final Deregulatory 'Push'

I. INTRODUCTION

Following the passage of the Depository Institutions Deregulation and Monetary Control Act of 1980 (DIDMCA), the Federal Home Loan Bank Board (FHLBB) continued to pressure Congress to take legislative action to permit thrift institutions to expand and diversify into new activities to generate earnings in order to maintain competitiveness in the lending markets (e.g. earn their way out of trouble).[1] The thrift industry received further legal authorization to diversify into new activities on the asset side under the Garn-St. Germain Act of 1982,[2] which was primarily a reactive attempt by Congress to assist the distressed thrift industry. This chapter evaluates this 1982 omnibus piece of deregulatory legislation (which proved to be the last major piece of deregulatory legislation in the 1980s).

II. THE BACKDROP

By October 1982 the general perception was that the earnings prospects of thrifts were distressed and the industry was in terminal crisis. The immediate objective of the Garn-St. Germain Act was to provide relief for troubled banks and thrifts by facilitating mergers and reorganizations of such institutions,

---

1 See 'Statement of Federal Home Loan Bank Board to Senate Committee on Banking, Currency, and Housing', Serial No. 97–37, on S. 1720 at 666.

2 See Pub. L. No. 97–320, 96 Stat. 1469 (1982). Under the Garn-St. Germain Act, federal S&Ls were granted limited powers to offer demand deposits, and money market accounts to compete with money market funds offered by securities firms. See Garn-St. Germain Act, § 312 (demand deposits) and § 327 (money market accounts), 96 Stat. 1469, 1496–1497, 1501. Federal S&Ls could further engage in lending with respect to commercial real estate, secured and unsecured commercial and agricultural loans, and ordinary consumer loans. See *ibid.* § 322 (commercial real estate lending), § 325 (secured and unsecured commercial and agricultural lending), and § 329 (consumer lending), 96 Stat, at 1499, 1501, 1502.

expanding the powers of the Federal Deposit Insurance Corporation (FDIC) and the Federal Savings and Loan Insurance Corporation (FSLIC), and establishing a federal program whereby troubled institutions could exchange capital notes with FDIC and FSLIC to obtain capital injections and increase their 'net worth'.[3]

The 1982 Act further expanded the loan and investment powers of thrift institutions, removed certain restrictions on the lending activities of national banks,[4] and liberalized the depository abilities of all banking and thrift institutions. The passage of the Garn-St. Germain Act also finalized the interest rate deregulation initiated under DIDMCA. The Act allowed depository institutions to open money market deposit accounts (MMDA) and set a timetable under which all depository interest rate limits would expire in 1986. Thus, for the first time since 1933, the US banks and thrift institutions were free from price restrictions, and able to compete openly for deposits with each other and non-bank financial institutions.[5]

The key failure of the Garn-St. Germain Act, however, was the very incompatibility of expanded asset powers with the deposit insurance amendments under DIDMCA. If Congress was willing to enact legislation to insure bank and thrift deposits, a necessary component of such legislation would be controls on the uses to which the banks and S&Ls could put the insured deposits. The Garn-St. Germain Act vastly expanded the asset powers of S&Ls without imposing any controls on deposit insurance, which implied a tacit acceptance that the S&Ls were no longer viable in the industry in which they were intended.[6]

The expansion of asset powers at the very least called for revisions to the deposit insurance scheme based upon the activities in which the S&Ls would engage, or the insurance funds would self-destruct. Notably, given the complex banking, monetary, and political conditions existing as of October 1982, the Garn-St. Germain Act was enacted without any serious debate.[7]

---

3 See, inter alia, Joseph J. Norton, 'The 1982 Banking Act and the Deregulation Scheme', 38 Bus. Law. 1627 (1983).

4 The Garn-St. Germain Act revised the rules on lending and borrowing by national banks, such as increasing the amount of loans that could be made to single borrowers. The Act further removed statutory restrictions on real estate lending by national banks and authorized the OCC to issue regulations concerning real estate lending. The former real estate lending provisions had required (1) maximum loan-to-value ratios for real estate lending under certain conditions; (2) certain types of real estate loans to provide for amortization of the entire principal amount of the loan within 30 years; and (3) set aggregate limits on real estate lending. The OCC proposed regulations to remove all limitations on real estate lending under the position that lending decisions should be left to national bank management and that the restrictions interfered with national banks ability to respond to changes in the real estate markets. The new rules became effective in 1983. See 48 Fed. Reg. 40,698 (9 September 1983). Although State laws continued to impose limitations on commercial bank real estate lending for State-chartered banks, the OCC regulation pre-empted these limitations for national banks.

5 See Edward L. Symons and James J. White, *Banking Law*, (2nd edn, 1984) at pp.45–46.

6 See Norton, *supra* note 3.

7 The FDIC should have initiated such a debate given the potential threat to the deposit insurance fund, but the FDIC Chairman (William Isaac) focused on regulating the mutual savings banks it supervised through capital standard maintenance by preventing them from attempting to 'grow' out of their problems and closing them down when their capital extinguished.

III. DIVERSIFICATION OF ASSET HOLDINGS

Title III of the Garn-St. Germain Act, the *Thrift Institutions Restructuring Act*, authorized thrift institutions to further diversify their asset portfolios with new investment powers. First, the Act authorized thrift institutions to invest up to 40 per cent of total assets in loans for non-residential commercial property.[8] Second, the Act authorized thrift institutions to invest in other thrift time deposits or savings accounts so long as the accounts were protected by deposit insurance.[9] Third, the Act authorized thrift institutions to invest without limitation in all local or State government debt obligations.[10] Fourth, the Act authorized thrift institutions to invest up to 10 per cent of total assets in commercial, corporate, business, or agricultural loan obligations.[11] Fifth, the Act authorized thrift institutions to invest up to 30 per cent of total assets in consumer loans.[12] Finally, the Act authorized thrift institutions to invest up to 10 per cent of total assets in tangible personal property.[13]

The explosion of thrift asset powers under the Garn-St. Germain Act represented the reaction of Congress to the 'negative' interest rate spread leading the S&L industry into terminal crisis.[14] Prior to the Garn-St. Germain Act, the S&L industry could only invest in certain assets allowed by then current law. These so-called 'legal assets' were principally single family mortgages, except for limited modifications enacted under DIDMCA. The Garn-St. Germain Act eliminated these restrictions and allowed S&Ls to invest in virtually any financial assets.

Thrift institutions concentrated their asset holdings in assets such as commercial and non-residential real estate loans,[15] as well as commercial loans,[16] direct real estate investments[17] (State-chartered institutions in some jurisdictions already enjoyed broad investment authority), joint ventures and subsidiary corporations, such as title insurance companies, mortgage

---

8 See Garn-St. Germain Act, *supra* note 2, at § 322, 96 Stat. at 1499 (codified as amended at 12 U.S.C. § 1464(c)(1)(B)).

9 *Ibid.* at § 323, 96 Stat. at 1499–1500 (codified as amended at 12 U.S.C. § 1464(c)(1)(G)).

10 *Ibid.* at § 324, 96 Stat. at 1500 (codified as amended at 12 U.S.C. § 1464(c)(1)(H)).

11 *Ibid.* at § 325, 96 Stat. at 1500 (codified as amended at 12 U.S.C. § 1464(c)(1)(R)).

12 *Ibid.* at § 329, 96 Stat. at 1502 (codified as amended at 12 U.S.C. § 1464(c)(2)(B)).

13 *Ibid.* at § 330, 96 Stat. at 1502 (codified as amended at 12 U.S.C. § 1464(c)).

14 Federal savings associations were granted expanded lending and investment authority by this Act, as an attempt to provide them with the flexibility necessary to maintain their role of providing credit for housing. See also 'Statement of Federal Home Loan Bank Board to Senate Committee on Banking, Currency, and Housing', Serial No. 97–37, on S. 1720 at 666, and see Pub. L. No. 97–320, 96 Stat. 1469 (1982). Under the Garn-St. Germain Act, federal S&Ls were granted limited powers to offer demand deposits, and money market accounts to compete with money market funds offered by securities firms. See, Garn-St. Germain Act, § 312 (demand deposits) and § 327 (money market accounts), 96 Stat. 1469, 1496–1497, 1501. Federal S&Ls could further engage in lending with respect to commercial real estate, secured and unsecured commercial and agricultural loans, and ordinary consumer loans. See *ibid.* at § 322 (commercial real estate lending), § 325 (secured and unsecured commercial and agricultural lending), and § 329 (consumer lending), 96 Stat. at 1499, 1501, 1502.

15 12 U.S.C. § 1464(c)(1)(B).

16 12 U.S.C. § 1464(c)(1)(R).

17 12 U.S.C. § 1464(c)(1)(B).

companies, development companies, and the like.[18] Congress desired to permit thrift institutions to diversify earnings into new assets and investments and thereby reach earnings levels beyond the 'negative spreads' and therefore out of terminal crisis. The question was whether this approach was the right approach, given the lack of risk-based controls on deposit insurance, and the volatile economic conditions imposed through Fed monetary policy.

Title III of the Garn-St. Germain Act further directed the Depository Institutions Deregulation Committee (DIDC), established under DIDMCA, to establish within 60 days of enactment of Garn-St. Germain Act, an account that was directly equivalent to and competitive with money market mutual funds. DIDC authorized depository institutions to establish money market deposit accounts (MMDAs) that were comparable to and could compete directly with money market mutual funds offered by investment banks.[19] The MMDA was eligible for deposit insurance. The MMDA was introduced to alleviate or reverse the massive disintermediation, which continued to work against the S&L industry. Section 327 of the Act established that the MMDA was limited in the number of transfers to and from such accounts, but was subject to lower reserve requirements for the non-personal time deposits. Finally, Section 326 of the Garn-St. Germain Act directed the DIDC to eliminate all interest rate differentials under Regulation Q by January 1984.[20]

IV. FDIC AND FSLIC POWERS TO ASSIST DISTRESSED INSTITUTIONS

The Garn-St. Germain Act also responded to banking and thrift agency lobbying and enhanced the powers of the FDIC and the FSLIC to provide assistance to distressed banking and thrift institutions through provisions for open bank (and thrift) assistance, emergency acquisitions, and net worth certificate programs. Title I of the Garn-St. Germain Act, the *Deposit Insurance Flexibility Act*, expanded the authority of the deposit insurance agencies for the banking and thrift industries, the FDIC and FSLIC, respectively, in order to assist financially distressed banking and thrift institutions. For instance, the FDIC and FSLIC were given expanded powers with respect to the forms of financial assistance those agencies could render to distressed institutions. In addition, these agencies were granted specific statutory procedures for effecting mergers and acquisitions of failed and failing banks and thrifts. These 'emergency acquisition powers' set to expire three years from the date of enactment, were granted a priority structure. The FDIC was authorized to engage in emergency interstate acquisitions of closed commercial banks or savings banks with assets in excess of

---

18 12 U.S.C. § 1464(c)(1)(N).

19 See Garn-St. Germain Act, *supra* note 2, at § 327, 96 Stat. at 1501 (codified as amended at 12 U.S.C. §. 3503(c)(1)–(3)).

20 *Ibid.* at § 326, 96 Stat. at 1500–1501 (codified as amended at various sections of 12 U.S.C.).

USD500 million, and interstate mergers and takeovers of mutual savings banks of the same size that were in distress. The FSLIC received similar authorization except that the asset size limitations applicable to FDIC did not apply to the FSLIC.[21]

A. Open Bank Assistance

The open bank assistance provisions authorized the deposit insurers (FDIC and FSLIC) to engage in transactions with institutions that were not subject to closure but were in need of assistance. The insurers were authorized to assist open banks to prevent the closing of an institution; to restore a closed bank to normal operations; or to mitigate the risk posed by severe financial conditions which threatened the stability of a significant number of insured institutions with significant financial resources.[22]

The FDIC and FSLIC were authorized to provide loans to failing institutions, to make deposits in or contributions to such institutions, to purchase the assets of and securities issued by such institutions, and assume the liabilities of such institutions.[23] In connection with a purchase and assumption transaction, the FDIC and FSLIC were authorized to engage in these transactions with either the troubled institution or the acquiring institution.[24]

In such transactions, the FDIC and FSLIC could guarantee either institution against loss by reason of the transactions or against loss with respect to any asset.[25] The amount of assistance was limited to the amount that the insurer determined to be 'reasonably necessary to save the cost of liquidating, including paying the insured accounts' of the troubled institution.[26] This restriction was removed, however, if the insurer determined that 'continued operation' of the institution is 'essential to provide adequate banking services in its community'.[27]

B. Emergency Acquisitions

The Garn-St. Germain Act further provided for emergency acquisitions. At the time, the Federal Reserve Board (FRB) did not permit banks or bank holding companies to acquire thrift institutions, so the thrift and banking industries remained separate. Most States prohibited entry by out-of-state

---

21 See generally, Norton, *supra* note 3.
22 See Garn-St. Germain Act, *supra* note 2, at §. 111, 96 Stat. at 1469 (codified as amended at 12 U.S.C. § 1823(c)(1)).
23 *Ibid.* § 111, 96 Stat. at 1469–1470 (codified as amended at 12 U.S.C. § 1823(c)(1), (c)(2)(A)).
24 *Ibid.*
25 *Ibid.*
26 *Ibid.* at § 111, 96 Stat. at 1470 (codified as amended at 12 U.S.C. § 1823(c)(4)(A)).
27 *Ibid.*

institutions, and federal law incorporated State law as to either bank or bank holding company acquisitions.[28]

The limitations primarily emanated from restrictions on geographic barriers to mergers and acquisitions. The emergency acquisition provisions authorized large thrift institutions and banking organizations to circumvent both provisions. The FDIC-insured banks could conduct emergency acquisitions with closed institutions of USD500 million or more in assets.[29] The thrift institutions could be subject to emergency acquisitions if 'severe financial conditions' existed which threatened the 'stability of a significant number of insured institutions possessing significant financial resources', if the institution were in default or could be restored to normal operating conditions, or if a default could be prevented.[30]

If the State banking agency objected to an extraordinary acquisition, the FDIC could proceed only if the board of directors of FDIC unanimously voted to proceed.[31] In any case, the FDIC or FSLIC was required to notify the State authority of the target institution. The State authority had 48 hours to object to the acquisition, but a unanimous vote of the FDIC or FSLIC board could pre-empt such objections.[32] Special rules applied to interstate acquisitions that involve an insured depository institution in default.

The interstate acquisitions of insured depository institution in default must be approved by the primary federal or State agencies of the parties to the acquisition.[33] The acquisition may not be finalized by FDIC unless the State banking authority approves such an acquisition.[34] Finally, the provisions applicable to banks in danger of default do not affect any other federal or State laws that require regulatory approval.[35] The application of State law

---

[28] See 12 U.S.C. § 36c (1982) (prohibiting branching by national banks except where permitted by State laws); § 1842(d) (1982) (prohibiting bank holding company expansion across State lines where not expressly permitted by State laws). The barriers to interstate banking began to erode under State laws and interstate arrangements where States permitted entry based on region or reciprocity by States whose institutions sought entry. These interstate arrangements were upheld by the US Supreme Court. See *Northeast Bancorp v. Board of Governors of the Federal Reserve System*, 472 U.S. 159 (1985). Since 1985, geographical barriers eroded gradually under such arrangements, and in 1994 Congress eliminated most of the remaining barriers to bank holding company expansion and to interstate branching, unless a given State 'opts out' of interstate branching laws. See 'Riegle-Neal Interstate Banking and Branching Efficiency Act of 1994', Pub. L. No. 103–328, 108 Stat. 2338 (1994).

[29] See Garn-St. Germain Act, *supra* note 2, at § 116, 96 Stat. at 1476–1477 (codified as amended at 12 U.S.C. § 1823(f)(2)(A), (f)(3)(A)). Banks could only be subject to purchase and assumption transactions. *Ibid.*

[30] *Ibid.* § 123(a), 96 Stat. at 1483 (codified at 12 U.S.C. § 1730a(m)(1)(A) (1988), repealed by Pub. L. No. 101–73, 103 Stat. 83 (1989)). Thrift institutions could be subject to either purchase and assumption transactions or mergers. *Ibid.*

[31] See 12 U.S.C. § 1823(f) (1982) (repealed 1986).

[32] See Garn-St. Germain Act, *supra* note 2, at § 123(a), 96 Stat. at 1483 (codified at 12 U.S.C. § 1730a(m)(1)(B) (1988), repealed by Pub. L. No. 101–73, 104 Stat. 183 (1989)); *ibid.* at § 116, 96 Stat. at 1477 (codified as amended at 12 U.S.C. § 1823(f)(2)(B), (f)(3)(B)).

[33] See 12 U.S.C. § 1823(f)(2)(A).

[34] See 12 U.S.C. § 1823(f)(3)(E).

[35] See 12 U.S.C. § 1823(f)(3)(F).

and federal law to an interstate acquisition involving an institution in default or in danger of default is addressed in several contexts.[36]

The FDIC could prohibit any interstate acquisition if it would result in a monopoly, or if it determines that the acquisition would threaten the safety and soundness of the acquirer and does not result in the future viability of the resulting depository institution.[37] The interstate and inter-industry acquisitions were subject to a hierarchy, with first priority given to in-state, same industry acquiring institutions; second priority given to interstate, same industry acquiring institutions; third priority given to same State interindustry acquiring institutions; and fourth priority given to out-of-state other industry acquiring institutions.[38]

The deposit insurers, in soliciting bids for distressed institutions, were required to find prospective purchasers determined 'in its sole discretion' to be qualified, and the insurers were then able to acquire the subject institution's assets and liabilities, the calculations and estimations of which were 'determinative'.[39]

C. Net Worth Certificates

Title II of the Garn-St. Germain Act, the *Net Worth Certificate Act*, conferred new powers to the FHLBB to address financially distressed thrift institutions[40] and established a program to assist distressed thrift institutions.[41] The net worth certificate provisions were designed by the Democratic majority of the House of Representatives, which generally sided with the thrift industry.

Title II provided a mechanism for capital assistance to insured banking and thrift institutions having net worth equal to or less than 3 per cent of assets and were to be in an amount equal to 50 per cent of operating losses for institutions with a net worth in the 2–3 per cent range;[42] 60 per cent of operating losses for institutions with a net worth in the 1–2 per cent range;[43]

---

36 See, e.g. 12 U.S.C. § 1823(f)(4)(A) (pre-empting interstate acquisition prohibition of the BHCA (the Douglas Amendment) and any State laws); 12 U.S.C. § 1823(f)(4)(D) (authorizing acquiring institution after two years to branch or acquire additional insured depository institutions in the same manner as other institutions in the respective State); and 12 U.S.C. § 1823(f)(4)(E) (acquiring institution under interstate acquisition not required to divest any other bank and cannot be prevented from acquiring any other insured depository institution or holding company).

37 See 12 U.S.C. § 1823(f)(7).

38 See Garn-St. Germain Act, *supra* note 2, at § 116, 96 Stat. at 1478 (codified as amended at 12 U.S.C. § 1823(f)(6)(A)-(B)); *ibid.* at § 123(a), 96 Stat. 1483–1484 (codified at 12 U.S.C. §. 1730a(m)(3)(A)-(B), repealed by Pub. L. No. 101–73, 103 Stat. 183 (1989)).

39 *Ibid.* at §. 116, 96 Stat. at 1477–1478 (codified as amended at 12 U.S.C. § 1823(f)(5), (f)(6)(D)); *ibid.* at §. 123(a), 96 Stat. at 1483–1484 (codified at 12 U.S.C. § 1730a(m)(2), (m)(3)(E) (1988), repealed by Pub. L. No. 101–73, 103 Stat. 183 (1989)).

40 *Ibid.* at § 123, 96 Stat. at 1483–1485 (codified as amended at 12 U.S.C. § 1730a). For example, prior to the passage of the Garn-St. Germain Act, Texas law required an 80 per cent loan-to-value ratio on many loans. After the passage of the Act, Texas S&Ls were treated in the same way as federal S&Ls.

41 *Ibid.* at § 122, 96 Stat. at 1480–1483 (codified as amended at 12 U.S.C. § 1729(f)).

42 *Ibid.* at § 203, 96 Stat. at 1492, repealed by *ibid.* § 206, 96 Stat. at 1496 (Sunshine Provision).

43 *Ibid.* at § 203, 96 Stat. at 1493, repealed by *ibid.* § 206, 96 Stat. at 1496 (Sunshine Provision).

and 70 per cent of operating losses in the less than 1 per cent range.[44] The net worth certificates did not involve the transfer of any tangible assets to the issuing institution. The 'troubled institutions' issued capital instruments ('net worth certificates') that were purchased by the respective insuring agency with promissory notes, and paid dividends equal to the interest due on the notes.[45] The net worth certificates were consummated as non-cash transactions.

The Act provided the FDIC and FSLIC with the authority to purchase net worth certificates from distressed institutions, which could be included as 'capital' by banking agencies and the FHLBB and therefore permit distressed institutions to continue operations until their financial health was restored. With respect to thrift institutions, the FHLBB had oversight jurisdiction over the FSLIC, and this procedure was used heavily to support the failing thrift industry. The procedure increased the capital of the institution receiving the net worth certificates and thereby allowed the institution to grow based upon that new capital and the applicable leverage ratio.[46] The income, capital, net worth or mutual capital certificates were issued to an S&L by the FSLIC, booked as capital and leveraged at a 33:1 assets to capital leverage ratio.[47] The net worth certificate program also permitted FDIC to purchase certificates to increase capital of insured banks. Qualifying institutions exchanged their own capital instruments for promissory notes and certificates issued by FDIC.[48] The determination of a period loss was restricted to operating losses as determined by the respective agency.[49]

The net worth certificates were treated similarly to preferred stock for purposes of liquidation priorities (higher priority than common stock but lesser priority than other creditors), and institutions were prohibited from paying dividends on their stock if they had net worth certificates outstanding.[50] The temporary net worth certificate program was set to expire in October 1986 under a 'Sunshine Provision' in the Act.

---

[44] *Ibid.* § 203, 96 Stat. at 1493, repealed by *ibid.* § 206, 96 Stat. at 1496 (Sunshine Provision).

[45] *Ibid.* § 203, 96 Stat. at 1493, repealed by *ibid.* § 206, 96 Stat. at 1496 (Sunshine Provision).

[46] The thrift institution would count the note from the FSLIC as an asset and the certificate as part of its net worth. This note-and-certificate exchange meant that the Bank Board was allowing thrifts to raise their reported net worth levels in a way that offered no added protection for the FSLIC. This provision of the Garn-St. Germain Act effectively blessed and expanded a program of note-and-certificate exchange that the FHLBB had previously initiated.

[47] This action was undertaken particularly by the FSLIC on many occasions often described generally as the 'Phoenix Program'.

[48] See 12 U.S.C. § 1823(i) (1982) (repealed 1986).

[49] *Ibid.* at § 203.

[50] See 12 U.S.C. § 1823(i)(1).

V. REAL ESTATE LENDING PROVISIONS FOR NATIONAL BANKS AND THRIFT INSTITUTIONS

A. National Banks

Historically, Congress imposed few restrictions on the lending activities of national banks, except in the area of real estate lending activities.[51] The former real estate lending provisions had required (1) maximum loan-to-value ratios for real estate lending under certain conditions; (2) certain types of real estate loans to provide for amortization of the entire principal amount of the loan within 30 years; and (3) set aggregate limits on real estate lending. Many of these restrictions were removed under Title IV of the Garn-St. Germain Act.[52]

The statutory restrictions removed included loan-to-value ratios, amortization requirements, aggregate lending limits, and maturity requirements. The Garn-St. Germain Act essentially provided that real estate lending activities for national banks were subject to the terms, conditions, and limitations prescribed by the OCC. The Act directed the OCC to issue regulations to cover real estate lending activities by national banks based on the general principles of safety and soundness applicable to all national bank lending activities. The OCC proposed regulations to remove all limitations on real estate lending under the position that lending decisions should be left to national bank management and that the restrictions interfered with national banks' ability to respond to changes in the real estate markets. The new rules, which clearly enhanced the ability of national banks to develop real estate lending products, became effective in 1983.[53]

Although State laws continued to impose certain limitations on commercial bank real estate lending for State-chartered banks, the OCC regulations pre-empted State law limitations such as LTV ratio requirements, prepayment schedules, maturity, aggregate loan limitations, and covenants and restrictions in leases to qualify the leasehold as security for real estate loans.[54] The most important of the real estate restrictions repealed under Title IV was the elimination of loan-to-value (LTV) requirements.[55]

---

[51] National banks are authorized to grant loans secured by real estate pursuant to § 24 of the Federal Reserve Act. See 12 U.S.C. § 371c.

[52] See Garn-St. Germain Act, *supra* note 2, at § 403. § 403 took effect on 15 April 1983, 180 days after 15 October 1982, the date of enactment of the Garn-St. Germain Act.

[53] See 48 Fed. Reg. 40,698 (9 September 1983) (codified at 12 C.F.R. Part 34).

[54] The OCC viewed many classes of loans made based on the security of real estate as excepted from § 24 of the Federal Reserve Act, 12 U.S.C. § 371c. These loans may be granted by a national bank under the 'bank powers clause' of the National Bank Act, 12 U.S.C. § 24 (Seventh) even if the bank takes a security interest in real estate for prudential or other reasons. See 12 C.F.R. § 34.3. Thus, even though a national bank may take an interest in real property, the OCC views such loans as exempt from State laws as set forth in text above because such State laws conflict with federal law, which grants exclusive authority over national banks to the OCC.

[55] See 12 U.S.C. § 1464(c)(1)(B).

B. Thrift Institutions

Title III of the Garn-St. Germain Act and provisions of DIDMCA previously discussed essentially provided federal thrift institutions with real estate lending powers comparable to national banks.[56] In order to provide national bank-type real estate powers to thrift institutions, Congress (1) removed the first lien restrictions on residential real estate loans; (2) expanded authority to make acquisition, development, and construction loans; and (3) eliminated the LTV ratio requirements. Federal thrift institutions therefore received authorization to conduct real estate lending activities, subject to the regulations of the FHLBB.

The Home Owners Loan Act (HOLA) and FHLBB regulations placed aggregate lending limits on real estate loans according to the type of loan or the collateral securing the loan.[57] These limits were additional to the lending limits applicable to the borrower imposed under other FHLBB lending regulations.[58] The FHLBB regulations set forth that loans were 'made on the security of real estate' if:

1. the security property is real estate under the law of the State in which the property is located;
2. the security interest of the thrift institution may be enforced as a real estate mortgage;
3. the security property is capable of appraisal;
4. the thrift institution relies substantially on the real estate as the primary security for the loan; and
5. the security property is a leasehold, the thrift institution may extend the leasehold for a period of five years after the term of the loan.[59]

1. *Aggregate Lending Limits and LTV Ratios*

The HOLA applied different aggregate lending limits to specific types of real estate loans, as distinguished from the Federal Reserve Act, following enactment of the Garn-St. Germain Act. First, loans secured by non-residential real property could not exceed 40 per cent of the thrift's assets.[60] Second, there was no aggregate lending limit with respect to residential loans which conformed to the HOLA requirements.[61] Third, loans secured by residential real property or farm property that did not comply with the HOLA limitations could not exceed 5 per cent of the thrift's assets.[62] Fourth, the LTV ratio could not exceed 100 per cent of the market value of the security property.

---

56 See DIDMCA, *supra* note 2 of Chapter One, at Title IV, § 401, 94 Stat. at 151; Garn-St. Germain Act, *supra* note 2, at Title III, Part B, 96 Stat. at 1469. The Home Owners' Loan Act (HOLA) expressly authorizes loans on improved and unimproved real estate, including residential real property and commercial property. See 12 U.S.C. § 1464(c)(1)(B).
57 See 48 Fed. Reg. 23032 (23 May 1983) (codified at 12 C.F.R. Part 545 et seq.).
58 See 12 C.F.R. § 563.9 et seq. (1983).
59 See 12 C.F.R. § 545.32 (1983).
60 See 12 U.S.C. § 1464(c)(1)(B).
61 *Ibid.* § 1464(c)(1)(B).
62 See 12 U.S.C. § 1464(c)(3)(B).

Except for this ceiling, the thrift institution boards of directors were required to establish LTV ratios for loans made on the security of real estate.[63]

Thus, the Act directly gave federal thrifts the authority to loan up to 100 per cent of appraised value on certain real estate assets, including single family residential loans.[64] The result was that the federal S&L charter was somewhat more flexible than the national bank charter, and clearly represented a more liberal requirement than existed for many S&Ls organized under State laws. For many S&Ls organized under laws of States having LTV requirements, this aspect of the Garn-St. Germain Act provided federal S&Ls with a competitive advantage. In response to this competitive advantage of federally chartered S&Ls over State-chartered counterparts, many States adopted legislation which allowed their S&Ls to also have the benefit of the federal laws.[65]

2. *Appraisals*

The FHLBB required that all real estate loans must be supported by the opinion of an appraiser except loans insured or guaranteed by a government agency, in which case the valuation of the security property by the agency was substituted for the appraisal.[66]

3. *Loan Charges and Repayment*

The FHLBB authorized thrift institutions to collect from the borrower the actual charges incurred in connection with making the loan and pay third parties rendering the services. Except for construction and improvement loans, repayment on real estate loans began not later than 60 days after the loan was disbursed.[67]

4. *Home Loans*

The 'home loan' was defined as a loan made on the security of a home or farm residence. The definition of 'home' included multifamily dwellings and units of a condominium or cooperative. Home loans could also be secured by combinations of home and business property, and combinations of farm residences and commercial farm real estate.[68] Home loans were required to be

---

63 See 12 C.F.R. § 545.32(d) (1983).

64 *Ibid.*

65 Prior to the Garn-St. Germain Act, federal law and many State laws had loan to value limitations. If an 80 per cent loan to value ratio was required by State law, the savings and loan could only lend 80 per cent of the appraised value of the property serving as collateral for the loan. For example, assume a real estate project is appraised at USD10,000,000. If an 80 per cent loan to value ratio limits the S&Ls lending authority, then the association can loan up to, but not exceeding, USD8,000,000 (i.e. 80 per cent of USD10,000,000). Federal law governing federal associations and each State law governing that State S&Ls had varying loan to value restrictions. When the Garn-St. Germain Act was implemented, federal loan to value restrictions of less than 100 per cent were eliminated in most instances. Pursuant to new rules, federal associations could then loan 100 per cent of the appraised value (or in our example, USD10,000,000, instead of USD8,000,000).

66 See 12 C.F.R. § 545.32(b)(1) (1983).

67 See 12 C.F.R. § 545.32(b)(2), (b)(5) (1983).

68 See 12 C.F.R. § 545.33.

repayable in at least semi-annual installments sufficient to liquidate the debt within 40 years, but amortization schedules on such loans were not required.[69]

The LTV ratio for home loans had to be established by a thrift institution's board of directors. The LTV ratio for a home loan which exceeded 90 per cent of the appraised value of the property had to be insured or guaranteed by a 'qualified private insurer' on that part of the unpaid balance that exceeded 80 per cent of the appraised value of the security property. Home loans that exceeded 90 per cent of the appraised value had to be approved by the thrift institution's board of directors.[70] Two significant limitations applied to loans secured by borrower-occupied property. First, due-on-sale clauses could be included in such loans. Second, prepayment penalties were generally a matter of contract between the thrift institution and the borrower to certain limits.[71]

5. *Home Improvement Loans*

Home improvement loans were defined as loans made for residential real property alteration, repair, or improvement.[72] The home improvement loan could be granted with or without security, with installments payable at least quarterly, and for a term not to exceed 20 years. The installments for home improvement loans were required to be equal except if the loan was a balloon payment loan, a graduated payment loan, or an adjustable mortgage loan. The FHLBB prohibited capitalization of interest for such loans.[73]

6. *Loans to Acquire or Improve Real Estate*

The FHLBB consolidated into one provision the investment limitations for riskier real estate lending activities, such as loans for the acquisition or development of real estate, loans on security of building lots and sites, and loans for the construction or rehabilitation of real estate. These loans could not exceed the LTV ratios adopted by a thrift institution's board of directors, and had to be repayable (1) within two years if the loans were for the construction or rehabilitation of an individual single family dwelling; (2) within three years if the loans were for the acquisition of a home; (3) within six years if the loans were for the construction or rehabilitation of multiple family dwellings, of non-residential real estate, or of more than one single family dwelling; (4) within six years if the loans were for the security of building lots and sites; (5) within eight years if the loans were to finance the development of real estate; and (6) within 15 years if the loans were on the security of building lots and sites for single family dwellings to be used as the borrower's principal place of business. In addition to limitations on single borrower loans, thrift institutions could not loan more than 2 per cent of its assets for the development of

---

69 *Ibid.* § 545.33.
70 *Ibid.*
71 See 12 C.F.R. § 545.34.
72 See 12 U.S.C. § 1464(c)(1)(J).
73 See 12 C.F.R. § 545.42.

any single project. Finally, if any portion of the security property is released from the lien securing the loan, the principal balance of the loan was reduced by an amount at least equal to that portion of the outstanding loan balance attributable to the value of the property to be released.[74]

7. *Combination Loans and Other Real Estate Loans*

The aforementioned loans authorized by FHLBB regulations could be combined with any other loan; subject to certain limitations regarding acquisition and development loans, the term of each loan began at the end of the term of the preceding loan.[75] 'Other real estate loans' consist of loans secured by residential real estate other than a home or non-residential real estate. Non-amortizing loans of this type could be repaid within five years, and partially amortizing loans could be repaid within 30 years. Semi-annual interest payments were required except that the contract could provide for deferral and capitalization of interest. Although the LTV ratios of such loans had to comply with FHLBB regulations and internal standards imposed by thrift boards of directors, the ratio could not exceed 100 per cent during the term of the loan from deferral and capitalization of interest.[76]

VI. CONCLUDING OBSERVATIONS: DRAWING TOGETHER THE EFFECTS OF LEGISLATIVE DEREGULATION AND TAX REVISION AND THEIR POLICY AND ECONOMIC IMPLICATIONS

The deregulatory legislation of DIDMCA and Garn-St. Germain Act clearly provided benefits to both banks and thrift institutions. In particular, the S&Ls achieved deregulation of the asset and liability sides of the balance sheet. The collective results of DIDMCA, the Economic Tax Recovery Act (ERTA), and the Garn-St. Germain Act, and the monetary and fiscal policies implemented during the period of 1980–1982, may be summarized as follows:

Thrift institutions were allowed to invest in many different types of investments with particular emphasis on inflation sensitive real estate lending activities;

Deposits were easy to raise because of DIDMCA and its allowance of banks and S&Ls to pay negotiated rates of interest on federally insured USD100,000 certificates of deposits, and deposit insurance would provide the incentives to engage in riskier activities under the Garn-St. Germain Act.

The elimination of interest rate ceilings under DIDMCA resulted in fierce competition for deposits and funding among the thrift and banking industries and between other

---

74 See 12 C.F.R. § 545.36.
75 See 12 C.F.R. § 545.37.
76 See 12 C.F.R. § 545.35.

financial institutions, notably securities firms, and riskier funding arrangements in an attempt to attract deposits.

The establishment of negotiable order of withdrawal (NOW) accounts and the introduction of liberalized reserve requirements under DIDMCA resulted in the destabilization of monetary policy and the Fed committing monetary policy errors which significantly worsened domestic economic conditions.

The conflict between anti-inflationary monetary policy and Reagan Administration fiscal policies resulted in recession and expanding deficits, increasing interest rates even as inflation abated, and the beginnings of sustained appreciation of the US dollar in foreign currency markets. The implementation of fiscal measures by the Reagan Administration, when coupled with DIDMCA and the Garn-St. Germain Act, created an enormous demand for real estate investments and lending activities, facilitating asset price bubbles in real estate markets setting the stage for a 'boom-bust' scenario in those markets.

The preoccupation of the Fed with monetary policy likely came at the expense of supervision and enforcement, as the largest money center banks set themselves up to exposure to the mounting LDC debt crisis.

The thrift industry was encouraged to use its new powers under the Garn-St. Germain Act (and ultimately, State laws) to invest its leveraged deposit base in the newly authorized legal assets to generate earnings and earn past their existing 'negative spreads'. Responding to these provisions, S&Ls invested heavily in real estate either directly through subsidiary corporations and joint ventures or indirectly through loans with so-called 'profits participations'. In particular, the Garn-St. Germain Act authorized many S&Ls to loan up to 100 per cent of the appraised collateral asset value, disregarding the more restrictive LTV limitations.

The Garn-St. Germain Act of 1982 brought to a close the first phase of the thrift industry crisis. For the next two years, the problems in the thrift industry appeared to be under control. The FHLBB resolved a number of problem institutions through purchase and assumption transactions.[77] As reviewed in Part Two of this volume, the FHLBB resolved numerous problematic institutions by promoting combinations through the adoption of regulatory accounting principles, which permitted institutions to record both the premium value of the institutions, measured by the excess of the liabilities assumed over the sum of the value of the assets plus the amount of assistance provided by the FSLIC, and the amount of assistance as assets on the books of thrift institutions, which augmented the capital of combined institutions. However, both prior to and following the Garn-St.

---

[77] During the 1981–1982 period, 730 thrift institutions, or approximately 17 per cent of a total of nearly 4,600 FSLIC-insured thrift institutions, were merged or liquidated. See Robert Trigaux, 'Congressional Study Calls Thrift Insurance Fund Fragile: Future Health Remains Closely Tied to Continued Low Level of Interest Rates, GAO Says', Am. Banker, 7 December 1983, at p.3.

Germain Act, concerns arose regarding the management difficulties experienced by thrift institutions in exploiting the newly authorized powers granted to them under DIDMCA and the Garn-St. Germain Act, respectively.

The US economy improved and interest rates declined during the 1982–1984 period and the thrift industry crisis for the most part remained out of the media limelight. The US economic expansion increased following the 1982 recession without any significant return of price inflation, which remained in the low single digits. The real rate of interest, the nominal market interest rate minus the rate of inflation, remained at very high levels, however. In 1983, inflation was at 3.2 per cent while the yield on three-month government securities was at approximately 9 per cent, the prime lending rate was at approximately 11 per cent, and interest rates on new mortgages exceeded 12.5 per cent.[78] The real rate of interest ranged from 6–8 per cent for corporate borrowers, but remained in the double digits for consumer and mortgage borrowers.[79] In the high interest rate environment, investors continued to shift into money market mutual funds, which increased from USD45 billion in 1979 to nearly USD207 billion by the end of 1982.[80] The tremendous growth in money market mutual funds damaged the relationship between money supply growth and economic growth because the Fed's main money supply aggregate, M-1, did not include institutional holdings in money market mutual funds.

The end result of this legislation was sustained asset value inflation, particularly in real estate. The DIDMCA, ERTA, and Garn-St. Germain Act established the foundation for asset value inflation and represented reactive responses to existing conditions. The Acts cumulatively fueled an inflation in real estate values through their collective impact on finance driven and tax driven pricing. In essence, DIDMCA deregulated the liability side of the balance sheet for the thrift industry, the Garn-St. Germain Act deregulated the asset side of the balance sheet for the thrift industry, and the ERTA generated enormous interest in real estate investment and acquisition through

---

78 See President's Council of Economic Advisors, *Economic Report of the President: 1984*, (1984) at p.299.

79 *Ibid.*

80 See Steven Greider, *Secrets of the Temple: How the Federal Reserve Runs the Country*, (Touchstone Books, 1988), at p.134.

significant tax incentives. The following tables reflect these acts of deregulation visually by illustrating their sequential impact on the balance sheet of a thrift institution:

Illustration 1. Pre DIDMCA, Garn-St. Germain and Deregulation as of 12/31/79

Assets	Liabilities
Loans (restricted to specific legal requirements)	Deposits (with ceilings on rates) Insured by FSLIC up to $40,000
Investments (restricted)	Capital (basically an FIR requirement of 5% of liabilities or a leverage ratio of 20 to 1 liabilities to capital)

Illustration 2. Post DIDMCA and Pre Garn-St. Germain and Deregulation

Assets	Liabilities
Loans (restricted to specific legal requirements)	Deposits (with ceilings on rates being phased out with no limits on $100,000 savings certificates) Insured by FSLIC up to $100,000
Investments (restricted)	Capital (basically an FIR requirement of 5% of liabilities or a leverage ratio of 20 to 1 liabilities to capital)

Illustration 3. Post DIDMCA, Post Deregulation and Post Garn-St. Germain

Assets	Liabilities
Loans (most restrictions lifted)	Deposits (ceilings on rates being phased out with no limits on $100,000 savings certificates) Insured by FSLIC up to $100,000
Investments (of all types unrestricted, for the most part)	Capital (FIR requirement reduced to 3% of liabilities or a leverage ratio of 33a to 1 liabilities to capital) (see Section 1) Capital is also redefined under regulatory accounting principles. (see Chapter Two)

Thus, DIDMCA, ERTA, and the Garn-St. Germain Act authorized the deregulation of thrift and bank balance sheets, and each fueled asset value inflation in real estate values during a period in which the Fed was engaged in direct combat against inflation and inflationary expectations. Similarly to the experiences of many developing and transition nations in the 1990s, these statutes opened the door to unparalleled and uncontrolled 'balance sheet' growth which made thrift institutions in particular appear more solvent and stable but significantly worsened the financial viability of the thrift industry and simply prolonged the inevitable boom-bust scenario in US real estate markets. These statutes were not the only factors fueling asset value inflation in the United States, however.

In the spirit of deregulation, the primary regulatory agencies of the thrift and banking industries eased regulatory constraints on their respective institutions, particularly with respect to enforcement of capital requirements and accounting standards, or otherwise engaged in patterns of forbearance, permissiveness and active encouragement during the period of 1980–1982. The deregulatory initiatives coupled with patterns of forbearance, permissiveness and active encouragement allowed many of the manifestations of crisis and asset value inflation to continue largely beyond the public scrutiny for quite some time, and accelerated asset value inflation and the thrift industry and banking crises in both explicit and subtle ways during this period.

In particular, the FHLBB promulgated extraordinary deregulatory measures which cumulatively served to distort the realities of the financial condition of the industry, instead of merely obscuring transparency of those conditions. The deregulatory measures are examined in Part Two.

Part II
Asset Value Inflation: Supervisory Deregulation and Regulatory Forbearance – The US Thrift Industry and Banking Experience

Introductory Note

The deregulatory legislation and monetary and fiscal policies reviewed in Part One facilitated the basis for rapid balance sheet growth in the thrift and banking industries, and generated asset value inflation in various economic sectors. As the banking and thrift industries became more competitive in the early 1980s, they also faced greater risks. For example, in order to cover the higher costs of funding imposed by anti-inflationary monetary policy, US banks and thrift institutions pursued more aggressive lending activities in search of higher yields.

The rising depository interest rates accompanying deregulation in the early 1980s facilitated high-risk lending activities leading to the first phase of the thrift industry crises, and precipitating various risk events which exposed cracks in the US banking system. These cracks included, for instance, competition to make loans to oil and gas producers which became so intense during the early 1980s that credit standards began to erode, resulting in rising loan defaults and the July 1982 collapse of Penn Square Bank of Oklahoma.

The Continental Illinois National Bank, which participated significantly in Penn Square Bank loans, was left with enormous losses after the Penn Square Bank collapse, and was subsequently forced to pay higher depository interest rates and to rely on a larger percentage of foreign sources for deposits. The most significant crack in the banking system was the Less-Developed Country (LDC) Debt Crisis, which manifested with the default of the government of Mexico in August 1982 and which threatened the integrity of the US banking system by late 1982.

The Depository Institutions Deregulation and Monetary Control Act of 1980 (DIDMCA), Economic Recovery Tax Act (ERTA), and Garn-St. Germain Act of 1980–1982 were supplemented by deregulatory policies adopted by the Federal Home Loan Bank Board (FHLBB) and federal banking agencies, respectively, in efforts to strengthen their constituent institutions' balance sheets and capital adequacy during the first phase of the thrift industry crises and LDC Debt Crisis, formally recognized as beginning in 1979 and August 1982, respectively.

Part Two reviews the deregulatory policies implemented by the FHLBB and banking agencies over the early 1980s. The deregulatory initiatives established by these agencies were intended to mitigate the effects of crisis and to sustain their constituent institutions until the emergence of more favorable economic conditions to facilitate growth and stability following the 'successful' campaign against inflation and inflationary expectations touched upon in Part One.

Chapter Four of this Part Two reviews the FHLBB deregulatory initiatives, a series of deliberate and overt attempts to manipulate capital and accounting guidelines in order to save the thrift industry from terminal crisis. As President Reagan assumed office in January 1981, his advisors recognized that the S&L industry was in dire straits crisis. President Reagan selected Richard Pratt as the new Chairman of FHLBB, who abruptly initiated deregulatory policies as part of a sustained campaign of regulatory forbearance and permissiveness that significantly worsened the fallout of the thrift industry crisis.

Chapter Five of this Part Two considers the banking agency deregulatory initiatives, a less deliberate pattern of regulatory assistance designed to enable growth and diversification in activities among the major banking institutions in lieu of massive exposure to LDC nations. The banking institutions were generally subsumed by overexposures to the LDC borrower nations, however, resulting in part from banking agency forbearance and permissiveness in regulatory enforcement. The banking agencies thereafter followed an unstated but clear policy of regulatory forbearance through the near absence of enforcement of rigorous capital adequacy standards, developed from 1983 through late 1985. The banking and monetary authorities devoted significant energies to resolving the LDC Debt Crisis, and these issues tended to preoccupy policymakers as the thrift industry worsened significantly during this period.

Chapter Six of this Part Two considers how these policies generated activities in the real estate sector that significantly augmented asset value inflation and magnified the actions taken by the FHLBB in this respect.

Chapter Seven of this Part Two reviews the monetary, fiscal, and exchange rate policies implemented over the period of 1982 – late 1985, which facilitated asset value inflation, clearly exacerbated the thrift industry and banking crises, and unfortunately jeopardized the US economy to a greater extent than the rampant inflation and inflationary expectations of 1979 to 1982. This chapter concludes by observing that the regulatory, monetary, fiscal, and exchange rate policies over the period from 1980 until late 1985, coupled with the monetary, fiscal, and exchange rate policies of the period from late 1982 until late 1985, set the stage for abrupt policy reversals and a massive shift from asset value inflation to asset value deflation beginning in late 1985 and continuing through the 1990s, particularly in the real estate sector.

4. US Thrift Industry: FHLBB Deregulation

I. INTRODUCTION

In 1980, the Federal Savings and Loan Insurance Corporation (FSLIC) insured approximately 4,000 State- and federally-chartered savings and loan associations (S&Ls) with total assets in excess of USD600 billion; and, the vast majority of these assets were held in traditional mortgage investments. While another 590 S&Ls with assets in excess of USD12.2 billion were insured by State-sponsored deposit insurance programs in Maryland, Massachusetts, North Carolina, Ohio, and Pennsylvania.[1] As previously reviewed in Part One, the thrift institutions were involved in the first phase of crisis because of upwardly spiraling interest rates and asset-liability mismatches on a systemic scale.

The deposit insurance provisions enacted under the Depository Institutions Deregulation and Monetary Control Act of 1980 (DIDMCA) during President Carter's Administration, which among other things increased deposit insurance from USD40,000 per depositor to the amount of USD100,000 per depositor, became one of the primary catalysts for the thrift industry crisis. First, deposit insurance enabled S&L operators to draw deposits from the public long after they were technically insolvent beyond the hope of bailout. Second, once S&L management had effectively removed their own money from distressed institutions, they had reason to speculate to the fullest extent possible with depositor funds in the hope of saving their respective institutions. If the speculation paid off, all was well; if the speculation lost, the government was obligated to pay back the depositors. The expansion of thrift asset powers simply extended the speculative avenues that S&L management could use with depositor funds to save their institutions. Unfortunately, the notion of changing the deposit insurance scheme soon after the enactment of DIDMCA was simply non-existent.

---

1 See US League of Savings Institutions, *Savings and Loan Sourcebook* (1982) at p.37.

Therefore, the Federal Home Loan Bank Board (FHLBB) perceived that it had little alternative but to do what it could through deregulatory initiatives to keep the S&Ls going until interest rates decreased and their mortgage portfolios were profitable once again. Beginning in late 1980, the FHLBB initiated a series of systematic relaxation of capital requirements directly and indirectly through relaxation of accounting procedures. Regulatory forbearance, or the exercise of judgment in applying supervisory mandates, occurred on both case-by-case bases and in formalized policies to S&Ls (and banks, as discussed later in this chapter) to continue operations below the mandatory capital requirements for substantial periods of time.[2]

This chapter analyses the 1980s US thrift and bank experiences vis-à-vis supervisory deregulation and regulatory forbearance.

II. REGULATORY STRUCTURE AND SUPERVISORY ENVIRONMENT

The federal regulatory structure of thrift institutions developed under a separate legislative framework from that for commercial banks in the early 1930s under the public policy of facilitating residential home ownership. The Federal Home Loan Bank Act of 1932 established the Federal Home Loan Bank System as a source of liquidity and funding for thrift institutions, comprised of 12 regional Federal Home Loan Banks under the supervision of the FHLBB. The Home Owners Loan Act of 1933 (HOLA) authorized the FHLBB to charter and regulate federal S&Ls and otherwise promote the expansion of residential mortgage lending. The National Housing Act of 1934 established the FSLIC to provide federal deposit insurance for S&Ls similar to the Federal Deposit Insurance Corporation (FDIC). The FSLIC was not established as an independent agency like the FDIC, however, and was subject to the authority of FHLBB. The deposit insurance functions were separated from the regulatory and supervisory functions under the FDIC for commercial banks, but were subject to authority of the same agency under the FHLBB for the thrift industry.[3]

The FHLBB examination, supervision, and enforcement practices were traditionally weaker than those of the federal banking agencies.[4] The S&L examination process and staff were generally not designed to function effectively in the new and complex environment of the 1980s following the enactment of

2 See L. William Seidman, *Full Faith and Credit: The Great S&L Debacle and other Washington Sagas* (Times Books, 1993).

3 See generally, Federal Deposit Insurance Corporation ('*FDIC*'), 'An Examination of the Banking Crises of the 1980s and Early 1990s', *History of the Eighties, Volume 1: Lessons for the Future*, (Washington D.C., 1998), at p.170.

4 Prior to the 1980s, thrift institutions had limited powers and failures were relatively uncommon. The FHLBB was a small agency with oversight authority for an industry that for all practical purposes functioned like a public agency. FHLBB examiners were generally under-compensated and the process was merely adequate to supervise the traditional S&L operation. See generally William K. Black, *Examination/ Supervision/Enforcement of S&Ls: 1979–1992* (1993).

DIDMCA and Garn-St. Germain Act, respectively.[5] In addition, the FHLBB's examination and supervisory functions were organized differently from the federal banking agencies, in that the examination function was totally separate and distinct from the supervisory function.[6] There existed no direct line of responsibility for dealing with a distressed institution, and the potential for conflicts of interest and communication failures by and between the supervisory and examination processes was enormous.[7] Finally, the FHLBB possessed enforcement powers similar to the federal banking agencies but utilized them much less frequently. The supervisory environment was generally not conducive to cease-and-desist orders and other prompt corrective actions.[8]

Unfortunately, these policies, arrangements, and precedents undermined the effectiveness of using enforcement actions to address problematic thrift institutions in the economic environment of 1980–1983, respectively. The vast number of insolvent or distressed thrift institutions in the early 1980s was entirely predictable because of the interest-rate mismatch dilemma addressed in detail in Chapter One. The Congressional response was to deregulate through legislation, and the FHLBB followed suit, engaging in a massive web of misguided deregulatory policies that set the stage for enormous industry losses and taxpayer bailout in the late 1980s.

III. CAPITAL REQUIREMENTS

The federal government was admittedly unprepared to deal with the thrift industry crisis.[9] The primary problems were the lack of adequate FSLIC

---

5 The examination philosophy was generally to identify compliance with rules and regulations, not general principles of safety and soundness. As most S&L assets prior to 1980 were fixed-rate home mortgages, credit quality issues were uncommon. Loan evaluations were generally driven by the appraisal process, as discussed *infra* in this chapter. The collateral affiliated with residential lending practices generally appreciated in the gradually inflationary environment during the 1960s and 1970s. Thus, losses on residential foreclosures were also relatively uncommon. See *History of the Eighties, Volume 1, supra* note 3, at p.171.

6 The supervisory oversight of the thrift industry was decentralized and separated from the examination function. The FHLBB designated each regional Federal Home Loan Bank president as the principal supervisory authority (PSA) for that region, and senior Bank staff acted as supervisory agents. The field examiners reported to the FHLBB instead of the regional PSA, however, and the PSA was not required to report to the FHLBB. Thus, as the regional Banks were owned by the institutions they supervised, they operated independently of the FHLBB regulatory process. See Black, *supra* note 4, at pp.2–12.

7 The system facilitated systemic distrust and disrespect between examiners, who were federal government employees, and the supervisory agents, who were employees of the privately owned regional Federal Home Loan Banks (FHLBs). The supervisory agents were generally paid far in excess of examiners, and were closely affiliated with the industry. See *History of the Eighties, Volume 1, supra* note 3, at p.172.

8 The S&Ls were traditionally subject to strict regulation, and prior to the 1980s were not generally susceptible to mismanagement. The S&L industry was significantly involved with its own supervision, and enjoyed a protected status with various political leaders. See *History of the Eighties, Volume 1, supra* note 3, at p.172.

9 See National Commission on Financial Institution Reform, Recovery, and Enforcement, *Origins and Causes of the S&L Debacle: A Blueprint for Reform: A Report to the President and Congress of the United States*, (1993) at p.32.

deposit insurance resources to close and liquidate insolvent thrift institutions, and the generally widespread perception that the industry should be granted regulatory forbearance until interest rates returned to normal levels, and thrift institutions could restructure their portfolios with new asset investment powers authorized under DIDMCA and the Garn-St. Germain Act, respectively.[10]

Thus, the federal legislative deregulation was initially accompanied by deregulatory actions of the FHLBB to decrease capital requirements for thrift institutions.[11] DIDMCA reduced net worth requirements by replacing the previous statutory net worth requirement of 5 per cent of insured accounts with a range of 3 to 6 per cent of insured accounts as determined by the FHLBB.[12] The resulting deregulation involved adjustments to capital reserves required by the FHLBB from 5 to 4 per cent of assets in November 1980,[13] and 4 to 3 per cent in January 1982.[14] In contrast, the commercial banking industry was required to have a percentage of assets, a larger base than insured deposits, as capital reserves. Just as S&Ls obtained vast new abilities to raise deposits under DIDMCA, the FHLBB increased nominal industry leverage from 20:1 to 33:1. The erosion of capital discipline that could have been provided by capital requirements was further exacerbated by two other FHLBB regulations, known as the 'five-year averaging' and '20-year phase-in' provisions. These provisions relaxed capital requirements for rapidly growing and newly-chartered thrift institutions, and were originally designed to allow for the gradual increase of reserves and net worth by mutual institutions financing residential mortgages in local real estate markets.

The 'five-year averaging' provision was adopted by FHLBB in December 1972, and authorized S&Ls to premise the determination of their minimum net worth and reserve requirements on average liabilities and deposits over the five year period (the year of the calculation and the previous four years) instead of on current liabilities and deposits.[15] This regulation provided the largest reduction of capital requirements for the fastest-growing thrift institutions.[16] The '20-year phase-in' regulation reduced capital requirements for a newly-chartered thrift institution by authorizing it to determine capital requirements by multiplying 3 per cent of liabilities by the fraction of 20 years that it had been covered by deposit insurance.

The first-year thrift institutions only needed to have one-twentieth of the normally required reserves and net worth. In permitting debt-to-equity ratios as high as 666:1, this regulation eliminated any meaningful capital restrictions on growth for the newly-chartered thrift institutions attempting

---

10 See *History of the Eighties, Volume 1, supra* note 3, at p.173.

11 See 12 C.F.R. § 563.13 (1981).

12 See *History of the Eighties, Volume 1, supra* note 3, at p.175.

13 See FHLBB, 'Net Worth Amendments', 45 Fed. Reg. 76111 (1980).

14 See FHLBB, 'Net Worth Amendments', 47 Fed. Reg. 3,543 (1982).

15 See 37 Fed. Reg. 26,579 (1972).

16 The five-year averaging rule encouraged rapid deposit growth at S&Ls because the net worth requirement was based on the average of the previous five years' deposits, not the institution's existing deposits. See National Commission, *supra* note 9, at pp.35–36.

to become competitive in the industry. Prior to November 1983, when the FHLBB eliminated use of the 20-year phase-in regulation for newly-chartered but not existing institutions, a new institution could leverage USD2 million in initial capital stock or pledged savings accounts to support nearly USD1.3 billion in liabilities after the first year of operations.[17]

The reduction in capital requirements in combination with the accounting practices authorized by FHLBB, discussed later in this chapter, permitted thrift institutions with little or no capital to engage in aggressive expansion. Notably, from 1980–1984, aggregate thrift assets increased from USD618 billion to nearly USD1 trillion, while during the same period aggregate industry capital levels (capital minus goodwill and other intangible assets) decreased from more than USD32 billion to less than USD4 billion.[18] Aggressive operators of thrift institutions had little to lose and much to gain by adopting strategies of rapid growth and significant speculative activities, particularly those institutions that were financially distressed. In 1984, the Task Force on Regulation of Financial Services, chaired by then-Vice President George Bush and including the key leaders of all federal financial regulatory agencies, recommended that the FHLBB be required to use the same capital requirements and accounting requirements for determining appropriate capital levels as the FDIC.[19] Notably, the legislation to implement this recommendation was not enacted until the passage of the Financial Institutions Reform, Recovery, and Enforcement Act of 1989 (FIRREA) in August 1989, discussed *infra* in Chapter Four, when aggregate thrift assets had increased to nearly USD1.25 trillion, more than USD400 billion higher than the level existing when the Task Group initially recommended tightening thrift institution capital requirements and accounting standards.[20]

IV. ACCOUNTING STANDARDS

A. Regulatory Accounting Principles

Regulatory accounting principles (RAP) were accounting standards established by regulatory agencies to monitor compliance with statutory and administrative requirements. With respect to federally insured depository institutions, RAP governed the financial reports submitted to the relevant federal agency. The appropriate intent of RAP was to require regulated

---

17 See FHLBB, 'Reserve Requirements and Policies Relating to Insurance of Accounts of de Novo Institutions', 48 Fed. Reg. 54,320 (1983).

18 See R. Brumbaugh, Jr., *Thrifts Under Siege: Restoring Order to American Banking*, (1988) at pp.50–52.

19 See 'Blueprint for Reform: The Report of the Task Group on Regulation of Financial Services', (1984) at p.82 (on file with author).

20 See generally Richard C. Breeden, 'Thumbs on the Scale: The Role that Accounting Practices Played in the Savings and Loan Crisis', at S71-S93, in *Annual Survey Issue: Financial Institutions and Regulations*, 'The S&L Crisis: Death and Transfiguration', Fordham Law Rev., Vol. LIX, No. 6 (May 1991).

institutions to determine earnings and net worth on a more conservative basis than under generally accepted accounting principles (GAAP). GAAP are established private sector accounting standards developed principally by the Financial Accounting Standards Board (FASB) and the American Institute of Certified Public Accountants (AICPA).[21] The development of accounting standards by these private sector entities occurs under the oversight jurisdiction of the US Securities and Exchange Commission (SEC). GAAP provides the framework for accounting measurements and disclosures that are required for the sale of securities and periodic financial reports under the federal securities laws and regulations.

The SEC's authority to regulate the accounting practices and disclosures includes registration statements and periodic financial reports of publicly-held holding companies owning banks and S&Ls, but the securities issued directly by depository institutions are exempt from the registration requirements of the Securities Act of 1933.[22] In addition, pursuant to Section 12(i) of the Securities and Exchange Act of 1934,[23] the federal agencies with regulatory jurisdiction over banks and S&Ls retain responsibility for administering the disclosure provisions for banks and S&Ls. The securities laws regulating accounting standards and disclosure requirements were interpreted and applied to thrift institutions by the FHLBB, and not the SEC. The FHLBB in turn abused this discretion in a number of ways that contributed to the erosion or manipulation of conservative accounting standards for thrift institutions and accelerated the eventual insolvency of a significant portion of the industry before the outside world grasped the magnitude of the S&L crisis.

The FHLBB developed RAP to replace GAAP for purposes of determining compliance with capital requirements that failed to meet the underlying intent of RAP. The FHLBB issued RAP that deviated from sound accounting principles and resulted in thrift management retaining far more flexibility and opportunities for accounting manipulation under RAP than conservatively applied GAAP. For instance, FHLBB RAP deviations included:

1. permitting the deferral of losses from the sale of assets with below-market yields;
2. permitting the use of net worth capital certificates, authorized by Congress, as substitutes for real capital;
3. permitting qualifying mutual capital certificates to be included as RAP capital;
4. permitting FSLIC members to exclude from liabilities in determining net worth certain 'contra-asset' accounts, including loans-in-process, unearned discounts, and deferred fees and credits;

---

21 The FASB issues guidance through Statements of Financial Accounting Standards (SFAS), interpretations, technical bulletins, Statements of Financial Accounting Concepts, and the minutes of the Emerging Issues Task Force (EITF). The AICPA issues guidance through Notices to Practitioners, Industry Audit and Accounting Guides, Statements of Position, Accounting Interpretations, Issue Papers, and Accounting Standards Executive Committee (AcSEC) Practice Bulletins.

22 See 15 U.S.C. §§ 77c(a)(2) (banks); 77c(a)(5) (thrift institutions).

23 See 15 U.S.C. § 78l(i).

5. permitting the inclusion of net worth certificates, qualifying subordinated debentures, and appraised equity capital as RAP net worth;
6. accelerating income recognition on certain real estate investments;
7. capitalizing losses on speculative forward and derivative commitments; and
8. amortization of acquisition costs in excess of net tangible assets over 40 years while recognizing income on the discounted market value of the acquired assets over ten years.[24]

Notwithstanding the development of significant deviations of RAP from GAAP by FHLBB, the responsibility does not rest solely with the FHLBB in this respect. The legal and accounting professions also contributed significantly to the development and implementation of these accounting practices by thrift institutions, and many firms subsequently became subject to enforcement actions and private litigation for their respective failures to fulfill their professional obligations. A conservative estimate of the impact of RAP accounting deviations was that 'by 1984, the difference between RAP and GAAP net worth for S&Ls stood at $9 billion,' which meant 'that the industry's capital position, or ... its cushion to absorb losses was overstated by USD9 billion.'[25]

B. Inflation of Reported Capital

1. *Deferral of Losses on the Sale of Assets*

The FHLBB's most significant divergence regarding RAP was a regulation that prompted thrift institutions to liquidate long-term mortgage loans that could be sold only at a substantial discount throughout the high interest rate period of the early 1980s. Both GAAP and RAP permitted such loans to be carried at historical cost without reflecting the enormous losses in market value that occurred given the high interest rates. The failure to represent economic reality effectively resulted in industry-wide overstatements of earnings and net worth. Although GAAP required immediate recognition of loss in the event that any loan assets were sold, the FHLBB regulation adopted in 1981 permitted thrift institutions to book the entire amount of losses realized on the sale of mortgage loans as an asset for purposes of RAP, and the accumulated loss would then be amortized over the remaining life of the assets sold.[26]

The FHLBB regulation is commonly known as 'FHLBB Memorandum R-49'. Under FHLBB Memorandum R-49, approved in September 1981, a thrift institution could sell a portfolio of mortgages with a USD200 million face amount for USD100 million, and could treat the realized loss of USD100

---

24 See *House Report*, at 298.
25 *Ibid.*
26 See FHLBB, 'Treatment of Gains and Losses on the Sale or Other Disposition of Mortgage Assets, Mortgage-Related Securities, and Debt Securities; Republication of Reserve Requirements', 46 Fed. Reg. 50,048 (1981).

million as an asset included in net worth. This treatment permitted the thrift institution to continue activities without injecting new capital even though the thrift enterprise suffered a decrease in real asset value of USD100 million. In addition, the thrift received a tax benefit from the loss transaction, as the sale resulted in the recognition of a USD100 million loss for tax purposes. The stated purpose of the regulation was to assist thrift institutions that could not effectively undertake mortgage disposition programs because GAAP required immediate recognition of a loss, but the loss deferral regulation went much further and essentially permitted thrift institutions to carry assets at historical cost on their balance sheets even after they had been sold. The loss deferral regulation created enormous divergences between GAAP and RAP measures of net worth.

The effects of Memorandum R-49 could be juxtaposed with even more beneficial tax treatment upon application of a provision of ERTA passed in August 1981, which permitted companies to effectively establish a 'safe harbor' system by which companies could carry back to any and all of the five previous years losses taken after 1980, which meant that the IRS would actually have to give thrift institutions conducting this activity a refund on back taxes.[27]

Therefore, Memorandum R-49 initially served as a tax shelter for S&Ls. The routine practice of thrift institutions was to exchange their mortgage portfolios for Federal National Mortgage Association (FNMA) and Federal Home Loan Mortgage Corporation (FHLMC) pass-through securities of the same fair market value (FMV), and to recognize the difference between the face value of the mortgage portfolio and the market value of the securities for which it was exchanged as a loss for tax purposes.[28] Memorandum R-49 soon served another purpose, however. The FHLBB and the staff of President Reagan's Housing Commission were convinced that the thrift crisis could be mitigated by diversifying thrift investments and activities away from mortgage lending. By encouraging S&Ls to sell their loss mortgages for tax reasons, the FHLBB essentially assisted S&Ls in obtaining funds for new investments and enhance their diversification of investments. Unfortunately, the investments selected by thrift institutions were not simply limited to FHLMC securities, however, as S&Ls also used the incentive to invest in speculative and exotic financial instruments, including over-the-counter market (OTC) mortgage-backed derivatives.[29]

The money center banks and investment firms ('dealers') marketed these instruments to S&L managers under the following scenario. First, the dealers would package the low-yielding mortgages held by S&Ls into mortgage-backed securities (MBS) without having the S&L recognize a loss on the constructive sale. Second, the S&Ls would invest the MBS proceeds from the constructive sale into high-yield debentures such as junk bonds under-written

---

[27] See Martin Mayer, *The Bankers: The Next Generation* (Penguin Books, New York, 1997), at p.379.

[28] This activity generated about USD1.5 billion of tax refunds, which the IRS vigorously disputed, but in ensuing litigation the courts ruled in favor of the S&Ls on grounds that the losses were real losses. See Mayer, *supra* note 27, at p.379.

[29] See Mayer, *supra* note 27, at pp.379–380.

by the same dealers, and the interest earned on these investments would be represented as S&L profits. The FHLBB's approval of such loss deferral techniques resulted in dramatic sales of junk bonds to S&Ls by notorious operators such as Michael Milken of Drexel Burnham Lambert, and for all practical purposes fueled the development of the junk bond market in the United States. Third, once the S&Ls held the junk bonds as investments, they could trade and profit from trading activities using the risk management and valuation models introduced to them by the same dealer firms.[30]

The Financial Accounting Standards Board (FASB) refused to accept such loss deferral techniques for S&L accounting, and determined them to be a gross misinterpretation of and inconsistent with GAAP.[31] The FHLBB pleaded with the FASB to endorse the practice to save the industry, but the FASB rebutted this lobbying with assistance from the SEC. The FASB refused to compromise on a wholesale basis with FHLBB on the loss deferral techniques.[32] The accounting firms nonetheless considered themselves protected by Memorandum R-49, however, and still blessed the balance sheets of S&Ls which incorporated loss deferral techniques.[33]

Finally, Memorandum R-49 eliminated the ability of S&Ls to survive in the economic environment from late 1982 onward as inflationary expectations mitigated and interest rates decreased to more rational levels. By encouraging the sale of mortgages that would otherwise recover their value if interest rates decreased as they did after August 1982, Memorandum R-49 guaranteed that the profits on mortgages from decreasing interest rates would not go to the S&Ls, but instead went to the dealer firms that purchased the mortgages as MBS from the thrift industry.[34]

2. *Loan Origination Fees*

Beginning in 1979, S&Ls were permitted to recognize income from construction loan origination fees under circumstances far more flexible than available under GAAP. Thrift institutions were permitted to recognize income from construction loan fees equal to 2.5 per cent of the total loan amount immediately upon origination of a loan. With respect to loans other than construction loans, thrift institutions could recognize income up to 2 per cent of the loan amount, plus USD400 if the institution's employees performed appraisal, attorney, or loan closing services for which no escrow fee was required.[35] For instance, for a USD50 million construction loan, RAP would permit a thrift to recognize USD1.2 million in loan fee income on the day of

---

30 *Ibid.* at 380.

31 See Martin Mayer, *The Greatest Ever Bank Robbery: The Collapse of the Savings and Loan Industry* (1990), at p.73 (reciting FASB arguments against endorsing the loss deferral rule to FHLBB Chairman Pratt and advising Pratt to 'stop concealing the condition' of thrift institutions).

32 The FASB eventually did compromise with FHLBB on the 40-year amortization of goodwill, however, discussed supra, by allowing such amortization over the 12-year average duration of mortgages. See Mayer, *supra* note 27, at pp.380–381.

33 See Mayer, *supra* note 27, at p.381.

34 *Ibid.* at p.382.

35 See FHLBB, 'Insurance of Accounts, Amendments Relating to Acquisition Credit Subject to Deferral', 44 Fed. Reg. 76,567 (1979).

closing. Conversely, GAAP permitted immediate recognition of loan fee income only to the extent of costs incurred in originating the loans, and the remainder of the fees were taken into income over the life of the loan if it remained current or upon sale of the loan asset. For purposes of RAP, the loan fee earnings were most significant for thrift institutions conducting large volumes of construction lending. The RAP treatment clearly encouraged many institutions to enter into additional construction loans, regardless of risk, in order to generate immediate income. Thrift institutions engaging in massive construction loan origination and underwriting could report enormous income in loan origination fees even though the loans themselves were extremely risky. Finally, thrift institutions had a powerful incentive to facilitate rapid growth in deposits that could be used as loans on real estate projects paying the highest origination fees. For instance, given the 'five-year averaging' and '20-year phase-in' regulations, a thrift accepting USD1 billion in new deposits would have to increase its capital merely by USD10 million, and simultaneously could generate up to USD25 million in income by using deposits to fund construction loans.

3. *Appraised Equity Capital*

Perhaps the most devastating regulatory change occurred in November 1982 when the FHLBB permitted S&Ls to credit themselves with appraised equity capital in determining net worth under RAP. The appraised equity capital represented the amount that certain capital assets (property and equipment) appreciated above their recorded depreciated cost.[36] The regulation permitted thrift institutions to recognize appreciation in the value of real estate even where those assets had not yet been sold, with a corresponding increase in net worth for purposes of RAP. Thrift institutions were permitted to utilize market value on a selective basis, in that only those adjustments which increased the value of certain assets were made, and there was no obligation to recognize the massive decreases in value of other assets.[37]

For instance, an S&L owning commercial property through foreclosure or direct investment of S&L deposits into commercial real estate (permissible in some States, such as California), could credit itself with any increase in the appraised value of that property and take that credit into capital allowing the recruitment of USD33 in deposits for each USD1 of appraised equity capital. The appraised equity capital regulation was simply a direct invitation for massive 'value' compounding. In various 'daisy chain' situations, S&Ls worked together to trade land and securities back and forth, incurring no tax liability because the trade of 'like assets' did not create taxable gain, at continuously escalating prices. These procedures originally developed in the State of Texas to protect the value of bad loans, and were called 'trading the dead horse for the dead cow'.[38]

---

[36] See FHLBB, 'Amendments to Net Worth and Statutory Reserve Requirements', 47 Fed. Reg. 52,961 (1982).

[37] See Breeden, *supra* note 20, at S80.

[38] See Mayer, *supra* note 27, at p.381.

The FHLBB acknowledged that the regulation at its inception significantly deviated from GAAP but asserted that it was intended to '... maintain public confidence in the industry during this period of financial and operational transition'.[39] The FHLBB itself was primarily responsible for reviewing financial statements and disclosure documents of federally-chartered thrift institutions as they offered shares of stock to the public but failed to restrict the release of statements with appraised equity capital to the public. The FHLBB further asserted that thrift institutions subject to the anti-fraud provisions of the federal securities laws should avoid releasing financial statements including appraised equity capital adjustments to the public.[40] The FHLBB was clearly mired in conflicts of interest regarding this regulation and other regulations. The FHLBB extended application of the appraised equity capital rule until its expiration in December 1986.

V. ACCOUNTING INTERPRETATIONS

A. Purchase and Goodwill Accounting

The FHLBB issued regulatory guidance under RAP that deviated from GAAP requirements which essentially permitted thrift institutions to misrepresent the true nature of their capital levels. The FHLBB also authorized regulations that resulted in serious misapplications of GAAP. The most egregious of these regulations involved treatments of goodwill that were designed to enhance the attractiveness of acquisitions of troubled thrift institutions (those whose liabilities exceeded the FMV of their assets). The accounting concept of 'goodwill' is based on a premise that when a business is acquired in an arm's-length transaction for an amount that exceeds the aggregate book value of its assets, there must be an intangible asset that accounts for the difference, thereby assuming that a purchaser will not pay too much for the acquired assets. The application of goodwill to acquisitions of troubled thrifts distorted this premise, however, as in many thrift acquisitions the purchasers assumed the excess liabilities of thrift that was incurring substantial losses at the time of acquisition. Many troubled thrift acquisitions, would probably not have occurred unless the FHLBB interpreted GAAP so as to permit such purchasers of insolvent or troubled thrifts to generate immediate accounting profits.

In the acquisition of a troubled thrift, the assets (long-term mortgages that had depreciated in value as a result of changes in interest rates) were recorded on the purchaser's books at FMV in accordance with GAAP. The difference between the original book value and the FMV (the 'discount') was recorded as income over the estimated life of the assets on an interest-method basis. The net liabilities (fair value of the liabilities reduced by the fair value of the assets acquired) were recorded as goodwill and expended on a

---

[39] See 47 Fed. Reg. at 52,962.
[40] *Ibid.* at 52,964.

straight-line basis over an amortization period.[41] GAAP principles specified that the amortization period for goodwill should be recognized over the appropriate period of benefit, not to exceed 40 years. If a thrift institution used the 40-year amortization period, the annual 'expense' for goodwill would be one-fortieth of the total amount. As the typical life of the purchased assets generally averaged ten years, using a 40-year amortization period resulted in the discount being recorded as income over a shorter period. The income from amortizing the purchase discount would exceed the expense from goodwill and the acquiring institution would generate net income over the first ten years of the acquisition. As the amount of such paper profits immediately following the acquisition was directly related to the amount of goodwill amortized over a longer period, the most significant increase to profits was realized by purchasers that had acquired the most troubled thrifts.[42]

The FHLBB guidance from 1974–1981 required thrifts to amortize goodwill over a maximum ten-year period.[43] In 1980, the FHLBB proposed a regulation to codify Memorandum R-31a and to require that the goodwill amortization periods match with the accretion of discounts on acquired assets, observing that the use of different amortization periods 'may give rise to distortions in net worth levels and computations'.[44] In 1981, the FHLBB abruptly reversed course and changed the accounting guidance and eliminated the restriction on acceptable goodwill periods.[45] The FHLBB release withdrawing the proposed regulation provided that the FHLBB determined to allow the application of [GAAP] in this area without *regulatory restriction*. Notably, this regulation was promulgated on the same day that FHLBB issued a proposed regulation to permit the deferral of losses on assets sold that significantly diverged from GAAP.

The FHLBB regulation permitted S&Ls that acquired other S&Ls to capitalize as goodwill the difference between the net worth of the acquired institution and the price paid for it, and to write off that goodwill over as many as 40 years. The logic behind goodwill as an asset is that businesses are rational, so when one company pays another company more than the FMV of the business being sought, the business must have 'intangible assets' such as a franchise, reputation, location, brand name, or customer list, that will generate future income. The intangible asset of a troubled or insolvent S&L in the 1980s was the *deposit insurance* offered by the US Government through FSLIC for minimal premiums not otherwise premised on risk-based principles.

Under the deposit insurance regime and the FHLBB's permissive capital standards, each dollar of goodwill booked into the acquiring S&L made possible the acquisition of at least another USD33 in the form of insured deposits. Therefore, an insolvent S&L with a portfolio of low-rate mortgages and distressed or non-performing loans would be 'worth' more to a

---

41 See Breeden, *supra* note 20, at S82.
42 *Ibid.* at S82.
43 See FHLBB Memorandum R-31a (8 March 1974).
44 See 45 Fed. Reg. 72,661, 72,662 (1980).
45 See FHLBB, 'Treatment of Goodwill Acquired in Mergers', 46 Fed. Reg. 42,274 (1981).

prospective purchaser than a solvent S&L because the goodwill asset that could be recorded as an asset by purchasing the insolvent S&L provided greater opportunities for expansion. The perversion of the situation is easily cognizable in that one insolvent S&L could acquire another insolvent S&L, and the two combined could suddenly show enough capital to remain solvent.[46]

The depreciation of goodwill over 40 years only legitimated a serious misrepresentation, because the average duration of a mortgage asset was (and still is) generally recognized as 12 years. As low-rate mortgages were paid off the S&L, instead of writing off the goodwill it had acquired by purchasing them at a price below their face value, could take profits and pay dividends to its owners and basically forget about the obligation to write off what was still after 12 years the surviving 70 per cent of the goodwill on its balance sheet. Because one year's reduction of the 'asset' goodwill produced a one-for-one reduction in the capital goodwill on the liability side of the balance sheet, the continuing write-offs of the remaining 70 per cent doomed the S&L to eventual downsizing or insolvency.[47]

B. FSLIC Acquisitions Programs: Supervisory Goodwill

Under GAAP, there exist circumstances wherein a business combination may be addressed using the 'purchase method' of accounting. The critical aspect of the purchase method of accounting under the FSLIC supervisory acquisition program was that it permitted the purchaser to designate the excess of the purchase price over the fair value of all identifiable assets acquired as an intangible asset termed 'goodwill'. The recognition of 'goodwill' as an asset is ordinarily logical because a 'rational purchaser' in a 'free market' would not purchase a business at a price in excess of the value of the business' assets unless there existed some intangible 'going concern' value that comprised the excess amount paid. Goodwill recognized under the purchase method as the result of an FSLIC-sponsored supervisory acquisition transaction was referred to as 'supervisory goodwill'.[48] The recognition of 'supervisory goodwill' under the purchase method was essential to the supervisory acquisition transactions because the FSLIC lacked sufficient funds to cover the difference between a failed thrift's liabilities and assets. Supervisory goodwill was the FHLBB's 'cash substitute' to encourage solvent thrifts to assume a failed thrift's liabilities, and consolidate the industry by moving insolvent thrifts into solvent institutions.[49]

The concept of supervisory goodwill was acceptable to acquiring institutions for several reasons. First, the FHLBB permitted acquiring institutions to include supervisory goodwill towards their capital requirements.[50] The

---

[46] See Mayer, *supra* note 27, at p.377.

[47] *Ibid.* at p.378.

[48] See *Winstar Corp.*, 116 S. Ct. 2432 (1996).

[49] See 'Savings and Loan Policies in the Late 1970s and 1980s', Hearings Before the House Committee on Banking, Finance and Urban Affairs, 101st Cong., 2d Sess., No. 101–176, at 227 (1990) (statement of FHLBB Chairman Richard Pratt); *Winstar Corp.*, *supra* note 48.

[50] See 12 C.F.R. § 563.13 (1981).

capital adequacy treatment was critical because in most cases the combined institution following the acquisition would have been immediately insolvent under federal regulations unless goodwill was included towards capital reserves. The treatment of supervisory goodwill from the acquiring institution's perspective, however, as regulatory capital was acceptable because it inflated the institution's reserves, and thereby allowed it to leverage into more loans and to possibly make greater profits. Second, the FHLBB permitted acquiring institutions to amortize goodwill assets over long periods of time, up to the 40-year maximum permissible under GAAP.[51]

The concept of amortization recognizes that intangible assets such as goodwill are useful for a limited period of time, and that a business must accordingly 'write down' the value of the asset each year to reflect its decreasing worth.[52] The amount necessary for the 'write down' is reflected on the business's income statement each year as an operating expense. As the acquiring thrift institution amortized its goodwill, however, it had to further account for changes in the value of its loan assets, which were its principal assets.[53] The loans acquired as assets of the failed thrift in a supervisory acquisition transaction were generally worth less than their face value because they were issued at interest rates below the market interest rates at the time of acquisition.[54] The differential or 'discount' appears on the balance sheet as a 'contra-asset' account – a deduction from the face value of the loan – to reflect market valuation of the asset. As loans are repaid at face value, the impact of the discount decreases over time as the loan's maturity date approaches. This process is called the 'accretion of the discount' and is reflected on a thrift's income statement as a series of capital gains.[55]

The FHLBB decided that goodwill was of transitory value to the thrift industry in this context and imposed a particular amortization period for its own regulatory purposes. The advantage to the acquiring thrift institution was dependent upon the fact that 'accretion of the discount' is the 'mirror image' of amortization of goodwill. In a normal case the failed thrift's primary assets were long-term mortgages that earned below-market rates of interest and had decreased in value to the point that the thrift's assets failed to exceed its deposit liabilities. The disparities between assets and liabilities from which the accounting goodwill was derived was nearly equal to the value of the discount from face value of the thrift institution's outstanding loan assets.[56] However, the thrift regulators normally agreed to supervisory acquisition terms that permitted acquiring thrifts to 'accrete the discount' over the average life of the loan assets, normally seven years.[57] Given that goodwill and discount were nearly equal in overall value, the more rapid accrual of capital gain from 'accretion of the discount' resulted in net profits

---

51 See Accounting Principles Board Opinion No. 17, P29, at 340 (1970).
52 See APB Opinion No. 17, P27, at pp.339–340.
53 See *Winstar Corp., supra* note 48, n7.
54 See William K. Black, 'Ending Our Forbearers' Forbearances: FIRREA and Supervisory Goodwill', 2 Stan. L. & Policy Rev. 102 (1990), at pp.104–105.
55 See *Winstar Corp., supra* note 48, n7.
56 See Black, *supra* note 4, at pp.104–105.
57 *Ibid.* at p.105.

(on paper) over the initial years following the supervisory acquisition transaction.[58]

Of course, the downside to an accelerating accretion schedule was that it exhausted the discount long before the goodwill asset had been fully amortized. Therefore, this treatment resulted in a net impediment on earnings over the medium term and long term.[59] Many thrift managers sought to take the short-term gains at all costs, while others sought to postpone recognition of the inevitable losses by pursuing further acquisitions.[60] The difference between amortization and accretion schedules therefore permitted acquiring thrift institutions to appear more profitable than they actually were.[61] After the merger, the goodwill would be amortized as an expense over a set period. The discount would be 'accreted' to income over the life of the loan, usually approximating ten years. Under RAP accounting, prior to June 1982, goodwill was amortized over the same ten-year period, but the accounting period changed dramatically. Under GAAP, the goodwill could be amortized over as many as 40 years. The expenses for the amortization of goodwill would be far lower than the income from the accretion of the discount for many years. This allowed thrift institutions to literally 'manufacture' earnings and capital by acquiring other thrift institutions.[62] Between June 1982 and December 1983, goodwill increased from nearly USD8 billion to USD22 billion, which represented approximately 67 per cent of total RAP capital.[63] The FHLBB actively encouraged use of this accounting treatment as a low-cost method of resolving troubled thrift institutions, but the liberal treatment of supervisory goodwill ultimately restricted the FHLBB from initiating enforcement actions on distressed or insolvent thrift institutions because the actions could only be based on RAP capital levels, not tangible capital.

1. *Capital Credits*

In addition, supervisory acquisition transactions frequently included separate inducements called 'capital credits'. The capital credit arose when the FSLIC injected cash to further a supervisory acquisition transaction and permitted the acquiring institution to include the FSLIC injection as a permanent credit to regulatory capital. By failing to require the thrift to exclude the FSLIC injection from the amount of supervisory goodwill generated by the transaction, the FHLBB effectively permitted 'double counting' of the cash as both a tangible and an intangible asset.[64] Capital credits thus inflated the acquiring thrift's regulatory capital and permitted leveraging of more loan assets.

---

58 *Ibid.* at p.105.
59 *Ibid.* at pp.104–105.
60 *Ibid.* at p.105.
61 See *Winstar Corp., supra* note 48.
62 See 'Capital Requirements for Thrifts As They Apply to Supervisory Goodwill', Hearing Before the House Committee on Banking, Finance and Urban Affairs, Subcommittee on General Oversight and Investigations, 102d Cong., 1st Sess., at 31 (1991).
63 See *History of the Eighties, Volume 1, supra* note 3, at p.174.
64 See, e.g., *Transohio Savings Bank v. Director*, OTS, 967 F.2d 598, 604 (D.C. 1992).

2. *FHLBB-Industry Agreements*

The accounting treatment afforded in supervisory goodwill acquisition transactions was the subject matter of express arrangements between regulators and the acquiring thrift institutions. The extent to which these arrangements deviated from prior norms is unclear, however, as acquiring institutions would reasonably have desired to bargain for the special accounting treatment. Although GAAP permitted the use of the purchase method in acquiring distressed thrift institutions, the relevant FHLBB regulations did not expressly provide that intangible goodwill assets created using the purchase method could be included as regulatory capital.[65] The rationale for recognizing goodwill is reversed in the supervisory acquisition transaction. Under normal conditions, goodwill is recognized as an asset with value because a rational purchaser would not pay more than the assets are worth. Under the supervisory acquisition transaction, however, the purchase is rational only because of the accounting treatment resulting in the shortfall.[66]

The reasoning behind supervisory goodwill clearly undermines or circumvents the entire purpose of having capital reserve requirements – to protect depositors and the deposit insurance fund.

Given the fundamental irrationality in this process, it was clearly prudent for the acquiring institution management to obtain agreements from regulators that they would continue to accept purchase accounting in determining compliance with regulatory criteria in the years following supervisory acquisition transactions. The advantageous treatment of amortization schedules and capital credits in supervisory acquisitions transactions were clear deviations from GAAP, and thus represented prime subjects for agreement with regulators.

The FHLBB exacerbated the thrift industry crisis by promising lenient regulatory treatment, through forbearance practices involving supervisory goodwill, to encourage healthy thrift institutions to acquire financially distressed institutions. The supervisory goodwill essentially created phantom assets that were included as capital for regulatory purposes. In subsequent legislation in 1989, reviewed *infra* in Chapter Four of this work, the policy of supervisory goodwill was reversed and strict capital requirements were imposed, which effectively terminated the FHLBB and FSLIC forbearance agreements with acquiring institutions, making several dozen institutions instantly insolvent.

The thrift institutions with such forbearance agreements filed lawsuits to challenge these terminations, arguing primarily that breach of a forbearance agreement is a government 'taking' under the US Constitution because the federal government was not motivated by a desire to avoid contractual

---

65 See 12 C.F.R. § 563.13(a)(3) (1981) (permitting thrift institutions to include as capital reserves any 'items listed in the definition of "net worth"'); 12 C.F.R. § 561.13 (1981) (defining 'net worth' as 'the sum of all reserve accounts ..., retained earnings, permanent stock, mutual capital certificates . . . , and any other non-withdrawable accounts of an insured institution.').

66 See Black, *supra* note 4, at p.104.

duties, and that the agreements were binding contracts upon which the institutions relied to conduct transactions with the government. The institutions argued that the FHLBB could not simply remove its regulations under Congressional authority when the promise that such regulations would remain in place was the substantive representations behind the transactions. The litigation was spearheaded by Glendale Federal Savings and Loan Association of Glendale, California, which counted as capital more than USD1 billion of goodwill acquired when the FHLBB persuaded its directors to purchase certain institutions.[67]

C. Effects of Accounting Deviations

The ability to extend the amortization period of goodwill effectively increased both the profitability of acquiring institutions on paper and the overall capital of the thrift industry by eliminating the capital deficiencies of insolvent or troubled thrift institutions. In 1982, approximately USD15 billion in goodwill was generated by supervisory acquisition transactions, which enabled thrift institutions to maintain in excess of USD500 billion in deposits and to make the same volume of loans therefrom without any tangible capital investments. Goodwill as a percentage of industry-specific GAAP capital increased from 6 per cent to approximately 82 per cent.[68]

D. SFAS No. 72 Interpretations

The FASB issued SFAS No. 72 in 1983, which applied to the acquisitions of S&L institutions.[69] SFAS No. 72 provided that

---

[67] The cases made their way gradually through the federal courts, and in 1996 the US Supreme Court ruled in favor of the institutions. *US v. Winstar*, 116 S. Ct. 2432 (1996), where the Supreme Court held the US Government responsible for the damages it had caused by breach of its contract with certain acquirers of troubled thrifts under the inducement of offering 'supervisory goodwill' and deferred loan losses in support of capital requirements. The *Winstar* decision opened the door for many other institutions with similar claims to file lawsuits against the government to receive compensation for the losses they incurred as a result of the breach of promises implemented by Congress in the 1989 legislation. See also, Winstar, *The Leverage or the Last Straw in Deciding the Savings Industry's Future*, Fall, (1996) Private Paper on file with the author, and R. Schmitt, 'Judge Orders US to Pay $908.9 Million to California Thrift Glendale Federal', WSJ, 12 April 1999, at A-4. The Glendale case is a part of the *Winstar* case and is one of the 126 similar suits which, if decided for the claimants, could add another approximately USD30 billion to the costs of the US thrift crisis.

[68] See William K. Black, 'Ending Our Forbearers' Forbearance: FIRREA and Supervisory Goodwill', Stanford L. & Pol'y Rev. 102 (1990), at p.106.

[69] Although the accounting treatment of goodwill was purportedly based on GAAP, the SEC refused to allow thrift holding companies reporting to the SEC to amortize goodwill over a period longer than 25 years, and shorter amortization periods were required when the transaction involved a troubled thrift. This position was adopted in SEC Staff Accounting Bulletin No. 42 issued in 1981. The FASB ultimately adopted the general concepts of SAB 42 as an industry-specific GAAP in SFAS No. 72. See Statement of Concepts No. 72, 'Accounting for Certain Acquisitions of Banking or Thrift Institutions' (Feb. 1983) ('SFAS No. 72).

'if, and to the extent that, the fair value of liabilities assumed exceeds the fair value of identifiable assets acquired in the acquisition of a banking or thrift institution, the unidentifiable intangible asset recognized generally shall be amortized to expense by the interest method over a period of longer than the discount on the long-term interest-bearing assets acquired is to be recognized as interest income.'[70]

SFAS No. 72 thus required that goodwill, to the extent that it results from the assumption of excess liabilities, be amortized on an interest method over the life of the assets acquired, and further required that regulatory assistance be netted out against goodwill. Thus, SFAS No. 72 eliminated any question that the differential amortization period on which acquiring thrifts relied to manufacture profits on paper in supervisory acquisition transactions were inconsistent with GAAP. SFAS No. 72 additionally precluded 'double counting' of capital credits by requiring that financial assistance from regulatory authorities had to be deducted from the cost of the acquisition before the amount of goodwill was determined.[71] The thrift acquiring institutions relying on capital credits thus had 'every reason for concern as to the continued availability of the RAP in effect at the time of the supervisory M&A transactions'.[72]

As the FSLIC lacked the funds to liquidate all troubled and insolvent S&Ls, the FHLBB decided to avoid the deposit insurance liabilities by encouraging solvent thrifts and outside investors to merge with or acquire failing thrifts in supervisory mergers and acquisitions.[73] The FSLIC assisted FHLBB by developing lists of prospective acquirers, making presentations, holding seminars, and attempting to promote generally the acquisitions of failing S&Ls. The supervisory acquisition transactions, in which the acquiring parties assumed the obligations of thrifts with liabilities that exceeded their assets, were not intrinsically viable to solvent thrifts. In addition, the FSLIC lacked the necessary cash to promote acquisitions through direct federal subsidies, although cash injections were often a part of supervisory acquisitions. The principal reason for the success of the supervisory acquisition program was that the acquisition would be subject to an accounting treatment that would assist the acquiring institutions to meet their capital reserve requirements imposed by federal regulations which were imposed by the FHLBB itself. In 1980–1986, nearly 300 supervisory acquisitions were completed, as opposed to only 48 liquidations.[74] There is substantial disagreement as to whether the policy of supervisory acquisitions actually incurred less cost to the government than outright liquidation of these failed thrifts.[75]

---

70 See Accounting Standards, Original Pronouncements (July 1973–1 June 1989), at p.725.

71 See SFAS No. 72, P9, at 10.

72 See *Winstar Corp., supra* note 48.

73 See GAO, 'Solutions to the Thrift Industry Problem', (GAO/GCD-89–47, 1989).

74 See GAO, 'Thrift Industry Forbearance For Troubled Institutions', 1982–1986 (GAO/GCD-87–78 BR, May 1987), at p.13.

75 See *Winstar Corp., supra* note 48.

VI. ACQUISITION, DEVELOPMENT AND CONSTRUCTION (AD&C) LOANS

In the early 1980s, thrift institutions engaged in transactions involving real estate development that stretched the permissible limits of lending activities. These transactions, called 'acquisition, development and construction loans' ('AD&C loans') were generally structured to give the lending institution a share of the risks and proceeds of investor participation instead of a normal loan return of market interest rates and eventual return of principal. These transactions, characterized as 'loans', should have actually been recorded as joint venture transactions under GAAP in order to reflect the economic substance of the transactions.

The thrift institutions had every incentive to record these transactions as loans instead of joint venture transactions in order to increase reported income by recognizing accrued interest income from the loan component of the transaction. Although institutions might be able to capitalize the interest payments under a joint venture transaction to increase the carrying cost of the asset, the benefits to the institution of this accounting treatment would be less than including the payments as interest income.[76] The AD&C loan debate evolved into a significant dilemma, as many thrift institutions subsequently incurred huge losses from risky investments inappropriately characterized as loans.[77] The temptation to report joint venture investments as loans, and obtain immediate recognition of fee income and accelerated recognition of interest payments, resulted in many accounting distortions of which the FHLBB was well aware but summarily failed to prevent in most cases, and even encouraged in many cases.

The AICPA issued a series of accounting guidelines beginning in 1983 to assist institutions and auditors in reviewing AD&C loan transactions.[78] In October 1984, the FHLBB issued a proposed statement of policy regarding the regulatory treatment of accounting for certain real estate activities, including AD&C loans.[79] This policy was not adopted until April 1985, and did not apply retroactively.[80] Nonetheless, the statement of policy emphasized that the characterization of AD&C transactions was 'best left to the insured institution and its independent public accountant'.[81] Although the

---

[76] See Breeden, *supra* note 20, at S83.

[77] See, e.g., 'Federal Home Loan Bank Board's Supervision and Failure of Empire Savings and Loan Association of Mesquite, Texas', before the House Committee on Government Operations, H.R. Rep. No. 953, 98th Cong., 2d Sess. at 32 (1984) (addressing AD&C loans of Empire Savings & Loan Association).

[78] See, e.g., Notice to Practitioners, 'Certain Real Estate Lending Activities of Financial Institutions' (November 1983) (AICPA guidance); Notice to Practitioners, 'ADC Loans' (November 1984) (AICPA guidance on AD&C Loans). The AICPA issued new guidance on these transactions in 1986 that was consistent with SEC accounting doctrine. See Notice to Practitioners, 'ADC Arrangements' (November 1986).

[79] See 49 Fed. Reg. 43,557 (1984).

[80] See FHLBB, 'Statement of Policy, Accounting for Acquisition, Development and Construction Loans', 50 Fed. Reg. 18,233 (1985).

[81] See 50 Fed. Reg. at 18,235.

statement of policy did bring the FHLBB regulations into line with AICPA guidelines, it was too little too late for enforcement purposes.

VII. FHLBB DEREGULATORY PERMISSIVENESS: 1980–1983

The Reagan Administration was more directly involved with the regulation of the thrift industry than of the banking industry in that the FHLBB and by implication FSLIC did not enjoy the relative political independence of the FRB or FDIC. During the early years of the Administration, members crafted policies of deregulation and forbearance and generally opposed any government cash distributions or the systemic closure of failed institutions to resolve the growing thrift industry problem. The Administration facilitated the capital adequacy and accounting interpretations previously reviewed and contributed directly to the lack of discipline that characterized thrift financial services activities and taxpayer bailout in the late 1980s and early 1990s. Notwithstanding the capital and accounting regulations and deviations previously reviewed, the FHLBB proposed and adopted various other 'deregulatory' provisions in the spirit of deregulation that greatly liberalized the powers of S&Ls over January 1980 – May 1983.

These regulations were promulgated by the FHLBB under the DIDMCA and Garn-St. Germain Act or otherwise on its own volition. Notably, the Garn-St. Germain Act actually codified various regulatory changes that Chairman Pratt had already initiated through the FHLBB. Many of these provisions liberalized real estate lending and were simply not well planned as to their long-term economic impact on the thrift industry or alternatively, if they were planned out at the time of passage or promulgation, the analysis on which they were based was flawed. By 1982, the FHLBB implemented rule changes to presumably facilitate S&L growth, and the S&L industry's assets did grow initially by 17 per cent.

A. May–December 1980

During the time period of May – December 1980, the FHLBB adopted at least 11 regulations which liberalized activities for S&Ls (both federal S&Ls and State S&Ls), including at least 30 elements that reinforced the inflation of the asset values. The most significant regulations and elements thereof are set forth as follows. First, in August 1980, the FHLBB authorized federal S&Ls to invest up to 3 per cent of their assets in service corporations.[82] Second, in October 1980, the FHLBB adopted regulations authorizing federal S&Ls to issue negotiable order of withdrawal (NOW) deposit accounts.[83] Third, in November 1980, the FHLBB also reduced the minimum period of maturity on time accounts from 30 to 14 days to increase funds available for home

---

[82] See FHLBB, 'Service Corporation Investment Authority', 45 Fed. Reg. 56029 (1980).
[83] See FHLBB, 'Negotiable Order of Withdrawal Accounts', 45 Fed. Reg. 66781 (1980).

financing,[84] and significantly expanded the real estate investment powers for thrift institutions in November 1980.[85]

This regulation

1. eliminated first lien mortgage requirements for residential loans, and allowed investments in real estate loans secured by junior mortgages;
2. eliminated previous statutory dollar restrictions on home loans and dollar limitations on multi-family dwelling mortgages;
3. eliminated geographic limitations on real estate loans, thereby eliminating restrictions on the ability of S&Ls to invest in loans outside their local areas if otherwise permitted to do so by its applicable regulatory agency;
4. extended the maximum term of residential mortgages to 40 years;
5. established a 90 per cent loan-to-value (LTV) ratio for multi-family dwelling mortgages;
6. increased from 60 per cent to 75 per cent the maximum LTV ratio on unamortized multi-family mortgages loans and increased the maximum term from three to five years;
7. extended from five to 15 years the maximum term for residential building lot and site loans and decreased the amortization requirement from 40 per cent to 30 per cent; and
8. permitted commercial real estate loans at 90 per cent LTV ratio and a 30-year maximum term with a 75 per cent loan-to-value ratio for unamortized loans.[86]

In November 1980, the FHLBB replaced the capital requirement of 5 per cent of insurable accounts plus 5 per cent of secured borrowings with a requirement of 4 per cent of total liabilities; reduced net worth requirements for institutions holding certain 'qualifying balances'; provided an exemption from capital requirements and reserve requirements for institutions that incurred losses due to sale of mortgages with interest rates of 7 per cent or less (this is the so-called 'deferred loss regulation'); and reduced statutory reserve requirements from 5 per cent to 4 per cent.[87] Finally, in December 1980, the FHLBB adopted regulations regarding the acquisition, exercise, and termination of trust powers by federal S&Ls.[88]

B. Calendar Year 1981

During calendar year 1981, the FHLBB adopted eight significant regulations that further expanded the powers of federal thrift institutions. The most significant regulations and elements thereof include the following. First, in March 1981, the FHLBB implemented DIDMCA provisions to authorize

---

84 See FHLBB, 'Maturity of Time Deposits', 45 Fed. Reg. 76103 (1980).

85 See FHLBB, 'Revision of Real Estate Lending Provisions', 45 Fed. Reg. 76095 (1980).

86 *Ibid.*

87 See FHLBB, 'Net Worth Amendments', 45 Fed. Reg. 76111 (1980).

88 See FHLBB, 'Trust Powers', 45 Fed. Reg. 82162 (1980).

federal S&Ls, without limitation, to invest in mutual funds holding assets that were otherwise permissible for federal S&L investment.[89] Second, in April 1981, the FHLBB authorized adjustable mortgage loan instruments and thereby replaced and subsumed all existing regulations with respect to renegotiable rate mortgage loans and variable rate mortgage loans.[90] In May 1981,the FHLBB also significantly expanded the list of activities in which federal thrift institutions could engage through service corporations without prior FHLBB approval.[91]

Third, in September 1981, the FHLBB amended regulations governing accounting requirements for all thrift institutions. These amendments permitted institutions to defer and amortize gains and losses in the disposition of mortgage loans, mortgage-related securities and debt securities to assist S&Ls caught in a negative spread (earnings squeeze) due to low yields derived from long-term, fixed-rate loans; and expanded net worth and statutory reserve exemptions to include losses due to the sale or other disposition of all mortgages, mortgage-related securities and debt securities.[92] Fourth, in December 1981, the FHLBB again reduced regulatory capital requirements from 4 per cent to 3 per cent, respectively. As of this date, the 20-year 'phase in' technique for de novo charters and the five-year averaging technique for existing associations (both previously discussed in this chapter) were still in effect, thereby effectively reducing capital requirements further.

C. Calendar Year 1982

During calendar year 1982, the FHLBB adopted 10 significant regulations which even further expanded the powers of federal thrift institutions. The most significant regulations and elements thereof include the following. First, in February 1982, the FHLBB:

1. removed limitations on aggregate borrowings by thrift institutions and gave full discretion to S&Ls to manage all liabilities according to their particular needs (the prior regulation limited aggregate amount of borrowings to 50 per cent of an institution's assets);
2. eliminated limitations on collateralization of non-federal home loan bank borrowings (the prior regulation limited the aggregate book value of all collateral securing outside borrowings to 25 per cent of assets);
3. eliminated requirements that S&Ls could not issue any long-term debt if, after giving effect to the issuance of the debt, the institution did not meet net worth requirements; and
4. eliminated limitations on distribution of maturities of all types of liabilities and requirements for prior notification to the principal

---

89 See FHLBB, 'Mutual Fund Investments', 46 Fed. Reg. 18686 (1981).
90 See FHLBB, 'Adjustable Mortgage Loan Instruments', 46 Fed. Reg. 24148 (1981).
91 See FHLBB, 'Service Corporation Activities', 46 Fed. Reg. 24526 (1981).
92 See Black, *supra* note 4.

supervisory agent when liabilities maturing in a three-month period would exceed 30 per cent of S&L assets, thereby leaving overall liability management to each association.[93]

Second, in September 1982, the FHLBB:

1. permitted all subordinated debt securities, mutual capital certificates and nonpermanent preferred stock to be included in order to fulfill existing capital requirements;
2. increased the ability of S&Ls to issue subordinated debt securities by revising eligibility and structural requirements; and
3. expanded the authority of the FHLBB to waive the form, term and offering requirements for subordinated debt securities.[94]

D. Calendar Year 1983

The ongoing deregulatory permissiveness and regulatory forbearance, however, ensured the situation would nonetheless result in terminal crisis. Chairman Pratt left FHLBB in March 1983, warning Congress in testimony that under the then-existing statutory and regulatory system in place the government would certainly share in any losses, while gains would accrue entirely to those who have interests in depository institutions. The rational course of action in these circumstances would be for the S&L industry to collectively engage in activities that may be excessively risky. Chairman Pratt was succeeded by Edwin Gray in March 1983.

In May 1983, the FHLBB implemented the Garn-St. Germain Act by authorizing federally chartered S&Ls to:

1. delete the LTV ratios for loans made on the security of real estate, thereby permitting real estate loans to be made in the amount of 100 per cent of the appraised value of the real property offered as collateral;
2. permit loans to be made in excess of 100 per cent of the value of the property serving as collateral as long as the excess portion is made under another source of the S&Ls investment authority, such as the authority to make unsecured loans;
3. allow LTV ratios on home loans to rise to 125 per cent of appraised value following loan origination due to negative amortization;
4. allow receipt of interest in the form of a share of the appreciation of the property serving as collateral or a share of the income generated from the property;
5. permit loans secured by multi-family dwellings and nonresidential real estate in amounts up to 100 per cent of appraised value for terms not to exceed 30 years, except that interest-only loans had to be repaid within five years;

---

[93] *Ibid.*
[94] *Ibid.*

6. eliminate the requirement that loans on the security of non-residential real estate must be first liens;
7. permit S&Ls to issue commercial and standby letters of credit;
8. invest in secured or unsecured loans for commercial, corporate business or agricultural purposes, with no special record keeping requirement;
9. clarify that lending limits were applicable only to funds actually advanced so that, among other things, loan commitments were not included in outstanding loan amounts and wraparound mortgages were counted only to the extent credit had actually been extended to the borrower; and
10. increase to USD500,000 the absolute minimum lending limit to permit more troubled institutions to make sizable loans that would help restore them to profitability as authorized under the Garn-St. Germain Act.[95]

VIII. CONCLUSIONS AND SUMMARY OBSERVATIONS

The FHLBB deregulatory measures largely represented the agency's implementation of powers deemed authorized under DIDMCA and the Garn-St. Germain Act, respectively. During the period of 1980–1983, nearly 120 thrift institutions with assets in excess of USD43 billion failed, and cost the FSLIC nearly USD3.5 billion to resolve, and from 1980–1982 there were also 493 voluntary mergers and 259 supervisory mergers of S&Ls, respectively.[96] As previously noted in Chapter Two, during the 1981–1982 period alone, nearly 750 thrift institutions, or approximately 17 per cent of the 4,600 FSLIC-insured institutions, were merged or liquidated.[97] Nonetheless, at year-end 1982 there were 415 thrift institutions with total assets in excess of USD220 billion that were insolvent based on the book value of their tangible net worth (defined as net worth excluding goodwill and other intangible assets).[98]

In December 1983, the General Accounting Office (GAO) reported that the thrift industry would face enormous dangers if short-term interest rates remained above 11.5 per cent, and as of November 1983, the federal funds rate alone was between 9 and 9.5 per cent.[99] By 1984, approximately 687 thrift institutions with USD360 billion in assets, constituting 22 per cent of the number of thrift institutions and 37 per cent of total industry assets, were insolvent on the basis of tangible net worth.[100]

---

95 *Ibid.*
96 See *History of the Eighties, Volume 1, supra* note 3, at p.168.
97 See Robert Trigaux, 'Congressional Study Calls Thrift Insurance Fund Fragile: Future Health Remains Closely Tied to Continued Low Level of Interest Rates, GAO Says', Am. Banker, 7 December 1983, at p.3.
98 See *History of the Eighties, Volume 1, supra* note 3, at p.169.
99 See 69 Federal Reserve Bulletin, December 1983, at A26.
100 See Lawrence J. White, *The S&L Debacle: Public Policy Lessons for Bank and Thrift Regulation* (Oxford University Press, 1991), at p.114.

Beginning in 1984 and continuing throughout Chairman Gray's tenure, however, regulatory and supervisory measures adopted by the FHLBB began the abrupt reversal of deregulation. Less than six months later, however, Chairman Gray understood that this presumption was incorrect, and that S&L management were all too eager to speculate in activities that were opened for them by FHLBB and the Garn-St. Germain Act. Chairman Gray attempted to control the situation, but received no help from the Reagan Administration nor the Treasury Department, which were largely committed to the deregulation doctrine and attempting to influence Fed monetary policy.

The Fed's anti-inflationary monetary policies discussed later in Part Two, generally succeeded in lowering market interest rates, which indeed elevated many distressed thrift institutions from the interest rate mismatch dilemma and returned them to notional solvency.

5. Banking Agency Deregulation and Forbearance

I. INTRODUCTION

The federal banking agencies actively responded to problematic trends and economic conditions through changes in monetary policy, and regulatory and supervisory intervention and forbearance practices. The OCC, FRB and FDIC were very active in expanding the regulatory and supervisory frameworks, particularly in response to the LDC debt crisis, and the Fed engaged in rigorous anti-inflationary monetary policy which shook the US and global banking systems to the core. The regulatory intervention and more importantly forbearance practices of the federal banking agencies resulted in significant capital impairment for the majority of the banking system involved in the LDC debt crisis, and for several particular banking organizations whose capital impairment threatened the safety and soundness of the banking system. The following factors and events, although not as blatant as the FHLBB deregulatory initiatives previously reviewed in this chapter, certainly contributed to the pervasive systemic capital impairment which existed throughout the 1980s.

This chapter reflects upon these and other issues respecting this banking agency deregulation and forbearance.

II. BANK ENTRY AND THE CHARTERING PROCESS

The reckless chartering of national banks by the OCC introduced many aggressive and inexperienced banking institutions to the US banking system which contributed to the instability and pervasive capital impairment in the 1980s.[1] The OCC is the only federal chartering agent for national banks. All other commercial banks, regardless of whether or not they become members of the Federal Reserve System, are chartered by individual State banking

---

[1] See FDIC, 'An Examination of the Banking Crises of the 1980s and early 1990s', *History of the Eighties, Volume 1: Lessons for the Future* (Washington D.C., 1998), at p.106.

agencies.[2] The chartering process is designed to assess a proposed bank's potential for successful operation. The process generally involves an examination of the proposed bank's capital contributions and reserves; the character and experience of its proposed management; the proposed bank's ability to achieve a certain level of profitability; and the proposed bank's role in the community.[3]

The chartering process became a relevant vehicle of regulatory competition in the 1980s between the OCC and State banking agencies in general, and between State banking agencies in particular. The OCC responded to pressure from Congress in 1980 and reversed its chartering policy to focus more on the institution itself and less on the ability of the community to support it.[4] The OCC asserted that enhanced market competition would better promote a safe and sound banking system that in turn would better serve consumers, and abruptly reversed policy to facilitate competition through the chartering process.[5]

Predictably, the number of national bank charters approved by OCC increased significantly under this policy reversal.[6] The new chartering policy resulted in a significant amount of national bank charters being granted in Texas and California in the early 1980s.[7] The Comptroller at the time, Robert C. Clarke, was a Texas constituent with a background in Texan politics. Many of the newly chartered Texas banks soon failed or otherwise became distressed institutions in need of resolution by the FDIC by the mid-1980s and contributed directly to the Texas banking and real estate crises which manifested by early 1985.[8] The OCC eventually tightened its 'shortsighted' chartering policy in response to the failing institutions, and national bank chartering declined by 1985 as economic conditions deteriorated and bank failures multiplied.[9]

The chartering processes used by State banking agencies for State non-member banks resembled those used by the OCC in most instances.[10] The State processes differed from the OCC in that chartering policies continued to focus on criteria concerning the effect of the proposed bank on the community and opportunities for public scrutiny of applications that had been

---

2 *Ibid.* at p.106.

3 *Ibid.* at p.106.

4 See, e.g., 'Majority Staff Study on Chartering of National Banks: 1970–1977', Senate Committee on Banking, Housing, and Urban Affairs, 96th Cong., 2d Sess. (1980) (congressional criticism of previous OCC chartering policies).

5 See, e.g. 12 C.F.R. § 5.20(c) (1980) (fostering competition through chartering of national banks).

6 See Eugene N. White, The *Comptroller and the Transformation of American Banking, 1960–1990* (1992), at pp.53–54. The OCC chartering policy generally absolved the need for public notice, comment, and hearing concerning applications for national bank charters. See 12 C.F.R. § 5.3 (1980).

7 See, e.g. Phillip L. Zweig, '37 Bank Openings in Texas This Month to Set Record', Am. Banker, 4 January 1983, at p.1; Jay Rothstein, 'Comptroller May Tighten Chartering Process', Am. Banker, 12 October 1983, at p.3.

8 See *History of the Eighties, Volume 1*, *supra* note 1, at p.107.

9 *Ibid.* at p.107.

10 National banks and State member banks received deposit insurance upon FDIC receipt of certification by the OCC or the FRB. *Ibid.* at p.109.

largely abandoned by the OCC in 1980.[11] The chartering processes were generally perceived as subjective in nature, however, which provided State chartering authorities with significant amounts of political and regulatory discretion in deciding whether to grant bank charters.[12]

The data collected during the period in question underscores that the change in chartering policy by OCC had a significant effect on national bank chartering, but national bank charters did not necessarily supplant State charters in this respect.[13] The FDIC's assessment of deposit insurance applications for State non-member banks addressed the same issues that were addressed in charter applications.[14] The FDIC adopted various policy positions regarding the levels of initial net capital required of applicant institutions,[15] and clarified policy for authorizing deposit insurance to institutions in 1987.[16] The FDIC capital requirements for all practical purposes pre-empted State laws and regulations regarding initial net capitalization that were less rigorous in this respect because of its inherent ability to deny deposit insurance to applicant State banks.[17]

III. PENN SQUARE BANK FAILURE AND BROKERED DEPOSITS AS SOURCES OF FUNDING

The Penn Square Bank failure in 1982 focused attention on many regulatory issues, notably the increasing use of brokered deposits by banking organizations and thrift institutions as sources of funding. In the Penn Square Bank failure, the amount of brokered deposits issued by the bank to raise funds had increased from less than USD20 million to $282 million just prior to the bank failing.[18] In 1983 the FDIC expressed concern that deposit brokers were

---

11 See, e.g. TEX.REV.STAT.ANN Banks and Banking §§ 342 et seq. (1991); CAL. Financial Code § 361 (1992); FLA.STAT.ANN. §§ 658.20–21 (1991).

12 See *History of the Eighties, Volume 1, supra* note 1, at p.109.

13 *Ibid.* at p.109.

14 The FDIC is not directly involved in the State chartering processes, but its role as provider of deposit insurance had a significant impact on these processes. The newly proposed State banks were generally not issued charters by State banking agencies unless they could obtain federal deposit insurance. State banking agencies were unlikely to grant bank charters without the FDIC approving the bank's application for federal deposit insurance, to the extent that deposit insurance was not already expressly required under State laws. *Ibid.* at pp.109–110.

15 The FDIC adopted a policy in 1980 requiring that the initial capitalization of banks applying for federal deposit insurance should be sufficient to provide a ratio of unimpaired capital to total estimated assets of 10 per cent after three years, and applicants with less than USD750,000 in initial capital were discouraged. The minimum initial net capital requirement was soon raised to USD1 million, and in 1992 to USD2 million. The initial net capital requirement was revised in 1992 to be sufficient to provide a ratio of Tier 1 capital to total estimated assets of at least 8 per cent after 3 years. See 57 Fed. Reg. 12,882 (13 April 1992).

16 See 52 Fed. Reg. 21,736 (9 June 1987).

17 See *History of the Eighties, Volume 1, supra* note 1, at p.110.

18 See, e.g. Phillip L. Zweig, 'Brokered Penn Square Funds Soared Just Before Collapse', Am. Banker, 19 November 1982, at p.3.

dividing investor funds into packages of USD100,000 and investing in the CDs of banking organizations and thrift institutions that were not deemed to be financially sound in order to earn higher commissions.[19]

In March 1984, the FDIC and FHLBB adopted a regulation that limited receipt of deposit insurance for brokered deposits placed through third party deposit brokers up to USD100,000 per deposit broker per bank.[20]

The OCC opposed the proposed regulation and, together with the Treasury Department, argued for a more supervisory approach that would permit a banking organization or thrift institution to accept up to twice its capital in brokered deposits if those deposits did not exceed 15 per cent of total deposits, but that no institution with a capital ratio under 3 per cent would be permitted to accept brokered deposits.[21] The FRB and Congress generally supported the FDIC and FHLBB, but shared similar concerns with the OCC that the regulation was overbearing and would limit legitimate practices regarding brokered deposits.[22] The FDIC and FHLBB planned to make the regulation effective on October 1984, but the securities industry trade group and institutions involved in brokered deposits sued the FDIC and FHLBB for exceeding their regulatory authority.[23] The federal district court hearing the case ruled in June 1984 that the FDIC and FHLBB had exceeded their authority, in that the federal statutes creating deposit insurance focused on ownership of deposited funds rather than on the manner in which deposits were arranged.[24]

The FDIC appealed the decision and imposed a temporary regulation that required banking organizations and thrift institutions that relied significantly on brokered deposits to file monthly reports regarding their holdings of brokered deposits.[25] Congress, the banking agencies, and the banking and thrift industries continued to debate the matter extensively.

In September 1984, a House of Representatives Subcommittee released a report on brokered deposits asserting that brokered deposits were an insignificant source of deposit growth for most rapidly growing institutions. The House Report suggested that the forceful use of existing supervisory powers on a case-by-case basis for excessive brokered deposit portfolios was the most effective regulatory policy; and that elimination of deposit insurance coverage for brokered deposit accounts would not achieve enhanced market

---

19 See, e.g. Caroline T. Harless, 'Brokered Deposits: Issues and Alternatives', *Federal Reserve Bank of Atlanta Economic Review* 69, No. 3 (1984), at pp.14–25.

20 Thus, the regulation would not have affected deposits placed by investors directly. The extent of deposit insurance under the regulation would have depended on the method of depositing the funds into the bank or thrift institution account rather than on the identity of the beneficial owner of that account. See 49 Fed. Reg. 13003 (1984) (to be codified at 12 C.F.R. § 330.13).

21 See *FDIC* Volume 1, *supra* note 1, at p.120; Lisa J. McCue, 'Agencies Propose Broker Limits', Am. Banker, 17 January 1984, at p.1.

22 See, e.g. US House Committee on Government Operations, 'Proposed Restrictions on Money Brokers: Hearing', 98th Cong., 2d Sess. (1984).

23 See *History of the Eighties, Volume 1, supra* note 1, at p.120; Andrew Albert, 'Securities Industry Sues to Void Broker Rules', Am. Banker, 13 April 1984, at p.1.

24 See *FAIC Securities, Inc. v. United States*, 595 F.Supp. 73 (D.D.C. 1984).

25 See *History of the Eighties, Volume 1, supra* note 1, at p.121.

discipline.[26] The FDIC disagreed with the conclusion of the House Report in that data concerning FDIC-insured banks revealed that more than 40 per cent of brokered deposits were held by institutions with less than adequate CAMEL ratings.[27] In addition, the Federal Reserve Bank of New York released a research paper which generally supported the contentions of the FDIC, but did not completely endorse the FDIC/FHLBB proposal.[28]

In January 1985, the Federal Appellate Court upheld the District Court's decision precluding the FDIC from ending deposit insurance on brokered deposits.[29] The FDIC continued to push the matter and debate continued in Congress, until the Court of Appeals refused rehearing in the case and the newly-incoming FDIC Chairman decided that a more conservative view of brokered deposits was appropriate.[30] The FDIC decided not to appeal the case and in December 1985 and June 1986 removed the temporary regulations on brokered deposits regarding deposit insurance and monthly reporting, respectively.[31] The use of brokered deposits nonetheless returned to the limelight in the fallout of the thrift crisis and portions of the regulations proposed by the federal banking agencies were incorporated in legislation enacted in 1989 and 1991, respectively, discussed *infra* in Chapter Four.[32]

IV. THE EXPANSION OF BANK POWERS

The development of the US banking system in the 1970s and early 1980s was characterized by sustained efforts by banking special interest groups to accelerate the expansion of bank powers into areas other than lending and other traditional banking activities. The federal banking legislation of the early

---

26 See US House Committee on Government Operations, 'Federal Regulation of Brokered Deposits in Problem Banks and Savings Institutions: Report', 98th Cong., 2d Sess., 1984.

27 See *History of the Eighties, Volume 1, supra* note 1, at p.121.

28 See Sherrill Shaffer and Catherine Piche, 'Brokered Deposits and Bank Soundness: Evidence and Regulatory Implications', Federal Reserve Bank of New York research paper no. 8405 (1984).

29 The appellate court affirmed the district court without opinion. See 753 F.2d 166 (D.C. Cir. 1985).

30 See *History of the Eighties, Volume 1, supra* note 1, at p.122; 'Mark Basch, Seidman Takes a Conciliatory Stance on Brokered Deposits, But Plans Curbs', Am. Banker, 6 November 1985, at p.1.

31 See *History of the Eighties, Volume 1, supra* note 1, at p.122.

32 The federal banking agencies also issued regulations that addressed many other areas of banking practice during this period. The regulations address areas to include insider lending transactions; management interlocks; and innovations such as highly leveraged transactions (HLTs) and guidelines for leveraged buyout loan portfolios. The FFIEC, established by Congress in 1978 as an organization to include all banking agencies, was used as a means for federal banking agencies to develop uniform regulatory standards on various practices. Most importantly, the banking agencies under FFIEC established significant revisions to regulatory financial disclosures, otherwise known as *Call Reports*. The federal banking agencies also focused on eliminating and simplifying many regulatory requirements that were unduly burdensome for their constituent institutions, and on streamlining the application procedures for new activities.

1980s did not provide national banks and bank holding companies (BHCs) with many new powers per se, but actions by the respective federal banking agencies interpreting relevant provisions of the National Bank Act,[33] Glass-Steagall Act,[34] and Bank Holding Company Act[35] generally attempted to fill the gap created by legislative gridlock.[36] In addition, State legislatures and State banking agencies were particularly active in responding to legislative gridlock and provided their constituent institutions with new powers as a means to stimulate economic growth.[37] The federal banking agencies, in particular the OCC, began to liberalize bank powers in the early 1970s,[38] but this trend did not fully develop until the early 1980s through liberal and even aggressive interpretations of the aforementioned banking law provisions that were challenged by securities industry trade groups but largely enforced by federal court decisions favoring the regulatory interpretations.[39]

The primary motivation behind the regulatory efforts to expand national bank and bank holding company powers was generally premised on financial innovations, domestic and international competition between and among financial institutions, and competition between the regulatory agencies.[40] The

---

33 See, e.g., 12 U.S.C. § 92 (National Bank Act provision authorizing national banks to conduct limited insurance powers); 12 U.S.C. § 24 (Seventh) (National Bank Act provision authorizing national banks to conduct activities determined to be within the 'business of banking' and 'investment securities' activities by the OCC).

34 See 12 U.S.C. §§ 24 (Seventh) (codifying § 16 of the Glass-Steagall Act and imposing limitations on national bank and State federal reserve member bank securities underwriting and dealing activities); 377 (codifying § 20 of the Glass-Steagall Act and imposing limitations on national bank and State federal reserve member bank (and their corporate affiliates) from becoming 'engaged principally' in securities activities affiliates within a holding company structure); 378 (codifying § 21 of the Glass-Steagall Act and prohibiting securities firms from engaging in depository activities) ; 78 (codifying § 32 of the Glass-Steagall Act and prohibiting interlocking management between national banks and State federal reserve member banks and firms 'primarily engaged' in securities activities); 12 U.S.C. § 335 (extending §§ 16 and 21 of the Glass-Steagall Act to State federal reserve member banks).

35 12 U.S.C. § 1843(c)(8) (Bank Holding Company Act provision authorizing bank holding companies to engage in non-traditional activities 'so closely related to banking or managing or controlling banks as to be a proper incident thereto' subject to approval by the FRB; the Garn-St. Germain Act of 1982 also codified various insurance activities permissible for bank holding companies in this section).

36 See *History of the Eighties, Volume 1, supra* note 1, at p.122.

37 The Federal Reserve Act of 1913 and the establishment of the FDIC under the Banking Act of 1933 imposed considerable federal regulation on State-chartered banks. States traditionally exercised wide regulatory authority over their institutions, however, and State-chartered non-member banks were generally considered exempt from the Glass-Steagall Act provisions. In addition, many States authorized their banks to engage in interstate banking activities during the 1980s, although Congress did not enact legislation to authorize interstate banking until 1994. Thus, the decision to become a State-chartered or a federally-chartered banking institution often raised issues of regulatory arbitrage concerning permissible bank powers.

38 The OCC's first attempt to expand bank powers to permit national banks to organize a common investment fund was rejected by the US Supreme Court on grounds that the arrangement too closely resembled an open-ended mutual fund in violation of the Glass-Steagall Act. See *Investment Company Institute v. Camp*, 401 U.S. 617 (1971).

39 See, e.g. Joseph J. Norton, 'Up Against the "Wall": Glass-Steagall and the Dilemma of a Deregulated ("Reregulated") Banking Environment', 42 Bus. Law. 327 (1987).

40 See *History of the Eighties, Volume 1, supra* note 1, at p.123.

banking agencies generally endorsed the concept that banks and bank holding companies should have additional powers to maintain their innovative competitiveness with other financial institutions, but also generally believed that Congress was the appropriate mechanism for true bank powers reform.[41] Without action from Congress, the banking agencies generally came under enormous pressure from their constituent institutions to expand bank powers.[42]

The OCC differed somewhat from the FRB and FDIC in that it had direct ties to the political apparatus as a de facto subsidiary of the Treasury Department. The OCC generally incurred more 'political' and 'constituent' pressure than other banking agencies, due to its direct link to the Executive Branch as a de facto subsidiary of the Treasury Department, to expand bank powers. The OCC was therefore quite responsive and the most aggressive banking agency in terms of expanding bank powers largely beginning in the early 1980s,[43] and the FRB increasingly permitted BHCs to enter into new activities in the late 1980s in regulatory competition with the OCC.[44]

The FDIC generally lacked jurisdiction to authorize State-chartered FRS member banks to engage in new activities, but possessed authority to regulate State non-member banks in this respect and in 1984 ruled that insured State non-member banks could establish or acquire subsidiaries that were engaged in securities activities.[45] The FDIC ruling simply represented an acknowledgment that State banking agencies and/or legislatures had the authority to permit and could continue to permit State-chartered banks to engage in such activities, to include securities underwriting, insurance underwriting, and real estate development.[46]

The reasons motivating State legislatures and banking agencies to permit expansion into new activities were more concerned with promoting competition with federally-chartered institutions, and not necessarily with prudential safety and soundness of the banking system, however.[47] The FDIC

---

41 *Ibid.* at p.123.

42 *Ibid.* at p.123.

43 For instance, during the early 1980s, the OCC authorized national banks to offer discount brokerage and investment advisory services, operate futures-commission merchant subsidiaries, and underwrite credit life insurance. See, e.g. Joseph J. Norton and Christopher D. Olive, 'The Ongoing Process of International Bank Regulatory and Supervisory Convergence: A New Regulatory-Market "Partnership"', 16 Annual Rev. of Banking Law 227 (1997), at pp.268–271 (reviewing national bank activities).

44 The FRB authorized new activities through Regulation Y, which implemented section 1843(c)(8) of the Bank Holding Company Act. See 12 C.F.R. § 225.25 (1991); Norton and Olive, *supra* note 43, at pp.272–274 (reviewing bank holding company activities).

45 See FDIC, *Annual Report* (1984), at p.39.

46 By 1990, generally half of the State banking agencies or State legislatures had authorized State-chartered banks to engage in one or more of these activities. See generally FDIC, 'State Powers Bank Study' (1991) (on file with author); Arthur E. Wilmarth, 'The Expansion of State Bank Powers, the Federal Response, and the Case for Preserving the Dual Banking System', (1990) 58 Fordham Law Rev. No. 6, at p.1132.

47 See *History of the Eighties, Volume 1, supra* note 1, at p.124; Richard Ringer, 'States Rush to Deregulate', Am. Banker, 9 May 1983, at p.7; Richard Ringer, 'Volcker Urges Care on Deregulation', Am. Banker, 10 May 1983, at p.1.

attempted to address these prudential concerns and proposed regulations in 1984 regarding State bank involvement in non-bank activities,[48] and in 1985 the FDIC proposed an amended rule that FDIC-insured banks were required to place insurance underwriting and real estate investment or development activities in separately capitalized subsidiaries to insulate them from the presumed increased risks.[49] The FDIC asserted that as federal deposit insurer it should have the authority to set such guidelines, but State banking agencies, State-chartered banks and industry predictably opposed the rule on various grounds.[50]

The OCC also opposed the FDIC proposed regulation because the OCC asserted potential FDIC jurisdiction over national banks.[51] The FRB was generally supportive of the FDIC proposed regulation and in particular on limiting real estate development activities, but favored restricting such activities to non-bank subsidiaries of bank holding companies rather than to direct subsidiaries of banks.[52] The FRB was also concerned with the potential legal issues involved in the FDIC regulation of State member banks and BHCs and their non-bank affiliates over which it presumably had jurisdiction, and asserted that if the FDIC pursued its regulation, it should exclude institutions regulated by the FRB.[53] The FDIC ultimately delayed implementing the regulation, and was unable to reach consensus with the FRB and in late 1987 withdrew the proposed regulation.[54]

Notwithstanding jurisdictional debate over regulation of State member banks and their respective powers, the 1980s was largely dominated by expansion of bank and BHC powers through the regulatory activism of the OCC and FRB, respectively, which generated a plethora of federal court litigation and US Supreme Court and federal appellate court precedent as the securities and insurance industry interest groups affected by such activism responded to

---

48 See FDIC *Annual Report* (1984), *supra* note 45, at p.41.

49 See FDIC *Annual Report* (1985), at p.57.

50 The State banking authorities, State-chartered banks, and industry associations all opposed the rule, and argued that the FDIC lacked jurisdiction and violated States' rights by preempting State laws. See *History of the Eighties, Volume 1, supra* note 1, at p.124.

51 *Ibid.* at p.124.

52 The FRB generally desired to limit real estate activities and preferred to limit State banking powers which arguably jeopardized the 'safety and soundness' of the banking system. *Ibid.* at p.124.

53 *Ibid.* at p.124.

54 See FDIC *Annual Report* (1987), at p.30. The FRB issued its own proposed regulation which provided that State member banks and State-chartered bank subsidiaries of bank holding companies would be prohibited from direct investment in real estate, and that real estate investment would be permissible only through separately incorporated real estate subsidiaries of bank holding companies that met certain capital requirements. See Barbara A. Rehm, 'Fed Weighs Restrictions on Real Estate', Am. Banker, 3 November 1987, at p.1. The FRB proposal attracted undue attention from Congress, which drafted legislation to limit the Fed from exercising control over subsidiaries of State banks within holding company structures, and similarly opposed by State banking agencies, State-chartered banks and industry. See, e.g., Barbara A. Rehm, 'House Measure May Foil Fed Efforts to Gain Control of State Bank Limits', Am. Banker, 10 April 1989, at p.1; John D. Hawke, 'Fed Needs New Approach to Real Estate', Am. Banker, 16 August 1989, at p.4. The proposal was ultimately not codified.

protect their constituent institutions.[55] The expansion of bank powers, fueled by financial innovations and competition, served the same purpose as the expansion of thrift institution powers under the DIDMCA and Garn-St. Germain Act, respectively, and FHLBB implementing regulations, by unleashing competitive forces that ultimately favored the money center banking organizations and introduced banks with less market power and experience to diminishing market share, new sources of risk, reduced earnings, and financial distress or failure. The money center banks were therefore able to diversify sources of risk and revenues, and eventually acquire or merge with other banks that could not survive in the enhanced competitive environment.

V. CAPITAL REQUIREMENTS AND FORBEARANCE

A. Evolution of Bank Capital Requirements

The emphasis on deregulation during the early years of the Reagan Administration facilitated regulatory policies based on the perception that capital requirements were necessary to maintain the safety and soundness of the banking system. Bank capital reserves were viewed as a viable layer of protection against unforeseen losses and therefore as a means to advance public confidence in, facilitate prudent growth of, and protect depositors of banking organizations.[56]

---

55 See, e.g., *Securities Indus. Ass'n v. Board of Governors of the Federal Reserve System* 450 U.S. 46 (1981) (permitting bank holding companies and their non-bank subsidiaries to engage in investment advisory services to closed-end investment companies); *Securities Indus. Ass'n v. Board of Governors of the Federal Reserve System* 468 U.S. 137 (1984) (permitting banks to engage in the placement of commercial paper issues); *Securities Indus. Ass'n v. Board of Governors of the Federal Reserve System* 468 U.S. 207 (1984) (permitting bank holding company ownership of retail securities brokerage activities); *Securities Indus. Ass'n v. Board of Governors of the Federal Reserve System* 839 F.2d 47 (2d Cir.), cert. denied, 486 U.S. 1059 (1988) (permitting bank holding company non-bank affiliates to engage in underwriting and dealing in certain bank-eligible securities).

56 In the 1970s, the federal banking agencies approached to capital requirements by establishing bank peer groups and target capital ratios for each group, and then adjusting those targets according to the circumstances of individual organizations. See Arnold A. Heggestad & B. Frank King, 'Regulation of Bank Capital: An Evaluation', Federal Reserve Bank of Atlanta Economic Review 67, No. 3 (1982), at pp.38–39. The agencies did not set specific numerical minimum capital requirements. Banking organization capital reserves steadily declined during the 1970s under this policy, and several large banking institutions failed and imposed substantial costs on the FDIC. See, e.g. FFIEC, 'Capital Trends in Federally Regulated Financial Institutions' (1980). The regulatory practices generally evolved in 1978 into a Uniform Interagency Bank Rating System (CAMEL system) and the related Federal Reserve Board rating system for bank holding companies (BOPEC system). See 'Banking Agencies Adopt Uniform Interagency Bank Soundness Rating System', [1978–1979 Transfer Binder] Fed. Banking L. Rep. (CCH) P97,451 (11 May 1978); Federal Reserve Board, 'Rating Systems – Bank Holding Companies', (1978) Fed. Reserve Reg. Serv., Vol. 1, at pp.4–865. These uniform systems utilized capital adequacy as one of a number of factors that are evaluated individually and then collectively by the banking agencies in applying a soundness rating for their own internal examination purposes. See Joseph J. Norton, 'Capital Adequacy Standards: A Legitimate Concern for Prudential Supervision of Banking Activities?', 49 Ohio St. Law J. 1300, 1320 (1989).

As reviewed in Chapter Two, the money center bank capital bases became increasingly vulnerable to the worsening economic conditions in LDC nations, given the oil price shocks and inflation in the US economy. These trends prompted federal banking agencies to work towards establishing more specific regulatory guidelines for capital requirements in 1980–1981.[57]

As of 1980, there were no generally formal and specific regulatory or statutory minimum capital requirements, except for the minimum capital requirement for forming a national bank, and substantial differences existed among the regulatory agencies on the correct approach to capital requirements. The various regulatory positions were largely separate internal examination tools for facilitating the assessment of bank safety and soundness and to informally urge bank management to improve capital positions.[58] The large banking organizations resisted regulatory initiatives to raise and codify capital requirements and tighten their respective definitions of capital, but the federal banking agencies realized that the money center banks were dangerously overexposed to LDC borrower nations and otherwise undercapitalized.

The most controversial issue by 1981 with respect to defining regulatory 'capital' for measuring capital requirements involved 'subordinated debt', which was as a means to inflate otherwise declining capital reserves.[59] The Federal Financial Institutions Examination Council (FFIEC) proposed rules dividing capital into *primary capital*[60] *and secondary capital*.[61] The FFIEC eventually proposed to include secondary capital within the definition of what constituted acceptable regulatory capital.[62] The FFIEC required, however, that average maturities of qualifying instruments had to be at least 7 years, and that acceptable secondary capital would be limited to 50 per cent of primary capital. Banks were generally divided into three groups based upon their asset size to determine capital requirements.

The FDIC strongly opposed the use of subordinated debt in determining capital requirements in the FFIEC proposed regulation, however.[63] The FDIC asserted that since subordinated debt could not be used to absorb unanticipated losses, it should be excluded, and voted against sending the proposed regulation to the federal banking agencies for approval.[64] The FDIC Board of Directors rejected the FFIEC proposal and uniform capital guidelines.[65] The first formal regulatory pronouncement on bank capital requirements came in 1981 with the public issuance of a Joint Policy Statement proposing 'Capital

---

57 See *History of the Eighties, Volume 1, supra* note 1, at p.111.

58 See Norton, *supra* note 56, at p.1321.

59 See, e.g. James G. Ehlen, 'A Review of Bank Capital and its Adequacy', Federal Reserve Bank of Atlanta Economic Review 68, No. 11, at p.54 (1983).

60 Primary capital included common and perpetual preferred stock, surplus, undivided profits, contingency and other capital reserves, mandatory convertible instruments, and loan-loss reserves. See 'FFIEC Notice of 17 June 1981', 46 Fed. Reg. 32,948 (23 June 1981).

61 Secondary capital included non-perpetual preferred stock, and subordinated debt (i.e. notes and debentures). See FFIEC Notice, *supra* note 60, at 32,948.

62 *Ibid.*

63 See *History of the Eighties, Volume 1, supra* note 1, at pp.111–112.

64 *Ibid.* at p.111.

65 *Ibid.* at p.112.

Adequacy Guidelines' by the FRB concerning State member banks and bank holding companies, and the OCC concerning national banks.[66]

The FRB and OCC joint statement was very similar to the FFIEC proposed rules, and banking organizations were thus divided into three groups based on asset size: multinational, regional, and community.[67] The multinational group, consisting of the 17 largest money center banks, however, were treated individually and had no mandatory capital requirements but were expected to reverse the trend of declining balances in their capital reserve levels.[68] The banking agencies purportedly informed the multinational banks that if they did not generally increase capital reserves, the regulatory agencies would set more precise capital standards and remove bank discretion from the process. Thus, the money center banks received favorable treatment, and the banking agencies set more precise capital standards for regional banks and community banks.[69] The FDIC adopted similar but more restrictive capital requirements.[70] Notably, as most FDIC-supervised banks had assets less than USD1 billion, the differences in capital adequacy regulation between the FDIC, OCC, and FRB were actually marginal at that time.[71]

B. LDC Debt Crisis

The concepts of regulatory intervention and forbearance on an industry basis were generally not used as openly by the FRB and OCC with banking organizations as they were with respect to the FHLBB and thrift institutions during

---

[66] See 'Joint News Release of the Comptroller of the Currency and Federal Reserve Board', reprinted in 1 Fed. Banking L. Rep. (CCH) P5554A, at 3406 (17 December 1981).

[67] *Ibid.*

[68] See The OCC and FRB identified 17 banking institutions as multinational institutions; regional banks were all other banking agencies with consolidated assets of USD1 billion or more, and community banking institutions were all others not otherwise included in these categories. See Norton, *supra* note 57, at p.1322, n101.

[69] The regional banks were defined as those holding assets of USD1 billion to USD15 billion. The regional banks were expected to maintain a primary capital-to-assets ratio of 5 per cent. The community banks were defined as those holding assets of less than USD1 billion. Community banks were expected to maintain a capital-to-assets ratio of at least 6 per cent. Banking institutions were further divided into three supervisory zones according to their total capital-to-assets ratios. Multinational and regional banks with ratios of 6.5 per cent were deemed 'adequately capitalized'; such banks with ratios of 5.5 per cent to 6.5 per cent were deemed 'possibly undercapitalized'; and such banks with ratios of less than 5.5 per cent were deemed 'presumed undercapitalized.' Community banks were similarly designated, except that their respective ratios were one-half of a percentage point higher. Banking institutions that were deemed within the 'presumed undercapitalized' or 'possibly undercapitalized' zones received greater attention from the agencies and were required to submit capitalization plans to increase their capital reserves. See Norton, *supra* note 56, at p.1322, n102.

[70] The FDIC used a single measure of capital, the ratio of adjusted equity capital-to-adjusted total assets. The FDIC established a 6 per cent minimum requirement for all State non-member banks regardless of respective asset size, but also established a minimum acceptance ratio of 5 per cent. Banks falling below this level were required to initiate specific programs to improve their capital levels. See FDIC, 'Statement of Policy on Capital Adequacy', 46 Fed. Reg. 62.693 (17 December 1981).

[71] See *History of the Eighties, Volume 1, supra* note 1, at p.112.

the 1980–1983 period, with the major exception being the LDC debt crisis. The US banking system came under enormous pressure with the LDC debt crisis, and many individual banking organizations were for all practical purposes critically undercapitalized given their LDC exposures. The largest portion of LDC claims originated with US money center banks, which specialized in managing large syndicated Eurodollar lending facilities,[72] and increased rapidly over the 1970s.

By the end of 1978, the 8 largest money center banks held approximately USD36 billion in outstanding LDC debt obligations of Latin America, which accounted for more than 200 per cent of their total capital and reserves.[73] The signs of impending crisis became clearer as the ability of LDC nations to continue servicing their debts (interest on short-term and long-term debt plus amortization of long-term debt) deteriorated rapidly. The second major oil price shock of 1979 intensified LDC debt-servicing problems.

In the period of 1979–1982, total Latin American LDC debt obligations more than doubled, increasing from USD159 billion to USD327 billion.[74] The US banks significantly increased their lending to LDC nations during this period, and the outstanding loans of the eight largest money center banks increased from approximately USD36 billion to USD55 billion.[75]

The banking agencies made some efforts to curtail LDC lending activities and facilitate diversification of foreign credit risk, partly through Interagency Country Exposure Review Committee composed of officials from the OCC, FDIC, and Federal Reserve, but these efforts had little effect on the growth of LDC lending activities.[76] The growth of LDC lending activities was likely facilitated by a liberal OCC interpretation of 'single borrower' limits wherein the OCC determined that public sector borrowers meeting certain conditions were not required to be counted as parts of a single entity.[77] The Reagan Administration and banking agencies may be collectively viewed as supportive of LDC lending activities by US banking institutions, notwithstanding the obvious risks that were well understood by the Federal Reserve and Treasury Department.

The LDC Debt Crisis formally began on 12 August 1982 when Mexico declared that it had run out of US dollar reserves and could not meet its interest obligations on international bank syndicated loan facilities.[78] The overzealous lending practices to LDC debtor nations by the various US and international banking organizations developed into a full-blown but largely secretive banking crisis when the LDC nations generally defaulted on their debt obligations. By year end 1982, approximately 40 nations were in arrears on their interest payments.[79] By October 1983, 27 nations owing nearly

---

[72] The medium-sized regional and other non-money center banks often participated in these lending facilities through loan participation arrangements.

[73] See *History of the Eighties, Volume 1, supra* note 1, at p.195.

[74] *Ibid.* at p.199.

[75] *Ibid.* at p.199.

[76] *Ibid.* at p.43.

[77] *Ibid.* at p.44.

[78] *Ibid.* at p.191.

[79] *Ibid.* at p.206.

USD240 billion had rescheduled their debt obligations to banks or were in the process of negotiating such rescheduling, and 16 of these nations were from Latin America, and the four largest nations, Mexico, Brazil, Venezuela, and Argentina, owed various commercial banks approximately USD176 billion, or approximately 75 per cent of the total LDC debt outstanding.[80] The LDC nations owed approximately USD37 billion of this amount to the eight largest US money center banks which constituted nearly 150 per cent of their capital reserve at that time.[81] The international banking crisis was only averted through the coordinated actions of central banks and international financial institutions; favorable examination and accounting treatment; incredibly complex borrower workouts involving hundreds of banking organizations; and the eventual securitization of LDC debt obligations.[82] The Federal Reserve and Treasury Department initiatives prior to and following the Mexican default all but guaranteed that none of the large US banking organizations at significant risk during the LDC Debt Crisis failed, however.[83] These reasons included the massive undertaking of a coordinated effort by the federal banking agencies, the Treasury Department, the international financial institutions, and central banks from other nations to keep LDC sovereign borrowers from defaulting on their loan obligations, and to prevent the largest multinational banking organizations from reaching a sustained position of capital impairment.[84]

The US banking agencies did not require large reserves to be set aside on restructured LDC loans or on the succeeding arrearages by other LDC nations, however.[85] This policy was determined to be necessary at the time because the total LDC portfolios held by money center banks was on average more than double the amount of aggregate capital and reserve at the end of 1982.[86]

---

80 See Philip A. Wellons, *Passing the Buck: Banks, Government and Third World Debt*, (1987) at p.225.

81 See, e.g., FFIEC, 'Country Exposure Report', at p.2 (December 1982).

82 The seven-year period after the Mexican default was devoted to restructuring existing loans, setting aside loss reserves, and attempting to protect the solvency of the US financial system. More than ten years passed after the crisis before the LDC debtor economies recovered and the money center banks cleared their balance sheets of such loans. Bank advisory committees were established to represent the banks in bilateral negotiations with the individual debtor nations for debt reschedulings which lasted throughout the 1980s.

83 See, e.g., GAO, 'Financial Crisis Management: Four Financial Crises in the 1980s', GAO/GGD-97-96 (May 1997), at pp.19–34 (addressing details of Federal Reserve and Treasury Department crisis management during Mexico debt crisis of 1982); Joseph Kraft, 'The Mexican Rescue', Group of Thirty (June 1984); Darrell Delamaide, *Debt Shock: The Full Story of the World Credit Crisis* (Doubleday, 1984).

84 The Federal Reserve, Treasury Department, European and Japanese central banks, and finance ministries, the IMF, and US and foreign commercial banks were involved in the ensuing crisis containment efforts. See GAO, 'Financial Crises Management', *supra* note 83, at pp.19–34; William R. Cline, 'International Debt and the Stability of the World Economy', Institute for International Economics (September 1983).

85 The European banking institutions generally had less exposure to LDC nations than US money center banks, however, and were in some instances able to establish 'hidden reserves' by agreement between regulatory authorities and the banks that were generally beyond public scrutiny. See L. William Seidman, *Full Faith and Credit: The Great S&L Debacle and Other Washington Sagas* (Times Books, 1993).

86 See *History of the Eighties, Volume 1, supra* note 1, at p.207.

Regulatory forbearance was granted to the largest US banks with respect to the establishment of reserves against LDC loans in default. According to FDIC Chairman William Seidman, this regulatory forbearance was clearly necessary as eight of the ten largest money center banks in the US could easily have been deemed insolvent and thereafter induced economic panic and political crisis.[87]

The strategy of regulatory forbearance was generally successful in preventing the insolvency of the US banking system and a major domestic or international financial crisis, as during this period no large US banks failed because of delinquent or non-performing LDC loans. The large banks were able to maintain funding and liquidity and obtain time to raise capital and increase reserves over the remainder of the 1980s. The regulators and commentators attempted to distinguish the notion of regulatory forbearance in the LDC Debt Crisis from the thrift industry crisis,[88] but the bottom line is that both crises occurred in the face of massive inflation caused by conflicting fiscal and monetary policy, abrupt policy reversals precipitating catastrophic asset value deflation and because of poor to non-existent regulation and supervision, obscured by manipulation of or lack of enforcement of the regulatory apparatus.[89] The LDC Debt Crisis ultimately resulted in a massive loss of wealth, largely shouldered by the shareholders of lending banks, under the plan designed by then-US Secretary of the Treasury Nicholas Brady.[90]

The LDC debt crisis provided the impetus for significant changes in bank capital adequacy regulation in 1983. As the LDC Debt Crisis unfolded, Congress perceived that the collective failure of banking agencies to impose more rigorous capital requirements against the enormous sovereign credit risks assumed by US banks in the 1970s and early 1980s represented a primary cause of the precarious state of multinational (and some regional) banking organization balance sheets and a sizable portion of adverse effects to the US economy.[91]

The stages of formal regulation of capital adequacy authority were initiated in 1981, but of course these standards generally excluded the money center banks, and the authority to set more precise capital requirements was

---

87 See Seidman, *supra* note 85, at pp.127–128. See also Robert A. Eisenbeis and Paul M. Horvitz, *The Role of Forbearance and Its Costs in Handling Troubled and Failed Depository Institutions, in Reforming Financial Institutions in the United States* (George G. Kaufman (ed.), 1993)), at pp.49–68 (reviewing regulatory forbearance in connection with LDC debt crisis).

88 See Seidman, *supra* note 85, at p.128 (distinguishing regulatory forbearance practices in the LDC Debt Crisis from thrift industry crisis).

89 Although between 1982–1986 the loan-loss reserves for the average international bank more than doubled, as of year-end 1986 they were only approximately 13 per cent of the total LDC debt exposures. In 1987, the money center banks began to recognize massive losses on LDC loans that were in some instances carried on their balance sheets at par value for over a decade. In May 1987, Citicorp was the first money center bank to recognize a loss on LDC debt, and established loan-loss provisions of US$3.3 billion, or more than 30 per cent of its total LDC debt exposure, and shortly thereafter all money center banks followed with similar provisions. By the end of 1989, the money center banks had total reserves on average of 50 per cent of their total outstanding LDC debt exposures.

90 See William R. Cline, *International Debt Reexamined* (1995), at pp.234–235.

91 See Norton, *supra* note 56, at p.1325.

challenged in federal court in 1983.[92] The case acted as a catalyst for Congress to enact the International Lending Supervision Act of 1983 (ILSA).[93] The participation of the US banking agencies in the Basle Committee deliberative process contributed to the passage of ILSA.[94]

The ILSA was intended to address the notion that US multinational and other major banking institutions engaged in substantial international lending activities without the benefits of a comprehensive supervisory framework; to assure that the US economy would not be adversely affected or threatened by imprudent lending practices or lax supervision; and to achieve the uniform adoption of effective and consistent supervisory policies and practices regarding international lending activities.[95] The ILSA required the federal banking agencies[96] to ensure that all banking institutions engaging in international lending activities achieved and maintained adequate capital levels by establishing minimum levels of capital for such institutions and by such other methods as the agencies deemed appropriate.[97] The ILSA also provided federal banking agencies with express enforcement powers to implement and enforce capital requirements through the issuance of capital directives, therefore largely overruling the *Bellaire* decision.[98]

The ILSA directed that any failures to maintain adequate capital requirements in this respect would be deemed 'unsafe and unsound' banking practice.[99] The ILSA required US banking agencies to work towards uniform capital standards on both the domestic and international levels, and largely

---

92 See *Bellaire v. Comptroller of the Currency*, 697 F.2d 674 (5th Cir. 1983). In Bellaire, the Court of Appeals set aside the relevant portion of an OCC cease-and-desist order requiring that the capital levels of a particular national bank be increased and maintained at a level not less than 7 per cent of its total assets. Prior to this case, the banking agencies assumed they would enjoy broad administrative discretion in enforcing capital requirements based on broad statutory authority to issue cease-and-desist orders under federal banking laws. The judicial review applied in *Bellaire* generally introduced uncertainty regarding the enforcement of capital requirements.

93 See Pub. L. No. 98–181, 97 Stat. 1278 (1983) (codified as amended at 12 U.S.C. § 3901).

94 In 1974, the major industrialized nations formed the Committee on Banking Regulations and Supervisory Practices (Basle Committee) with the primary purpose of harmonizing bank practices to improve the quality of international bank regulation and supervision. See Joseph J. Norton, 'The Work of the Basle Supervisors Committee on Bank Capital Adequacy and the July 1988 Report on "International Convergence of Capital Measurement and Capital Standards"' 23 Int'l Law. 245 (1989). By 1978 the Basle Committee formulated guidance on capital adequacy and risk exposure, and in 1988 the Basle Committee published the Final Report on 'International Convergence of Capital Measurement and Capital Standards,' which established minimum requirements for core capital and supplementary capital, risk weightings, and targets for leveraging core capital and risk-weighted ratios, to mitigate counterparty credit risk. See Committee on Banking Regulations and Supervisory Practices, 'Final Report on International Convergence of Capital Measurement and Capital Standards' (15 July 1988) (on file with author).

95 See Norton, *supra* note 56, at p.1325; Cynthia C. Lichtenstein, 'The U.S. Response to the International Debt Crisis: The International Lending Supervision Act of 1983', 25 *Virginia Journal of International Law* (1985), at pp. 401–435

96 The ILSA applied to members of the FFIEC, including the FRB, OCC, and FDIC. See 12 U.S.C. § 3902.

97 See 12 U.S.C. § 3907(a).

98 See 12 U.S.C. § 3907(b)(2)(B).

99 See 12 U.S.C. § 3907(b)(1).

eliminated the forbearance practices and permissiveness which had existed up to that point.[100] Therefore, the ILSA facilitated the convergence of domestic capital requirements by the three banking agencies and for multilateral efforts of bank regulatory agencies with the Basle Committee forum.

In June 1983, the banking agencies issued a series of amendments to the 1981 capital guidelines.[101] The amendments were designed to bring the multinational banks that were otherwise excluded from regulation under the 1981 guidelines under a uniform 5 per cent minimum ratio of primary capital to total assets and to broaden the definition of secondary capital components for bank holding company purposes. The agencies opined that banking organizations with a 'higher than average percentage of assets exposed to risk' or a 'higher than average amount of off-balance sheet risk' would be expected to hold additional primary capital to compensate for increased risk levels.[102]

The federal banking agencies shortly thereafter proposed separate capital adequacy regulations in 1984.[103] The FDIC and OCC proposed regulations were similar in setting the minimum primary capital-to-assets ratio for all 'well-managed' banks at 5.5 per cent, and the minimum total capital ratio at 6 per cent. The FRB's proposal retained the current 'zone' concept with respect to total capital levels but set the same minimum primary capital ratio for all institutions at 5.5 per cent. The FDIC pressed for a higher total capital ratio of 9 per cent, consisting of 6 per cent equity and up to 3 per cent subordinated debt. The FRB and Treasury Department purportedly endorsed the FDIC proposal, but the proposal was ultimately not codified as regulation. The banking agencies articulated various reasons for the emphasis on capital adequacy with respect to prudent bank management and regulation. The agencies emphasized that the erosion of bank capital bases since the 1960s was aggravated further by

1. the deregulation of interest rates on bank deposits;
2. the weakening of loan portfolios resulting from the shocks in the domestic and international economies with the related declines in bank profitability notwithstanding increased levels of risk within the banking system;
3. the increased competition for financial services within the banking industry and between other financial services industries (securities, insurance);

---

100 The ILSA provided that: 'The Federal banking agencies shall consult with the banking supervisory authorities of other countries to reach understandings aimed at achieving the adoption of effective and consistent supervisory policies and practices with respect to international lending.' See 12 U.S.C. § 3901(b).

101 See 'Joint Press Release of Comptroller of the Currency and Federal Reserve Board', reprinted in 1 Fed. Banking L. Rep. (CCH) P5461 (13 June 1983).

102 *Ibid.* at P5462, 3355.

103 See FRB, 'Capital Maintenance', 49 Fed. Reg. 30,317 (1984) (codified at 12 C.F.R. Pts 208, 225 and 263) (proposed 30 July 1984); OCC, 'Minimum Capital Ratios', 49 Fed. Reg. 34,838 (1984) (codified at 12 C.F.R. Pt 3) (proposed 3 September 1984); FDIC, 'Capital Maintenance', 49 Fed. Reg. 29,399 (1984) (codified at 12 C.F.R. Pt 325) (proposed 20 July 1984).

4. the dramatic increase in off-balance sheet activities and risks undertaken by banking institutions; and
5. the perceived growth of interdependence within the banking system whereby financial distress of one institution could have severe repercussions on other institutions within the banking system.[104]

The banking agencies issued final regulations in 1985 with the purpose of generally complying with ILSA. But these regulations did not achieve full uniformity and transparency. Although the banking agencies made further refinements and clarifications to the components of regulatory capital and agreed to use a common approach of primary and secondary capital, the agencies were not in full agreement.[105]

C. Risk-Based Capital Requirements

The banking agencies finalized the 1985 capital regulations, but the imposition of enforceable capital ratios motivated the banking industry to utilize 'financial innovation' to circumvent them by expanding into off-balance sheet activities, such as letters of credit, loan commitments, swaps and derivatives, as such activities were not subject to capital requirements.[106] The 1985 capital regulations did not propose specific treatment for off-balance sheet risks, notwithstanding a dramatic increase in such activities, but placed the banking industry on notice that regulations would be forthcoming in this respect.[107]

Although more restrictive uniform capital requirements were achieved following ILSA, the banking agencies generally downplayed them as insufficient. The US banking organizations were generally at the time not required to disclose specific aspects of off-balance sheet activities in financial reports. The accounting rules in existence for such activities left vast discretion to the organizations in deciding how, whether, and when to disclose information to the banking agencies or the public at large. Banking organizations were generally unrestrained in the amount of off-balance sheet activities that they could conduct. Most of the off-balance sheet activities were 'authorized' as permissible by the banking agencies issuing self-interested deregulatory interpretations of applicable provisions of the National Bank Act, the

104 See Norton, *supra* note 56, at p.1327.

105 The FDIC and OCC proposals were largely unchanged, while the FRB retained the supervisory 'zones' previously established for supervision purposes but implemented the 5.5 per cent minimum primary capital ratio and 6 per cent total capital ratio, respectively. The capital regulations also formalized the enforcement powers of the agencies by including comprehensive regulatory provisions regarding the issuance of capital directives and the enforcement of capital requirements. The regulations further incorporated the notion of risk assessment as an evaluation tool for banking agencies on a case-by-case basis. See FRB, 'Capital Maintenance', 50 Fed. Reg. 16,057 (1985) (codified at 12 C.F.R. Pts 208, 225 & 263); OCC, 'Minimum Capital Ratios', 50 Fed. Reg. 10,207 (1985) (codified at 12 C.F.R. Pts 3 & 7); FDIC, 'Capital Maintenance', 50 Fed. Reg. 11,128 (1985) (codified at 12 C.F.R. Pt 325).

106 See *History of the Eighties, Volume 1, supra* note 1, at p.114.

107 See Norton, *supra* note 56, at p.1331.

Glass-Steagall Act, and the Bank Holding Company Act, as appropriate. The regulatory interpretations enabled banking organizations to engage in off-balance sheet activities either directly, through the holding company structure, or indirectly through subsidiaries and affiliates.

The explosion of off-balance sheet activities at multinational banks prompted the banking agencies to abruptly change the capital adequacy regulatory framework to one involving *risk-based* capital requirements. The banking agencies generally attempted to establish uniform risk-based capital requirements by issuing regulations for all US banks by mid-1986, although not explicitly required by ILSA.[108]

Although the specific agency proposals were not exactly similar, the proposals were largely similar and definitely facilitated the development of uniform capital requirements. Nonetheless, several notable differences in underlying policy were evident.[109] The US banks of course did not favor the new risk-based capital proposals, arguing that they would place US banks at a competitive disadvantage to other international banks, but these arguments were diminished after the US banking agencies joined their international counterparts in 1986 in the Basle Committee forum to establish a common set of risk-based capital requirements.

The LDC Debt Crisis, conceived largely through lax enforcement of capital standards by the federal banking agencies, was addressed through forbearance practices and permissiveness similar to those followed by the FHLBB. The near insolvency of the US banking system facilitated the adoption of risk-based capital standards which evolved into the current system of capital adequacy regulation in existence at the present time. Nonetheless, historical review generally does not compare the practices of the federal banking agencies and the FHLBB, and instead singles out the FHLBB as having committed egregious errors with respect to its deregulatory initiatives.

---

[108] The agencies issued preliminary risk-based capital standards that were essentially quite similar. The risk-based capital requirements initially focused on credit risk incurred by banking organizations with respect to certain activities and linked capital requirements to the levels of risk incurred through such activities. The risk-based framework entailed the conversion of off-balance sheet activities into *on-balance sheet credit equivalents* and assigned risk weightings. The framework was originally contemplated and debated at the international level through the Basle Committee forum, but all US banking agencies issued preliminary risk-based capital proposals in 1986. See FRB, 'Bank Holding Companies and Change in Bank Control; Capital Maintenance; Supplemental Adjusted Capital Measure', 51 Fed. Reg. 3,976 (1986) (to be codified at 12 C.F.R. Pt 225) (proposed 31 January 1986) (FRB proposing to amend Appendix A to Regulation Y, 12 C.F.R. Pt 225, as set forth in 50 Fed. Reg. 16,057 (1985) and further noting that other countries were acting or had acted to establish risk-based capital standards); OCC, 'Minimum Capital Ratios; Risk-Based Capital Standards for National Banks', 51 Fed. Reg. 10,602 (1986) (to be codified at 12 C.F.R. Pt 3); FDIC, 'Capital Maintenance; Supplemented Adjusted Capital Proposal', 51 Fed. Reg. 6,126 (1986) (to be codified at 12 C.F.R. Pt 325) (proposing to amend the prior regulation set forth in 50 Fed. Reg. 11,128).

[109] For instance, the FRB and FDIC asserted that the risk-based capital requirements should supplement the already-existing capital requirements, while the OCC asserted that the risk-based standards should supplant them. Moreover, the OCC's definition of primary capital (or soon-to-become 'Tier 1 capital') included loan-loss reserves, a position adopted in 1987, but contrary to that of the FRB. Finally, the banking agencies also differed on treatment of risk-weightings for longer-term government securities.

The truth is that regulatory forbearance practices and permissiveness, whether deliberate through deregulatory initiatives or indirect through insufficient enforcement of standards, were widespread in the US banking industry during the early 1980s to a far more serious extent than in the thrift industry. Of course, as the federal banking agencies came under pressure for their poor performance leading up to the LDC Debt Crisis and its impact on the US banking system, the FHLBB deregulatory initiatives entered the political crossfire on grounds that thrift institutions were receiving 'special treatment' through deregulation.

D. Differences in Bank-Thrift Capital Requirements

The federal banking agencies implemented capital guidelines for banks under ILSA, however, and it became apparent that notable differences existed between the capital requirements of banks and those of thrift institutions. In particular, the OCC observed that many commentators pointed out the 'continuing inequities' between banks and S&Ls and urged the banking agencies to work with FHLBB to achieve uniform capital requirements for all financial institutions.[110] The FRB and FDIC, acting under powers granted by the DIDMCA, responded to these charges by requiring higher capital ratios for S&Ls.[111]

The FHLBB moved to increase thrift capital requirements in 1985 and phase out provisions allowing for significant leverage, and acknowledged that 'inadequate capitalization' was a primary problem faced by the S&L industry and thrift institutions undertaking notable asset growth.[112] In 1986 the FHLBB further amended capital requirements for FSLIC-insured thrift institutions to increase capital requirements to 6 per cent of total liabilities within a transition period.[113] These requirements were designed to raise thrift capital ratios to parity with the capital requirements of commercial banks.[114]

Notwithstanding the interest in designing uniform capital requirements for all domestic banks, the rules for banks were simply inappropriate for wholesale application to thrift institutions. First, the nature of S&L business was quite different from that of banks, particularly with respect to the nature of their asset portfolios. Thrift institutions served traditionally smaller clients, while banks generally provided financing for larger institutions on a domestic and international basis. The banks also engaged in various financial services activities, while thrift institutions primarily engaged in less diversified mortgage lending.

---

110 See OCC, 'Minimum Capital Ratios', 50 Fed. Reg. 10,207, 10,209 (1985).

111 See FRB, 'Capital Maintenance', 50 Fed. Reg. 16,057, 16,063 (1985) (final rule); FDIC, 'Capital Maintenance', 50 Fed. Reg. 11,128, 11,130 (1985) (final rule).

112 See FHLBB, 'Net Worth Requirements of Insured Institutions', 50 Fed. Reg. 6891 (1985) (to be codified at 12 C.F.R. Pts 561, 563, 570, 571 and 584).

113 See FHLBB, 'Regulatory Capital (Net Worth) Requirements of Insured Institutions', 51 Fed. Reg. 33,565 (1986) (to be codified at 12 C.F.R. Ch. V and Pts 561 and 563).

114 See FHLBB, 'Regulatory Capital Requirements of Insured Institutions', 51 Fed. Reg. 16,550 (proposed 5 May 1986) (to be codified at 12 C.F.R. Pts 561, 563 and Ch. V).

Second, banks historically exploited comparative advantages over thrift institutions, particularly with respect to offering floating-rate products subject to repricing while thrift institutions were prevented from doing so by restrictive State laws.

Third, reserve or loan-loss forbearance practices were substantially different between banking and thrift industries. Many banks until the late 1980s would frequently reschedule defaulting debts while maintaining artificially low loan-loss reserves, particularly with respect to foreign loans to commercial and sovereign borrowers, thus presenting their non-performing assets in an optimistic manner. Thrift institutions generally did not or could not provide their non-performing assets with options to reschedule loans.

Fourth, the effects of inflation over the late 1970s and early 1980s coupled with competition from government sponsored enterprises (GSEs) for mortgage lending business undermined the profitability of all thrift institutions.

Finally, the notion that capital standards and measurements must differentiate depending on the types of assets and markets utilized by institutions applies strongly between banks and S&Ls. The adoption of uniform capital requirements by FRB, OCC, and FDIC in 1986 and the movement to risk-based capital requirements in accordance with the Basle Committee process over the late 1980s did not directly include FHLBB for the reasons set forth above.

VI. CONCLUDING NOTE: STATE BANKING AGENCY DEREGULATION

The federal deregulatory initiatives were supplemented by similar initiatives in various States, particularly California, Texas, and Florida. The impact of the deregulatory changes in State laws was substantial, as over 50 per cent of all thrift institutions were chartered under State laws.[115] The US State legislatures and regulators either originated or responded with their own form of deregulation to maintain the value of State-sponsored thrift franchises. In California, changes were made in statutory and regulatory limitations whereby California S&Ls were permitted to invest an amount equal to 100 per cent of their assets into an investment subsidiary for investment purposes (which could, in turn, leverage that capital). In Texas, the percentage of assets permitted to be invested in an investment subsidiary was 10 per cent, with the ability to increase that percentage up to 50 per cent with the approval of the Commissioner of the Department of Savings and Loans of the State of Texas.

State statutes and regulations were liberally construed to allow investments in many types of speculative investment ventures, such as ski resorts, golf courses, airplanes, casinos, and the like. During calendar years 1980 and 1983, State governments enacted legislation that granted powers similar to or

---

[115] See *House Report*, *supra* note 26, at p.297.

broader than those established under the DIDMCA to thrift institutions organized under their respective State laws. Some of these States greatly expanded the percentage of assets that could be placed in commercial real estate loans, commercial loans and direct equity investments.[116]

In States such as Texas, with legislation that authorized State-chartered S&Ls to exercise the greater of State or federal powers as to any action, expansion of the powers of federal S&Ls had the effect of expanding the powers of State S&Ls. The States reacted in response to the federal emphasis on deregulation, which encouraged State S&Ls to convert to federal S&Ls to achieve the more liberal treatment afforded to federal savings and loans under DIDMCA and the Garn-St. Germain Act.

---

[116] See Strunk and Case, *Where Deregulation Went Wrong, United States League of Savings Institutions* (Washington, D.C., 1988), at p.56.

6. Commercial Real Estate and the Thrift and Banking Crises

I. INTRODUCTION

In many ways the US 1980s S&L bank crises was tied to the largely artificial rise and fall of commercial real estate prices. These prices (values) were largely impacted by dysfunctional and uncoordinated federal governmental regulation. This chapter provides a backdrop to this unfortunate phenomena.

II. THE REAL ESTATE BOOM (REVISITED)

In the 1980s, the S&L industry was critical to the flow of savings and investments in the US economy, and represented the main engine driving the residential real estate market. One of the primary causes exacerbating the S&L crisis, however, was the entry of S&Ls into commercial real estate development to compete with national banks following the enactment of DIDMCA and the Garn-St. Germain Act, respectively.

The demand for commercial real estate projects increased dramatically in the early 1980s, and reached speculative levels in many regional markets. Real estate lending activities by commercial banks and thrift institutions increased to meet this demand, as deregulation and other factors generated an environment in which commercial real estate lending was quite profitable for financial institutions.

The commercial real estate industry was generally cyclical, and when combined with the aggressive lending practices of banks and thrift institutions, the real estate markets were destined for asset value inflationary and deflationary cycles. The 'bust' cycle commenced following the enactment of the Tax Reform Act (TRA) in 1986, eventually resulting in massive losses for the banking and thrift industries, respectively.

The risks inherent in commercial real estate markets are worth exploring in connection with this section. First, the demand for commercial real estate is affected by local economic factors and regional developments, coupled with national economic conditions. Second, information about specific projects, with respect to construction costs, terms, pricing, and other transactional data, is generally unavailable to the general public. Third, most real estate projects are highly leveraged, funded primarily with debt as opposed to equity capital by respective investors, and leveraged investments are quite sensitive to changes in interest rates and overall credit liquidity in the lending markets. Fourth, government tax and other policies contribute 'policy risk' with respect to changing tax rates and depreciation allowances which can dramatically alter the profitability of real estate investments. Fifth, the long duration of projects coupled with macroeconomic changes in the economy over time can result in sustained periods of volatility in real estate lending activities, where the availability of credit for real estate lending fluctuates, causing prices of existing properties and the volume of new investments to similarly fluctuate. Finally, the structure of real estate loan agreements involves complex lending risks characterized by non-recourse financing provisions prohibiting lenders from recouping losses from other borrower assets, and little internal expertise to deal with foreclosed commercial real estate properties in terms of sales and management.[1]

As reviewed in Part One, the DIDMCA and Garn-St. Germain Act facilitated bank and thrift expansion into commercial real estate lending activities, and the enactment of favorable tax provisions for real estate development under ERTA facilitated the conditions for a sustained real estate boom in the United States. In the early 1980s, supply and demand for commercial real estate were in relative balance, and investment returns were enhanced by gradual asset value inflation over the 1970s which facilitated demand for real estate.[2] Thus, commercial real estate markets experienced an unprecedented 'boom' period which affected different regions of the US during the early- to mid-1980s.[3]

The regions in which the 'boom-bust' scenario occurred included the Southwest, the Northeast, and California. In Texas, major real estate markets experienced the boom cycle in the late 1970s and early 1980s, accelerated in part by local economic growth fueled by rising oil and gas prices.[4]

Banks and thrift institutions made many aggressive loans in the commercial real estate market and generally increased portfolio resources towards more real estate loans over the 1980s. The changes in bank and thrift real estate lending portfolios resulted in the overall deterioration of quality in loan portfolios, which compounded the amount of commercial real estate lending losses. First, banks and thrift institutions in competition for lucrative real estate lending commitments liberalized underwriting standards and relaxed terms on commercial loan contracts, and therefore assumed greater credit risk.[5] The enhanced competitive environment for banks and thrift institutions fueled commercial real estate lending activities, which generated

---

1 See FDIC, 'An Examination of the Banking Crises of the 1980s and Early 1990s', *History of the Eighties, Volume 1: Lessons for the Future,* (Washington D.C.,1998) at p.138.

2 *Ibid.*.

3 See *History of the Eighties, Volume 1, supra* note 1, at p.142.

4 See, e.g. Patric H. Hendershott and Edward J. Kane, 'Causes and Consequences of the 1980s Commercial Construction Boom', *Journal of Applied Corporate Finance* (Spring 1992).

5 See *History of the Eighties, Volume 1, supra* note 1, at pp.153–154.

large up-front fees and immediate income, especially with respect to construction-related lending activities.[6] As commercial real estate lending expanded, the underwriting standards for land, construction, and mortgage lending were liberalized significantly with respect to establishing adequate LTV ratios[7] and ensuring that income generated by a project was sufficient to cover interest and principal payments on borrowed funds.[8] The underlying component on which these liberalizations were premised was the value of the real estate collateral underlying the lending transaction as determined by the real estate appraisal process.

III. US REAL ESTATE VALUES, 1980s AND 1990s

Documentation of the rise, and then fall of real estate values in America, and in particular in the regions of America corresponding to the onset of banking distress in the 1980s, is difficult. Professor Lawrence J. White made this same observation in his study of the savings and loan debacle.[9]

Unlike more readily marketable assets whose values are regularly recorded in centralized markets and reported promptly in readily available venues, most real estate properties are illiquid and determination of the values are heavily dependent on reports of comparable sales information to estimate value. Residential real estate transactions are a more reliable source of market data. Sales information is less likely to be considered sensitive or confidential. Real estate loans secured by residential real estate are more easily standardized and values depend more on interest rates than on underlying real estate collateral values. The effects of interest rate volatility on fixed interest rate loans (the primary investments of S&Ls until problems of negative spread and disintermediation led to deregulation) is manifest in the illustrations earlier in this chapter.

'Real estate values in the entire United States peaked in 1985 and then declined by 10 per cent. For office buildings in the South, however, the price index peaked in 1983 and then fell by over a third. Finally, the price index for all commercial properties in the Southwest sub-region – covering the States

---

6 The competitive environment resulted from various factors, including (1) the removal of deposit interest rate ceilings; (2) the authorization of expanded lending and investment powers to thrift institutions; (3) the increase in the number of newly chartered national banks; (4) pressure from shareholders to improve earnings; and (5) the loss of sizable commercial lending markets to the commercial paper (securities) markets. Thus, banks and thrift institutions engaged in riskier lending practices in order to increase revenue and maintain market share during this period.

7 Many banks and thrift institutions raised their maximum LTV ratios, which decreased the amount of borrower's equity at risk, increased risk to the lending institution, and fueled investor demand for real estate development projects.

8 Many banks and thrift institutions also liberalized the frequency and timing of principal payments, or when interest payments went into default, the unpaid interest was frequently added back to the unpaid principal, or 'capitalized'.

9 Lawrence H. White, *The S&L Debacle: Public Policy Lessons for Bank and Thrift Regulation* (Oxford University Press, 1991), at p.110.

of Arkansas, Louisiana, Oklahoma and Texas – peaked in 1983, slipped only slightly for two years, and then fell by almost a third.[10] Professor White's compilation also showed that 'oil prices fell modestly after 1981 and then skidded sharply after 1985'. As Professor White also noted, 'Since many real estate projects of the early 1980s were based on assumptions of a *continuing rise* in real estate values, even a leveling of prices would have had serious consequences for their viability. A severe price decline meant devastation for these projects – and for their investors and lenders. Thrifts were prominent among these two groups. Also, the real estate investments of the rapidly growing thrifts were probably of lower quality than those of the pension funds included in the FRC index, so it is likely that the property values of the former group fell earlier and by more than the declines that are indicated in Illustration 6.

'Thus, the rapid growth of thrifts assets, much of it in new types of loans and investments, would have spelled serious trouble for the FSLIC in any event. The timing of the Tax Acts of 1981 and 1986 and of the decline in the price of oil, with their consequences on the prices of real estate in the South and Southwest, made a potentially bad situation substantially worse.[11]

The Frank Russell Company Index, referred to by Professor White, has been taken over by the National Council of Real Estate Investment Fiduciaries (NCREIF), and is now published as the NCREIF Property Index.[12] Professor White's observation that 'the real estate investments of the savings and loans were probably of lower quality than those of the pension funds in the FRC Index' is a vast understatement. Typically, real estate investments held by S&Ls and banks during this period consisted of raw land; land under development; and projects under construction, yet uncompleted, unleased and unsold to an end user. These investments were leveraged, many by over 100 per cent. By contrast, the properties in the FRC Index (now the NCREIF Index) were fully completed *income producing* apartments, office buildings, retail shopping centers, R&D/office buildings and warehouse facilities. Further, the Index properties were *unleveraged*, that is, properties owned by voting members of NCREIF (institutional members) free of any debt, in order to eliminate the effects of mortgage indebtedness upon valuation. The real estate properties in the NCREIF Index are 'investment grade' real estate properties.[13]

The loans in the S&L and bank portfolios were almost entirely short and intermediate term and were supported also by the general credit of the borrower and guarantors. Further, real estate projects under development or

---

10 *Ibid.* at p.110.

11 *Ibid.* at pp.110–111.

12 The NCREIF Property Index measures the historical performance of income-producing properties owned by commingled funds on behalf of the qualified pension and profit-sharing trusts, or owned directly by these trusts and managed on a separate account basis. The starting date for the Index is 31 December 1977. In order to eliminate the effects of mortgage indebtedness upon valuation, only unleveraged properties (properties owned free of any debt) are included. The data incorporated in the Index is drawn from the performance of properties managed or owned by voting members of the National Council of Real Estate Investment Fiduciaries (NCREIF).

13 *The NCREIF Real Estate Performance Report*, Third Quarter, 1996.

construction are in a state of transition, and therefore their values are also in transition. Loans secured by land have valuable collateral only when the underlying land has prospect for development or for sale to another for speculation, or for use in a development context. In short, the values of real estate collateral in bank and S&L portfolios are somewhat ephemeral, by the nature of the collateral, in direct contrast to the more stable values of the institutional investments owned by NCREIF members and reported in the NCREIF Index. As a further complication to bank and S&L portfolios collateralized by real estate, when economic conditions necessitate the shrinkage of those institutions' balance sheets as reflected in this chapter's illustrations, the higher quality, more marketable or more institutional assets are the first to be collected or disposed of through sale or refinancing to facilitate such balance sheet shrinkage.

In this context, then, it is instructive to examine some additional information kindly provided by NCREIF. The following illustration shows rolling 4-quarter returns for NCREIF real estate in comparison to prevailing rates of inflation, beginning with the fourth quarter of 1981 and continuing through to the end of 1991. Although the effects of FRB chairman Volcker's War on Inflation are evident from the end of 1981 onward, the rate of decline in real estate values exceeds the decline in the rate of inflation for the period, particularly from mid-1989 onward.

Illustration 4[14]

Rolling 4-Quarter Returns and Inflation

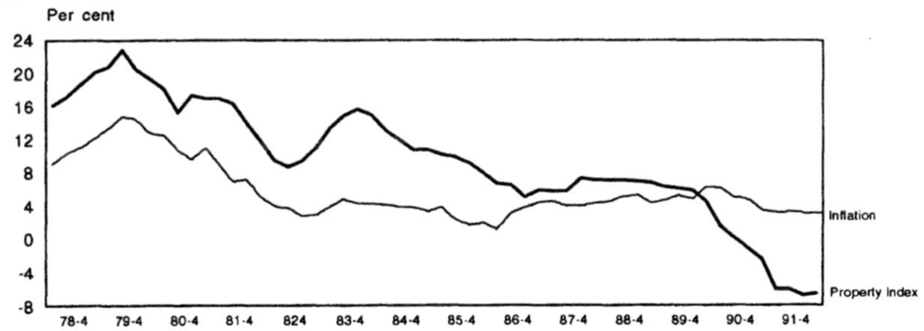

The next illustration reflects the decline of the NCREIF Property Index over the same time period, but split into two components of the Index: income and appreciation.

[14] *The Russell-NCREIF Real Estate Performance Report*, Third Quarter 1992 Results, at p.3.

Illustration 5[15]

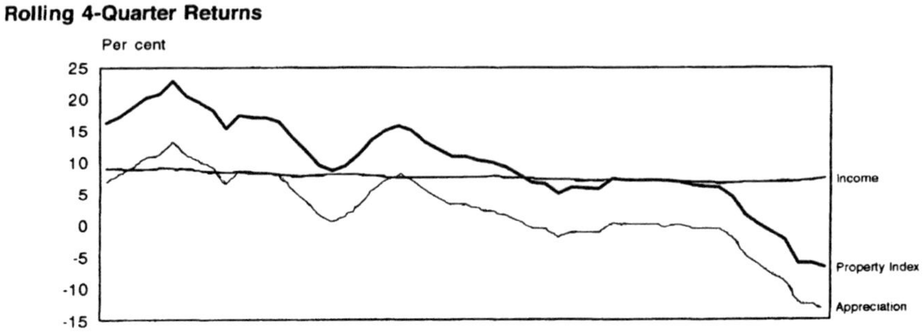

The foregoing chart illustrates dramatically the relative consistency of the Index in contrast to the drastic drop in the appreciation component of the Index, diverging at the beginning of the period, with a brief synthesis in mid-1983, before literally dropping off the chart. This graph illustrates the increasing irrelevance, over the pertinent period, of income in real estate valuation and the effect of the collapse of values based on the actual or comparable sales data. This pattern is reinforced by the following graph which depicts the NCREIF Property Index and its components, income and appreciation over the longer period, 1979 through 1996, the entire period relevant to this work.

Illustration 6[16]

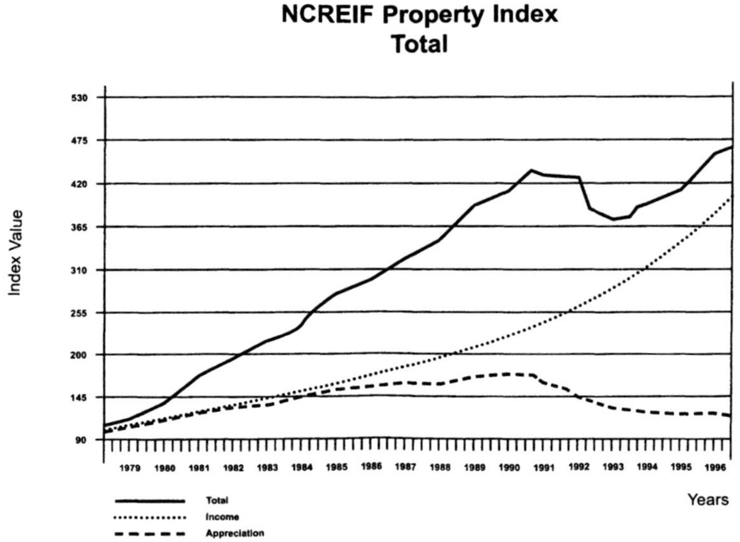

---

15 *The Russell-NCREIF Real Estate Performance Report*, Third Quarter 1992 Results, at p.3.

16 *The NCREIF Property Index, Detailed Quarterly Performance Report*, Second Quarter 1996, Section I, *Index and Market, Total Index Values*, Page 2, 30 June 1996.

Although income from NCREIF Index properties continued to increase at a relatively constant rate for the period, the drop-off of appreciation through 1993 until appreciation stabilized indicates that the American commercial real estate market in this period experienced a collapse independently of, and despite the consistent rise in income. Also, as noted by Professor White, the results were dramatically worse in the regions of the country affected by more general economic recessions, as they occurred, beginning in the Southwest and continuing to the East, Mid-Atlantic, Northeast, Midwest and finally the West.

The capitalized value of property income was, and remains the most important and reliable component of real estate valuation. It is interesting to note that while Index values dropped, the market appeared to ignore income for valuation purposes, even though income is the most important component for such valuation. Conversely, when regulatory authorities began to develop their own valuation methods for purposes of examinations, they relied almost exclusively on capitalized income, even for real estate that produced no current income. To do this, the regulators calculated the present value of future sales at current 'depressed values', (determined by reference to the then rapidly falling rate and incidence of comparable sales and values) deducting the present value of future property burdens, such as taxes, insurance, maintenance costs, assessments from utility and improvement districts, et cetera.

The results, in many cases, produced 'negative values'. The foregoing information foreshadows more radically and progressively depressive valuations for properties which lacked capitalized current income as a component of valuation, i.e. real estate assets such as those comprising real estate collateral for bank and S&L portfolios, for the same period, and which, by their nature were more illiquid, and therefore more difficult to value by reference to comparables to the extent that comparables then existed. The collapse of real estate values illustrated in this section, correlate directly to the foundation for values at the beginning of the period as discussed in Part One, and to the subsequent collapse of values as to be explored in Part Three.

IV. REAL ESTATE APPRAISALS

The aggressive lending practices of banks and thrift institutions were generally based on prevailing practices involving real estate appraisals. The underlying assumption throughout growing real estate markets in the early 1980s was that commercial real estate collateral values would continue to increase and demand for such properties would remain robust. The US banking and S&L regulations generally required (and still require) appraisals on each parcel of real property which becomes the subject of a loan or investment. During the 1980s, however, real estate appraisals were subject to only infrequent and inconsistent regulation by the federal and State banking and thrift authorities, and a growing number of real estate loans were made by banks and thrift institutions based on relatively informal appraisals.[17] In the early 1980s, appraisals were prepared by many different types of individuals, collectively referred to as 'appraisers'. Many appraisers were independent. Some appraisers were licensed; some were not licensed. Some appraisers were experienced; some not experienced.

Although most appraisers were independent of any bank or S&L for which they performed appraisals, some appraisers were hired by banks and S&Ls as employees. There were few rules governing appraisals in the early 1980s, and the appraisal industry was essentially unregulated.[18] All real estate values against which banks and S&Ls extended credit or made investments, however, were required to be supported by appraisals. Following the Garn-St. Germain Act, many S&Ls could loan up to 100 per cent of the appraised value of real estate loan collateral. The cushion of restrictive LTV ratios was abandoned.

The FMV for any parcel of real estate is typically the value at which an independent seller would be willing to sell, and an independent buyer would be willing to buy, the parcel of real estate. If there is no willing buyer and willing seller, the market value of the real estate parcel can only be established by an appraiser or appraisers based upon 'comparable values' or through calculation of present value based upon future income. To the extent there are no rules or only a few specific rules that must be followed by appraisers in establishing appraised value, the appraisal process, and given appraised values become highly subjective. One method of establishing value is through the use of comparative sales information. If a sale of a contiguous parcel of real estate sells at a certain price, this information can be an indication of value for the parcel being appraised. The comparative sales information are recognized as 'comparables'. The 'comparables' are typically the best indicators of market value for real estate under such conditions.

In an inflationary period, comparables reflexively indicate increased values for all similar properties in 'close proximity' and what is 'similar' is in the eyes of the appraiser. If banks and thrift institutions are dependent on appraised values or recent market value sales in determining the market value of any parcel of real estate for loan or investment purposes during an inflationary period, the market value of any particular parcel of real estate will rise and if sold at a higher price, will affect all values of 'similar' property

---

17 See, e.g. 'Impact of Appraisal Problems on Real Estate Lending, Mortgage Insurance, and Investment in the Secondary Market', (1986) H.R. Rep. No. 99–891, 99th Cong., 2d Sess.

18 Congress investigated the entire appraisal process and found many problems. One was the failure to have a uniform licensing requirement for appraisers. Incredibly, it was not until 1990 that uniform standards were adopted for appraisers and appraisals by the regulators of banks and S&Ls pursuant to legislation enacted in 1989, discussed *infra* in Chapter Four. Appraisals are critical to the banking and savings and loan industry. The best indication of appraised value is the market value of the appraised property as determined by a buyer and seller acting freely. Yet, if there is no standard definition of 'market value' for all lenders including banks and S&Ls, then there is a strong likelihood that 'market value' for one lender's appraiser may be totally different from 'market value' for another lender's appraiser. Furthermore, depending upon the assumptions used, the same appraiser could arrive at different 'market values'. Therefore, 'marking to market' real estate values when the market is in distress is not only a risky business, it also invites the abuses evident in the 'credit crunch' of the early 1990s.

in 'close proximity'. In other words, in inflationary times, appraised values and market values reflect and add momentum to increasing values. It is one comparable built on another, giving momentum to value inflation. Asset value inflation was transmitted through the financial statements of all US financial institutions by comparables during the early 1980s. The transmission of the value inflation spread quickly, as lenders and borrowers transacted over continuously increasing real estate appraisal values and repeatedly leveraged profits generated from these values.

As part of the deregulatory initiatives to allow thrift institutions to earn past their 'negative spread' the FHLBB, under the authority of DIDMCA, reduced the capital requirements for each S&L insured by the FSLIC from 5 per cent of assets to 3 per cent of liabilities. For every dollar of 'capital' an S&L could raise USD33 dollars of deposits. The leverage ratio was therefore 33 to 1. The higher leverage could and did lead to a 'tax-finance' driven increase in real estate asset values. With the same amount of capital, S&Ls could raise a greater dollar amount of assets. With a greater amount of deposits, an S&L could invest in a greater dollar amount of assets. With more demand for real estate assets came higher values for real estate; resulting in an inflationary push in asset values, particularly real estate values. With high leverage ratios and very little capital, S&Ls could raise large amounts of deposits and invest heavily in real estate related investments.

Thus, the financing incentives coupled with tax incentives of ERTA forced the price of real estate higher through a combination of (a) direct fundings of loans and real estate purchases by the S&Ls and (b) the indirect, more subtle effects of appraisals based on comparables. In order to remain competitive, banks also made real estate loans and funded through these loans real estate acquisitions, the values of which had been or were being affected by this finance and tax push. Through funding loans, both banks and thrift institutions earned fees and interest, and generated earnings which resulted in higher share values and increased trading activity for the shares of publicly held banks and thrift institutions; and higher dividends and higher value of the banks and thrift institutions whose shares were privately held, respectively.

Real estate values continued to rise and earnings of banks and S&Ls continued to flourish in the early 1980s as the asset portfolios of banks and S&Ls (particularly Texas institutions) increased geometrically through leverage ratios and real estate asset value inflation. For those banks and S&Ls that did not jump wholesale into speculative real estate lending activities, their stock values, earnings and market value decreased relative to competitor institutions. In order to generate continued earnings, new real estate loans and investments were made by banks and S&Ls to 'new entry developers' (i.e. those developers with little or no history in the development business). Real estate projects were increasingly financed and developed through this process, based on projections of continued asset value inflation and continued market liquidity, supported by the rate of absorption in the early 1980s. Overbuilding and asset value inflation became the norm for most US regional real estate markets, and virtually all banks and S&Ls participated in some manner in this competitive speculation.

V. APPRAISAL METHODS AND STANDARDS

In the early 1980s, there were three basic methods of valuation used by appraisers: (1) 'replacement cost', (2) 'income basis evaluation'; and (3) 'existing market conditions or comparables'. Of the three methods, the best indication of real property market value is what a buyer would agree to pay for the particular parcel of real property *or a comparable piece of real property*. In other words, the appraisals of particular parcels of real property were (and still are) greatly influenced by sales prices/market values of comparable properties. Most appraisers developed statistical data that reflected sales prices and recent appraised values of properties. In inflationary periods, the appraisals reflexively incorporated increasing prices of comparable properties in arriving at FMV. In the finance and tax driven price increases of the early 1980s, these comparables exaggerated the asset value inflation and thereby affected all real estate properties in the applicable market. Although the powers of S&Ls to make real estate loans and investments were greatly expanded by State and federal statutes and regulations, the appraisal standards applicable to S&Ls remained unchanged through the early 1980s.

The appraisal standards in force were established in FHLBB Memorandum R41 adopted by the FHLBB on 7 June 1977 as the S&L industry was primarily engaged in single-family residential mortgage lending. The FHLBB appraisal standards were totally inadequate for other commercial real estate transactions, and therefore the quality and reliability of appraisals varied significantly between appraisers.[19]

In addition, real estate appraisals were heavily relied upon by banking and S&L personnel and required by regulation during the 1970s and 1980s, but there were virtually no qualification standards as to who could perform such appraisals. Although many appraisers were licensed as members of organizations such as the American Institute of Real Estate Appraisers or the Society of Real Estate Appraisers, many appraisers did not obtain licenses at all. The failure to implement and enforce qualification standards for appraisers rendered the quality and reliability of appraisals inconsistent at best. Nonetheless, real estate appraisals were heavily relied upon by banks and thrift institutions in the decision-making process for granting loans or confirming asset/collateral prices and in turn, appraisal values became 'swept up' in the reflexive, upward spiraling market of real estate.

VI. APPRAISALS AFFECTING APPRAISALS

Many real estate appraisals were greatly affected by previous appraisals conducted on the same property or comparable properties. The effects of

---

[19] See, e.g. US House Committee on Government Operations, 'Impact of Faulty and Fraudulent Real Estate Appraisals on Federally Insured Financial Institutions and Regulated Agencies of the Federal Government: Hearings', 99th Cong., 1st Sess. (1985).

previous appraisals on current appraisals were analogous to the effects of compounding interest. The elements of a free market based on supply and demand became heavily influenced by reflexive and increasing real estate appraisal values, that generated the impetus for speculative real estate market valuation 'bubbles' throughout regions of the United States. The widespread availability of financing and tax incentives similarly fueled the 'compounding appraisal' value effect and consequential speculative growth of real estate price bubbles. In addition, many banks and S&Ls relied upon 'in-house appraisers' to evaluate real estate values, which generally reported to the very department of the institution that was making the loans. In many such cases, the 'in-house appraiser' became unduly influenced by the 'hot real estate market', perceptions of 'unending inflation' and constant pressures of senior management to generate earnings through loan origination fees. This corrupted the very notion of 'appraiser independence' and resulted in serious conflicts of interest regarding valuation on a systemic basis throughout the bank and thrift industries.

VII. CONCLUDING NOTE: THE PRACTICE OF NON-RECOURSE FINANCING

The favorable tax treatment afforded to real estate acquisitions and dispositions under ERTA fueled enormous speculative growth in the real estate market during 1981–1985. One provision of the then-existing federal tax code authorized non-recourse financing to be spread among all partners or joint venturers in a given real estate project, thereby creating a tax basis in the interest of that partner or joint venturer. This tax basis allowed the benefits of accelerated depreciation provided by ERTA, reviewed in Chapter Two, to pass through to all the partners or joint venturers on a pro rata basis. Conversely, recourse financing was treated quite unfavorably in comparison. Thus, thrift institutions generally agreed to such non-recourse provisions in real estate financings to remain competitive, which fueled a real property acquisition boom and sustained asset value inflation during the early 1980s. The Garn-St. Germain Act authorized the '100 per cent' financing practices by federally-chartered S&Ls, and many State laws (allowing State-chartered S&Ls to conduct the same activities otherwise permitted of federally-chartered S&Ls) authorized State-chartered S&Ls to engage in '100 per cent' financings. The '100 per cent' financings authorized S&Ls to advance up to 100 per cent of appraised value (i.e, LTV ratio of 100 per cent). By reason of this tax provision, perverse incentives existed for borrowers to contract for the purchase of a real estate project, negotiate a period of six months to close, obtain a new legitimate appraisal on the project from a qualified appraiser, and borrow from the S&L an amount in excess of the purchase price because the appraised value for the project would then exceed the purchase price. The borrower could therefore retain the excess loan proceeds and invest them in another project as equity. These practices and others similarly situated accelerated real estate asset value inflation.

Part III
Asset Value Deflation: Supervisory and Legislative Reregulation

Introductory Note

The legislation, deregulation and rule-making of the early 1980s that supported the adoption of DDMCA and Garn-St. Germain, fueling asset value inflation, stopped in the mid 1980s. Rule-making and regulation slowly resumed, with a different emphasis: 'reregulation'. Reregulation precipitated asset value deflation. This message is the focal point of Part Three.

In 1985, the thrift industry problems returned to the public medium. The General Accounting Office (GAO), charged under the 1982 Garn-St. Germain legislation to monitor the net worth certificate program, audited the FSLIC's annual report and the audits revealed that the range of mechanisms for deferring the payments of deposit insurance, such as net worth certificates, FSLIC guarantees of payments of insurance in supervisory mergers, and Federal Home Loan Bank advances, rendered determinations of the solvency of the FSLIC much more difficult.[1]

The GAO Report was the first in a series of reports in 1986 that repeatedly criticized the FHLBB initiatives in resolving distressed or failed institutions, from the net worth maintenance programs to the forbearance agreements.[2] Thus, year-end 1985 marked the beginning of the second phase of the thrift industry crisis, and the primary factor was no longer interest-rate mismatch dilemmas but rather asset quality problems, particularly real estate.

The problems were particularly evident in Texas, where the collapse of oil prices in 1985 and 1986 resulted in a cycle of downward spiraling real estate values, facilitated by tax legislation which largely reversed the incentives enacted under the ERTA in 1981. The collapse in real estate prices predictably caused real estate lending portfolios to deteriorate, particularly those of thrift institutions. Similar problems evolved in other oil-producing States, such as Oklahoma and Louisiana, as well as Florida and California. These States had all amended their thrift industry laws to extend to thrift institutions chartered under State laws a new range of powers even broader than those extended to federally-chartered thrift institutions under the Garn-St.

1 See GAO, 'Examination of the Federal Savings and Loan Insurance Corporation's Financial Statements For the Years Ended December 31, 1984 and 1983' (1985).

2 See GAO, 'Thrift Industry: Forbearance For Troubled Institutions 1982–1986' (1987); GAO, 'Thrift Industry: Cost to FSLIC of Delaying Action on Insolvent Savings Associations', (1986): GAO, Thrift Industry: 'Net Worth and Income Capital Certificates' (1986).

Germain Act. In Texas the real estate market difficulties weakened the commercial banking industry and the thrift industry alike, and eventually resulted in a number of FDIC and FSLIC rescue operations.

The FHLBB issued warnings that the FSLIC was indeed insolvent and in need of recapitalization to resolve problems in the thrift industry.[3] The FHLBB Board Members consistently and publicly expressed their reservations about the warnings, and the thrift industry consistently, publicly, and officially downplayed the problems.[4] The thrift industry's objective was apparently to block congressional funding of the FSLIC and thereby deny the FHLBB the authority to facilitate mergers and acquisitions of smaller thrift institutions by larger ones or of thrift institutions in general by commercial banks.[5]

As the thrift industry crisis and need for FSLIC recapitalization became significant political issues, the Reagan Administration and Fed were nonetheless generally preoccupied with addressing international debate over the appreciation of the dollar, which was essentially undermining the competitiveness of US manufacturing sectors in the international trade markets and creating serious imbalances between global and currency blocs.

The unprecedented international economic imbalances and appreciating dollar were symptoms of both incompatible national monetary and fiscal policies, but also of a world monetary system without direction and stability. By the mid-1980s, there was little support for the notion that floating exchange rates were inherently beneficial, given the imbalances caused by the appreciating dollar.

The Reagan Administration's support for floating exchange rates was the necessary component of its domestic monetarist approach, in that the theoretical insulation of floating rates from foreign economic developments, since exchange rates were postulated to adjust quickly and autonomously to levels which reflected the new comparative economic fundamentals under the monetarist doctrine, released the Administration to utilize purely domestic monetary operations, and sustain the 'benign neglect' approach to exchange rate policy.[6] The monetarist models were universally determined to have failed the challenge, and the prime recognition was that the short-term behaviour of floating exchange rates was not determined by current account deficits, but rather by capital account flows, which reflect the differentiating views of a multitude of investors.[7]

The Reagan Administration and the Fed soon realized that the exchange rate policy of benign neglect was causing intolerable damage to US manufacturing and agriculture sectors, and that such damage had its due effect on other sectors in the economy. The dollar had soared beyond all levels that the

---

3 See, e.g., Nina Easton and Barlett Naylor, 'At Last, Relief is in Sight for the Nation's S&L Fund', Am. Banker, 27 May 1986, at p.17.

4 See, e.g., Nina Easton and Bartlett Naylor, 'Thrift Group Attacks FSLIC Bailout: But US League Opposition to Treasury Plan Faces Uphill Battle', Am. Banker, 15 December 1986, at p.2.

5 *Ibid.*

6 See S. Solomon, *The Confidence Game: How Unelected Central Bankers Are Governing the Changed World Economy* (Simon & Schuster, 1995), at p.294.

7 See, e.g., Peter B. Kenen, *Managing Exchange Rates*, Royal Institute of International Affairs (Council on Foreign Relations Press, New York, 1988), at p.8.

Fed and Treasury believed possible on the strength of global capital inflows to the US to sustain federal deficits, and that by any reasonable measure of the underlying international competitiveness of the US economy, the dollar had to come down.[8]

The appreciation of the dollar also was a problem for the entire world. After the Bretton Woods system disintegrated in the early 1970s, the dollar remained the primary monetary medium for international finance and commerce. The dollar exchange rate was the most important pricing determinant for allocating investments among nations, and for influencing inflation, growth and employment. The dramatic appreciation of the dollar from 1980 onward affected other nations like a 'third oil shock'.[9]

The same borrowed capital inflows that caused dollar appreciation and economic stimulus had as its counterpart the capital outflows from other nations and economic recession, and generated inflation through currency depreciation. The international capital flows into the dollar effectively imposed a set of policy limitations that compelled foreign governments to maintain domestic interest rates higher than otherwise desired, which exported the US economic conditions around the world.

The appreciating dollar caused foreign governments to tighten monetary and fiscal policies that were already tightened in response to the inflationary pressures generated by the second oil price shock of 1978–1979. In the early 1980s, Japan and Germany tightened fiscal policy as the Reagan Administration expanded budget deficits. The enormous fiscal policy clash was a central force behind the appreciating dollar and world economic imbalances.[10] Thus, democratic world leaders pressed the Reagan Administration for joint intervention to depreciate the dollar and control expanding budget deficits, but the Administration adhered to the concept of benign neglect.

Shortly after taking office in 1981, the Reagan Administration announced a non-intervention policy to affect the exchange rate value of the dollar – the Treasury Department would intervene only in exceptional circumstances to address disorderly market volatility.

The Administration advocated that dollar appreciation was not the problem of the United States, and that government intervention in floating exchange markets violated the monetarist doctrine and the concept of deregulation, respectively.[11] From 1981 through January 1985, the Treasury Department intervened in the currency markets on a minimal basis, at a fraction of the cost incurred by foreign central banks that actively intervened against the dollar.[12] The international debate over the appreciating dollar was the same international burden-sharing struggle that ensued during the LDC Debt Crisis resolution, between markets and ad hoc policy coordination

8 See generally Yoichi Funabashi, *Managing the Dollar: From the Plaza to the Louvre* (Institute for International Economics, Washington, D.C., 1989).

9 See *Confidence Game, supra* note 6, at pp.277–278.

10 See generally *C. Fred Bergsten, 'Economic Imbalances and World Politics'*, Foreign *Affairs*, Spring 1987.

11 See *Confidence Game, supra* note 7, at p.287.

12 See generally I.M. Destler & Henning C. Randall, *Dollar Politics* (Institute for International Economics, Washing, D.C., 1989), at p.23.

among nations. The main observation, however, is that the foreign nations suffered the most severe consequences of the misaligned dollar, even before the US itself. Beyond the US, the powerful economic effects of currency exchange rate values required immediate policy responses.[13]

For most foreign central banks, the exchange rate was the most important operational guidance for conducting monetary policy (raising or lowering interest rates). The more powerful central banks that normally did not target exchange rates, such as the Bundesbank and the Bank of Japan, were often forced to adjust their monetary policies given dramatic changes in the dollar exchange rate. In contrast, the Fed was clearly preempted from adjusting monetary policy in response to the moving dollar exchange rate, and the FOMC generally did not consider the exchange rate to be a dominant factor in directing monetary policy. The end result was that the dollar generally reacted to domestically oriented shifts in monetary policy, while other nations generally react to the dollars.[14]

By 1985, the only question was how fast and how hard the dollar would land, and these questions would be dictated by global currency markets. The Treasury Department returned to direct interventions in the foreign exchange markets, and initiated a series of policy consultations with the Fed to create a united front against the appreciating dollar. The use of pressure by the Executive Branch to influence monetary policy through exchange rate policy underscored federal law and custom which required the Fed to accept that the President and Secretary of the Treasury had primary responsibility for exchange rate policy (managing the international value of the dollar) and the Fed was obliged to assist the Executive Branch in this respect, even if that meant altering monetary policy.[15] As the dollar continued to appreciate in late summer 1985, the Treasury Department triggered an aggressive and open effort to bring down the dollar.

The visible result of this campaign was the 'Plaza Accord' of 22 September 1985, where the G-5 nations (US, Germany, Japan, France, and Britain) agreed to coordinate efforts to address exchange rate imbalances. The Plaza Accord effectively prevented the Fed from any near-term tightening of monetary policy, as raising interest rates would cause the dollar to appreciate higher in violation of the text and spirit of the Plaza Accord.[16]

This agreement represented the most aggressive and persistent effort towards coordinated intervention to influence exchange rates since the breakdown of the Bretton Woods system.[17] It further portrayed an attempt to regain at least some official control over exchange rates, and the primary institution in this respect was the Treasury, not the Fed.

---

13 See *Confidence Game*, *supra* note 6, at p.289.

14 *Ibid.*

15 See generally, Stephen Marris, *Deficits and the Dollar: The World Economy at Risk* (Institute for International Economics, Washington, D.C., 1985).

16 See W. Greider, *The Secrets of the Temple: How the Federal Reserve Runs the Country* (1987), at pp.684–687.

17 See P. Volker and T. Gyohten, *Changing Fortunes: The World's Money and the Threat to American Leadership* (1992) at pp.228–229.

The Plaza Agreement set G-5 exchange rate policy and supported it with intervention. In order to be successful, however, official intervention could not directly conflict with monetary policy, as changes in domestic interest rates would normally have a significant effect on the impact of exchange rate transactions.[18]

The Plaza Accord resulted in sustained efforts to depreciate the dollar, and set the stage for international reform of exchange rate policy, which altered power relationships among governments and within governments at the same time. The Fed was effectively forced to surrender a significant degree of independence to establish and implement domestic monetary policy in lieu of Executive Branch exchange rate intervention. If the leading governments agreed to coordinate and maintain stable exchange rates, the Fed and other central banks could no longer independently establish interest rates or restrict money supply growth to satisfy their own objectives.

The paradox was that in order to establish a fixed value for the 'domestic dollar' (by eliminating inflation) the Fed had to permit the destabilizing appreciation of the 'international dollar' (as an exchange rate). The exchange rate reforms initiated by the Treasury Department thereby forced the Fed to balance its objectives and manage the money supply so that the domestic dollar was not distorted at the expense of the international dollar. This effectively forced the Fed to coordinate monetary policy more closely with the fiscal policy set by the elected government. In other words, the Fed's decisions would have to harmonize with the broader economic goals of the elected political leaders, by implicitly losing a significant degree of independence exercised during 1979–1982 to eliminate inflation.[19]

In summary, one may review this history and reach the conclusion that whatever was fundamentally wrong with the US economy by late 1985 had not been fixed by the Fed's monetary policies or the Reagan Administration's supply side economics. In many ways, these policies and concepts actually compounded the underlying problems. The public was told, and evidently believed, that the Fed had saved the US economy, when in truth the Fed arguably guided the economy into greater weakness and sustained contraction. The Fed and Reagan Administration policies imposed significant damage on many economic sectors and by implication the global economy through contagion processes, and the US public at large, but generally evaded questions that necessarily arose from their policies.

---

18 The objectives for conducting monetary policy are not necessarily framed in terms of the amount of foreign exchange intervention. If that intervention either enlarged or contracted the monetary base, the central bank would normally offset it by domestic monetary policy actions. This is called 'sterilized' intervention, as the initial purchase of foreign exchange is offset by the central bank by the sale of another asset, such as Treasury bills, so that monetary reserves and monetary policy remain unchanged by the intervention. Conversely, unsterlized intervention means that the central bank, when purchasing or selling foreign currency, permits the resulting change in its assets to work its way through to a change in the money supply and interest rates. For instance, if the Fed created dollars to purchase yen, those dollars would, as in any open market purchase, increase bank reserves and ultimately the amount of money in circulation by some multiple of that reserve increase; interest rates would tend to decline, other things being equal.

19 See Greider, *supra* note 16, at pp.688–690.

The Fed's concern with the depreciating dollar was based on the concept that rapid dollar depreciation could trigger inflationary expectations, and necessitate even further monetary tightening (higher interest rates) to mitigate those expectations.

The Plaza Agreement resulted in rapid dollar decline: by January 1986 the dollar declined sharply by nearly 25 per cent from its peak in 1985.[20] By the beginning of 1986, the organized effort to realign exchange rates under the Plaza Agreement had run its course. The coordinated international efforts to encourage dollar depreciation through direct intervention in the foreign exchange markets all but ceased.

In 1986, the international financial authorities focused on the need to sustain the upward momentum of the global economy. Despite the dollar depreciation, the enormous US trade and current account deficits continued to rise into 1986. The Fed reduced the discount rate by 1 per cent in February 1986, and the exchange markets did not react violently, as the dollar had already depreciated by nearly 25 per cent from September 1985 – January 1986.[21] The rapid dollar depreciation did not result in inflationary expectations, however, as the inflation rate dropped to little more than 1 per cent in 1986 as oil prices collapsed.

By 1987, however, the American trade and balance of payments *deficits* reached the greatest levels in history, reflecting the unprecedented slide of the American dollar. The 1987 American trade balance reached a negative UDS159.49 billion. The American trade deficit reached USD50.3 billion. On 17 January 1985, 'An attack on sterling leads to an emergency G-5 meeting in Washington, which agrees that the dollar is 'grossly overvalued' and that this warrants 'concerted action'.[22] On 5 February 1985, the 'Chairman Volcker expresses concern to Congress that the world's largest and richest economy might soon become the world's largest debtor (as does indeed occur in 1986)'.[23] On 3 September 1986, 'in a single day, the dollar falls by more than 4 per cent, the largest daily drop since flotation began'.[24] On 21 and 22 February 1987, at the meeting of the G-7 finance ministers at the Louvre in Paris, 'they declare that the dollar has fallen far enough and agree to cooperate in stabilizing it ... The United States promised to reduce its government deficits from 3.9 per cent of GNP in 1987 to 2.3 per cent GNP in 1988 by cutting public spending.'[25] On 17 April 1987, at the annual meeting of the OECD finance ministers, 'Baker (then American Secretary of the Treasury

---

20 See Volker, *supra* note 17, at p.246.

21 The greater interest in achieving exchange rate stability was represented at the G-5 meeting of finance ministers at the Louvre Palace in Paris in February 1987. The communiqué reached there set precise exchange rate ranges around agreed upon but not publicly acknowledged exchange rate levels between the dollar and other G-5 currencies, and those ranges would be defended by intervention and other measures. The exchange rate ranges soon needed to be adjusted, however, with respect to the yen and thereafter with the stock market crash in October 1987.

22 See Volcker, *supra* note 17, at p.356.

23 *Ibid.*

24 *Ibid.* at p.357.

25 *Ibid.* at p.358.

James Baker) declares that a US trade deficit of USD100 billion is not politically sustainable'.[26]

America appeared to be due for a 'change in macroeconomic policies'. The country had accumulated unsustainable fiscal and current account balances; had become heavily reliant on volatile short-term external financing, and have been embodied in a defense of an exchange rate that was out of line with underlying fundamentals (leading to abrupt corrections in asset prices and creating a boom and bust cycle). These are precisely the conditions leading to systemic finance crises in *emerging economies*, later recognized by the G-10 Working Party on Financial Stability in Emerging Market Economies in 1997.[27]

---

[26] *Ibid*. at p.357.

[27] 27. See Group of Ten, *Financial Stability in Emerging Countries: A Strategy for the Foundation, Adoption and Implementation of Sound Principles and Practices to Strengthen Financial Systems* (April 1997). See also Group of Seven, *Report of G7 Finance Ministers to Kölm Economic Summit* (18–20 June 1999).

7. The Immediate Post-Deregulatory Years (with summary observations)

I. INTRODUCTION

The years immediately following the passage of the Garn-St. Germain Act were characterized by legislative and deregulatory stalemate for most purposes. No significant instances of banking legislation were enacted after the Garn-St. Germain Act, and the major deregulatory reforms initiated by FHLBB and the banking agencies largely occurred in the early 1980s. As previously reviewed in Part Two, the banking agencies pressed on with the development of capital adequacy requirements and were otherwise preoccupied with fallout of the LDC Debt Crisis. In addition, significant litigation ensued between the banking and securities industries over newly authorized securities activities for banks and bank holding companies. The thrift industry crisis, while continuing to grow under the oversight of FHLBB, was largely obscured from public view. The more important policy ramifications occurred with respect to fallout from the Fed's vigorous anti-inflationary monetary policies implemented prior to year-end 1982.

The interconnection between the Fed's tightening of monetary policy and the Reagan Administration's expansion of fiscal policy was one of policy conflict, the fallout of which dramatically affected the US economy and engendered a sustained appreciation of the dollar. The policy conflicts would have a dramatic effect on the banking and thrift industries because of the forces they unleashed, in terms of the rapidly expanding federal deficit, the sustained period of high real interest rates and the sustained appreciation of the dollar.

This chapter considers and evaluates these post deregulatory matters.

II. MONETARY POLICY AND THE END OF INFLATION

As reviewed in Parts One and Two, the Federal Reserve imposed the strictest monetary discipline ever attempted in US history over late 1979–1982, and generally succeeded in driving price inflation from the US economy. The recession caused by the strict monetary discipline, however, was generally far worse than expected. By abruptly reversing policies and abandoning the monetarist operating technique, the Fed took the US economy to the brink of devastation. The claims of citizens and politicians regarding the impact of the recession did not serve as guidance for monetary policy, but rather guidance from the financial markets, particularly money center banks, dominated the monetary policy sphere.[1] The Fed officials undoubtedly misjudged the severity of the US and global economic trauma caused by anti-inflationary monetary policy. The stringent monetary policy depressed the US economy in 1982 far more than the Fed predicted or anticipated (about five percentage points below its own forecast for nominal GNP).[2] The Fed either knowingly or unwittingly went to the extremes in pursuit of monetary discipline.[3] By October 1982, given the partial abandonment of the monetarist operating technique, the Fed generally reversed course and pumped liquidity into the financial system in order to restart the economy and avert additional banking failures under the strain of the LDC Debt Crisis.[4] The immediate result was recovery of profits for financial institutions as financial markets, particularly

---

1 Of course, there were no disinterested players in the monetary policy sphere. The bond markets and financial institutions representing them collectively and implicitly instructed the Fed to squeeze the real economy tighter to further enhance the value of financial assets and resolve inflationary expectations. The money center banks advising the Fed through the Federal Advisory Council did not necessarily advocate policies in the national interest but injurious to themselves, and much guidance issued by the Council and otherwise available from the banking sector was certainly self-interested to a significant degree. The course decided by the Fed clearly enhanced some political and financial interests while seriously injuring others. Thus, the central fallacy inherent in the notion of 'central bank independence', as advocated by the Fed, was the notion that monetary policy was disinterested and separate from politics in a way that other government policies were not. Thus, the ancillary distortion surrounding the notion of 'central bank independence' was the notion that some political interests – the financial markets, banks, and investors – were appropriate guides to the Fed in deciding the proper course for monetary policy, and others were not.

2 See S. Solomon, *Confidence Game: How Unelected Central Bankers Are Governing the Changed World Economy* (Simon & Schuster, 1995), at p.161.

3 See W. Greider, *Secrets of the Temple: How the Federal Reserve Runs the Country* (Touchstone Books, 1988), at p.530.

4 By October 1982, the Fed abandoned the monetarist operating system in a public sense. At the October 1982 FOMC meeting, the FOMC determined that M-1 was surging explosively but given the fragile state of the banking system, the Fed disregarded the monetary aggregates and continued to push interest rates lower. The move was justified by technical explanations, namely the expected distortion of M-1 due to the proliferation of NOW accounts following DIDMCA. In the FOMC Directive, the disregard for M-1 was described as only temporary, but historical review indicates that the FOMC implicitly knew that the monetarist operating technique and the accompanying self-imposed restraint was forever abandoned. Although the FOMC minutes were normally not released to the public for six weeks, in this case they were promptly leaked to the press, and three days later the Fed emphasized the move by reducing the discount rate again. The money center banks reduced their prime rate to the lowest level in two years. The powerful stimulus of lower interest rates ensured that the economic contraction was about to end, and the Reagan Administration for the most part left the Fed alone. Thus, the end of 1982 largely resulted in the disintegration of monetarism and wholehearted pursuit of Friedman economics. No longer was there a 'single guide' to monetary policy, but the discount rate was implicitly the key indicator of monetary policy decisions.

the stock market, rallied and continued to appreciate until Black Monday, the 19 October 1987 stock market crash.[5]

The celebratory reaction of the financial markets represented a critical restoration of credibility in the Fed and Chairman Volcker. The prevailing view was that Volcker was responsible for much of the financial successes perceived to have occurred under the first Reagan Administration, and had little to do with the original 'supply side' economics perpetrated by the Administration.[6] The Fed thereafter embarked on the most aggressive sustained expansion of money supply in history, and over the next nine months the M-1 aggregate accelerated explosively: from July 1982 – March 1983, the money supply expanded at an equivalent annual growth rate of 15 per cent, more than twice the Fed's official money supply growth targets.[7]

The Fed engaged in seven interest rate reductions over a five-month period, and by December 1982 the discount rate declined to 8.5 per cent. Thereafter, notwithstanding the continuing strains on the economy, the Fed discontinued further easing, and kept the discount rate essentially frozen for the next 15 months until 1984.[8] By early 1983, the LDC Debt Crisis preoccupied Congress and the Fed, which largely focused efforts on expanding influence and stabilizing the precarious position of the money center banks and the process of debt rescheduling for LDC nations that inevitably followed from 1983 onward.[9]

III. MONETARY AND FISCAL POLICY CONFLICT

The Fed desired to maintain progressive economic growth without a resurgence of inflation during this period, but the Reagan Administration pursued fiscal stimulus through deficit spending, particularly in connection with the defense industry. The contradictory elements present in the Reagan Administration's policies since 1981 revealed themselves once again, and the economic growth was therefore largely fueled by tax cuts and fiscal deficit spending. If the Fed simply accommodated fiscal stimulus, it would possibly result in resurgence of price inflation. If the Fed restrained the money supply and US economy once again, however, it could likely preclude economic growth.

The Fed was therefore caught in a policy struggle with the Reagan Administration during the early 1980s. Congress enacted a series of secondary tax increases and additional spending cuts during this period, but fiscal policy generally remained intent on generating further enormous annual fiscal deficits.[10] Although separate functions, monetary policy was subject to direct

---

5 See *Confidence Game*, *supra* note 2, at p.162.
6 *Ibid.* at p.163.
7 See Greider, *supra* note 3, at p.538.
8 *Ibid.* at pp.544-545.
9 *Ibid.* at pp.545-555.
10 By 1983, the federal budget deficit surpassed USD200 billion or nearly 5.6 per cent of GNP.

pressures from fiscal policy in part because the Fed had a customary and quasi-legal obligation to assist the Treasury Department in borrowing money.[11] As larger fiscal deficits forced the Treasury Department to increase borrowings in the early 1980s, however, the pressure on the Fed to accommodate the larger debt issues grew more intense. If the Fed refused to provide sufficient liquidity, the US Government borrowings could squeeze the supply of available credit in the private economy, interest rates would sharply increase, and private borrowings would diminish and economic growth would suffer.[12]

In the extreme, if the Fed was too accommodative in the process, inaction could 'monetize the debt', a circular notion wherein the Fed essentially bailed out the Treasury by permissively allowing inflation of the dollar, and this generally occurred in the early 1980s.[13]

Although the Fed was obligated to support the orderly sale of new Treasury debt issues, the Fed would not deliberately retard economic growth and generate inflationary expectations in pursuit of this objective. The Fed purportedly warned Congress in the early 1980s to take corrective action on the deficit spending, and the Fed resolved not to yield to the cumulative pressures of the growing debt. Congress and the Reagan Administration could not count on the Fed to intentionally monetize the debt and bail them out of their fiscal deficits. Instead, the Fed 'compromised' and held domestic interest rates at a high level in the midst of economic recovery. This unprecedented strategy satisfied the Fed's obligation to support Treasury debt issues. If interest rates were sustained at high enough levels, the Treasury would have no problems issuing new government debt securities because

---

11 When the Treasury sold government bonds, borrowing to finance federal deficits, the financial markets had to absorb the new debt issues, or else the creditworthiness of the federal Government could come into question. The Fed's monetary officials were responsible for insuring 'orderly markets' for government securities, and they regularly coordinated with Treasury officials when large new debt offerings were made so the government bonds would be sold quickly and interest rates would not be detrimentally affected. The Fed could generally ensure successful Treasury offerings by pumping sufficient liquidity into the banking system to purchase the debt issues and still remain able to serve other banking needs.

12 The relationship between money creation and government debt support was the principal reason behind the Fed reluctantly accepting a passive role in supporting the federal Government borrowings during World War II. The Fed expanded money supply to ensure that Treasury could sell enormous debt offerings to finance the war efforts, and interest rates were not allowed to rise above 2 per cent. The famous Treasury-Fed Accord of 1951 released the Fed from its subordinate status, but the Fed nonetheless retained the fundamental obligation to ensure that the government could market its debt offerings. See Greider, *supra* note 3, at p.559.

13 The Treasury borrowed money from the private sector by selling new Treasury notes and bonds. The Fed then diluted the value of this debt by purchasing old Treasury notes and bonds from the private sector and paying for them with newly created money. The Fed, in effect, held more and more Treasury debt instruments in its own clandestine portfolio, and the result was an expanded money supply and potential inflationary expectations. Although no government would openly pursue this policy, and the Fed did not consciously monetize Treasury debt holdings, but the process could, and did, occur in a far more gradual and ambiguous manner. During the early 1980s, deficit-driven inflation occurred in approximately this manner.

the higher returns available in the US financial markets would attract global capital to purchase new debt issues. The expanding debt required to finance the Reagan Administration's enormous deficits would be absorbed by foreign governments and financial institutions (particularly those of Japan), and the world's largest creditor nation thereby became the largest debtor nation very quickly.[14] The cost of this compromise was that real interest rates remained at artificially high levels when under normal conditions the reduced inflation would generate downward pressure on interest rates. The Fed engaged in a 'dual strategy' to maintain high real interest rates to attract foreign capital to absorb Treasury debt offerings and sustain the Reagan Administration fiscal deficits, and much of this capital came from Japan.

IV. THE REAL INTEREST RATE DILEMMA

The bizarre conflict between monetary policy and fiscal policy generated extraordinary real interest rates that did not reflect the macroeconomic conditions of the US economy, but attracted ample capital to finance the expanding budget deficit.[15] This scenario was certainly not explained as 'government policy', and it was widely understood that nominal interest rates were declining gradually from their peaks in 1981 and 1982. The actual consequences for the US economy were quite the opposite, however, because real interest rates (the true measure of the cost of money) were not falling at all. In other words, nominal interest rates were not falling as fast as price inflation, and the difference implied that the real return for 'credit providers' (lending institutions) increased dramatically, and the bond markets and money center banks flourished.[16]

In 1983, the nominal interest rates were deliberately kept from subsiding in proportion with the decline in price inflation by Fed monetary policy, and real interest rates increased to higher levels than even the extraordinary levels reached in 1981–1982 when the Fed was actively depressing the economy to combat inflation.[17] Thus, the increasingly enormous Treasury debt issues were generally purchased by foreign institutions, at the expense of unfavorable borrowing terms imposed on the US economy (high interest rates).

By March 1983, the discount rate remained fixed at 8.5 per cent, the same level as in December 1982, and the FOMC rejected numerous requests by regional Federal Reserve Banks to lower the discount rate. In rejecting the Federal Reserve Bank requests, the Fed effectively defined the new strategy of countering the economic stimulus generated by the fiscal deficits from Congress and the Reagan Administration. The high interest rates would

---

14 See *Confidence Game*, *supra* note 2, at p.167.

15 See Greider, *supra* note 3, at p.561.

16 See, e.g., Henry Kaufman, *Interest Rates, the Markets, and the New Financial Order* (1986).

17 See, e.g. Oliver J. Blanchard and Lawrence H. Summers, 'Perspectives on High World Real Interest Rates', (1984) *Brookings Papers on Economic Activity*, 2.

attract foreign investors for Treasury debt financing, but those rates also held back economic recovery. The Fed intended to restrain growth and keep the US economy from reaching full capacity and full employment.[18]

In 1983, fiscal stimulus was quite active, and the Fed permitted significant growth in the money supply, resulting in increased economic activity. The FOMC decided to raise interest rates in May 1983, however, notwithstanding clear divisions in the FOMC.[19] The modest tightening caused swift response in the money markets in terms of increasing interest rates, but the economic recovery continued explosively. The Reagan Administration economic revival was powered by government borrowings, however, and the US government's debt burden was expanding much faster than real economic growth.[20] The concept of 'supply-side' economics was revealed, as foreign nations and institutions supplied most of the capital to finance government borrowings and economic stimulus.[21]

V. BEGINNINGS OF DOLLAR APPRECIATION

The massive demand for US financial assets initiated a cycle of dollar appreciation during 1983 in response to high foreign demand for dollar-denominated Treasury debt securities, and the competitive export positions of certain US economic sectors in international markets were gradually undermined.[22] The dollar appreciation was primarily caused by sustained high interest rates generated by the Fed, and high demand for dollar-denominated financial instruments, particularly Treasury debt issues, to finance the fiscal policies of the Reagan Administration.

The only means to 'apply brakes' to the appreciating dollar was to reduce interest rates to allow foreign exchange rates to rebalance with the dollar. The Fed realized that backing off of high interest rates would effectively yield control to the expanding budget deficits. Thus, as appreciation of the dollar spread havoc throughout US export industries and generally reduced competitiveness, the Fed did little to intervene relative to the dollar.[23]

---

18 See Greider, *supra* note 3, at pp.561–565.

19 The perceived pressure on borrowing nations in the LDC Debt Crisis from increasing interest rates was a dominant factor in the dissenting votes not to tighten further. In addition, the perceived pressure on US trade sectors caused by appreciation of the dollar that would result from increasing interest rates also supported the dissenting votes.

20 See Greider, *supra* note 3, at pp.566–569.

21 See *Confidence Game*, *supra* note 2, at p.167.

22 The appreciation of the dollar was nearly as explosive in 1984, and by early 1985 the dollar appreciated to nearly 45 per cent above 1980 levels against the German Deutschmark. The strength of the economic recovery eventually ran its course in the face of generating an enormous trade deficit. The Fed nonetheless believed that backing off of high monetary targets and attempting to mitigate the situation by lowering interest rates would only jeopardize the larger goal of eliminating inflation and inflationary expectations. See P.Volcker and T. Gyohten, *Changing Fortunes: The World's Money and the Threat to American Leadership* (1992), at p.179.

23 See Greider, *supra* note 3, at pp.594–596.

The Treasury Department was responsible for formulating exchange rate policy, and the political pressure of various interest groups increased the need for government intervention or other action to depreciate the dollar. The FOMC determined that the appreciating dollar was a 'regrettable but unavoidable side effect' of the collision between monetary policy and fiscal policy. The central force driving the appreciating dollar was the Fed's determination to keep interest rates abnormally high, even higher than competing interest rates in foreign financial markets.

US financial assets paid higher interest rates, and global capital sought out the highest return. As long as the Fed maintained such wide differentials, the global capital would naturally migrate towards the United States, where investments in dollar-denominated assets held the highest interest rates. In order to mitigate this order of affairs, the Fed would have to bring down interest rates and increase the money supply, the very thing the Fed was unwilling to do given the expanding federal deficits. If the Fed attempted to bring the dollar down with a highly expansive monetary policy, this would result in destructive consequences. The Fed argued that the only solution was to reduce the federal budget deficit.

By the end of 1983, the dollar appreciation resulted in significant political uproar from certain major US exporting corporations, increased unemployment, and 'Japan bashing', notwithstanding the fact that the appreciating dollar did not affect all economic sectors equally and detrimentally, and actually benefited certain sectors, such as the defense industry, retailing operations, and financial markets.[24]

VI. COLLISION OF MONETARY, FISCAL AND BENIGN EXCHANGE RATE POLICIES

In March 1984, the FOMC moderately tightened the money supply, and resorted to targeting the M-1 aggregate once again, permitting interest rates to freely move up and down. The FOMC move resulted in mortgage interest rates and other such rates increasing sharply, and the economic expansion was confronted with higher interest rates, much to the satisfaction of the financial markets and the detriment of the Reagan Administration.[25]

The dollar appreciated higher in international foreign exchange markets, given the increasing interest rates, which further increased the competitive damage already incurred by export sectors of the US economy. The significant effect of this tightening presented the Fed with the prospect of attempting to restimulate the economy to avert another recession.[26]

In April 1984, the Fed increased the discount rate to 9 per cent, the first such change since December 1982, following in step with the tightening that

---

[24] See Greider, *supra* note 3, at pp.597–600.
[25] See *Confidence Game, supra* note 2 at p.168.
[26] See Greider, *supra* note 3, at p.615.

the FOMC had previously authorized.[27] In May 1984, the commercial banks raised the prime rate for the second time in 6 weeks, to 12.5 per cent. The Reagan Administration reacted predictably and argued that the Fed would produce another recession if it did not immediately reverse the monetary policy actions.[28] In May 1984, the bond market had difficulty absorbing a USD4.75 billion Treasury bond issue, and the Reagan Administration publicly attributed blame to the Fed monetary policy actions for this disruption.[29] The Reagan Administration declared their 'Fed bashing' a success, however, as the Fed refrained from any further decisions to tighten money and credit until after President Reagan was reelected in November 1984. The real reason behind the Fed's monetary restraint was a much larger event, however; the potential collapse of the US banking system precipitated by crisis in the Continental Illinois National Bank.

VII. CONTINENTAL ILLINOIS NATIONAL BANK DEBACLE

The crisis involving the Continental Illinois National Bank (CINB), the seventh largest banking institution in the US at the time, was and still is the largest US bank resolution in history. The crisis focused attention on the degree and effectiveness of supervision and whether the banking agencies, particularly the OCC, could conduct legitimate risk assessment and take enforcement action against the larger and more influential banking institutions. The economic dislocation that such a large bank failure could bring about also facilitated increased scrutiny of the bank supervisory process.

The CINB resolution forced the banking agencies to recognize that large institutions could fail and that the means of dealing with such a failure were inherently controversial. The debate centered on whether large banks received or should receive differential treatment than smaller regional or local banking institutions. The policy debate of differential treatment engendered the label 'too big to fail' (TBTF).[30]

The CINB engendered a growth strategy throughout the 1970s as an aggressive commercial lending institution, and by 1981 the bank was the largest and fastest growing commercial and industrial lending institution in the United States.[31] The CINB was representative of the aggressive 'managed liabilities' lending strategy discussed *supra* in Part One, and its significant growth and utilization of leverage were lauded by industry and analysis

---

27 See *Confidence Game, supra* note 2, at p.168.

28 See Greider, *supra* note 3, at p.616.

29 *Ibid.* at p.617.

30 See FDIC, 'An Examination of the Banking Crises of the 1980s and Early 1990s', *History of the Eighties, Volume 1: Lessons for the Future* (Washington D.C., 1998), at p.236.

31 See US House Committee on Banking, Finance and Urban Affairs, Subcommittee on Financial Institutions Supervision, Regulation, and Insurance, 'Inquiry Into Continental Illinois Corp. and Continental Illinois National Bank: Hearings', 98th Cong., 2d Sess. (1984).

alike.[32] By year-end 1981, the CINB's financial profile evidenced aggressive lending strategies through high loan-to-assets ratios, origination of loans at below-market interest rates, and lending in risky and cyclical economic sectors, particularly the energy sector.[33]

The optimism surrounding CINB ended abruptly in July 1982, when the institution was diagnosed as a troubled money center lending institution during the Penn Square Bank debacle. CINB and other 'upstream' banks pressed the banking agencies to resolve the situation without implementing a deposit payoff, a course of action clearly preferred by the FRB and OCC, but Penn Square Bank's largest creditor banks refused to inject funds into or otherwise waive their claims on the bank.[34] The refusal of the larger creditor banks to participate directed that the contingent liabilities that the FDIC would have incurred in resolving the failure made every course of action unfeasible except deposit payoff. By insisting that Penn Square Bank be liquidated in 1982, with enormous losses for 'upstream' participating banks such as Continental Illinois Bank, the FDIC merely set in motion the eventual failure of confidence in the US banking system.[35]

The non-performing loans incurred by CINB and its loss of credibility in the money markets, necessary sources of funding for the managed liabilities lending strategy, encountered by CINB increased in scope during 1983, and the larger institutional investors in CINB gradually liquidated their holdings in the bank. The first quarter of 1984 revealed that CINB's non-performing loans had increased to approximately USD2.3 billion, with the majority of the increase coming from LDC loans.[36] The deterioration in CINB's condition and earnings, and its reliance on the Eurodollar markets for funding, made the institution vulnerable to an electronic run on deposits and money market investments that occurred in May 1984. The US banking agencies clearly feared a systemic disruption in US banking, and readily admitted that the CINB could not be allowed to fail without orderly intervention. The OCC, meanwhile, took the extraordinary position on behalf of the bank that it had not 'sought assistance' for the bank and that it was unaware of 'any significant changes in the bank's operations' that would serve as the basis for rumors of pending insolvency.[37] The bank run commenced in earnest, however, and by mid-May 1984, the Fed provided nearly USD3.6 billion in discount window funds to supplement lost deposit liquidity.[38]

---

[32] See *History of the Eighties, Volume 1, supra* note 30, at p.237.

[33] See *History of the Eighties, Volume 1, supra* note 31, at pp.239–240.

[34] See generally Phillip L. Zweig, *Belly Up: The Collapse of the Penn Square Bank* (1985).

[35] The Penn Square Bank debacle proved to be CINB's undoing, as approximately half of the total USD1.1 billion in problem loans with which Penn Square Bank resulted in total losses. In addition, CINB had approximately USD1.2 billion in other problem loans and more than USD1 billion exposure in LDC debtor nations that the banking agencies did not classify as problematic.

[36] See *History of the Eighties, Volume 1, supra* note 30, at pp.242–243.

[37] *Ibid.* at p.243.

[38] *Ibid.*

The largest bailout in US banking history resulted, as the FDIC injected USD4.5 billion in immediate new capital into the bank, and assumed liability for the majority of its bad loans while it searched for a new owner to take over the institution.[39] The most controversial aspect of the bailout package was that the 'government' (i.e. the FDIC) promised to protect all of CINB's depositors and general creditors from any losses, regardless of the USD100,000 limit on deposit insurance while the search for a permanent solution was devised, which established the precedent that the larger money center banks were simply 'too big to fail'.[40]

The policy implications of the CINB scenario were enormous, and clearly established that the largest money center banks would in all likelihood never be allowed to fail, whatever the eventual cost to the federal government. In hearings before the House of Representatives, the OCC even conceded that the largest multinational banks would not be allowed to fail.[41]

The critical issue raised in the ensuing debate over the bailout, however, largely focused on the concept of regulatory and supervisory forbearance that was still evident from the LDC Debt Crisis, in that the banking agencies clearly understood that CINB had enormous problems but had failed to initiate decisive action or otherwise adequately demand resolution of those

---

39 The banking agencies initially developed a temporary financial assistance package in the amount of USD2 billion, as the FDIC provided USD1.5 billion, and participated an additional USD500 million to a group of commercial banks in the form of interest-bearing subordinated notes at a variable interest rate of 100 basis points higher than that on one-year US Treasury bills. The FRB stated that it would meet any liquidity needs through discount window lending, and a group of major US banks agreed to provide more than USD5.3 billion in unsecured funding while a permanent solution was devised. *Ibid.* at p.244.

40 In July 1984 the banking agencies agreed on a complex and controversial solution consisting of the FDIC's purchase of USD4.5 billion in nonperforming or defaulted loans from CINB. The FDIC then entered into a servicing contract with CINB whereby the bank managed the loans on behalf of the FDIC. The loan transfer involved a charge-off to the bank of nearly USD1 billion, but the permanent assistance plan injected USD1 billion in capital into CINB through the FDIC's acquisition of preferred stock in the holding company, which the holding company was then obligated to downstream to CINB as equity. The CINB continued to receive liquidity support from the FRB and commercial bank unsecured lending facility, and the FDIC replaced CINB's top management and board of directors. See OCC, FRB, and FDIC, 'Permanent Assistance Program for Continental Illinois National Bank and Trust Company', PR-87-84 (26 July 1984).

41 As a practical reality, the number of protected banks was probably the top fifty or one hundred banks, as the systemic effects of one of their failures on the banking system would be regarded as generating excessive systemic risk. See Greider, *supra* note 3, at pp.623-629. The FDIC, however, could not find an acquirer for the institution after further analysis indicated that Continental Illinois Bank amassed nearly USD4 billion in troubled or non-performing loans, not the USD2.7 billion originally indicated. Thus, in late July 1984, the Continental Illinois Bank was 'nationalized,' the FDIC acquired 160 million shares of the bank's stock, fired management and installed new executives, for nearly USD5.5 billion (excluding the short-term liquidity borrowings from the Fed). The assumption was that the FDIC would 'run' the bank until it was operating profitably and an acquiring institution stepped forward. As of early 1986, the FDIC reported a loss of USD1.24 billion on the bad loans it assumed from the institution, but the real cost to the public was many times greater.

problems. In particular, the OCC was heavily criticized for its ambiguous examination processes and loan evaluations. The FRB was similarly criticized on the grounds that although its supervision of the holding company identified potential risks from reliance on money market funding, the agency was inconsistent in communicating these matters to the bank over time.[42] The criticism also focused on the fact that the FRB continued to approve the holding company's applications to expand its activities, notwithstanding the fact that numerous FRB examinations had criticized CINB's capitalization, asset quality and funding.[43]

The banking agencies defended themselves and articulated that their actions concerning CINB, including formal regulatory agreement between the OCC and CINB to address the bank's asset and liability management, loan administration, and funding problems and otherwise suggest prudential limitations, were overtly rejected or breached by CINB management.[44] The bottom line, however, was that the banking agencies were likely unable to effectively resolve such problems when they first became apparent in 1982, and that taking more dramatic actions while the money center bank was in distress would likely have triggered the eventual bailout in any event. In other words, the policy implications from the CINB debacle was simply that the regulation and supervision of money center banks resulted in more careful and special treatment, and that such institutions were clearly 'too big to fail' (TBTF) or perhaps more accurately stated as 'too big to liquidate'.[45]

The banking agencies thereafter attempted to use a policy of 'constructive ambiguity' to prevent any institutions or depositors from certainty that they would be protected under TBTF.[46] The TBTF policy was invoked four times

---

42 See, e.g. US House Committee on Banking, Finance and Urban Affairs, Subcommittee on Financial Institutions Supervision, Regulation and Insurance, 'Continental Illinois National Bank: Report of an Inquiry into its Federal Supervision and Assistance', Staff Report, 99th Cong., 1st Sess. (1985).

43 See *House Staff Report, supra* note 13, at pp.7-10.

44 See *History of the Eighties, Volume 1, supra* note 30, at pp.246-247.

45 The criticism largely concerned the acquisition of 80 per cent ownership in a national bank by the government as part of the bailout, which effectively nationalized the bank, and the combined protection of all depositors and creditors, including CINB bondholders, under the FDIC assistance plan. The concept of 'open bank assistance' to failed and failing banks deemed 'essential' to the bank's 'community', first enacted into law in 1950 (and augmented by the Garn-St. Germain Act, discussed *supra* in Chapter Two of this work), also received heavy criticism. See 12 U.S.C. sec. 1823(c)(1). After 1950, the FDIC operated under a 'cost test' to determine whether to close such institutions and pay off insured depositors (liquidation) or use an alternative method if said method was expected to be less costly to the deposit insurance fund. The FDIC was also authorized to use an alternative method under 'essentiality' considerations noted above, in that the statutory language was vague enough to provide FDIC with discretion to extend 'essentiality' beyond the immediate local economic dislocation, which was done with respect to the CINB bailout.

46 The regulatory agencies acknowledged that the markets knew that the largest banking institutions would always be viewed as 'too big to fail'. See, e.g., L. William Seidman, *Full Faith and Credit: The Great S & L Debacle and Other Washington Sagas* (Times Books, 1993), at p.150.

following the CINB bailout, however, until legislation enacted in 1991 imposed limitations on this policy.[47]

VIII. ECONOMIC FRAGILITY AND GOVERNMENT FORBEARANCE

The LDC Debt Crisis, the CINB debacle, and outright depression in the agriculture and energy sectors of the US economy sent tremors through the US banking system and directly influenced the Fed's monetary policy actions all prior to year-end 1984, which had damaging consequences for the US economy.

The largest money center banks experienced difficulties similar to those of CINB with respect to raising short-term funds in the money markets. Interestingly, the US banking system suffered from the aftershock of the very policies that they had previously urged the Fed to pursue, the stringent tightening of money supply and the rapid deceleration of price inflation that had destroyed or undermined other business enterprises. The money center banks experienced record profits in 1980–1981 when the Fed pushed interest rates to unprecedented levels. The severity of the anti-inflationary tactics did not give borrowers time to adjust to the new reality of 'disinflation', however, and the banking system soon experienced significant numbers of non-performing or troubled loans in their lending portfolios.

---

47 Notwithstanding the debate engendered by the CINB bailout, banking agencies were reluctant to tolerate the sudden and uncontrolled failure of large banking institutions and therefore generally opted to implement managed asset / liability disposition, merger, or recapitalization approaches. The concepts of systemic risk and logistical problems associated with liquidating large banking institutions were several reasons for adopting this position. See, e.g. Statement of John P. LaWare, US House Committee on Banking, Finance and Urban Affairs, Subcommittee on Economic Stabilization, 'Economic Implications of the "Too Big To Fail" Policy: Hearing', 102d Cong., 1st Sess. (1991); E. Gerald Corrigan, 'A Perspective on Recent Financial Disruptions', Federal Reserve Bank of New York Quarterly Review 14, No. 4 (Winter 1989-1990). The TBTF policy was used in cases involving First National Bank and Trust Company of Oklahoma City (USD1.6 billion in assets at time of failure) in 1986; First Republic Bank of Dallas, Texas (USD32.2 billion in assets at time of failure) in 1988, and Mcorp of Houston, Texas (USD15.7 billion in assets at time of failure) in 1989, and the Bank of New England Corporation (USD21.9 billion in assets at time of failure) in January 1991, respectively. See US House, 'Economic Implications of the "Too Big To Fail" Policy', *supra*, at p.83. The FDICIA legislation of 1991, discussed infra in Chapter four of this work, imposed limits on regulatory activities associated with TBTF but left banking agencies with discretion to invoke it under certain circumstances. See, e.g. Larry D. Wall, '"Too-Big-To-Fail" After FDICIA', Federal Reserve Bank of Atlanta Economic Review 78, No. 1 (Jan./Feb. 1993).

The TBTF policy was replaced in 1991 and 1992 by a policy of holding the federal funds rate down to permit troubled big banks to 'earn out' of their problems. The banks maintained a prime rate of interest of approximately 6 per cent, while the Fed dropped the federal funds rate to 3 per cent, and while also allowing the banks to invest in Treasury securities yielding 5 per cent to 6 per cent, thereby giving the banks a full 200 to 300 basis points to revitalize capital levels. See B. Riley, *Financial Times*, 4 November 1995; and R. Koo and N. Weinberg, *Forbes*, 9 February 1998, at p.52. The government thereby allowed the FDIC to avoid the continuing avalanche of bank failures originally predicted for 1991 and 1992.

The recession of 1982 translated into the fragility and failure in the US banking and thrift systems by 1984, two years after economic recovery was initiated. Indeed, the FRB, OCC, and particularly the FHLBB, went to extraordinary lengths to ensure that bank and thrift regulations were not zealously enforced during 1983–1984. The FRB, OCC and FHLBB instructed federal bank and thrift examiners to apply capital requirements and accounting standards with 'compassion' for the 'special circumstances' that troubled banks and thrifts encountered.

The FHLBB policies of 1980–1984, reviewed previously in this chapter, were very clear in this respect, and there was little doubt that if the bank examiners applied standards without such 'compassion' on non-performing loans and such, it would have caused enormous problems for the banks.[48]

The unexpected fallout of the CINB bailout nearly induced a serious Fed monetary policy error in summer 1984. After May 1984, the daily level of discount window borrowing subsided dramatically, as US banks stayed away en masse to avoid the perception of fragility by the market as occurred with CINB.[49] As a result, the Fed took out reserves through the open market and expected banks to borrow through the discount window, but witnessed an absence of such borrowings, ordinarily a signal of excess money supply. The federal funds interest rate continued to increase at least one full percentage point higher than the Fed intended, however, a signal of tightening money supply.[50]

These confusing signals resulted in the federal funds rate increasing 150 basis points by July 1984 and resulted in further deceleration of the economy, as M-1 went from 11 per cent growth in June 1984 to 1 per cent contraction in July 1984. The real short-term interest rates increased to the highest levels since 1979, however, nearly double the 1982 levels. The real interest rates were nearly four times higher than the normal cost of money during a normal expansionary cycle, and the rising real interest rates caused further appreciation of the dollar, compounding the damage to US exporting industries. By September 1984, the economic boom was over, and the FOMC eased interest rates in October 1984 (conveniently just prior to the re-election of President Reagan).[51]

Interestingly, US individuals and institutions continued borrowing at an unprecedented and dangerous pace during this period of high real interest rates, despite the Fed's deliberate actions to restrain economic growth during

---

48 The FRB and the Treasury in effect ensured that the bank examiners did not attend to their duties too zealously. This was especially true in the areas of agricultural lending and the rules for declaring international loans past due. This response was consistent with the FRB's and OCC's preoccupation with the refinancing of the LDC debt throughout 1983-1984. The FRB and OCC only gradually began to tighten procedures as the Continental Illinois crisis passed, and banks avoided taking actions that could trigger direct regulatory intervention, such as normal borrowing functions at the discount window.

49 See *Confidence Game*, *supra* note 2, at p.172.

50 *Ibid.* at p.172.

51 *Ibid.* at p.173.

1983–1984.[52] The monetary easing, falling interest rates, and lower inflationary expectations generated another burst of speculation in financial markets through highly leveraged takeovers, venture capital finance, mortgage-backed securities, and swaps and derivatives.

The general rationale behind the contradiction of market activity versus government intervention was based on the hidden consequences of financial deregulation under the 1980 DIDMCA and the 1982 Garn-St. Germain Act, respectively, and the Reagan Administration's tax legislation under the ERTA and stimulative fiscal policies. These legislative enactments, coupled with the phased-in removal of interest rate ceilings under Regulation Q through 1980–1986, fueled the economic recovery in 1983–1984 notwithstanding the sustained high real interest rate levels. The economic recovery during this period was unlike any other in the modern US economic experience, as the punishing interest rate levels were not enough to prevent lenders and borrowers from establishing new credits in an undisciplined manner. In addition, the Fed's management of the LDC Debt Crisis over 1983–1984 resulted in the gradual reduction in exposures of US banks, while the LDC nations' foreign (dollar-denominated) debt as a measure of GNP actually increased from 38 per cent in 1981 to 61 per cent in 1984, as those nations actually borrowed more to make interest payments on old debt obligations, with the new borrowings undertaken at higher interest rates.[53]

The significant question mark during the economic recovery of 1983–1984 was the appreciating dollar. The Reagan Administration seemingly ignored the rising dollar, and did not utilize exchange rate policy to address the dollar

---

52 The total outstanding debt, both public and private, at the end of 1984 was nearly USD7.1 trillion, nearly doubled since 1977. The domestic debt levels had increased by more than 25 per cent in 1983–1984 alone. Thus, debt was growing much faster than the economy as a whole. The outstanding debt was nearly 60 per cent of GNP. The Fed's monetary policy was unable to restrain this massive borrowing, the central contradiction of Volcker's tenure as Fed Chairman. See Greider, *supra* note 3, at pp.638-639.

53 There was almost no public discussion of the underlying causes or how to remove the political economy from the debilitating consequences. The obvious solution was that the government should impose other kinds of controls on the banking and credit markets, legal limits that would contain the supply of credit, so the Fed would not have to rely solely on the extreme punishment of high interest rates, which eventually bankrupted the borrowing sector. The new controls could take on many forms, from interest-rate ceilings to income-tax penalties to direct regulation by the Fed of how banks and other lending institutions allocated their lending activities. If Congress desired lower interest rates from the Fed, it could have created different mechanisms to control the expansion of credit. In the Reagan Administration era of free markets and deregulation, however, there was no political opportunity for Congress to pursue this solution, and the political influence of commercial banks pushed in the other direction, towards less government intervention and freedom from legal restraints. The largest money center banks sought the power to operate nationwide branches, a consolidation of power that would inevitably result in the centralization of political influence of banking in a small number of elite and very large institutions. These institutions further pressed for entry into other business sectors, where they could employ enormous advantages over competitors since, given their special status as commercial banks, they would still be protected by the government from failure. The 1980s established that attempting to control credit by manipulating interest rates alone was fundamentally ineffective, and additionally was inequitable given the effect on income distributions, as it punished borrowers and rewarded lenders excessively.

and guide the Fed to assist in this respect. As the stratospheric levels of the dollar in foreign exchange markets became evident, however, powerful interest groups aligned with exports and trade imposed increasingly greater political pressure on bringing down the dollar. Upon taking office, the new Treasury advisors to the Reagan Administration became fully engaged in exchange rate policy efforts, already initiated by other G-5 governments, to restrain further appreciation of the dollar. The speculative growth in financial instruments transactions and diminishing but still cognizable economic growth stimulated by Reagan Administration deficits and Fed de facto accommodation set the stage for President Reagan's re-election in November 1984.

Although the Fed remained non-partisan, Chairman Volcker was successful in alleviating inflation and facilitating economic growth despite structural budget deficits and financial sector instability. The Fed's monetary policy actions kept inflation subdued, but the economic expansion initiated by fiscal stimulus was also held in check by the Fed's tight monetary policy, which prevented the resurgence of inflation.[54] The appreciating dollar destruction to the domestic economy, however, was an unfortunate side effect of the Fed's monetary-fiscal policy conflict as the Fed tightened credit to restrain the economy. The clash between the expansive budget deficits and anti-inflationary monetary policy produced real dollar interest rates that were often five percentage points higher than outside the United States.[55]

The global markets poured capital into the United States, which propelled the dollar and the US foreign deficits, a sustained trend that the Fed largely failed to anticipate. By January 1985 the recession was over and the economy was growing but after the election-year boom such growth diminished.

The Fed's continued control over the economy produced disappointing results, as the economy settled into a pattern of uneven advances, weakening one quarter, then surging in the next, then weakening again. The Fed eased or restrained in measured steps, and averted recession but failed to emerge from the dislocated pattern. Notwithstanding the slowing of US economic

---

[54] The essence of monetary policy, notwithstanding the complexities, was always a choice of values. The Fed was necessarily preoccupied with technical issues, but the implicit question at the core of their decisions could never be reduced to scientific solution, with a right answer or a wrong answer. The real questions were which economic objectives were of highest priority. The concept of 'neutral money', characterized by the absence of inflationary or deflationary cycles, was ultimately an illusion, nothing more than a statistical artifice that concealed harsh realities. The Fed was celebrated for accomplishing what it took to be its highest purpose, the elimination of dollar inflation. Neutral money was the golden mean, what everyone thought they wanted. Yet the ideal was merely an economic abstraction and it was not necessarily neutral, it was simply an averaging of gains by certain sectors of the economy and losses of other sectors that produced the comforting illusion of balance. The condition of neutral money conveyed a satisfying sense of social order, but the reality was continuing disorder. In the real economy, neutral money resulted in an inequitable division of advantage where certain economic interests continued unrestrained in their ability to raise prices and wages, while others were consigned to permanent decrease and were bound to fail if the condition persisted. The illusion of neutral money was most persuasive to those who were not destroyed by it, a paradox of economic order that was perpetrated by economics, a core belief of democratic capitalism. The disposition was to believe that a neutral dollar gave no artificial advantage to anyone, a disposition that was simply wrong.

[55] See *Confidence Game*, *supra* note 2, at p.176.

growth and foreign interest rate differentials, however, the dollar continued to appreciate, surging 20 per cent during the period of July 1984 – February 1985.[56]

The US federal budget deficits continued expanding, but the Reagan Administration seemed not to recognize the damage being done to the US manufacturing economy by the appreciating dollar until early 1985, when urgings from the United Kingdom guided the Treasury to shift views and articulate a desire to see the dollar depreciate, following which it engaged in concerted interventions to bring the dollar down.[57]

IX. EXCHANGE RATE AND MONETARY POLICY IN 1985

The US economy weakened in early 1985, but the Fed eased monetary policy only slightly, reducing the discount rate once in May 1985, and denied multiple requests from the Federal Reserve Banks for further reductions in the discount rate. Thus, short-term interest rates declined only slightly through the year and the economy continued in the uneven pattern of growth and stagnation. In 1985, most of the petitions for interest rate reductions came from the Dallas Federal Reserve Bank, where oil, agriculture, and real estate sectors were caught in the spiral of asset value deflation.

Most of the major Texas banks and thrift institutions were also endangered, but the Fed did not alter monetary policy and continued to press Congress to enact controls on the federal deficits and the Treasury to address the appreciating dollar in foreign exchange markets. The appreciating dollar peaked in February 1985, having increased nearly 50 per cent since 1980, and began subsiding gradually.[58] The Fed argued that any sudden depreciation in the dollar on foreign exchange markets could trigger price inflation, and refused to lower interest rates because it did not want to challenge the bond markets.[59] By July 1985, the FOMC found that M-1 expanded in excess of 16 per cent, with the economy barely expanding at all (less than 1 per cent). The increase in money supply balances was not being used to support real economic activity, but for speculative financial transactions. The falling

---

56 *Ibid.* at p.290.

57 *Ibid.* at p.291.

58 *Ibid.* at p.174.

59 The continuing fears of inflation were reflected in extraordinarily high long-term interest rates demanded in the bond markets, and if the Fed eased monetary policy, the bond markets could react by pushing long-term rates higher on inflationary expectations. The bond markets were therefore ultimately guiding the US Government's economic policy. The general desire for a more robust economy was stifled by a particular financial interest group. The bond market and its investors held an enviable position of influence, and were hardly disinterested, and profited directly from imposing their inflationary expectations on the financial markets. In fact, in the four years since 1981, the bond market returns averaged 18.5 per cent in those years, the most profitable era for the bond markets in the 20th century. The preferred status of the bond markets and their influence over the Fed's monetary policy simply supported the economic myth of stable money. By embracing neutral money as the goal, the Fed had unwittingly deferred to the bond market.

interest rates, deregulation, and innovation helped trigger an explosion of financial transactions relative to real economic activity, which created a surge in the demand for money and credit, including M-1, to support them.[60] The banking, oil, and real estate sectors were in precarious positions. The FOMC decided to ignore M-1 and permit the money supply to grow, and by the end of 1985 the money supply increased by 11 per cent, but the economy remained weak and uneven. The bottom line was that M-1 was not a constant value, but a variable that held little certainty for measurement of the economy. In short, the sole focus on M-1 through the monetarist operating technique was a costly illusion for the US economy, and the Fed finally and permanently abandoned it in 1985, based largely on concerns of the appreciating dollar.[61] The key political event of late 1985 was the Reagan Administration's public acknowledgment that the appreciating dollar and external imbalances that came with it were a serious problem and that alleviating them required joint currency intervention with coordinated policy changes, manifested through the meeting and statement of the G5 to address the dollar in September 1985.

X. CONCLUDING OBSERVATIONS: THE END OF THE DEREGULATION ERA AND ASSET VALUE INFLATION

The dynamics of deregulatory and forbearance policies adopted by the FHLBB and banking agencies during 1980–1982 clearly represented misguided government intervention and set the stage for uncontrolled expansion of thrift and bank activities. These policies set the stage for extended asset value inflation during this period, especially when considered in conjunction with the monetary and exchange rate policies reviewed in Chapter Two. The end of inflation arrived by year-end 1982, and the government agenda commenced with abrupt policy reversals in monetary policy and addressing conflicts between monetary and fiscal policy. In addition, the banking agencies became sincerely preoccupied with the LDC Debt Crisis which bloomed by August 1982. The FHLBB and thrift industry seemed geared to 'growing' out of their problems under the deregulatory framework adopted through legislation and regulatory policies reviewed in this chapter. The period of 1983–1985 was dominated by monetary and exchange rate policy reversals and conflicts, legislative gridlock, and a

60 See *Confidence Game, supra* note 2, at p.177,

61 From 1974-1979, M-1 grew by an average of 7 per cent, during a period of excessive money supply growth and surging inflation. From 1979-1984, however, M-1 also grew by 7.4 per cent, during a period of tight money and reducing inflation. This anomaly represented the true end of Milton Friedman's monetarist doctrine as a credible theory of monetary policy, as recent history eliminated the logic of reliance on the M-1 aggregate as a disciplinary force in monetary policy. The collapse of monetarism as a practical theory had far reaching implications. The concept was simply a method for the Fed and other economic sectors to claim that concentration on the abstraction of money supply alone was appropriate and to ignore the consequences for the rest of the economy.

seeming desire to address the underlying problems in the thrift and banking industries over a sustained period of time as the economy wrestled with the lasting impact of inflation and mitigating inflationary expectations. These trends created the impetus for sustained artificial asset value inflation, particularly in the real estate market, and contributed greatly to the degree and severity of thrift industry and banking crises. The policy actions taken during the period of 1983–1985 with respect to the general impact of the deregulatory legislation and regulatory policies on the thrift and banking industries, coupled with monetary, fiscal and exchange rate policies, are critical. These policy actions set the foundation for the commencement of abrupt policy reversals in the form of 'reregulation' in the banking and thrift industries and exchange rate policies to halt the appreciating dollar.

As the banking and thrift industries entered the 1980s, interest rates and inflationary expectations continued to remain at extremely high levels. The Reagan Administration captured the overreaching theme of deregulation in an environment where inflation caused short-term interest rates to increase dramatically, thereby causing real estate values to inflate. The banking and thrift industries entered this era with great expectations under the legislative framework accorded under the DIDMCA and Garn-St. Germain Act, respectively. Unfortunately, by 1983 the thrift and banking industries were consumed by distress, and particular economic sectors principally relied upon by the thrift and banking industries for earnings and lending security were beset with asset value inflation manufactured by various aspects of misguided government intervention.

A. Thrift Industry Crisis

The period from year-end 1982 to year-end 1985 was characterized by the extremely rapid growth of the thrift industry, as the industry responded to the new legislative and regulatory scheme. The combination of misguided FHLBB policies, particularly the permitted diversification of S&Ls into other businesses, the onset of RAP accounting deviations, unchecked regulatory forbearance, and the increase in deposit insurance to USD100,000, all generated through combined political lobbying by S&L industry and the Reagan Administration's blind adherence to the doctrine of deregulation (which dominated the misguided FHLBB policies), together with extreme anti-inflationary monetary policy came to be a lethal combination and not only accelerated the demise of the S&L industry but also generated many problems in the banking industry.

In the early 1980s, borrowers, banks and S&Ls each unwittingly reinforced the inflation in real estate values fueled by the effects of DIDMCA, the Garn-St. Germain Act, ERTA, State deregulation, 'comparable' market appraisals, increased leverage and US monetary policy. In an inflationary period of increasing values and increasing earnings, banks and S&Ls, *by reason of how 'banking', 'leverage' and 'capital' were defined*, flourished and grew, causing a natural inflationary push.

Increases in the leverage ratios; the momentum arising from comparables, competition, and the capitalist quest for increased stock values through higher earnings accelerated the inflationary process. Entrepreneurs were encouraged to acquire S&Ls and operate them as giant real estate companies. Regulatory and examination forces of State and federal regulatory bodies, however, were not expanded to effectively handle the regulation of the broadened powers arising from DIDMCA and the Garn-St. Germain Act. In addition to new powers, there was a quantifiable risk increase as the amount of deposit insurance rose two-and-one-half times from USD40,000 per account to USD100,000.

The thrift industry was poised to endure and even compete until interest rates stabilized and the one-product business of long-term mortgage lending was no longer subject to market pressures caused by interest rate mismatches. In reality, the thrift industry was only several years away from failure. The primary driving force that set the stage for thrift industry failure was the initial lack of FSLIC resources necessary to close down all of the insolvent thrift institutions.

This was complemented by the perception that the institutions were insolvent 'on paper only' and that the interest rate environment would soon change to alleviate the interest rate/asset-liability mismatch dilemma. As this chapter plainly shows, the forces and causes of thrift industry crisis were diverse and interconnected, and no single cause or force can be said to have unilaterally resulted in crisis.

B. Consensus Points on the Thrift Industry Crisis

The general consensus by the mid-1980s was that the following eight forces or causes resulted in significant capital impairment and otherwise played significant roles in the ongoing thrift industry crisis:

(i) the continuing interest rate mismatch problem exacerbated by economic conditions, systemic issues, and political and monetary policy deference to more powerful global interests and financial institutions at the expense of the S&L industry;
(ii) government intervention in the form of inappropriate regulatory actions or omissions in the form of basic failures of supervision by the FHLBB that ultimately sustained the worsening condition of the industry until failure was imminent;
(iii) the structure of the federal deposit insurance system that generally encouraged thrift institutions to engage in more aggressive risk-taking activities without requiring corresponding risk-based assessments;
(iv) the declining prices of residential and commercial real estate which were indirectly caused by untimely legislation affecting the tax treatment of real estate investments;
(v) the imprudent and inappropriate use of expanded powers accorded to thrift institutions by management;
(vi) the internal fraud and mismanagement committed by some thrift directors and officers;
(vii) the development of government-sponsored enterprises ('GSEs') to compete with S&Ls in long-term mortgage lending activities on an

unlevel playing field, and of powers accorded to banks and BHCs that were not otherwise available to S&Ls; and

(viii) uncontrolled State legislative and regulatory initiatives for the States' constituent S&Ls.

The most prevalent examples of regulatory intervention and forbearance arose through the FHLBB policies and instances of regulatory intervention and forbearance either on behalf of the industry or particular institutions. Many of the problematic instances of regulatory intervention and forbearance were significant underlying causes of the thrift industry crisis. The FHLBB policies were primarily designed to sustain the highly distressed thrift industry and keep the FSLIC from becoming officially insolvent until the surrounding political, interest rate, and real estate environments were more conducive to thrift institutions.[62]

C. The Trigger Points of Insolvency and the Onset of Policy Reversal

The growth among thrift institutions during the early 1980s was particularly evident in the States whose economies were stimulated by surging energy and commodity prices in the early 1980s, especially in Texas. The Texas thrift institutions were among the most aggressive in terms of growth, concentrated in a relatively small number of institutions. One of the most egregious examples of such institutions, Empire Savings and Loan Association of Mesquite, Texas, grew between 1981–1983 from approximately USD13 million in assets to over USD300 million.

In 1983, even when interest rates declined sharply and returned many thrift institutions to profitability, 10 per cent of the thrift industry was still insolvent on a GAAP basis and 35 per cent of the thrift industry assets were controlled by institutions that were insolvent on a tangible basis, but these institutions were nonetheless permitted to grow with the remaining solvent institutions.[63]

Three events in 1984 occurred which caused great concern in the banking and thrift industries. First, Empire Savings and Loan of Mesquite, Texas, failed and investigators uncovered a pattern of various criminal activities. The bailout eventually cost the US taxpayers nearly USD300 million.[64] This failure coupled with the FHLBB's joint efforts with the FDIC to eliminate

---

[62] The calendar years 1984-1985 were dominated by notable thrift failures. For instance, in 1984 the FHLBB closed Empire Savings of Mesquite, Texas, and the American Savings of Stockton, California, failed. In 1985, the State-chartered thrift systems in Ohio and Maryland suffered systemic withdrawals of deposits in 1985 that nearly liquidated their State deposit insurance systems.

[63] See *History of the Eighties, Volume 1, supra* note 30, at p.180.

[64] The Empire Savings and Loan Association, based in Texas and previously proclaimed as one of the most successful associations in the United States in 1982 based on earnings and growth, was placed into conservatorship by the Department of Savings and Loans of the State of Texas in March 1984. The Texas authorities uncovered instances of 'land flips' and other patterns of fraudulent and criminal activities.

deposit insurance for brokered deposits, made clear that the process of policy reversal from deregulation to reregulation would commence in earnest in the thrift industry. Second, the saga of Penn Square National Bank, which was placed in receivership by the FDIC on 5 July 1982, continued to unfold. The Penn Square Bank debacle eventually claimed an enormous victim in 1984, the Continental Illinois National Bank, N.A., which became technically insolvent through deposit withdrawals and funding illiquidity and was restructured by the FRB and OCC, with the assistance of the FDIC.

In the Continental Illinois National Bank experience, the regulators discovered the fragility of all banks, even large money center banks, when both investor and depositor confidence is lost. Third, the massive American Savings & Loan Association of Stockton, California suffered a fate quite similar to that of Continental Illinois National Bank.

These events prompted the FHLBB to adopt regulations affecting S&L powers in 1984 which expanded and then contracted the authority of federal S&Ls. The FHLBB began to tighten the thrift regulatory system in 1984 by imposing a number of regulations designed to (1) restrict rapid growth and direct investments made by thrift institutions with low net worth; (2) increase net worth standards; and (3) reform accounting practices.[65]

Most importantly, the FHLBB imposed a regulation that restricted growth at undercapitalized thrift institutions to a rate equal to the interest credited on existing deposits. The institutions that met their net worth requirements could not grow at rates exceeding 25 per cent per year without supervisory approval. The high growth period was also characterized by weak or non-existent examination and supervisory processes. The States that enacted liberal thrift institution laws, such as California, Florida, and Texas, lacked effective supervisory processes and were politically influenced by the industry.

These events, together with ancillary events such as the failure of the 'Butcher Banks' in Tennessee,[66] the failures of the so-called 'I-30 corridor savings and loans' in Garland, Texas[67] and the runs on the State-chartered thrifts in Ohio and Maryland[68] in March 1985, generated enormous concern and focus on systemic banking and thrift crisis issues in the US Congress. The banking and S&L regulatory agencies by implication adopted this focus and reacted to these concerns, and the cumulative effect of this reactionary phase

---

65 See National Commission, 'Origins and Causes, of the S&L Debacle: A Blueprint for Reform', (1993), at pp.98-99 (listing regulations).

66 The 'Butcher Banks' were those banks, principally domiciled in the State of Tennessee, that were owned by Jake Butcher, a close associate of former US President Jimmy Carter.

67 The 'I-30 corridor savings and loans' were those numerous savings and loans that participated, directly or indirectly, in the vast overbuilding of condominium units on the shores of Lake Ray Hubbard in Garland, Texas along Interstate 30. See generally 'Hearings on Adequacy of Federal Home Loan Bank Board Supervision of Empire Savings and Loan Association', before the Committee on Government Operations, US House of Representatives, 98th Cong., 2d Sess. (1984).

68 In March 1985, massive thrift institution failures initiated in Ohio, and in May 1985 S&L failures in Maryland eventually caused losses to State deposit insurance funds and State taxpayers of USD185 million. The Ohio and Maryland S&L failures resulted in the termination of State deposit insurance funds.

was a significant reversal in policies both in Congress and among the regulatory agencies which resulted in a policy sequence of legislation and 'reregulation' to address the perceived problems.

As the FHLBB attempted to mitigate the pressure on the thrift industry through deregulation and accounting deviations, the enormous number of failed S&Ls threatened the FSLIC with deposit liabilities that could exhaust its capital base. The total reserves of FSLIC decreased from USD6.46 billion in 1980 to USD4.55 billion in 1985,[69] as the FHLBB estimated that it needed USD15.8 billion to close down all institutions deemed insolvent under GAAP.[70] By the mid-1980s there were over 4,000 distressed thrift institutions, the majority of them bankrupt, and the FSLIC simply did not have enough funds to bail them all out. The FSLIC was for all practical purposes insolvent itself, and needed to be recapitalized to address the growing thrift industry crisis.

D. Banking Crises

In the 1980s, the federal banking agencies actively responded to problematic trends and economic conditions through changes in monetary policy, and regulatory and supervisory intervention and forbearance. The OCC, FRB and FDIC were very active in forbearance practices, particularly in response to the LDC debt crisis, and in expanding the regulatory and supervisory frameworks to authorize banks and bank holding companies to engage in new activities. The Fed conducted monetary policy that directly conflicted with fiscal policies of the Reagan Administration, which facilitated the sustained appreciation of the dollar through 1985. The regulatory intervention and, importantly, forbearance practices of the federal banking agencies resulted in significant capital impairment for the majority of the banking system in the LDC debt crisis, and for several particular banking organizations whose capital impairment threatened the safety and soundness of the banking system. After deregulation, commercial banks also faced certain competitive pressures from the thrift industry with respect to aggressive diversification into real estate lending and investment activities.

E. Banking and Monetary Priorities and Regulatory Capture

The thrift industry crisis was exacerbated by continued focus on the ongoing banking system and banking organization crises involving the commercial banking sector and fallout of anti-inflationary monetary policies conducted by the Fed during the 1980s. In addition, Congress and the primary federal banking agencies handled various individual institution and systemic banking crisis issues during the 1980s that actually dwarfed the S&L industry problems. In other words, the focus on monetary policy and commercial

---

[69] See GAO, 'Thrift Industry Forbearance For Troubled Institutions 1982-1986', at p.12 (1987).

[70] See GAO, 'Troubled Financial Institutions: Solutions to the Thrift Industry Problem', at p.108 (February 1989).

banking sector crises dominated the agenda of reform during this period and shifted attention away from the S&L crisis until the S&L industry had largely failed.

The end result is that the S&L crisis was ultimately manageable through financial bailout, while the commercial banking crises were systemic in nature and could not necessarily be managed by financial bailout altogether because they were simply too large and complex to comprehend. In addition, the international banking organizations and sovereign borrowers were far too large and interconnected to permit failure and international financial institution bailout.

The US Congress and federal banking regulators continued to be preoccupied with various banking and financial market events resulting in systemic risks which opened cracks in the international financial system and influenced monetary policy. The bottom line is that these banking and financial market events dominated the regulatory, supervisory, and monetary spheres of influence and the S&L crisis was an unfortunate sideline event which did not present the same nature of systemic risk to the US economy or international financial system at this time. In the era of financial deregulation, the Fed lacked the political self-confidence to sincerely restrain the largest money center banks.

As an institution, the Fed is an assembly of unelected technocrats with no political base of their own. Although ostensibly free of politics, the Fed technocrats are actually dependent for political protection on the banks that the Fed was supposed to control, the constituency of banks dominated by the largest money center banks. When the Fed fails to fulfill its regulatory obligations, the excuse invoked is that they were too vulnerable to the informal pressures of politics. The Fed is not that different from other 'captive' regulatory agencies. Therefore, in the hardest cases, the Fed proved to be far less powerful, and much more political, than it pretended to be.[71] As the magnitude of the S&L crisis increased exponentially into the late 1980s, the crisis would soon rise to the forefront of US regulatory and supervisory policies through remedial legislation enacted by Congress.

The monetary policy actions administered by the Fed designed to combat inflation nonetheless fueled value inflation in various assets, particularly real estate, during this period. With a continued striving for greater earnings, banks and S&Ls sought greater fee producing loan volume. The booming real estate market, influenced by deregulatory finance and tax-driven pricing, became a logical place to quench the thirst for greater S&L loan volume.

According to basic economic principles, as banks and S&Ls make more and more loans, the money supply increases exponentially, unless controlled by monetary policy. If uncontrolled or partially controlled, the result is a greater supply of money seeking an increasing number of deals. If totally controlled, the result is a stabilizing of the money supply and a limitation on the growth, but at whose expense? If demand for real estate lending is booming and perceived as safe based upon existing conditions, the available

---

[71] See Greider, *supra* note 3 at pp.526-527.

money will seek real estate as an investment opportunity as opposed to any other investment alternative. In retrospect, the question became whether the economic indicators relied upon by the Federal Reserve were sufficiently sensitive to identify this inflationary push and increase in money supply. Since most indices then relied upon by the Federal Reserve in establishing monetary policy excluded commercial real estate transactions, the answer is that the Federal Reserve was not really cognizant of the circumstances or effects of this specific, massive inflation.

F. Legislative Gridlock

The 1982 Garn-St. Germain Act represented the second phase of deregulatory legislation for the banking and thrift industries. The crucial aspect of expansion of powers that was eliminated from the Act over tremendous debate, however, was a provision to authorize banking organizations to engage in bank-ineligible securities activities and to own mutual funds.

The debate over expanded powers into the securities and insurance industries dominated the legislative agenda during 1982–1986 and ended in legislative gridlock, as the vested interests involved were too powerful to force consensus on the issues. The Reagan Administration strongly believed that product deregulation was the crucial element of banking industry reform, and the Senate Banking Committee continued to make expansion of bank powers the top priority during this period.

The vested interests proved too much for expansionary reform, however. The securities, insurance, and real estate industries all battled against banking organization entry into their industries and engaged in extensive lobbying to halt legislation authorizing such entry. The banking industry was itself often not united on entering these markets, as the money center banking organizations were more interested in acquiring the right of entry than smaller institutions were, and the implications for banking industry competition complicated bank trade association agendas.

The members of Congress that supported expansion of powers and the key members of the Reagan Administration often did not address the issues from a united perspective. The differences in perspective were driven by political interests and the Treasury Department and the banking agencies themselves, as their respective positions tended to advocate the preservation of their perceived importance in financial market regulation. For instance, the arguments focused on how and through what entity the new powers would be carried out, and which regulatory agency would supervise and regulate the execution of the new powers. In addition, certain members of Congress that were considered influential in the banking industry in certain instances opposed the acquisition of new powers under the position that such powers entailed too much risk to banking organizations, particularly those related to the Glass-Steagall Act.

Finally, the banking agencies had different positions on how new powers should be regulated and supervised, and these positions were incorporated into the larger debate concerning major reform of the financial regulatory apparatus. The competing interests in this debate ensured legislative gridlock in 1982–1986 and such gridlock continues today.

G. The Beginnings of Reregulation

In 1985, the general consensus recognized that the FSLIC was insolvent and that most thrift institutions' capital and asset bases were greatly overstated as a result of Fed monetary policy operations and FHLBB deregulatory initiatives, forbearance, and permissiveness. Thus, although the FHLBB did introduce several regulations addressing growth, net worth, and accounting reforms in 1984, the true reregulation of the thrift industry commenced in earnest in 1985. The FHLBB personnel of the early 1980s were replaced with tough new regulators appointed to key positions.

The FHLBB adopted new real estate appraisal standards that were often applied on a retroactive basis,[72] which predictably resulted in reduced asset values and comparables across the real estate sector. The FHLBB also adopted more stringent capital adequacy standards to require greater capital provision,[73] when the aim should have been to preserve existing capital. The FHLBB further adopted 'growth restriction regulation'[74] and 'classification of asset' regulations, respectively.[75] These reregulatory measures were reactionary attempts by the FHLBB to respond to Congress and take tough but untimely actions to preserve the thrift industry and itself, and treat the systemic thrift industry crisis as one that could be cured by simply tightening the rules.

However, these measures failed to take into account their cumulative effect on the dynamics of the real estate industry and its interrelation with the value of assets held by thrifts institutions. The bottom line is that the sudden change in regulatory approach largely caused property values to depreciate quickly and insidiously in a downward spiral.

The FHLBB reregulatory initiatives resulted in:

1. a precipitous decline in available financing from thrift institutions;
2. revised appraisal standards which generated lower appraised values that, by way of comparables, caused further reductions in values;
3. the evaporation of existing capital from asset value deflation;

---

72 These standards are currently located at C.F.R. § 563.17-1a(c)(1). The Code sets forth three appraisal standards that, at a minimum, must be included in the appraisal policies of every insured institution and service corporation. First, the appraisal must be based upon the definition of market value as set forth in the regulation. This definition contemplates the consummation of a sale as of a specified date and the passing of title from buyer to seller under open and competitive market conditions requisite to a fair sale. Second, the appraisal must be presented in a narrative format. The appraisal report must be sufficiently descriptive to enable a reviewer to readily ascertain the estimated value reported and the rationale for that estimate. The analysis is required to be as detailed and in depth as the complexity of the real estate requires. Third, an appraisal must contain a sales history of the real estate appraised. Generally, sales within the three previous years must be disclosed.

73 See 50 Fed. Reg. 6891 (1985) (codified at 12 C.F.R. § 563.13 (1985)).

74 See 12 C.F.R. § 563.98 (1990). This section established new restrictions for equity risk investments by savings associations. The limits for investments were based on tangible capital in relation to total liabilities. In addition, permissible investments were described and diversification was required.

75 See FHLBB Memorandum No. R41C; Fed. Banking L. Rep. (CCH) § 40.185.176.

4. incipient negative leverage;[76] and
5. the substantive shifting of loan portfolio holdings of many financial institutions to consist primarily of non-amortizing term loans which were due to be paid in full at maturity.[77]

The legislation and 'reregulation' commenced in 1985 represented a direct contradiction to the attitudes and policies established under DIDMCA, ERTA, the Garn-St. Germain Act, and FHLBB deregulatory initiatives and regulatory forbearance and permissiveness, as reviewed in Parts One and Two. The policy sequence reversal also precipitated massive asset value deflation, particularly in the real estate sector. Most importantly, Congress enacted significant remedial legislation for distressed and failed thrift and banking institutions from 1987–1991.

The structure of this series of legislative enactments consisted of clearly identifiable levels of interests and strands of government intervention, and the banking regulatory agency-institution partnership made most evident in FHLBB-thrift industry relations and FRB-money center bank relations shifted and evolved. At times these interests collided, particularly given the fallout from Fed monetary policy operations to attack inflation over 1979–1982. These collisions unquestionably exacerbated the US thrift industry crisis which continued to unfold, particularly in Texas banking and thrift institutions, and which spread throughout the capital base of other US businesses and financial institutions.

The reregulation of thrift and banking institutions and elimination of tax incentives for real estate investment eliminated the finance/tax push on real estate values and caused those values to collapse and capital to 'evaporate' from the US financial system, precipitating an asset value deflation crisis in real estate which began slowly, but quickly gathered momentum. Nonetheless, the monetary policies, legislation and regulatory initiatives of the early 1980s that fueled value inflation, stopped in the doldrums of 1985–1986. Slowly, regulation and rule-making resumed, but with a different emphasis, as the US banking and thrift industries entered the era of reregulation, and with reregulation came asset value deflation.

---

[76] Thus, for each dollar of capital loss, thrifts were required to shrink assets USD33, and banks USD15. Shrinkage was difficult, however, since the depreciating values meant that there were no buyers or new financing available. When shrinkage did occur, it usually was from the sale of earning assets, and the loss of income from those earning assets' further reduced capital, requiring still more asset shrinkage.

[77] The majority of these loans were not paid at maturity. As a result, the institutions were deprived of a major source of asset shrinkage.

8. Supervisory and Legislative Reregulation in the Thrift Industry

I. INTRODUCTION: THE STAGE FOR DISASTER

As the Reagan Administration, Congress, and the Fed concerned themselves with exchange rate imbalances, mitigating fiscal deficits, and lingering fragility in the banking system following the aftermath of the LDC Debt Crisis, Congress and the bank and S&L regulatory authorities, particularly the FHLBB, failed to recognize the massive systemic build-up of asset value inflation inherent in thrift and bank portfolios, particularly in real estate collateral (despite warnings to the contrary). Instead, Congress and the regulators perceived the thrift and bank problems as involving fraud, unsafe and unsound banking practices, excessive greed, and criminal behavior.

Perhaps as the thrift and banking crises became more transparent in 1984 in the cases of Empire Savings Bank, Penn Square Bank, and Continental Illinois Bank (as discussed in Part Two, above), there was some justification in this line of thinking, as there were instances where such behavior occurred. Of course, regardless of whether the thrift and banking crises were a cumulative USD100 billion problem or a USD1.5 trillion problem, the primary question is how could such losses be caused by those factors alone, in such amounts, given the high degree of regulation and supervision in the US thrift and banking industries.

Nonetheless, the political atmosphere was dominated by those very factors, and by 1985 the stage was set for abrupt policy reversals in addressing the thrift and banking crises. As Congress investigated the Empire Savings and Continental Illinois National Bank debacles, the FHLBB commenced a forceful program of S&L reregulation. The initiation of criminal investigations, removal actions, supervisory agreements and cease and desist orders were the initial tools of reregulation, and new rules and regulations followed promptly.

These reactions set the stage for two major pieces of US banking and thrift legislation in 1987 and 1989, which among other things 'reregulated' the thrift industry and shifted accountability for many issues from government policy failures to industry participants. As the banking regulators methodically went about their business, the FHLBB reregulation program commenced at a furious pace. The rules and regulations involving banks did not change quite as dramatically as those involving S&Ls over 1985–1986, notwithstanding the lasting impact of the Penn Square Bank and Continental Illinois Bank debacles. The S&L balance sheets were far more leveraged than banks, particularly with respect to the effects of asset value inflation and severe asset price bubbles in specific sectors, namely real estate.

The initial reregulatory actions taken by the FHLBB, although perhaps appropriate in another place and at another time, were simply inappropriate given the state of the US economy and exchange rate imbalances at this time. A softer and more gradual approach based upon an awareness of the asset value inflation brought about by a deliberate government initiated process of finance and tax driven asset value inflation was necessary. Instead, the FHLBB, having no apparent sense of history or context, adopted in 1985 and 1986 a number of rules and regulations that essentially reregulated the S&L industry and began to precipitate asset value deflation.

Analyses of this new scheme of supervisory and legislative 'reregulation' forms the focal point of this chapter.

II. FHLBB REREGULATION

A. Calendar Year 1985

In March 1985, the FHLBB substantially strengthened the minimum capital requirement.[1] The effect was to increase the capital requirements immediately for most S&Ls. This policy was in direct opposition to the policy the FHLBB had pursued in the early 1980s. At the same time, the FHLBB adopted regulations severely limiting direct investment.[2] The effect was to limit investments that could be made by most S&Ls. Again, this policy was in direct opposition to the policy the FHLBB had pursued in the early 1980s. In April 1985, the FHLBB adopted more restrictive accounting policies relating to loans for acquisition, development and construction (so-called 'AD&C loans').[3] These policies limited the lumping of front-end fees received on these loans into the association's income. The effect was not only to reduce income in the current fiscal year with respect to AD&C loans made in that

---

1 On 31 March 1985, the FHLBB substantially revised the minimum net worth (capital) requirement making the requirement much stronger. The FHLBB revisions (1) required that minimum net worth be calculated more often; (2) prohibited institutions from increasing their deposit liabilities in any two consecutive quarters at an annual rate of in excess of 25 per cent; and (3) eliminated the advantage of calculating the capital requirement on a five year deposit average basis or by use of the 20-year phase-in technique. See 50 Fed. Reg. 6891 (1985).

2 On 31 March 1985, the FHLBB also adopted a direct investment limitation regulation to limit by quantity and quality of the investments an insured institution could make in real estate, service corporations, operating subsidiaries and equity securities. See 50 Fed. Reg. 6912 (1985).

3 On 29 April 1985, the FHLBB adopted a statement of accounting policy relating to acquisition, development and construction loans (so-called 'AD&C loans') which severely limited the amount of income that savings and loan associations could book with respect to front end fees paid for such loans. See 50 Fed. Reg. 18,233 (1985).

fiscal year, but also in many instances to restate income for previous fiscal years thereby reducing the earning for those previous years.

In August 1985 and September 1986, the FHLBB adopted restrictive appraisal standards. These appraisal standards, required appraisers to comply with very strict new definitions of 'value'. The effect of these standards, particularly Memorandum R-41C, was to deflate 'values' on collateral assets securing not only new loans, but also loans previously made and reflected on the books of associations.[4] In November 1985, the FHLBB adopted a regulation that further restricted the amount of loans that could be made to any 'one borrower'.[5] Finally, in December 1985, the FHLBB adopted a 'classification of assets' regulation which established a new, more restrictive basis for calculating reserves.

In effect, thrift institution examiners could classify any loan as 'doubtful' and require a reserve of 50 per cent of the outstanding balance of the loan. For loans classified by the examiner as 'loss', the reserve was increased to 100 per cent.[6] Many such 'examiners' applying this subjective regulation were young and inexperienced, often having been out of college no more than two or three years.

B. Calendar Year 1986

In April 1986, the FHLBB terminated the delegation of authority to principal supervisory agents to permit newly organized thrift institutions to change their capital requirements from the newly organized institution requirement to the standard requirement. On 14 August 1986, the FHLBB issued its Memorandum R-41c which set forth new very controversial standards and reporting requirements utilized by the FHLBB in determining compliance with appraisal requirements. On 28 October 1986, the FHLBB increased the loan documentation requirements with respect to real estate loans and established for the first time minimum documentation requirements for other types of loans.[7]

---

4 On 30 August 1985, the FHLBB adopted appraisal and underwriting procedures for real estate lending which were more strict than previously existed. See FHLBB Memorandum R-64 (citation). It further tightened the appraisal standards by adopting Memorandum R-41C on 11 September 1986.

5 On 27 November 1985, the FHLBB tightened its loan to one borrower regulation making it more restrictive. See 50 Fed. Reg. 45,988 (1985).

6 On 9 December 1985, the FHLBB adopted its classification of asset regulation requiring the establishment of specific reserves of 50 per cent and 100 per cent of assets classified 'doubtful' or 'loss' respectively. See 50 Fed. Reg. 53,275 (1985). This regulation, in effect, gave examiners complete control over an association's capital. By designating a loan as a 'loss' and requiring a 100 per cent reserve, an examiner could eliminate most, if not all, of an association's capital thereby rendering it insolvent and subject to closure. There was little opportunity for appeal.

7 See, inter alia, J. Norton and S.C. Whitley, *Banking Law Manual* (1984), 1986 Supplements.

C. Calendar Year 1987

In January 1987, the FHLBB adopted new regulations that significantly changed the existing net worth rules and imposed substantial new capital requirements. These changes generally (1) increased all thrift institutions' minimum net worth (now to be called 'regulatory capital') requirement from 3 per cent of liabilities to 6 per cent of liabilities; (2) required an institution to have additional capital equal to up to 10 per cent of its aggregate direct investment and 4 per cent of all land loans and non-residential construction loans; and (3) revised regulatory capital computation to reflect more accurately an institution's interest rate risk exposure.[8]

In April 1987, the FHLBB amended the direct investment limitation regulation to impose stricter threshold requirements before associations could make investments and required capital deficient institutions (determined on the basis of newly issued minimum capital regulations) to obtain prior regulatory permission to make direct investments. In June 1987, the FHLBB adopted a statement of policy concerning the standards under which the FSLIC determines when to file lawsuits and pursue claims against directors and officers of insured associations that have failed. The FHLBB made further amendments to the direct investment limitation regulation to expand its scope and further restrict association activity.[9]

D. Reregulation and Asset Value Deflation

The FHLBB reregulation program initiated in 1985 proceeded to alleviate asset value inflation pressures as institutions were necessarily forced to begin reducing aggressive real estate lending activities, disposing of assets, and reserving increasing amounts of capital. The FHLBB activities were reactionary in nature, and reflected the environment in Congress that thrift management was generally to blame for the state of affairs in the thrift industry, instead of the misguided and conflicting government monetary, fiscal and exchange rate policies. Members of Congress also understood that the effects of prior FHLBB deregulatory initiatives and regulatory permissiveness and forbearance practices in the early 1980s, which undoubtedly fueled asset value inflation, were manifesting themselves in thrift balance sheets, the result of which was that many thrift institutions presented a far clearer picture of solvency and soundness on paper than existed in reality. The debate within Congress and pressure on the FDIC and FSLIC for clear accounting determinations made it clear that the FHLBB would likely not survive the decade intact as a regulatory institution. The 'bottom line' is that the FHLBB reregulatory initiatives were reactionary attempts to mitigate a situation that was already far out of control, and served as the catalyst, together with exchange rate instability, for an abrupt reversal of asset value inflation to a phase of asset value deflation. The FHLBB set asset value

---

8 *Ibid.*, 1987 Supplements.

9 *Ibid.*

deflation in motion, but the real impetus for these phenomena in the real estate industry arrived under ill-timed tax legislation in 1986.

In addition, State legislators and regulators generally responded to federal thrift reregulation during this period with their own form of reregulation, and State statutes and regulations were strictly construed. For instance, in Texas many changes were made to state statutes and regulations, and a State government task force was designated to investigate the Texas aspects of the S&L crisis.[10] The other States experiencing mounting thrift industry problems, such as California and Florida, preceded in a similar manner. The States initially reacted in this way in response to pressures from the FHLBB and the federal examination staff, but the State regulatory bodies ultimately joined the reregulation efforts as a reflexive response to the actual and perceived excesses in the S&L industry. The State reregulation efforts, similarly to the federal efforts, were simply too little too late and merely reinforced the downward pressure on real estate and asset value deflation.

III. LEGISLATIVE REREGULATION – THE BEGINNINGS

By 1986, there was pressure for congressional action, especially as certain provisions of the 1982 Garn-St. Germain Act were set to expire (i.e. the net worth certificate program). The Reagan Administration remained largely disengaged from the thrift industry crisis, but in early 1986 a new Undersecretary of the Treasury developed a proposal for injecting USD15 billion into the FSLIC through a combination of increased premiums imposed on thrift institutions, purchases of FSLIC obligations by the Federal Home Loan Banks, and primarily by the formation of a financing corporation that would issue obligations that it would then use to purchase zero coupon bonds of the FSLIC.[11] By mid-1986, however, other legislative matters were troubling the banking industry and members of Congress, including the expansion of banking industry powers and abrupt reversals in tax policy from 1981.

A. The Tax Reform Act of 1986

Notwithstanding repeated warnings from the real estate industry, Congress passed the Tax Reform Act of 1986 (TRA).[12] The TRA eliminated virtually all of the tax benefits and incentives built into the US tax laws by

---

10 See, e.g., Eugenie D. Short and Jeffery W. Gunther, *The Texas Thrift Situation: Implications for the Texas Thrift Industry* (1988).

11 See S. Langbein,'The Thrift Crises and the Constitution', 53 Wash. & Lee L. Rev., at p.197.

12 See Tax Reform Act of 1986, Pub. L. No. 99–514, 100 Stat. 2085 (1986). The 60 per cent deduction for long-term capital gains were repealed; residential real estate was to be depreciated over 27.5 years under the straight-line method, non-residential real estate was to be depreciated over 31.5 years under the straight-line method; the investment tax credit was repealed; the Rehabilitation tax credit was substantially reduced; 'at risk' rules now applied to real estate; and losses from 'passive activities' could be offset against income from other passive activities.

ERTA,[13] and none of the ERTA benefits and incentives were 'grandfathered' under this legislation. These benefits and incentives were either phased out or eliminated, effective 1 January 1986, for the tax year 1986 and all future tax years. Thus, the easy tax write-offs that once made aggressive or otherwise marginal real estate development profitable were all but eliminated in an abrupt policy reversal.

In particular, 1986 was the last year that real estate developers could take advantage of the faster depreciation allowed under the old law. Under the TRA, the depreciable life for real estate improvements was extended from 19 years to 31.5 years.[14] The 'at risk' rules were also revised to limit tax write-offs to the amount actually invested.[15] The deductibility of interest used to finance investment property was limited to the amount of net investment income. Moreover, new 'passive loss' rules required that losses from an activity in which an individual did not materially participate could be deducted only from income derived from a passive activity.[16] Prior to these rules, an investor could deduct these losses from any income, including salary.[17] In addition, the capital gains tax exclusion was repealed,[18] which increased the maximum tax rate from 20 per cent to 28 per cent.[19] Finally, the investment tax credit was eliminated[20] and the rehabilitation credit substantially reduced.[21]

As a result of the initial finance/tax incentives for real estate investment and development under ERTA resulting in asset value inflation given the US monetary policy and economic environment of the early 1980s, and the subsequent removal of the finance/tax incentives under the TRA, there followed a spiraling depression in real estate values with valuation losses often exceeding 50 per cent, rivaling even the October 1987 stock market debacle. There was not a shift of wealth, but a massive loss of wealth, in the form of real estate asset value deflation.

---

13 Don Williams, Chief Executive Officer of the Trammell Crow Company, a Dallas, Texas based real estate company (the largest in America) went to great efforts to convince Senators Packwood and Rostenkowski, the primary sponsors of this tax legislation, that the impact of this legislation would be draconian on the American real estate market. Coupled with the decrease in oil prices from a peak of more than USD34 per barrel in 1981 (curiously, the same year as the Economic Tax Recovery Act of 1981 (ERTA) was passed) to a nadir of slightly under USD10 per barrel in early 1986 (curiously the same year as the Tax Reform Act of 1986 (TRA) was passed) the real estate industry in the oil belt was massacred. Real estate prices plummeted. Banks and S&Ls that loaned against the high real estate values saw their capital diminish and faced insolvency. Their officers and directors were blamed for unsafe and unsound lending practices, fraud, etc.

14 See TRA § 201 (amending 26 U.S.C. § 168).

15 See TRA § 503 (repealing 26 U.S.C. § 465(c)(3)(D), which excluded the holding of real property from the application of the 'at risk' rules).

16 See 26 U.S.C. § 469.

17 See 26 U.S.C. § 165.

18 See TRA § 301 (amending I.R.C. § 1202).

19 See 26 U.S.C. § 302(a)(1).

20 See 26 U.S.C. § 211.

21 See 26 U.S.C. § 251. The rehabilitation tax credit for certified historic structures was reduced from 25 per cent to 20 per cent, a credit of 10 per cent was provided for substantial rehabilitation of building placed in service before 1936, there was to be no credit for any buildings placed in service after 1935, that were not certified historic, and the credit was subject to the limitations on passive losses and credits.

In other words, the tax laws were changed in such a manner that the inflationary tax push pricing of real estate created by ERTA was not only eliminated for all future tax years as to any new investments in real estate, but also as to any existing investments.[22] This action coupled with the elimination of tax exempt financing for many real estate projects under TRA made the deflationary impact of this legislation on real estate values inherently predictable.[23] The resulting loss of capital in the S&L industry alone was widely

---

22 See, e.g., Lawrence H. White, *Competition and Currency: Essays on Free Banking and Money* (1989) at p.109:

> 'At the end of 1984 the US Department of the Treasury issued a proposed revamping of the tax code. The proposal aimed at eliminating tax loopholes and other advantaged positions while lowering overall tax rates. The proposal – discussed and revised during the following two years – was finally passed by the Congress as the Tax Reform Act of 1986. Real estate investors' ability to shelter other income with their 'passive' (depreciation-related) losses was restricted. *This last provision was applied to existing real estate projects as well as prospective ones.* Such changes in the tax code – to the extent that they were unanticipated by real estate markets before, say, 1985 – *could only mean a decrease in real estate values.*' (Emphasis added).

Professor White also applies the same rationale to oil prices. In the paragraph immediately following the above quoted paragraph, he states:

> 'Movements in the price of oil reinforced this effect, at about the same time. After hitting their $34 per barrel peak in early 1981, oil prices drifted gradually downward during the next few years, settling to a $24 per barrel level in 1985. They then fell sharply in early 1986, dipping briefly below $10 per barrel during the summer. They subsequently rose modestly and fluctuated in a range around $15 per barrel. Thus, not only did the price of oil fail to rise to the heights that many had expected, but it fell to levels that were only half of those of the early 1980s. *Again, this change could only mean a sharp fall in real estate values in the oil belt.*' (Emphasis added.)

23 In 1979, the Internal Revenue Code was amended to allow for the issuance of industrial development bonds (IDBs) by government and quasi-governmental bodies. The use of these bonds were expanded into many areas of real estate. Take, for example, a 500-acre piece of raw land. A quasi-governmental body, say an industrial district, would be formed under State law having jurisdiction over the 500 acres. The district would issue bonds and provide the proceeds of those bonds to a real estate developer to develop and build the infrastructure (i.e. roads, utilities, etc.). The bonds were to be serviced and repaid from revenues generated from ad valorem taxes assessed by the district. The bonds were purchased by investors because of their higher yields and tax exempt features. Once the infrastructure improvements had been completed by the developer and paid for with the proceeds of the bonds, the owner of the 500 acres had at least a partially developed site. Typically, the owner of the 500 acres would be the developer. The owner/developer would then borrow money from a savings and loan (S&L) or a bank to fully develop the 500 acres into finished industrial lots for resale. Because of the newly developed infrastructure funded with bond proceeds, the 500 acres appraised value had greatly appreciated. The lender gladly loaned needed funds to the developer. The developer finished the project and sold the lots to industrial users. From 1979 through to 1986, many projects were financed in this manner with many variations. On 31 December 1986, the music stopped ... the favorable tax treatment for industrial revenue bonds was eliminated by the Tax Reform Act of 1986. This was another blow to real estate, since what had been a ready source of funding for real estate (namely the industrial revenue bonds and their tax exempt characteristics) dried up. A question remains for many of the holders of the industrial revenue bonds issued during this 1979–1986 time period: how will ad valorem taxes assessed by the district cover the servicing of their bonds when real estate values are declining and much worse, real estate is not selling. Believe it or not, this question is still playing out in the 1990s not only for districts that issued industrial development bonds, but also cities and countries that issued their own municipal bonds.

estimated to equal or exceed approximately USD10 billion, and required either massive new capital infusions or a massive shrinkage of assets or a combination thereof. Since new capital is predictably hard to raise in a depressed and declining market, shrinkage of assets became the only effective response, but disposing of real estate assets into a depressed and declining market simply created more losses and magnified the financial problems of S&Ls and banks.

The TRA had a far more devastating impact on asset value deflation, however. As real estate values declined, financial institutions became concerned about the value of real estate collateral securing their loans. The real estate lending market began to 'dry up'; new loans and refinancing became much more difficult to obtain; and liquidity for real estate investments, refinancing and loan renewals generally diminished.

As liquidity diminished, investors could not protect their real estate investments, and foreclosures and deeds in lieu of foreclosure occurred en masse. Although no cash proceeds were received through repossession, investors ironically faced enormous tax liabilities arising from so-called 'phantom income' generated from 'recapture', 'debt forgiveness', and 'debt in excess of basis' problems.[24] The end result of the increased tax liabilities (to the extent paid) was further decreased liquidity for real estate investment, lending activities and (to the extent not paid) tax liabilities to the IRS which could be collected through foreclosure on all assets of the investor, including the investor's home. Investors could not discharge these tax liabilities by filing for bankruptcy.

Although it was generally anticipated that gross tax revenues from individuals would substantially decrease by reason of the TRA, this did not occur. The apparent reason for this unanticipated result was the phantom income generated by the incidence of recapture, debt forgiveness and debt in excess of the basic phenomena. Neither Congress nor the IRS anticipated the impact of these phenomena or the increased tax revenues, and collectively failed to understand the impact of TRA upon real estate values.

B. The Competitive Equality Banking Act of 1987

The banking industry continued pressing for expanded powers, particularly the right to engage in securities activities notwithstanding the Glass-Steagall Act provisions.[25] As reviewed in Part One, above, the securities activities of banks were of special concern to the large money center banking institutions as competition intensified with securities firms through the losses of deposits to money market mutual funds and traditional lending activities to commercial paper markets.

---

24 These are concepts respecting 'US tax consequences of debt restructure and foreclosure'.

25 As reviewed *supra* in Chapter Three of this work, the Glass-Steagall Act consists of §§ 16, 20, 21, and 32 of the Banking Act of 1933 and introduced statutory divisions between the banking and securities businesses. These provisions are now codified at 12 U.S.C.§§ 24 (Seventh), 377, 378a, and 78 (1997).

Since the early 1980s, non-banking entities developed institutions known as 'non-bank banks' which exploited the definition of the term 'bank' in the Bank Holding Company Act.[26] The FRB sought to exercise jurisdiction over the non-bank banks, but the OCC approved of non-bank banks, and eventually the FRB's challenge was quashed by a decision of the US Supreme Court.[27] The commercial banking industry nonetheless maintained pressure on Congress to expand bank affiliations with non-banking activities,[28] but Congress did not respond and the Reagan Administration remained detached as the primary interest before Congress was by then the recapitalization of the FSLIC and mounting thrift industry problems.[29]

By early 1986, the regulatory agencies, principally the FRB, issued a number of deregulatory rulings reinterpreting the Glass-Steagall Act and afforded banks expanded opportunities to engage in securities activities, and initiated legislation to close the non-bank bank loophole. The Reagan Administration finally drafted legislation to assist the thrift industry, but the plan became entangled in the congressional debate over expanded banking powers and the non-bank banks and failed to become law.[30]

During the period of 1986–1987, thrift industry losses compounded as real estate values declined following the enactment of the TRA and affected various regions of the United States.[31] Many insolvent thrift institutions were permitted by the FHLBB to remain open and grow, notwithstanding recent reregulatory initiatives. These initiatives, coupled with the devastating effects of TRA on the real estate market, set the stage for accelerating losses to accumulate.

Texas thrift institutions were the most aggressive in terms of growth, and their demise was particularly notable. In 1987, losses at Texas thrift institutions alone consisted of more than 50 per cent of all thrift losses in the United States, as 14 of the 20 largest thrift failures were premised in Texas. The Texas State economy entered major recession, oil prices fell by nearly 50 per cent, and real estate market prices collapsed.

---

26 In order to be deemed a 'bank' under the Bank Holding Company Act, a company had to engage in both taking deposits and commercial lending. See 12 U.S.C. § 1841(c). The 'nonbank banks' refrained from engaging in one of these activities, and their affiliated holding companies therefore circumvented the limitations on nonbanking activities imposed by the Bank Holding Company Act. See generally Jonathan R. Macey and Geoffrey P. Miller, *Banking Law and Regulation* (1993), at pp.300–301.

27 *See Board of Governors of the Federal Reserve System v. Dimension Financial Corp.*, 474 U.S. 361 (1986).

28 The banking industry was somewhat divided over the expansion of bank powers between the money center banking contingency and independent banking contingency. See Langbein, *supra* note 1, at p.198; Philip T. Sudo, 'Small Banks Add to Chorus Against Glass-Steagall Reform', Am. Banker, 2 March 1987, at p.9.

29 See Langbein, *supra* note 11, at p.198; Robert M. Garsson, '100th Congress Preps For Financial Service Struggle: FSLIC Aid Still Dominates Hill Agenda, While Industry's Divisions Remain Keen', Am. Banker, 5 January 1987, at p.8.

30 See Langbein, *supra* note 11, at pp.198–199.

31 See, e.g. 'Oversight on the Condition of the Financial Services Industry', Hearings Before the Committee on Banking, Housing and Urban Affairs, 100th Cong., 2d Sess. (1988).

By year-end 1987, insolvent Texan thrift institutions accounted for 44 per cent of the assets in all insolvent S&Ls, and the unprofitable Texan S&Ls accounted for over 60 per cent of all losses in the entire United States.[32] The condition of the Texan thrift institutions resulted in higher interest rates being paid for all financial institutions in Texas, as the market required payment of a 'Texas premium' to maintain deposit bases.[33]

The FSLIC, struggling with solvency since early 1985, reported overall net annual losses of USD6.6 billion and reserve fund deficits of USD13.7 billion by 1987.[34] The Senate Banking Committee began by reviving the FSLIC recapitalization plan in 1987 along with a comprehensive bill that also provided for expanded banking powers. However, congressional infighting resulted in the elimination of the bank powers provisions, implementation of a one-year moratorium on the grant by regulatory agencies of any additional securities, insurance, or real estate powers, and prohibition on non-bank banks. The FSLIC recapitalization efforts were stalled by powerful S&L special interest groups which argued that the FHLBB reregulatory initiatives were too harsh and arbitrary, but these provisions remained in the bill, although the recapitalization figure was pared down to the point where key figures involved with the bill realized that the authorized amount would be inadequate.[35]

1. *FSLIC Recapitalization*

The Competitive Equality Banking Act of 1987 (CEBA) [36] was enacted in August 1987 as a comprehensive piece of banking legislation, with its genesis in the recapitalization of FSLIC, but clearly the product of serious infighting and compromise between the Reagan Administration, Congress, and the commercial banking and thrift industries. Within the 11 titles of CEBA, Congress addressed a wide range of banking issues, some of which were under consideration since the enactment of the Garn-St. Germain Act of 1982.

The CEBA was enacted in large part to address problems that had manifested within thrift institutions and banking organizations alike. Notwithstanding the FSLIC recapitalization, the CEBA as originally drafted would have primarily granted banking institutions additional powers in securities, insurance, and real estate activities, but the legislation was revised to create

---

32 See FDIC, *History of the Eighties, Volume 1: Lessons for the Future* (Washington D.C., 1998) at p.183.

33 See, e.g., Eugenie D. Short and Jeffery W. Gunther, *The Texas Thrift Situation: Implications for the Texas Financial Industry* (1988).

34 See Joint Committee on Taxation, 'Current Tax Rules Relating to Financially Troubled Savings and Loan Associations' (JCS 3–89), at p.2 (16 February 1989); General Accounting Office, 'Troubled Financial Institutions: Solutions to the Thrift Industry Problem', GAO/GGD-89–47 (December 1988).

35 See Langbein, *supra* note 11, at p.200.

36 See Pub. L. No. 100–86, 101 Stat. 552 (1987) (codified as amended, in scattered sections of 2, 12, 15 and 31 U.S.C.).

a temporary but comprehensive moratorium on banking agencies' ability to authorize these additional powers.[37]

The most significant provisions of CEBA (1) recapitalized the FSLIC with USD10.875 billion;[38] (2) required the application of generally accepted accounting principles (GAAP) to all banks and S&Ls whose deposits were federally insured by the FDIC or the FSLIC;[39] and (3) established the Qualified Thrift Lender (QTL) Test which required S&Ls to devote 60 per cent of their assets to residential housing-related lending activities and investments, and thereby reduced the investment flexibility enjoyed by thrift institutions since the Garn-St. Germain Act. The FHLBB augmented the reregulatory initiatives adopted in 1985 through early 1987 and adopted additional restrictive regulations under authority vested in CEBA.

Commencing on 31 December 1987, with the establishment of a classification of asset procedure consistent with the classification practices of federal banking agencies, the FHLBB adopted more restrictive regulations dealing with troubled debt restructures, the qualified thrift lender test, appraisal rules and policies and accounting standards, which greatly exacerbated the thrift industry crisis and accelerated asset value deflation.[40]

---

37 Similarly to the Garn-St. Germain Act, CEBA also originally contained provisions to include expanded powers for banking organizations, but the failure to reach consensus resulted in the elimination of such provisions from CEBA. More importantly, CEBA did include a six-month moratorium on the authorization of new powers in securities, insurance, and real estate activities by any of the federal banking agencies. The reason behind the moratorium was to provide Congress with time to reconsider the issue and reach timely consensus, but this failed to materialize. The CEBA moratorium on new bank powers was intended to provide time to develop a legislative solution to the issue, but Congress failed to act on the issue prior to the end of the moratorium. Thus, in 1988 the Glass-Steagall Act became a key issue once again, but Congress again failed to act on the issue. The Glass-Steagall Act focus therefore shifted from Congress to the federal banking agencies and the courts. The federal banking agencies increasingly authorized bank entry into these areas on an accelerated basis, and the banking organization and thrift institution crises tended to replace expanded powers into securities, insurance, and real estate activities as key issues before Congress.

38 The primary factor behind the passage of CEBA was to provide financial assistance to the FSLIC, the resources of which were being depleted by distressed and failing thrift institutions. CEBA provided USD10.875 billion towards the recapitalization of FSLIC and established a forbearance program for certain 'well-managed' thrift institutions. CEBA also imposed more restrictive and prudential accounting, appraisal, reserve, and capital standards for thrift institutions.

39 Despite the mandate that banks and savings and loans be subject to the same GAAP accounting rules, the FHLBB took the position that the GAAP that applied to savings and loans was different. Incredibly, there was then considered to be a 'bank GAAP' and a 'savings and loan GAAP', for regulatory purposes.

40 On 31 December 1987, the FHLBB adopted rules and guidelines to govern and clarify the procedures to be followed by an insured institution that engaged in troubled debt restructurings. In the calendar year 1988, the FHLBB was even more active in reregulation. On 1 January 1988, the FHLBB implemented the qualified thrift lender test. On 1 January 1988, the FHLBB implemented CEBA provisions by adopting regulations to allow troubled, but well-managed, S&L associations to be exempted temporarily from certain capital requirements. As a practice matter, five forbearances were granted by the FHLBB. On 5 February 1988, the FHLBB implemented CEBA provisions giving the FHLBB authority to vary an insured association's minimum capital requirement on a case-by-case basis. The regulations also implemented the new FHLBB authority to issue capital directives to enforce the minimum capital requirements. On 30 March 1988, the FHLBB amended the capital requirements to force a more rapid increase in capital by revising the method of computing required increases in capital.

Most importantly, however, the CEBA superseded most of the FHLBB's deregulatory capital requirements adopted in the early 1980s which facilitated excessive growth and speculative activities. CEBA amended previous thrift legislation under the Home Owners Loan Act (HOLA) to require conformity between thrift regulations to many existing federal banking agency regulations.[41] CEBA also required the FHLBB to promulgate accounting standards adopting and implementing GAAP 'to the same degree that generally accepted accounting principles are used to determine compliance with rules and regulations of the [FRB, OCC and FDIC]' for both federally-chartered and State-chartered thrift institutions regulated by it, by December 1993.[42]

Thus, CEBA appeared to eliminate RAP and contemplate one set of GAAP rules for thrifts and banks alike. The distinction was not elaborated upon in CEBA, however, and regulatory authorities continued to apply varying GAAP standards and interpretations to thrift institutions and banks. The FHLBB proposed further reregulatory initiatives to implement the remaining CEBA provisions in 1987.[43] Therefore, the enabling capital and accounting regulations and guidance promulgated by the FHLBB in the early 1980s to permit thrift institutions to grow on paper and alleviate the interest rate mismatch dilemma were abruptly reversed under CEBA.

Title IV of CEBA, entitled the *Thrift Industry Recovery Act*, established several other requirements that further unified standards between the thrift and banking industries. In addition to requiring convergence of accounting standards, CEBA also amended HOLA and the National Housing Act that required federally chartered and FSLIC-insured thrift institutions to adopt asset classification systems and appraisal standards comparable to those required by federal banking agencies.[44] Notably, however, the concepts of subordinated debt and goodwill were excluded under CEBA and could therefore continue to be used for purposes of determining capital reserve requirements, permissible loss deferrals, and other regulatory requirements.[45]

The FHLBB eventually implemented CEBA to require the preparation of several financial reports in accordance with GAAP.[46] CEBA further allowed for forbearances from strict enforcement of capital requirements for thrift institutions with more than 0.5 per cent net worth, provided that the weak

---

41 See CEBA, § 402(a), 101 Stat. at 605, codified at 12 U.S.C. § 1467.

42 See CEBA § 402(b), 101 Stat. at 606, codified at 12 U.S.C. § 1724.

43 See, e.g., 'Appraisal Policies and Practices', 52 Fed. Reg. 39,070 (1987) (codified at 12 C.F.R. Pts 563 and 571) (proposed Oct. 2, 1987); 'Classification of Assets', 52 Fed. Reg. 39,087 (1987) (codified at 12 C.F.R. Pts 561, 563 and 571) (proposed 2 October 1987); 'Minimum Capital Requirements for Individual Insured Institutions', 52 Fed. Reg. 39,105 (1987) (codified at 12 C.F.R. Pt 563) (proposed 5 October 1987); 'Troubled Debt Restructuring', 52 Fed. Reg. 39,112 (1987) (codified at 12 C.F.R. Pts 563 and 571) (proposed 5 October 1987); 'Uniform Accounting Standards', 52 Fed. Reg. 39,145 (1987) (codified at 12 C.F.R. Pts 561, 563, and 563c) (proposed 2 October 1987).

44 See CEBA § 402, 101 Stat. at 605–608.

45 See CEBA § 402, 101 Stat. at 608.

46 See FHLBB, 'Accounting and Reporting Requirements', 57 Fed. Reg. 40,085 (1992) (codified at 12 C.F.R. Pts 545, 562, 563, 563c and 571).

capital positions were attributable to 'economic conditions in a designated economically depressed region' or to losses incurred by certain minority-owned institutions.[47] Finally, the FHLBB was empowered under CEBA to establish minimum capital requirements on a 'case-by-case' basis, in a manner consistent with the underlying convergence requirements of the ILSA.[48]

2. *Distressed and Failed Banking Organizations and Thrift Institutions*

The remaining provisions of CEBA were designed to facilitate the resuscitation or acquisition of failed or distressed thrift institutions and banks. Most importantly, the CEBA provisions expanded and finalized the emergency interstate acquisition statutes originally adopted under the Garn-St. Germain Act of 1982. Both failed and distressed institutions were eligible for interstate acquisition. The distressed thrift institutions were included under these provisions within a new category of troubled institution: a bank 'in danger of closing'. If an insured bank's chartering authority rendered an 'in danger of closing' determination, the bank became eligible for interstate acquisition. The FDIC's authority to authorize and assist large emergency interstate acquisitions was expanded under CEBA: either an entire BHC or a part thereof could be part of an interstate acquisition if a large bank subsidiary was deemed to be 'in danger of closing'. CEBA further authorized the FDIC to establish 'bridge banks' or temporary national banks for up to three years to address instances wherein an immediate acquisition could not be arranged but circumstances surrounding liquidation of the institution were questionable. The FDIC could not establish a 'bridge bank', however, until the insured bank was closed.[49]

3. *Post-CEBA: The Thrift Crisis Unfolds*

The period between the enactment of CEBA and the beginning of 1989 was the time when public attention multiplied with respect to the thrift industry crisis. Although CEBA recapitalized the FSLIC with resources to address insolvent thrift institutions, the amount was clearly inadequate. The thrift industry failures through 1988, primarily in Texas, were increasingly large, and assistance amounts exceeded USD1 billion with regularity. By August

---

47 See CEBA, § 404, 101 Stat., at 609–612.
48 See CEBA § 406, 101 Stat., at 614–616.
49 The CEBA also addressed several other problem areas. First, the CEBA extended the Net Worth Certificate Program initiated under the Garn-St. Germain Act for another five years. Second, the CEBA established a loan-loss amortization program for agricultural banking organizations that (1) had assets of USD100 million or less; (2) adopted a capital restoration plan; and (3) maintained their required percentages of agricultural lending. These banks could therefore amortize their loan losses incurred after 31 December 1983. All three federal banking agencies purportedly opposed the loan loss deferral programs, but the program was nonetheless enacted into law by Congress. Finally, CEBA provided that insured deposits were backed by the 'full faith and credit' of the US Government. Although this policy had previously been articulated, it had never before been placed into statute and therefore made binding on the United States.

1988, estimates were that the Texas thrift industry had plunged into collective insolvency that cost the FSLIC approximately USD12 billion.[50]

The FHLBB, under new chairman Danny Wall, consistently downplayed the crisis, in contrast to the previous FHLBB regime, but FHLBB members publicly disagreed with the new chairman.[51] The media espoused many reports involving insider abuse, fraud and embezzlement, mismanagement, and unethical dealings of professionals involved with failing thrift institutions.[52] The public estimates of the cost of a thrift industry bailout increased steadily over the months into 1988.

The insolvent FSLIC thereafter engaged in what came to be known as the 'Southwest Plan' (discussed below) to resolve institutions with various arrangements, the common theme of which required capital in the future through net worth maintenance agreements, yield maintenance agreements, and capital asset guarantees which made estimates of the amount of FSLIC insolvency or the magnitude of the crisis somewhat difficult and speculative at best. The series of transactions conducted under the Southwest Plan by politically-connected acquiring institutions or investors who were exploiting tax incentives adopted in 1981, but were expiring in 1988, resulted in a magnified public outcry of charges of regulatory favoritism and corruption.[53]

In 1988, the FHLBB, under Chairman Wall, resolved over 220 thrift institutions with assets in excess of USD115 billion, many under the Southwest Plan using minimal cash outlays, and maximum use of promissory notes, guarantees, and tax advantages. All of these generally made these transactions more expensive than they would have been if the FSLIC had been equipped with sufficient resources to carry out its objectives, and further obfuscated the institutions' underlying economic situation.[54]

IV. CONCLUDING NOTE: THE FHLBB's SOUTHWEST PLAN

In February 1988, the FHLBB introduced the 'Southwest Plan' to consolidate and repackage insolvent Texas-based thrift institutions and sell them

---

[50] On 18 August 1988, the FHLBB announced a USD1.3 billion bailout of 12 Texas thrift institutions that were acquired by LSST Financial Services Corporation. The following day, the FHLBB announced a combination of 8 Texas thrift institutions with USD2.4 billion in assistance, which were combined into a single thrift institution in an apparent revival of the FSLIC 'Phoenix' program of the early 1980s.

[51] See Langbein, *supra* note 11, at p.201.

[52] For instance, the closing of Lincoln S&L Association, the institution whose insolvency resulted in the resignation of the Speaker of the House of Representatives for corruption, the investigation of five US senators, the resignation of a key regulatory authority, and the imposition of millions of dollars of fines against and suspension of partners in one of the most distinguished New York law firms, Kaye Scholer Fierman Hays & Handler, involved an estimated injection of public funds in excess of USD2.5 billion.

[53] See generally GAO, 'Failed Thrifts: Bank Board's 1988 Texas Resolutions' (1989).

[54] See *History of the Eighties, Volume 1, supra* note 32, at p.186.

to the highest bidders. The rationale behind the Southwest Plan strategy was to resolve insolvent thrift institutions quickly and conserve funds for the insolvent FSLIC. The FHLBB used various methods to pay for the difference between assets and liabilities of failed thrift institutions absorbed into the Plan process, such as FSLIC notes, tax incentives, and income, capital, value, and yield guarantees. The FHLBB sold approximately 205 thrift institutions under the Southwest Plan with assets in excess of USD100 billion.

A. Rationale for Transactions

The FHLBB understandably preferred supervisory mergers and acquisitions over liquidations as the method of choice for resolving failed or failing S&Ls, as invitations to healthy S&Ls to acquire failed or failing institutions produced more than 200 mergers during 1981–1982. These 'supervisory mergers' were arranged under Assistance Agreements and forbearance letters that included incentives such as long-term goodwill amortization covered in Chapter Two.

Goodwill was not only 'an indispensable tool' in making the mergers look attractive, but was required to authorize the merger because the immediate write-off of the shortage would simply render the merged entity insolvent again, and in some cases would also have rendered the acquiring institution insolvent. In addition, special provisions allowed the mergers to be tax-free in numerous respects, helping the FHLBB create an enticing offer without violating a statutory requirement that FSLIC assistance in each case could not exceed the cost of liquidation.[55]

The merger alternative was a painfully slow one considering that by 1987 in Texas alone, '[a]lmost 40 per cent of the State's 281 savings and loans were insolvent and losing money at the rate of US$500 million a month'.[56] Thus, the Southwest Plan was conceived as a plan to revitalize this process and repackage insolvent and failing thrifts for sale to private investors.[57] The bulk of the thrift institutions absorbed under the Plan were located in the southwestern area of the United States, hence the name 'Southwest Plan'.

Under the Southwest Plan, for investments equal to 3 per cent or less of the thrifts' combined assets, the acquiring institutions received, in addition to the goodwill, amortization and tax benefits, other enticements such as cash contributions from the FSLIC that were allowed as capital credits; a government guarantee to cover future losses on current assets; and the ability to use past and future tax losses to shelter profits from the acquiring institution's other businesses or from assets subsequently placed in the thrifts.[58]

The US Congress explicitly provided the FHLBB with the authority to use special tax incentives to assist in the sale of distressed thrift institutions under

---

55 See generally GAO, 'Failed Thrifts: Bank Board's 1988 Texas Resolutions' (1989).

56 See B. Fromson, 'The Screwiest S&L Bailout Ever,' *Fortune* (19 June 1989), at pp.114–115.

57 *Ibid.* at p.118.

58 *Ibid.*

the ERTA of 1981,[59] which were applied in numerous transactions perpetrated by the FHLBB under the Southwest Plan through assistance agreements entered into with failing thrift institutions in 1988. The only hitch was that the thrift institution tax provisions were set to expire in 1989. Thus, a frantic 'string of sell-offs' occurred in late 1988, just as the tax provisions were about to expire.

In 1988 and 1989, the FSLIC resolved nearly 200 insolvent thrift institutions in 96 assisted transactions, and the FSLIC entered into long-term agreements obligating the US Government to continue to make assistance payments to the 91 institutions that remained after the restructuring connected with these transactions.[60] Accordingly, for negligible cash investments, the new owners were prepared to reap enormous profits in the future while the government assumed most of the risk and lost significant tax revenues.[61] Certain transactions also allowed purchase prices to be spread over three to ten years, with investment recoupment predicted within two years of purchase.[62]

B. Structure of Transactions

The actual structure of the Southwest Plan transactions may be illustrated as follows:

---

[59] For instance, Section 597 of the Internal Revenue Code, enacted in 1981, provided that government financial assistance to distressed thrift institutions would be exempt from taxation, and that the receipt of such assistance would not trigger any reduction in basis for an institution's assets. See I.R.C. § 597. See Daniel M. Crane, 'Double Dipping: Congressional Tax Policy and the Savings & Loan Crisis', (1993) 13 Virginia Tax Rev. 101, at p.102.

[60] See 'Tax Aspects of Government-Assisted Savings and Loan Acquisitions', Hearings on H.R. 1135, H.R. 1338, H.R. 1326, and H.R. 561, before the Committee on Ways and Means, 102nd Cong., 2d Sess. at 37 (1992).

[61] See Wallace *et. al.*, 'The Great S&L Fire Sale Bailouts', U.S. News & World Rep. (9 January 1989), at pp.11, 14.

[62] See Fromson, *supra* note 56. Ronald O. Perelman invested USD315 million into a USD7.1 billion-asset S&L, solvent but with net operating losses of USD1.2 billion. In return for the payment, to be spread over ten years, he received a USD5.1 billion guarantee to cover the thrift's bad assets, and tax benefits worth USD900 million. Of course, Perelman did undertake the business risk of keeping the big S&L running. But how risky was that? So generous were the terms of the deal that to lose money on it, he would have had to let the thrift founder and go bankrupt within 18 months a near impossibility, financial analysts say. For the first 90 days of 1989 alone, Perelman's rate of return on the capital invested is estimated at over 80 per cent.

Illustration 7.

Southwest Plan

Aquisition Structure

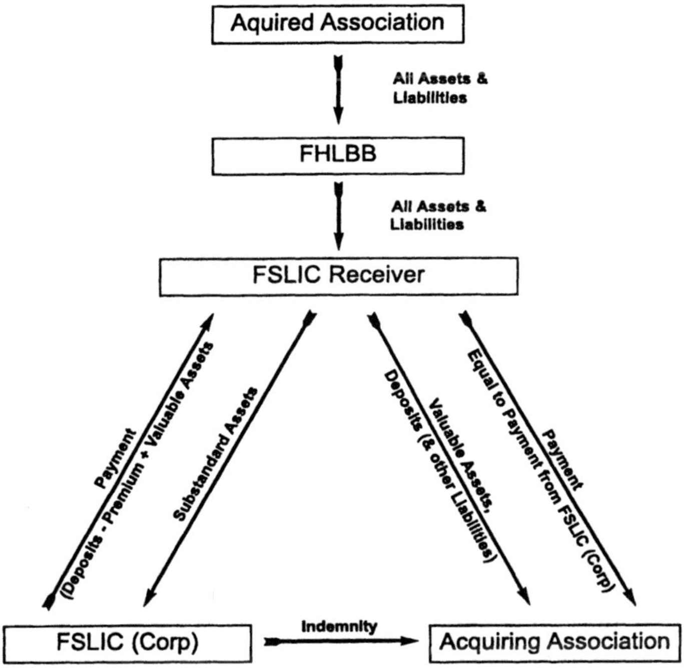

Under the Southwest Plan,[63] insolvent thrifts were consolidated as follows. First, the insolvent thrifts were closed by the FSLIC and *all* of their assets subject to *all* their liabilities were transferred to the FSLIC as Receiver. FSLIC as Receiver then transferred certain of these assets ('Acquired Assets' in the form of loans, real estate owned, etc.) to a newly formed thrift ('New Thrift') subject only to depositor liabilities and secured liabilities ('Assumed Liabilities') which were assumed by the New Thrift. The contingent and unsecured liabilities, executory contracts and other similar types of obligations ('Unassumed Obligations') were avoided or disaffirmed.

The FSLIC as Receiver kept these Unassumed Obligations which became claims against the estate of the insolvent thrift and any assets retained by the FSLIC as Receiver. As part of the ERTA of 1981, three special tax provisions were enacted to facilitate the acquisition of failing thrift institutions. The first

---

63 Much of this section is based upon the author and his law firm's actual involvement in structuring and implementing such plan (documents substantiating the information in this section of this chapter are in the law firm's possession).

provision permitted the acquisition of insolvent thrift institutions to qualify as tax-free 'G' reorganizations without regard to the continuity of interest rule.[64]

This provision gave the acquiring institution a carryover basis in the assets of the acquired thrift institution. The second provision permitted the preservation of net operating loss carry forwards (NOLs) through the 'G' reorganizations for tax purposes (at least through 31 December 1988).[65] The third provision provided that any assistance payments received from the FSLIC would be received tax-free and not require any downward adjustments.[66]

The initial Southwest Plan transactions were structured so the FSLIC retained 100 per cent of the tax benefits, with an emphasis on real estate and other assets held by insolvent thrifts. In later Southwest Plan transactions, part of the tax benefits were given up by the FSLIC with the result that, as noted above, so-called 'tax efficient users' were attracted to these transactions.[67] Thus, the Southwest Plan transactions were typically structured as a combination of allocation of tax benefits, coupled with a sharing of the gains and losses from maintaining and disposing of the assets acquired by the New Thrift.

The allocation of tax benefits and gain-sharing techniques failed to attract significant new capital into the thrift industry, however. The FSLIC elected to grant three types of assistance (each tax-free) over a term of ten years to induce owners of newly formed thrifts to acquire the Acquired Assets subject to the Assumed Liabilities. The first type covered the then-existing deficit net worth reflected by the excess of the Assumed Liabilities over the Acquired Assets.

This deficit was 'plugged' by a note (the 'Initial FSLIC Note') issued by FSLIC, which typically included a rate of interest equivalent to a fixed number of basis points above the Texas cost of funds. The determination of this deficit was based upon the book value of the Acquired Assets and Assumed Liabilities as reflected on the then-existing books and records of the insolvent thrifts, the subject of the consolidation, with all reserves and losses reversed.

The second type involved the concept of 'loss coverage', where the FSLIC essentially indemnified the New Thrift against any and all liabilities arising out of the acquisition, other than the Assumed Liabilities and other liabilities incurred or created by the New Thrift after the transaction closed. Further,

---

64 See I.R.C. § 368(a)(3)(D) (1988).

65 See I.R.C. § 382(l)(5)(F). This section allowed net operating loss carry forwards of insolvent thrift institutions to be used without the general annual use limitation imposed by section 382 on NOL carry forwards following an acquisition. See Crane, *supra* note 59, at p.104.

66 See I.R.C. § 597. Under the terms of the 1988 acquisition transactions, the FSLIC agreed to reimburse the acquiring institutions for any losses incurred on the disposition of certain assets held by a given distressed institution. For instance, if an asset with a book value of USD100 was sold for USD60, FSLIC would reimburse the acquirer for the USD40 differential between the book value and FMV of the asset. Under Section 597 of the Internal Revenue Code, the USD40 assistance payment was received tax free with no reduction in basis. The acquiring institutions interpreted § 597 and several other sections of the Code to allow a USD40 loss deduction, the effect of which was to completely disregard the direct assistance paid to compensate them for the loss in determining whether they were entitled to an allowable deduction. This practice came to be known as 'double dipping'. See Crane, *supra* note 59, at p.102.

67 See generally Derek A. Bloom, 'Tax Planning for an Acquisition of a Troubled Thrift Institution', 16 Journal of Corporate Taxation 313 (1990).

any loss arising by reason of disposition of the Acquired Assets below book value was covered by FSLIC through an assistance payment.

In general, all Acquired Assets were assets covered ('Covered Assets') against loss by the FSLIC. The FSLIC also paid an interest factor on the average book value of all Covered Assets equal to a certain amount of basis points over the Texas cost of funds.

With respect to the loss coverage described above, the FSLIC possessed the ability to cover these losses and satisfy any indemnities with cash or by delivering an additional FSLIC note(s) (the 'Additional FSLIC Notes') to the New Thrift, included interest rates equivalent to the yield maintenance rate. The New Thrift could thereafter build incentives into its assistance agreement by being able to participate in the value of the Acquired Assets. For example, certain New Thrifts had the ability, with respect to assets they acquired, to participate in any proceeds from disposition of those assets based upon an adjusted book value (i.e. a sum less than book value). Although these formulas were quite complicated, the main result was that the New Thrift was able to participate in proceeds generated from disposition of Acquired Assets at a level less than book value, while still obtaining yield maintenance and being covered as to loss based upon book value.

Under the FSLIC assistance agreements, two memorandum accounts were generally established. One memorandum account was entitled Special Reserve Account I (SRA I) and the other memorandum account was entitled Special Reserve Account II (SRA II). The SRAs each had debit and credit columns, respectively. The debit columns reflected money owed by the FSLIC to the New Thrift, and the credit columns reflected money owed by the New Thrift to the FSLIC. The SRA accounts were used to book the tax benefits, shared gains, settling of indemnifications, covered losses and other results for purposes of settling money owed by FSLIC to the New Thrift or vice-versa. The SRA I account primarily addressed capital issues, such as coverage of loss or indemnification against loss. The SRA II account primarily addressed an income concept, which considered the total yield maintenance as a debit, and offset that debit with any net operating income from the Covered Assets and increased that debit by any net operating loss from the Covered Assets.

The FSLIC typically required a 20 per cent interest in the New Thrift as consideration for the assistance package. The 20 per cent interest requirement was usually achieved through the issuance of warrants or preferred stock. Additionally, the FSLIC required cash contributions of capital generally ranging from 1.5 per cent of Assumed Liabilities up to 3 per cent of Assumed Liabilities.

C. Effects and Implications

In summary, the Southwest Plan Transaction involved numerous functional assistance packages offered by the FSLIC, coupled with an allocation of tax benefits, which together represented both an 'asset play' and an ability to avoid all liabilities other than depositor liabilities and secured liabilities. The assets acquired were then free from any exposure other than depositor liabilities and secured liabilities, and the assets were covered by the FSLIC against loss and subject to yield maintenance. The settling of money owed by or to the New Thrift was accomplished through debit/credit entries in the SRA I and II accounts. The FSLIC required new capital equal to 1.5 per cent to 3 per cent of Assumed Liabilities. Under the Southwest Plan, the FSLIC reserved claims against the former officers, directors and other institution-related parties. In addition to the major structural attributes of a Southwest Plan Transaction, the Acquirer was generally paid a fee for managing and disposing of non-performing assets.

The majority of these arrangements were undertaken on a tax-free basis. The FHLBB issued forbearance letters of varying durations which provided for the goodwill allowance as well as permission to operate below prescribed regulatory capital standards for a certain length of time; permission to engage in certain activities not normally approved for thrifts; and time to correct regulatory violations of the old thrift, such as the ownership of unauthorized subsidiaries. The Southwest Plan brought some of the largest US corporations and institutional investors into the supervisory merger and acquisition arena. These investors acquired many potentially rich assets within the shells of failed or failing thrift institutions for fractions of their face value with limited risk, as the FSLIC guarantees covered most of the risky loans already on thrift balance sheets.[68] The Southwest Plan generated enormous amounts of controversy throughout Congress, and subsequent audits raised many questions about these transactions in terms of fairness and conflicts of interest.

Notwithstanding the Southwest Plan controversies, the FSLIC reached the point of terminal insolvency. As early as 1981, regulators realized that FSLIC could not possibly meet its obligations to depositors in all insolvent S&Ls, and likewise could not possibly inject enough capital into the many failing S&Ls around the country to restore them to a sound financial footing.[69] From 1980 through 1988, the FSLIC arranged 333 acquisitions and resolved, through liquidation, merger, conservatorship or receivership, another 584 S&Ls, totaling USD180 billion in assets.[70] By January 1989, however, the FSLIC was insolvent with net deficits of USD50 billion, and incurred additional liabilities in excess of USD37 billion from resolutions of 223 problem thrifts closed in 1988 alone.[71] When the FHLBB reported that another 578 S&Ls would probably still require action, Congress at last acknowledged that taxpayers would have to pay for the clean-up.[72]

---

68 See William E. Sheeline, 'The Big Names in S&L Buyouts', *Fortune* (26 September 1988), at p.10.

69 See Paul G. Gaston and Jerry Stouck, 'OTS Argument that FIRREA Relieves Regulators of Binding Contractual Commitments is Bad Policy', (1990) 55 BNA Banking Rep. 861. Gaston and Stouck, partners with the Washington, D.C. law firm of Spriggs & Hollingsworth, are attorneys for Glendale Fed. Savings Bank, the only surviving S&Ls of the three cases consolidated under the *Winstar* litigation.

70 See M. Haisten, 'Winstar: The Leverage or the Last Straw in Deciding the Savings Association Industry's Future?', *Financial Institutions–Banking Law Paper* (1996), at p.8 (on file with author).

71 See US General Accounting Office, 'Thrifts and Housing Finance: Implications of a Stricter Qualified Thrift Lender Test', (1991).

72 See Haisten, *supra* note 70, at p.9.

FDIC Chairman Seidman decided to re-examine supervisory mergers and acquisitions of distressed institutions that occurred in 1988 under the Southwest Plan at a total cost to taxpayers of USD44 billion, and other political interests in Washington were also growing increasingly concerned.[73] The General Accounting Office underscored through various reports that it would have been a far less expensive undertaking to close down the otherwise insolvent thrift institutions and pay off the respective depositors under the Southwest Plan, especially since the obligation to cover losses was unlimited and GAO and others thought that estimated loss figures were too conservative.

Following the completion of Southwest Plan deals and intense subsequent scrutiny thereof by year-end 1988, Congress took notice and promised a 'top-to-bottom review' of the thrift industry situation in 1989.[74] Notwithstanding the controversy generated by the Southwest Plan and thrift industry crisis, there was virtually no action in Congress given the pending Presidential election.

Both political parties avoided the thrift industry crisis in campaign debates for fear of being mutually blamed for aggravating the crisis. The Reagan Administration and key Republican Party leaders supported legislation under the Garn-St. Germain Act and deregulatory measures that expanded the powers of thrift institutions, and the expansion of powers clearly backfired given the timing and context in which the expansion was granted. The enormous budget deficits generated in the mid-1980s also contributed to political problems for the Reagan Administration, and facilitated deferring action on the thrift industry crisis. The deferral of action by the Reagan Administration and political infighting clearly exacerbated the thrift industry crisis over 1985–1988. In addition, the Democratic Party controlled Congress during this period, and their involvement in exacerbating the thrift industry crisis was evident in supporting the thrift industry in delaying a federal bailout early on and consistently understating the severity of the problem. Finally, there were numerous charges of corruption and impropriety with respect to certain congressional leaders that intervened inappropriately in certain regulatory actions dealing with the resolution of individual thrift institutions.[75]

In November 1988, George Bush was elected President of the United States, and remarkably the S&L and banking crises were not significant issues (in fact, they were non-issues) during the election campaign and Presidential debates. Following the election, the delays underwent an abrupt reversal as the new Bush Administration and Congress became increasingly anxious to resolve the thrift industry crisis as quickly as possible with little

73 See Fromson, *supra* note 56, at p.114.

74 Notwithstanding the alarming S&L crisis, thrift institutions remained the nation's predominant mortgage lenders in 1988, originating 49 per cent, or USD160.7 billion, of all residential mortgages. Of the 2,949 FSLIC-insured S&Ls at year-end 1988, 70 per cent were actually deemed profitable by GAAP standards. Thus, the S&L crisis was actually 'concentrated' in the remaining 25 per cent having capital reserves below 3 per cent by GAAP standards, or 754 thrifts. Congress nonetheless enacted massive industry-wide reform.

75 See Langbein, *supra* note 11, at p.202.

political fallout. In February 1989, three weeks after taking office, the Bush Administration unveiled its massive and complex proposed 'bailout plan' which led to the enactment of comprehensive remedial federal legislation in August 1989.

9. The 1989 FIRREA Legislation: The Culmination of Legislative Reregulation in the 1980s

I. INTRODUCTION

Notwithstanding (or perhaps because of) the increasingly stringent and restrictive federal government 'reregulation', the thrift industry (and many banks) continued to be recognized as insolvent or in distress. As a direct political response, following the election of President Bush, the US Congress enacted the Financial Institutions Reform, Recovery, and Enforcement Act of 1989 (FIRREA).[1] This chapter analyses FIRREA as the culmination of federal legislative reregulation in the 1980s for US banking institutions.

FIRREA represented the most comprehensive restructuring of the US financial institution and deposit insurance apparatus in US financial history. The 1989 legislation totally reorganized the thrift industry with abrupt policy reversals in all substantive areas and shifted allocation of responsibility for the 'severity' of the crisis away from government policymaking to the industry itself. Most importantly for purposes of this work, FIRREA rendered the most significant changes in the supervision and regulation of the thrift industry since its establishment in 1933.[2]

The FIRREA legislation itself engendered little controversy, despite the comprehensiveness and abrupt policy reversals throughout its text. In fact, FIRREA has the least legislative history of any of the significant banking and thrift legislation and is relatively simple, notwithstanding the political and interest group competition that produced it.[3]

---

1 See Pub. L. No. 101-73, 103 Stat. 183 (1989).

2 On FIRREA generally, see, inter alia, D. Gail and J. Norton, 'A Decade's Journal From 'Deregulation' to 'Supervisory Regulation': The Financial Institutions Reform, Recovery and Enforcement Act of 1989,' 45 Bus. Law. 1103 (1990).

3 See S. Langbein,'The Thrift Crisis and the Constitution,' 53 Wash. & Lee L. Rev., at 204.

II. REVIEW OF FIRREA OBJECTIVES

A. In General

The congressional objectives of FIRREA were to prevent the total collapse of the S&L industry, eliminate the causes of the S&L crisis, and restore public confidence in the thrift industry and banking system. Congress enacted FIRREA to focus on reforming thrift institutions and providing bank regulatory agencies with expanded enforcement powers. FIRREA is widely understood as the principal shift towards supervisory reregulation of thrift institutions and banking institutions prompted by the widespread thrift crisis.

Although the genesis of FIRREA is found in the real estate depression of Texas and other southwestern States of the United States that overwhelmed the thrift industry and rendered the FSLIC insolvent, FIRREA affected all US financial institutions and professionals serving the financial institutions industry. The FIRREA legislation was enacted on a 'fast track' basis by Congress and, notwithstanding the absence of debate over the thrift industry crisis during the Presidential campaign, was clearly President Bush's top priority following his inauguration in January 1989.

The principal purposes of FIRREA as set forth in Title I included:

1. restoring public confidence in the savings and loan industry in order to ensure a safe, stable, and viable system of affordable housing finance;
2. strengthening capital, accounting, and other supervisory standards to improve thrift industry regulation and supervision;
3. limiting thrift investment powers and other activities that posed unacceptable risks to the deposit insurance funds;
4. strengthening the enforcement policies of federal regulators of depository institutions; and
5. strengthening the civil sanctions and criminal penalties for committing fraud or gross negligence against depository institutions and their depositors.

The primary objectives through which FIRREA would restore public confidence in the thrift industry consisted in part as follows. FIRREA abolished the FHLBB and established the Office of Thrift Supervision (OTS) with responsibility for supervisory and regulatory authority over federal and State S&Ls and S&L holding companies.[4] The OTS received all of the powers and authorities that were vested in the FHLBB immediately prior to the

---

[4] FIRREA amended the Home Owner's Loan Act of 1933 by dissolving the FHLBB and replacing it with the Office of Thrift Supervision within the Department of the Treasury similarly to the OCC to regulate and supervise the thrift industry. See FIRREA, *supra* note 1, at § 301(3)(e)(1), 103 Stat. at 278 (codified at 12 U.S.C. § 1462a(e)(1)).

enactment of FIRREA that were not otherwise expressly transferred to another entity or repealed.[5]

FIRREA also established the Federal Housing Finance Board and charged it with the primary responsibility of overseeing and supervising the activities of the Federal Home Loan Banks. To further the congressional intent of separating supervisory and examination activities from other functions of the Federal Home Loan Banks, FIRREA prohibited the OTS from delegating to any federal home loan bank or director, officer, or employee thereof the power to examine, supervise, initiate enforcement action against or otherwise regulate any S&L association or holding company. The Federal Housing Finance Board was established under Title VII of FIRREA as an independent agency in the Executive Branch to oversee and supervise each of the Federal Home Loan Banks, and succeeded the FHLBB in this respect.

FIRREA further improved the supervision of thrift institutions by strengthening capital, accounting, and other regulatory and supervisory standards, and additionally limited investments and other activities of thrift institutions that presented unacceptable risks to the federal deposit insurance funds.

FIRREA also dissolved the FSLIC and charged the FDIC with responsibility to insure S&L deposits, examine S&L institutions and their affiliates as necessary for deposit insurance purposes; issue regulations to preclude S&Ls from engaging in certain risky activities; and initiate enforcement actions against S&Ls as appropriate. FIRREA further promoted the independence of the FDIC from the institutions the deposits of which it insured, by establishing an independent board of directors, adequate funding, and appropriate powers within the FDIC. FIRREA further created the FSLIC Resolution Fund to be managed by FDIC and mandated the transfer of all reserves, assets, debts, and obligations and other liabilities of the FSLIC (other than those already transferred to the Resolution Trust Corporation (RTC)), including the assets and liabilities for which a receiver was appointed prior to January 1989.

Moreover, FIRREA established the RTC as an instrument of the US Government, and appointed the FDIC as the exclusive manager of the RTC, to manage and resolve all S&Ls for which a conservator or receiver was appointed during the period of January 1989 – August 1992, and to manage all of the assets of such institutions under the Federal Asset Disposition Association.

One of the most important and fundamental provisions of FIRREA for purposes of this work, however, are those which established new capital standards for the thrift industry. The Bush Administration and Congress clearly underscored the perception that the primary cause of the thrift crisis was capital inadequacy, and that only by requiring S&Ls to put their own

5 See J. Norton and S.C. Whitely, *Banking Law Manual*, at Ch. 2A-21 (1984, 1990 version). Thus, Title III of FIRREA abolished the FHLBB and established the OTS, Title IV provided for the transfer of the separated functions and activities from FHLBB to the OTS, and Title VII separated the regulatory and supervisory functions of FHLBB from the credit provision functions.

money at risk would any incentives exist to operate thrift institutions in a prudent manner while insuring the existence of sufficient capital levels to absorb losses in times of economic distress. The thrift capital standards were modeled upon those imposed on national banks, and thrift capital requirements were intended to be on parity with national bank capital standards by January 1995.[6] Thus, FIRREA required the OTS to establish uniformly applicable capital standards for S&L institutions under a new reregulatory regime of regulatory parity with national banks. Title III of FIRREA provided the FDIC with broader discretion to enforce thrift capital standards by restricting equity investments of S&Ls; tightening the 'qualified thrift lender requirements' under The Home Owners Loan Act (HOLA) (as amended by 1987 Competitive Equality Banking Act (CEBA)); and subjecting the thrift industry to the 'affiliate transaction' rules under the Federal Reserve Act (as amended by CEBA).

Title III of FIRREA tightened the thrift regulatory framework in a number of ways, several of which deemed most important are elaborated upon further below.[7]

In addition, Congress mandated the phasing out of 'goodwill' as a recorded asset on thrift institution balance sheets. As previously noted in Chapter Three, the recording of goodwill as an asset was strongly encouraged by the FHLBB in the early 1980s through supervisory merger transactions with push down accounting treatment as a means to artificially bolster thrift balance sheets. Under FIRREA, Congress required that the FHLBB's long-standing policy on goodwill, now a significant asset on the balance sheets of many thrift institutions, be summarily eliminated, a complete and abrupt policy reversal. Therefore, for each dollar of goodwill phased out under FIRREA, a dollar in assets evaporated from thrift balance sheets and by implication a dollar in capital or earnings was necessary to replace it.[8]

B. Capital Requirements and Accounting Compliance

The enactment of FIRREA, by mandating higher capital levels on parity with national banks and restricting the use of RAP by thrift institutions, eliminated most of the capital and accounting policies established by FHLBB in the early 1980s. FIRREA required thrift institution capital requirements to be at least as rigorous as those for national banking organizations and mandated even more rigorous accounting standards for thrift institutions. All relevant substantive definitions established by the OCC in its capital regulations were required for inclusion in OTS capital standards.[9]

FIRREA also repealed the provisions of prior laws that permitted capital forbearances for institutions lacking sufficient capital but not insolvent,[10]

---

6 See FIRREA, *supra* note 1, at §301.
7 See Lawrence J. White, *The S&L Debacle: Public Policy Lessons for Bank and Thrift Regulation* (Oxford University Press, 1991) at p.179.
8 See *U.S. v. Winstar*, 116 S. Ct. 2432 (1996).
9 See FIRREA, *supra* note 1, at § 301.
10 See 12 U.S.C. §§ 1467a, 1730i (1988).

and permitted institutions engaged in approved capital recovery plans to continue in this respect.[11] FIRREA mandated the convergence of capital and accounting standards for S&Ls and other banks through the incorporation of GAAP standards to the same extent that they were used to determine compliance with regulations prescribed by the federal banking agencies.[12] Although CEBA provided some incentive towards convergence of capital requirements and accounting standards between S&Ls and banks, FIRREA actually raised capital requirements for S&Ls and otherwise required such convergence.

FIRREA established three separate capital standards and directed S&Ls to be in compliance with each of them: (1) a leverage limit in the form of a 'core capital' requirement of not less than 3 per cent of total assets;[13] (2) a required threshold of 1.5 per cent of 'tangible capital';[14] and (3) a risk-based capital directive that would not in the aggregate result in materially lower levels of capital being required of S&Ls than would be required under the risk-based capital standards applicable to national banks.[15] In determining 'core capital', 'tangible capital', and 'risk-based capital', institutions could include 90 per cent of the FMV of 'readily marketable purchased mortgage servicing rights' on terms not less stringent than under the capital standards applicable to State non-member banks and national banks, subject to certain limitations.[16] Thrift institutions and banks alike were generally not permitted to include unidentifiable intangible assets in regulatory capital.[17] Congress intended to permit thrift institutions to include contributed assets in regulatory capital, such as land valued at FMV, in connection with supervisory transactions as appraised equity capital at the discretion of the OTS, if such treatment was no less stringent than the treatment provided by the OCC to national banks.[18]

The three capital standards were required to be complied with by all S&Ls, but merely meeting the minimum ratios was not the expectation of the newly

---

[11] See FIRREA, *supra* note 1, at § 302.

[12] See Norton and Whitely, *supra* note 5, at 2A-20.

[13] See FIRREA, *supra* note 1, § 301, 103 Stat. at 303 (codified at 12 U.S.C. § 1464(t)(2)(B)). The core capital requirement is the ratio of a designated part of capital to total assets. The S&Ls were required to maintain a minimum ratio of core capital to assets of not less than 3 per cent. The components of core capital were essentially those established by the OCC for national banks, subject to exceptions for supervisory goodwill and purchased mortgage servicing rights. See Norton and Whitely, *supra* note 5, at 2A-93.

[14] See *ibid*. § 301, codified at 12 U.S.C. § 1464(t)(2)(B). The 'tangible capital' requirement is the ratio of tangible capital to total assets. S&Ls were required to maintain tangible capital (essentially core capital minus all intangible assets except for purchased mortgage servicing rights) or not less than 1.5 per cent. See Norton and Whitely, *supra* note 5, at 2A-93.

[15] See *ibid*. § 301, codified at 12 U.S.C. § 1464(t)(2)(C). The risk-based capital requirement is a ratio of an institution's capital to specified weighted values of the individual components of that institution's assets and off-balance sheet items. The maximum risk-based capital requirement for thrift institutions increased to 8 per cent by 1993, and the assets divided among five risk-weight categories as set forth in the Basle Committee Capital Accord. See 54 Fed. Reg. 46,869, 46,871 (1989) (codified at 12 C.F.R. §§ 567.2, 567.6).

[16] See FIRREA, *supra* note 1, at § 301.

[17] See *ibid*., at § 221(4) (codified at 12 U.S.C. § 1828(n)).

[18] See H.R. Conf. Rep. No. 222, 101st Cong., 1st Sess. 405 (1989).

charged thrift regulatory agency, the OTS (notably a sister agency with the OCC under the US Treasury Department jurisdiction). FIRREA authorized the OTS to impose capital levels more stringent than the minimum levels on a case-by-case basis as consistent with FIRREA[19] and OCC capital regulations.[20]

The OTS announced at the outset that the thrift capital standards would differ from those of national banks because of statutory requirements, the unique mutual structure of many S&Ls, the concentration of risks of thrift asset portfolios, and the OTS experience.[21] FIRREA nonetheless required the OTS to 'prescribe and maintain uniformly applicable capital standards for savings associations' within statutory requirements.[22] The statute required thrift institutions to 'maintain core capital in an amount not less than 3 per cent of the savings association's total assets.'[23] FIRREA further instructed the FRB, OCC, FDIC, and OTS to establish uniform accounting standards to be used for determining the capital ratios of all federally insured depository institutions and other regulatory purposes.[24]

In order to discourage thrift institutions from conducting activities in subsidiaries that were not otherwise permissible for national banks, FIRREA mandated that S&L investments in, and loans to, any subsidiary engaged in such activities be deducted from the institution's capital, phased-in over a period of years.[25] Finally, for purposes of determining compliance with capital standards, the assets and liabilities of subsidiaries were required to be consolidated with the assets and liabilities of the parent association unless all of the association's investments in and extensions of credit to the subsidiary were deducted from the association's capital.[26]

---

19 See FIRREA, *supra* note 1, at § 301.

20 The OCC repeatedly asserted in publications concerning capital adequacy that the levels set forth in regulations for national banks were minimum levels and that banks were expected to maintain risk-based capital levels in excess of those levels. See, e.g. 54 Fed. Reg. 4,168, 4,169 (1989). The reason for this expectation was that the Basle Committee standards generally focused on credit risk and did not incorporate other risks, such as interest rate risk. See Norton and Whitely, *supra* note 5, at 2A-94.

21 See 'Regulatory Capital', 54 Fed. Reg. 46,865 (1989) (codified at 12 C.F.R. Pts 561, 563 and 571).

22 See 12 U.S.C. § 1464(t)(1)(A).

23 See 12 U.S.C. § 1464(t)(2)(A).

24 See *ibid.* § 1215, 103 Stat. at 529, repealed by Federal Deposit Insurance Corporation Improvement Act of 1991 (FDICIA), Pub. L. No. 102-242, Title I, § 121(b), 105 Stat. 2236, 2251, and superseded by FDICIA § 121(a), 105 Stat. 2250-52 (codified at 12 U.S.C. § 1831n).

25 See FIRREA, *supra* note 1, at § 301. This requirement did not apply to 'includable subsidiaries' such as those (1) engaged solely in mortgage banking activities; (2) engaged in such impermissible activities, but solely as an agent, unless the FDIC revoked the subsidiary's exemption for safety and soundness reasons; (3) insured depository institutions or companies where the sole investments are insured depository institutions and otherwise acquired prior to May 1989. *Ibid.* at § 301.

26 See FIRREA, *supra* note 1, at § 301.

During the phase-in period of the 'core capital' requirement, certain 'eligible savings associations' were permitted to include 'qualifying supervisory goodwill'[27] in core capital up to specified percentages.[28] FIRREA generally defined 'core capital' to exclude 'unidentifiable intangible assets', such as goodwill.[29] Thus, although FIRREA provided a 'transition rule' permitting thrift institutions to include 'qualifying supervisory goodwill' toward half of the 'core capital' requirement, this provision was phased out by 1995.[30]

The tightened capital requirements reflected the judgment of Congress that 'to a considerable extent, the size of the thrift crisis resulted from the utilization of capital gimmicks that masked the inadequate capitalization of thrifts.'[31] FIRREA introduced a scheme of enforcement actions to be initiated against thrift institutions for failure to maintain capital standards, in the form of (1) asset growth limitations; (2) required capitalization plans; (3) capital directives imposing discretionary restrictions, such as on payment of dividends and compensation; and (4) sanctions and penalties for engaging in 'unsafe and unsound' practices.[32]

Under FIRREA the convergence of capital and accounting standards was officially in place for thrifts and banks with little consideration for the immediate consequences to the S&L industry. Thrift managers and real estate professionals were alarmed by the impending effect of the abrupt convergence requirements.[33] The federal banking agencies were largely indifferent to the effect of FIRREA on the thrift industry.[34]

The impact of FIRREA capital requirements upon thrift institutions that had acquired failed thrifts in exchange for recognition of supervisory goodwill was fast and painful. The OTS issued regulations implementing the new capital standards with a bulletin stating that FIRREA 'eliminates [capital and accounting] forbearances' previously permitted to certain thrifts.[35] The OTS directed that 'all savings associations presently operating with these forbearances ... should eliminate them in determining whether or not they comply

---

27 'Qualifying supervisory goodwill' was defined as supervisory goodwill existing as of 12 April 1989, amortized on a straight-line basis over the shorter of twenty years or its remaining amortization period in effect as of that date. See FIRREA, *supra* note 1, at § 301. 'Supervisory goodwill' is goodwill resulting from the pre-12 April 1989 acquisition, merger, consolidation, purchase of assets or other business combination of a 'problem institution', one which at the time of the transaction was subject to special regulatory controls, posed particular supervisory concerns or failed to meet the regulatory capital requirements, or of an S&L whose FMV of assets was less than the FMV of liabilities at the time of the combination transactions. See 54 Fed. Reg. 46,869 (1989) (codified at 12 C.F.R. § 567.1).

28 See FIRREA, *supra* note 1, at § 301.

29 See 12 U.S.C. § 1464(t)(9)(A).

30 See 12 U.S.C. § 1464(t)(3)(A).

31 See House Report on FIRREA, 101st Cong., lst Sess. (1989), 310 (see note 68 *infra*).

32 See FIRREA, *supra* note 1, at § 301.

33 See 'The Unintended Effects of FIRREA on the Home Building Industry and Other Related Matters', before the Subcommittee on General Oversight and Investigations of the House Committee on Banking, Finance and Urban Affairs, 101st Cong., 2d Sess. (1990).

34 *Ibid.*

35 See OTS, 'Capital Adequacy: Guidance on the Status of Capital and Accounting Forbearances and Capital Instruments Held by a Deposit Insurance Fund', Thrift Bulletin No. 38-2, 9 January 1990.

with the new minimum regulatory capital standards.'[36] Notwithstanding the transitory phase-in statutory exception, many thrift institutions immediately failed to comply with regulatory capital requirements and became subject to seizure and enforcement actions by the OTS or FDIC as appropriate.[37]

Notwithstanding the capital and accounting interpretations reviewed above, FIRREA nonetheless failed to address material policy deficiencies. For instance, FIRREA did not render the registration requirements of the Securities Act applicable to publicly-offered securities of thrift and banking institutions, and did not shift the administration and enforcement of Securities and Exchange Act disclosure requirements for thrift and banking institutions from the thrift and banking agencies to the Securities and Exchange Commission (SEC). The S&L crisis underscores that continuing to exempt thrift and banking institutions from the application of the federal securities laws was probably poor policy.[38]

In addition, FIRREA did not mandate any movement towards greater use of market value accounting in the financial reports distributed by thrift and banking institutions, respectively. The FHLBB, during the period for which it permitted the use of questionable accounting practices under RAP, was simultaneously responsible for protecting the federal deposit insurance fund (FSLIC) and reviewing thrift financial statements that were distributed to public investors.

The dual responsibility represented a serious conflict of interest, as each dollar of equity that thrift institutions could raise from public investors obviously benefited the FSLIC. Predictably, the FHLBB consistently resolved this conflict in favor of the underfunded (and by 1987 the insolvent) FSLIC.[39] The former FHLBB Chairman Pratt testified before Congress, in defending the FHLBB treatment of goodwill:[40]

> The [FHLBB] was caught between a rock and a hard place. While it did not have sufficient resources to close all insolvent institutions, at the same time, it had to consolidate the industry, move weaker institutions into stronger hands, and do everything possible to minimize losses during the transition period. Goodwill was an indispensable tool in performing this task.

As the FHLBB was preoccupied with minimizing losses to the FSLIC, it apparently evaluated accounting standards in terms of how well they protected the FSLIC. The FHLBB treatment of goodwill was relaxed to render

---

36 *Ibid.*

37 See W. Black,'Ending Our Forbearers' Forbearance: FIRREA and Supervisory Goodwill', 2 Stan. L. & Policy Rev. 102, at p.107 ('FIRREA's new capital mandates have caused over 500 S&Ls . . .to report that they have failed one or more of the three capital requirements.')

38 Thrift and banking institutions, among other financial institutions, are excluded from the registration requirements of the Securities Act for public offerings of securities. § 12(i) of the Securities and Exchange Act provides that thrift and banking agencies have the authority to 'administer and enforce' the registration requirements of § 12, the periodic reporting requirements of § 13, the proxy and tender offer provisions of § 14, and the insider reporting and trading liability provisions of Section 16. See 15 U.S.C. § 78l(i).

39 See Testimony of Richard T. Pratt, Chairman, FHLBB, before the House Committee on Banking, Finance, and Urban Affairs, 101st Cong., 2d Sess. at 5 (1990).

40 *Ibid.*

it a better 'tool' to protect the FSLIC. Moreover, as GAAP came to be an inhibition against mortgage disposition programs, the FLHBB adopted the loss deferral regulations against the counsel of FASB (and the SEC as its oversight authority). The S&L crisis demonstrated the dangers in utilizing a reporting system for financial institutions premised on historical cost accounting.

As GAAP did not reflect the massive unrealized losses in S&L portfolios, the institutions that were clearly insolvent on an economic basis nonetheless continued to operate and report a positive net worth. The absence of viable financial information on the thrift industry made it difficult for investors and Congress to make a meaningful assessment of the real economic value and risk exposures of thrift institutions, and otherwise facilitated policies of regulatory forbearance.

C. Qualified Thrift Lender Test

As previously alluded to in this chapter, the CEBA legislation established the 'qualified thrift lender' test (QTL), designed to encourage S&Ls to commit to the role of providing housing-related lending activities. The CEBA conditioned an insured institution's ability to obtain the maximum level of Federal Home Loan Bank advances, and S&L holding companies' rights to engage in non-traditional thrift activities, upon maintaining QTL status.[41]

The CEBA defined a QTL as an insured institution whose housing-related lending activities, or 'qualified thrift investments' equaled or exceeded 60 per cent of its total tangible assets, and further required the institution to maintain that percentage on an average basis in three out of every four calendar quarters and in two out of every three years.[42] FIRREA reflected the intent of Congress to force the S&L industry into engaging in even more housing-related and consumer-related lending activities,[43] and tightened the QTL test by increasing assets devoted to housing-related lending activities from 60 per cent to 70 per cent.[44] The types of assets defined as 'qualified thrift investments' were also narrowed under FIRREA, commensurate with the intent to preclude the inclusion of additional assets by regulatory authorities.[45]

Finally, FIRREA directed that the qualified thrift investments be measured against the institution's 'portfolio assets' (total assets minus the value of thrift premises, furnishings, and equipment used to conduct business, liquid assets required to be held by regulation, and goodwill and other intangible assets) instead of 'total tangible assets'.[46] The institutions that failed to maintain QTL

---

41 See 12 U.S.C. §§ 1430(e), 1730a(c)(3) (1987).

42 See 12 U.S.C. § 1730a(o)(1) (1987). Regulations promulgated by the FHLBB followed the statute but expanded upon the definition of 'qualified thrift investments'. See 12 C.F.R. § 583.27 (1987).

43 See H.R. Rep. No. 54, 101st Cong., 1st Sess., Pt 1, at 436 (1989).

44 See FIRREA, *supra* note 1, at § 303(a). The QTL test was amended to require institutions to meet it as measured by a daily or weekly average for the two year period beginning 1 July 1991, and for each two-year period thereafter, rather than on a quarterly basis. See FIRREA, *supra* note 1, at § 303(a)-(b).

45 See FIRREA, *supra* note 1, at § 303(a).

46 *Ibid.* at § 303(a).

status were required under FIRREA to convert to a bank charter or otherwise become subject to severe restrictions on their activities and investments.[47] The revised QTL provisions further reduced the investment flexibility of thrift institutions, and when coupled with the amended capital standards (increased to be no less stringent than the standards applied to national banks), the revisions to the QTL test effectively increased S&L capital requirements.

D. Deposit Insurance Reorganization

Title II of FIRREA dramatically altered the deposit insurance system by replacing the insolvent FSLIC with the Savings Association Insurance Fund (SAIF),[48] and Title IV provided for the transfer of functions and activities of the FSLIC to the FDIC and/or RTC (discussed below). The SAIF insured all depository institutions formerly insured by the FSLIC.[49] Title II of FIRREA also dissolved the permanent insurance fund for banking organizations and replaced it with the Bank Insurance Fund (BIF) to insure all formerly covered banking organizations.[50]

The SAIF and BIF are maintained separately under FIRREA and used by the FDIC to carry out deposit insurance objectives. FIRREA required that BIF and SAIF levels had to be increased until the ratio of insurance funds to total insured deposits reached 1.25 per cent of insured accounts. The reserve ratio was to be maintained at that level thereafter unless the FDIC Board of Directors determined that the potential risks required a higher level be maintained with a maximum level of 1.5 per cent. The US deposit insurance scheme was reorganized and otherwise transferred fully to the FDIC.[51]

Unlike the House-passed version of FIRREA (H.R. 1278), the final version of FIRREA did not provide FDIC with authority to establish risk-based deposit insurance premiums, or premiums determined upon the risk to the insurance funds by an institution's assets and liabilities held or activities engaged in. FIRREA mandated that the FDIC produce a report on the viability of risk-based premiums by January 1991, but barred their imposition without specific approval of Congress.[52] The FDIC may terminate or

---

47 *Ibid.* at § 303(a).

48 *Ibid.* at § 211(6), 103 Stat. at 219 (codified at 12 U.S.C. § 1821(a)).

49 *Ibid.* at §§ 401, 211(3), 103 Stat. at 354, 219 (codified at 12 U.S.C. § 1821(a)(4)-(7)).

50 *Ibid.*, at § 211(m)(6), 103 Stat. at 218-219 (codified at 12 U.S.C. § 1821(a)).

51 *Ibid.*, at § 211(4)(a)-(c), 103 Stat. at 218-219 (codified at 12 U.S.C. § 1821(a)). § 206 of FIRREA also contained significant 'cross-guarantee' provisions. The cross-guarantee provisions were intended to protect the deposit insurance funds by requiring insured financial institutions that were liable for losses incurred by the FDIC and for losses that the FDIC reasonably anticipated incurring with respect to (1) the default of a commonly controlled insured depository institution; or (2) any assistance provided by the FDIC to any commonly controlled depository institution close to default. Thus, financially sound affiliates of BHCs that controlled failed thrift institutions could be required to pay part of the loss incurred by the FDIC in resolving the failed institutions. The cross-guarantee provisions applied to institutions controlled by the same BHC, or to one depository institution controlled by another. The FDIC had the authority to waive such liability if it determined that the waiver was in the best interest of the BIF or SAIF.

52 See Norton and Whitely, *supra* note 5, at 2A-26.

temporarily suspend deposit insurance of a given institution by notifying the respective institution's regulatory agency and following a notice and due process procedure set forth in FIRREA.

III. RESOLUTION TRUST CORPORATION

Title V of FIRREA amended the Federal Home Loan Bank Act to establish the Resolution Trust Corporation (RTC) under the management and control of the FDIC and its personnel.[53] FIRREA also established an Oversight Board[54] to develop a strategic plan for RTC operations.[55] The representative offices of the Oversight Board managed and resolved all cases involving depository institutions that were insured by the FSLIC (i.e. thrift institutions) prior to the enactment of FIRREA and that had a conservator or receiver appointed between 1 January and 9 August 1989 or that would be appointed prior to 9 August1992.[56]

The RTC was responsible for managing the Federal Asset Disposition Association and conducting operations in a manner that maximized the return from the sale or disposition of failed thrift institutions and their assets, primarily real estate holdings.[57] The RTC was simultaneously directed to minimize the effect of sale or disposition transactions on the US real estate and financial markets[58] and to make the most efficient use of federally acquired funds.[59] The Resolution Funding Corporation (REFCORP) was established to finance the functions and activities of RTC.[60]

The RTCs objectives were set forth in a strategic plan which the Oversight Board submitted to Congress by year-end 1989. The strategic plan and implementing policies and procedures promulgated by the Oversight Board contained, among other things, the following:

1. factors to determine the order in which failed institutions are resolved;
2. standards for selecting an appropriate resolution action;

---

53 *Ibid*. at § 501(b)(1)(C), 103 Stat. at 364 (codified at 12 U.S.C. § 1441(a)).
54 *Ibid*. at § 501(a)(14)(A)-(B), 103 Stat. at 367 (codified at 12 U.S.C. § 1441(a)).
55 *Ibid*. at § 501(a)(3)(A)(i)-(iv), 103 Stat. at 364 (codified at 12 U.S.C. § 1441(a)).
56 *Ibid*. at § 501(b)(3)(A), 103 Stat. at 369 (codified at 12 U.S.C. § 1441(a)).
57 *Ibid*. at § 501(b)(3)(C)(i), 103 Stat. at 369 (codified at 12 U.S.C. § 1441(a)).
58 *Ibid*. at § 501(b)(3)(C)(ii), 103 Stat. at 369 (codified at 12 U.S.C. § 1441(a)).
59 *Ibid*. at § 501(b)(3)(C)(iii), 103 Stat. at 369 (codified at 12 U.S.C. § 1441(a)).
60 REFCORP was a government corporation subject to the general supervision and direction of the Oversight Board authorized to borrow USD20 billion from the US Treasury and issue USD30 billion in bonds and similar debt obligations. The interest on funds borrowed from the Treasury or the bonds issued by REFCORP were paid from proceeds received by the RTC from liquidation of institutions and assets under FDIC management, net earnings of Federal Home Loan Banks, and lastly from the Treasury. REFCORP was required to purchase zero coupon bonds from the Treasury in a sufficient amount such that upon their maturity the principal amount of the borrowings from the Treasury and the issued bonds could be retired. See FIRREA, *supra* note 1, at § 511.

3. factors to be considered in deciding whether non-performing assets should be transferred to an acquiring institution or a failed institution or retained for disposal;
4. plans for disposing of assets;
5. staffing plans of RTC, including an assessment of the extent to which asset management functions would be performed by or through public and private entities;
6. standards for adequate competition and fair, consistent treatment of offerors;
7. non-discrimination standards;
8. utilization of standard market analysis, valuation, and appraisal practices to establish market value of assets;
9. guidelines to determine if no reasonable recovery of an asset's value is anticipated, in which case the RTC could consider potential public uses for the asset; and
10. policies and procedures to avoid political favoritism and undue influence in contracts and decisions.[61] Most importantly, the RTC was required to actively review all means to reduce costs under assistance agreements entered into by the FSLIC between January 1988 and August 1989 to resolve insolvent institutions, generally under the Southwest Plan (discussed previously in Part Three).

The RTC had to evaluate the costs with respect to capital loss coverage, yield maintenance guaranties, forbearances, and tax consequences, and determine whether the bidding and negotiating procedures used in the Southwest Plan were sufficiently competitive.[62] With respect to real estate asset dispositions, the RTC established a Real Estate Asset Division to develop policies and programs for the management and disposition of all of the real property assets of the institutions that were subject to RTC jurisdiction. The RTC Oversight Board established a National Advisory Council and various regional advisory boards to advise the RTC on policies and programs for the real property asset disposition.

FIRREA required the following objectives in disposition of assets: (1) maximizing net present value; (2) minimizing impact on the local real estate and financial markets; and (3) maximizing preservation of residential real property for low- and moderate-income individuals. Special policies and procedures were developed for the disposal of assets in 'distressed areas' as designated by the FDIC as having depressed real estate markets, including Texas, Arkansas, Colorado, New Mexico, Louisiana, and Oklahoma.[63] The RTC was prohibited from selling real property assets located in distressed areas without obtaining at least the 'minimum disposition price', initially defined as 95 per cent of the market value established by the RTC, with the percentage subject to change by the FDIC Board of Directors.[64]

---

61 See Norton and Whitely, *supra* note 5, at 2A-36.
62 *Ibid.* at 2A-36.
63 See FIRREA, *supra* note 1, at § 501(a).
64 *Ibid.* § 501(a).

The RTC General Operating Policies adopted in the area of asset disposition included the following:

1. the FDIC retained the flexibility to sell or otherwise dispose of a failed institution's problem assets before selling its franchise;
2. acquirers were generally expected to assume the operating expenses and all performing loans;
3. where markets were liquid and values could be readily ascertained, the FDIC favored early sales of assets at appraised values;
4. in determining acceptable prices, 'fire sale' or liquidation value appraisals were not to be used; and
5. reliance was placed on the private sector to assist in the disposition of problem assets, with appropriate incentives and controls maintained in the management of problem assets.[65]

The RTC was also directed to contract with private parties, including real estate and loan portfolio asset management, property management, auction marketing, and brokerage services, when practical and efficient in the disposition of assets.[66] The RTC adopted rules governing conflicts of interest with private parties performing services for the RTC consistent with federal ethics legislation, to protect the RTC from third party abuses in the disposition of assets, such as preferential or above-market rate transactions with insiders, related parties or affiliates.

By mid-1990 the RTC spent approximately USD59 billion and borrowed approximately USD26.6 billion for working capital, and by late 1990 had resolved 320 failed thrift institutions with assets totaling approximately USD114.8 billion. The OTS continued to supply RTC with many more failed or failing thrift institutions, however; for instance, during November 1990, the RTC accomplished acquisitions for seven thrifts, but in one ten-day period that month the OTS had put four more into its hands.[67]

The massive industry-wide reforms, however, did not fundamentally alter the structure of federal assistance in supervisory mergers of failing or failed thrift institutions and banks. The increasing volume of bank failures, as opposed to thrift failures, which occurred over 1990–1992 followed essentially the same merger and assistance structure represented by the Southwest Plan transactions. This process publicly represented a 'resolution' of the failed or failing financial institutions, but the ever-increasing bundle of 'covered assets' resulted over time in a bifurcated banking system. The result of the merger would be a 'healthy' or 'good' bank, and a 'bad bank', consisting of non-performing or 'covered' assets to be managed and disposed of by a division of 'good' bank management in conjunction with the FDIC on behalf of itself, the former FSLIC and the RTC.

Under FIRREA the liquidation of FSLIC came 'full circle' and marked a turning point in the government's treatment of failing S&Ls and financial

65 See Norton and Whitely, *supra* note 5, at 2A-41-42.
66 See FIRREA, *supra* note 1, at § 501(a).
67 See Pratt Testimony, *supra* note 39.

institutions. From 1980–1988, the S&L crisis was being managed as a 'workout program' within a 10-year time horizon by the FSLIC.[68] FIRREA mandated a massive liquidation program through the RTC. The magnitude of the change in policy and direction cannot be overstated. However, the FHLBB Chairman warned that:

'[T]he legislation [FIRREA] misses a very important point. It is not a savings and loan bailout, and it is not a FSLIC crisis. What we have in this country is we have a real estate collapse, and if we don't attack the problem and deal with the real estate collapse we are just going to be throwing money after money trying to deal with this issue ...'[69]

IV. THE ENFORCEMENT SUPERPOWERS

Congress considered the enforcement provisions of FIRREA as the focal point of the legislation. Title IX of FIRREA, the *Enhancement Enforcement Powers Act of 1989*, significantly enhanced the reach of the banking agencies' civil enforcement authority, dramatically increased the civil and criminal penalties for depository institution-related offenses, and rendered attorneys, accountants, and other professionals performing services for depository institutions potential targets of enforcement actions.[70]

A. The Concept of 'Institution-Affiliated Party'

The civil enforcement provisions of FIRREA generally extend to an 'institution-affiliated party', defined as:

1. directors, officers, agents, and controlling stockholders (other than BHCs) of depository institutions;
2. any independent contractor (attorneys, accountants, appraisers) who knowingly or recklessly participates in any violation of law or regulation, any breach of fiduciary duty, or any unsafe or unsound practice, which caused or is likely to cause more than a minimal financial loss to, or a significant adverse effect on, the insured depository institution;
3. any shareholder (other than BHCs), consultant, or joint venture partner who participates in the conduct of the affairs of an insured depository institution; and

---

68 See 'Full Faith and Credit for FSLIC Notes,' Hearings Before the House Committee on Banking, Finance and Urban Affairs, 100th Cong., 2d Sess. (1988).

69 See 'Financial Institutions Reform, Recovery and Enforcement Act of 1989', Hearings Before the Subcommittee on Financial Institutions Supervision, Regulation, and Insurance, of the House Committee on Banking, Finance, and Urban Affairs, 101st Cong., 1st Sess. at 60 (1989) (testimony of FHLBB Board Member).

70 G.N. Olson, 'The Repressiveness of the FDIC Superpowers: Complications From the Insolvency of the Federal Deposit Insurance Funds', Working Paper on file with the SMU Institute of International Banking & Finance (Dallas, TX).

4. any other person determined by the appropriate federal banking agency, (by regulation or on a case-by-case basis) who participates in the conduct of the affairs of an insured depository institution.[71]

This term and the term 'insured depository institution' which includes any bank whose deposits are insured by the FDIC, resulted in a uniform regime of federal banking agency enforcement and broadened the scope of individuals and entities covered under this regime. The persons against whom civil enforcement proceedings may be initiated (institution-affiliated parties) are the same whether the action is initiated by the FDIC, OTS, or OCC, and whether the institution is an S&L or national bank.[72]

B. Cease and Desist Orders and Affirmative Corrective Actions

FIRREA required federal banking agencies to mandate affirmative actions to correct violations or practices through issuance of cease and desist orders. The agencies were granted the specific authority to require an institution and institution-affiliated party to:

1. make restitution for, or provide reimbursement, indemnification or guarantee against any loss if the institution or party was unjustly enriched, or if the violation or practice involved a reckless disregard for the law, applicable regulations, or prior agency order;
2. restrict the growth of the institution;
3. dispose of any specific loan or asset;
4. employ qualified officers or employees that the agency may direct; and
5. take other action as determined appropriate.[73]

The agencies were further authorized to place limitations on the activities or functions of an institution or institution-affiliated party.[74]

C. Burden of Proof for Temporary Cease and Desist Orders

The burden of proof required for the issuance of temporary cease and desist orders was significantly reduced. Under prior law, the federal banking agencies were required to find that the act in question involved a 'substantial' erosion of assets, 'seriously' weakened the condition of the institution, or 'seriously' prejudice the interests of depositors. FIRREA substituted the word 'significant' for 'substantial' and deleted the word 'seriously'.[75] The term 'significant' covered anything more than a minimal or nominal erosion of

---

71 See FIRREA, *supra* note 1, at § 204(f) (codified at 12 U.S.C. § 1813(u)); FIRREA, *supra*, note 1, at §901(b)(1) (codified at 12 U.S.C. § 1818)).

72 See Norton and Whitely, *supra* note 5, at 2A-117.

73 *Ibid*. at § 902(a) (codified at 12 U.S.C. § 1818(b)(6)).

74 *Ibid*. at § 902(a) (codified at 12 U.S.C. § 1818(b)(7)).

75 See FIRREA, *supra* note 1, at §902(a)(2) (codified at 12 U.S.C. § 1818(c)(1)).

assets.[76] Temporary orders may be issued for any of the affirmative corrective actions previously set forth,[77] and if the institution's books and records are so incomplete or inaccurate that the appropriate agency is unable to determine the financial condition of the institution through the supervisory process.[78] Thus, banking agencies were authorized to initiate meaningful enforcement actions against institutions or institution-affiliated parties prior to completion of the administrative process preceding a final cease and desist order.[79]

D. Suspension, Removal, or Prohibition Orders

FIRREA authorized the federal banking agencies to order the suspension, removal, or prohibition of any institution-affiliated party when several components are met. First, there is a determination that the person has directly or indirectly violated any law, regulation, final cease and desist order, or other condition previously imposed by the respective agency; engaged in any unsafe or unsound practice; or committed any act, omission, or practice of that person's fiduciary duty. Second, by reason of the violation, practice, or act, the institution has suffered or will probably suffer financial loss or other damage; the interests of the institution's depositors have been or could be prejudiced; or the person involved has received a financial gain or other benefit. Third, the violation, practice, or act involved personal dishonesty; or demonstrates willful or continuing disregard for the safety and soundness of the institution.[80] The institution-affiliated parties may be temporarily suspended or prohibited from acting as an institution-affiliated party upon the agency's determination that such action is necessary to protect depositors.[81]

Most importantly, persons who are removed or suspended from office or prohibited from continuing participation in the affairs of an insured depository institution are also prohibited from holding any office in, or participating in the affairs of, any other insured depository institution, including banks and S&Ls, except with the written approval of the agency which issued the order and the agency which regulates the institution with which the person proposes to affiliate.[82] Congress intended that such proposals to resume any affiliation otherwise prohibited be closely scrutinized and granted only when 'there is no doubt that such an approval is justified by the complete rehabilitation of an individual'.[83] Although FIRREA states that the

---

76 See H.R. Conf. Rep. No. 222, 101st Cong., 1st Sess. 439 (1989).

77 See FIRREA, *supra* note 1, at § 902(a)(2) (codified at 12 U.S.C. § 1818(c)(1)).

78 *Ibid.* at § 902(a)(2) (codified at 12 U.S.C. § 1818(c)(3)).

79 See Norton and Whitely, *supra* note 5, at 2A-118.

80 See FIRREA, *supra* note 1, at § 903(a)(1) (codified at 12 U.S.C. § 1818(e)(1)).

81 *Ibid.* at § 903(a)(2) (codified at 12 U.S.C. § 1818(e)(3)). Persons who are subject to such an order are prohibited from (1) participating in any manner in the conduct of the affairs of any federally insured depository institution; (2) voting, soliciting, or transferring the right to vote the shares of stock in any federally insured depository institution; (3) violating any voting agreement previously approved by the appropriate agency; and (4) voting for a director or serving or acting as an institution-affiliated party. See FIRREA, *supra*, at § 903(a)(3) (codified at 12 U.S.C. § 1818(e)(6)).

82 See FIRREA, *supra* note 1, at § 904(a) (codified at 12 U.S.C. § 1818(e)(7)).

83 See H.R. Cong. Rep. No. 222, 101st Cong., 1st Sess. 440 (1989).

'industry-wide' prohibition applies only to individuals, the agencies were authorized to extend its application to entities if deemed appropriate by the respective agency.[84]

Therefore, under these provisions, attorneys and entire law firms could be subject to the industry-wide prohibition and therefore be precluded from representing any insured depository institution.[85] FIRREA also extended the enforcement jurisdiction of federal banking agencies to reach institution-affiliated parties even after their resignation or termination of employment from, or participation with an insured depository institution, as such persons may be subject to orders and civil money penalties imposed by banking agencies for six years from the date the person ceases or ceased to be an institution-affiliated party.[86]

E. Civil Money Penalties

FIRREA established a civil money penalty section applicable to all FDIC insured institutions.[87] FIRREA expanded the bases on which federal banking agencies may impose civil money penalties against institutions and institution-affiliated parties and vastly increased the amounts of the penalties. The FIRREA civil money penalty framework consists of three tiers of violations and penalties, the most severe of which address knowing and/or reckless violations causing substantial loss to the institution.[88] The banking agencies were given fairly wide discretion to determine the amount of a respective penalty within the FIRREA statutory guidelines.[89]

FIRREA also carved out special civil money penalties for insured depository institutions that fail to file timely required reports or for filing false and misleading reports, under a similar three-tier framework.[90] FIRREA further carved out special civil money penalties for violations of, and conspiracies to violate, certain criminal statutes relating to financial institutions.[91] Finally, the increased money penalties could be applied retroactively if pre-August

---

84 See FIRREA, *supra* note 1, at § 904(a) (codified at 12 U.S.C. § 1818(e)(7)).

85 See Norton and Whitely, *supra* note 5, at 2A-121.

86 See FIRREA, *supra* note 1, at § 905(a) (codified at 12 U.S.C. § 1818(i)(3)).

87 *Ibid*. at § 907(a) (codified at 12 U.S.C. § 1818(i)(2)).

88 *Ibid*. at § 907(a) (codified at 12 U.S.C. § 1818(i)(2)).

89 The banking agencies must consider various mitigating factors, including (1) the size of the financial resources of the institution or person involved; (2) the amount of good faith shown by the institution or person involved; (3) the gravity of the violation; (4) the history of previous violations; and (5) other matters as justice may require. See FIRREA, *supra* note 1, at § 907(a) (codified at 12 U.S.C. § 1818(i)(2)).

90 See FIRREA, *supra* note 1, at § 911(b)(2) (codified in various sections of 12 U.S.C.).

91 *Ibid*. at § 951. The criminal statutes for which civil money penalties could be recovered include (1) bank bribery; (2) misapplication and embezzlement relating to banks and S&L; (3) placing false statements in the records of a bank or S&L by an insider; (4) making false statements to the FDIC to induce it to enter into certain transactions; (5) making false statements to a federally insured depository institution to obtain credit; (6) mail fraud and wire fraud affecting a federally insured financial institution; and (7) financial institution fraud. See FIRREA, *supra*, note 1, at § 951(c).

1989 conduct was not already subject to administrative proceedings under the respective banking agency.[92]

F. Personal Liability of Directors and Officers

FIRREA mandates that directors and officers of insured depository institutions may be held personally liable for monetary damages in civil actions brought by, on behalf of, or at the request or direction of the FDIC, prosecuted wholly or partially for the benefit of the FDIC acting as conservator or receiver, or upon a suit or claim purchased from, assigned by or otherwise conveyed by the conservator or receiver.[93] The plaintiff bringing suit must generally prove gross negligence or similar conduct, or conduct demonstrating a greater disregard of a duty of care than gross negligence, as such terms are defined under State law.[94] This particular provision generated nearly a decade of voluminous litigation in the federal courts, as the FDIC, RTC, and private litigants sought indemnification from directors and officers through this avenue of approach. The complexities in application of Section 1821(k) generated wide divisions among the federal courts as to the burden of liability, which the US Supreme Court only resolved in 1997.[95]

G. FDIC Enforcement Provisions

FIRREA mandated that the enforcement provisions under the Federal Deposit Insurance Act[96] are applicable to S&Ls subsidiaries and affiliates, whether wholly or partially owned, in the same manner that such enforcement provisions are applicable to S&Ls themselves.[97] FIRREA provided the FDIC with special authority to recommend that OTS initiate enforcement actions against S&Ls for violations of the Change in Control Act provisions of the Federal Deposit Insurance Act[98] and for violations of the transactions with affiliates or insider loan provisions of the Federal Reserve Act.[99]

The FDIC may act unilaterally to address the violation if the OTS fails to take the recommended action or otherwise address the concern, if the FDIC determines that the S&L is in an unsafe or unsound condition or that failure to take action will result in a continuation of unsafe or unsound practices.[100] The ability of the FDIC to terminate or even to threaten to terminate an institution's deposit insurance is a powerful enforcement tool. FIRREA enhanced the ability of the FDIC to use this enforcement tool by (1) reducing the notice

---

92 See FIRREA, *supra* note 1, at § 907(l).
93 *Ibid.* at § 212 (codified at 12 U.S.C. § 1821(k)).
94 *Ibid.* at §212, 12 U.S.C. § 1821(k).
95 *See Atherton v. Federal Deposit Insurance Corporation* 519 U.S. 213 (1997).
96 See 12 U.S.C §§ 1818(a)-(s), (u).
97 See FIRREA, supra note 1, at § 902(a) (codified at 12 U.S.C. § 1818(b)(8)).
98 See 12 U.S.C. § 1817(j).
99 See 12 U.S.C. §§ 371c, 371c-1, and 375b.
100 See FIRREA, *supra* note 1, at § 912 (codified at 12 U.S.C. § 1818(t)). In 'exigent circumstances' the FDIC Board of Directors may order the FDIC to act without regard for any waiting period for OTS compliance. *Ibid.*

requirement for issuing notice of intent to terminate deposit insurance from 120 days to 30 days;[101] and (2) temporarily suspending deposit insurance of an institution after consultation with the relevant banking agency if the institution has no tangible capital.[102]

V. CERTAIN FIRREA RESTRICTIONS

FIRREA imposed various restrictions on thrift activities and operations.

A. Restrictions on Thrift Activities

Congress considered the loan and investment powers of thrift institutions, especially the powers of State-chartered institutions, to be another primary cause of the thrift industry crisis.[103] FIRREA significantly restricted the activities of federally chartered S&Ls, and four of these restrictions actually required significant action that most S&Ls could not possibly meet. First, FIRREA required S&Ls to comply with the 'single-borrower' lending standards applicable to national banks.[104] This provision effectively reduced 'the maximum size loan to a single borrower from 100 per cent of an S&L's net worth to 15 per cent.'[105] FIRREA thus required thrift institutions to follow national bank limitations on single borrower lending transactions and on transactions with affiliates. Second, except for acquisitions by 'qualified affiliates', FIRREA prohibited S&Ls from acquiring any new 'junk bonds' and

---

[101] *Ibid*. at § 926(1) (codified at 12 U.S.C. § 1818(a)(2)).

[102] *Ibid*. at § 926(7) (codified at 12 U.S.C. § 1818(a)(8)).

[103] See, e.g., S. Rep. No. 19, 101st Cong., 1st. Sess. 8-9 (1989).

[104] See FIRREA, *supra* note 1, at § 301. National banks lending limits to single borrowers was generally limited to 15 per cent of the bank's unimpaired capital and surplus. In addition, national banks could also have outstanding to one borrower loans and extensions of credit equal to 10 per cent of the bank's unimpaired capital and surplus if the loans and extensions of credit were fully secured by readily marketable collateral having a market value at least equal to the amount of the outstanding loans and credit (marketable securities). See 12 U.S.C. §84(c) (1989). The national bank lending limits were not new to the thrift industry, as they governed the amount of commercial loans (other than real estate secured) thrift institutions could make to any one borrower prior to FIRREA. See 12 C.F.R. § 563.9-3 (1988).

[105] The new legislation effectively repealed a portion of the FHLBB 'loans-to-one-borrower' regulations that permitted thrift institutions to make real estate secured loans to any one borrower in an amount up to 100 per cent of the institution's net worth. See White, *supra* note 7, at p.179. This rule change had many implications for the borrower, one of which was that in some instances the S&L could not complete its funding obligations on a project. This rule was even imposed where, half way through construction of a project, the lender could no longer fund the project. Application of the rule caused enormous difficulties for contractors, suppliers and laborers on the affected project resulting in work stoppage, lien filings, delays and litigation.

were otherwise required to divest their existing junk bond holdings by 1 July 1994.[106] Investments in commercial paper and corporate debt securities were also curtailed.[107] Third, FIRREA lowered the maximum permitted holdings of non-residential real estate by any S&L such that the level was four times the net worth of the association rather than 40 per cent of assets as previously permitted under the Garn-St. Germain Act.[108] Fourth, FIRREA imposed restrictions on the use of brokered deposits by thrift institutions and banks alike.

Banks and thrifts that did not meet the minimum capital requirements and were deemed 'troubled institutions' were prohibited under FIRREA from accepting deposit accounts, directly or indirectly, by or through a 'deposit broker' or otherwise rolling over or renewing 'brokered deposits'. The FDIC otherwise retained the authority to utilize on behalf of or otherwise approve the use of brokered deposits by troubled institutions.[109] In addition, FIRREA authorized the FDIC to determine by regulation or order that a specific activity engaged in by thrift institutions poses a serious threat to the deposit insurance fund (SAIF). In that event, the FDIC could prohibit any SAIF member institution from directly engaging in such activity, in consultation with the OTS.[110] Finally, FIRREA restricted the activities of State-chartered

---

106 See FIRREA, *supra* note 1, at § 222; White, *supra* note 7, at p.179. 'Junk bond' was defined as any corporate debt security that was not rated in one of the four highest categories by at least one nationally recognized statistical rating organization at the time the investment was acquired by the institution or its subsidiary. *Ibid.* at § 222. Junk bonds did not include bona fide loan participations issued in the ordinary course of business. The term 'qualified affiliate' is defined as any affiliate of the institution other than a subsidiary. *Ibid.* Thus, the entity investing in junk bonds was required to be separately capitalized from the institution and subject to the 'affiliate transaction' requirements of Sections 23A and 23B of the Federal Reserve Act. See H.R. Conf. Rep. No. 222, 101st Cong., 1st Sess. 401 (1989). FIRREA also provided mechanisms to facilitate divestiture of junk bond holdings by well capitalized S&Ls by exchanging their junk bond holdings for certain qualified notes issued by their respective holding companies. See FIRREA, *supra*, at § 222.

107 FIRREA restricted the authority of federal thrift institutions (and by implication State thrift institutions) from investing in, selling, or holding commercial paper and corporate debt securities by providing that the amount of such investments collectively with the amount of consumer loans held by a given institution could not exceed 30 per cent of the thrift institution's total assets. See FIRREA, *supra* note 1, at § 301. The prior laws also restricted federal thrift institution's aggregate amount of commercial paper and corporate debt securities that a given institution could invest in, sell, or hold. See HOLA, at § 5(c)(2)(B) (codified at 12 U.S.C. § 1464(c)(2)(B)). Under FIRREA, commercial paper and corporate debt securities permissible for investment, sale, or holding are only those defined and approved by the OTS. See FIRREA, *supra*, at § 301.

108 See FIRREA, *supra* note 1, at § 301. The OTS could permit individual institutions to make investments in non-residential real estate loans in excess of the 400 per cent of capital level if it determined that such investments would not pose significant risk to the safe and sound operations of the institution and if such lending was consistent with prudent operating practices. *Ibid.*

109 *Ibid.* at § 224(a); H.R. Conf. Rep. No. 222, 101st Cong., 1st Sess., at 508 (1989); Office of Thrift Supervision, Thrift Bulletin 35 (26 October 1989).

110 *Ibid.* at § 221(4), 12 U.S.C. § 1828(m)(3).

thrift institutions essentially to those activities permitted for federally chartered S&Ls.[111]

State-chartered thrift institutions could not engage directly in any type of activity or in any activity in a given amount not otherwise permitted for federal S&Ls and could not engage in a permissible activity in an amount greater than that permitted for federal S&Ls unless they met and remained in compliance with the phased-in capital standards and the FDIC determined that the activity would pose no 'significant risk' to the deposit insurance fund.[112] State-chartered thrift institutions were also precluded from directly acquiring or retaining any equity investment of a type or in an amount not permissible for federal thrift institutions.[113] This limitation was intended to preclude State thrift institutions from making direct investments in real estate, equity securities, and other equity investments such as common stock, preferred stock, options, warrants, and interests in general or limited partnerships, notwithstanding State laws to the contrary.[114]

B. Restrictions on Thrift Subsidiaries, Affiliates and Insiders

FIRREA imposed new requirements governing the activities of S&L subsidiaries and limiting or restricting certain previously authorized activities.[115] Most importantly, thrift institutions must provide FDIC and OTS with statutory notice and information before establishing or acquiring control of a company or commencing new activities through subsidiaries, and these agencies maintain the same enforcement powers against subsidiaries as they have with respect to insured S&Ls.[116]

FIRREA authorized the OTS to require an institution to terminate certain activities or operations, or otherwise divest itself of control of the subsidiary, if it determines that the institution's continued ownership or control of or relationship to the subsidiary constitutes a serious risk to the safety and

---

111 Prior to the enactment of FIRREA, the HOLA governed federal S&Ls while the NHA governed all insured savings institutions, both federal and State chartered. The existence of two separate statutes reflected the dual nature of the thrift industry, but resulted in instance where federal and State S&Ls were treated quite differently. FIRREA eliminated some of those differences by repealing sections of the NHA or transferring NHA provisions to the HOLA and making them applicable to all S&Ls those provisions of HOLA which authorize examination by the OTS or prescribe or limit certain activities where Congress determined such prohibitions or limitations were equally appropriate for all S&Ls, whether federal or State chartered. See Norton and Whitely, *supra* note 5, at 2A-21-22.

112 See FIRREA, *supra* note 1, at § 222. The test of 'significant risk' was defined as not the relative or absolute size of the potential loss to the insurance fund, but whether there is a significant risk that the insurance fund would suffer any loss if the State association engaged in the activity. See H.R. Conf. Rep. No. 222, 101st Cong., 1st Sess. 400-401 (1989).

113 *Ibid.* at § 222.

114 See S. Rep. No. 19, 101st Cong., 1st Sess. 22 (1989). Congress intended that the regulatory authorities would judge the substance and not the form of the transaction. Thus, a transaction that is technically a loan or other permissible transaction could be recharacterized as an equity investment if it is an equity investment in substance. See H.R. Conf. Rep. No. 222, 101st Cong., 1st Sess. 401 (1989).

115 See FIRREA, *supra* note 1, at § 221(4) (codified at 12 U.S.C. § 1828(m)).

116 *Ibid.* at § 221(4) (codified at 12 U.S.C. § 1828(m)(1)-(2)(A)).

soundness of the institution or is otherwise inconsistent with safety and soundness principles. Upon the OTS making such a determination, the FDIC is authorized to order the divestiture.[117]

FIRREA also made significant changes to the statutory treatment of transactions between thrift institutions and its affiliates by extending statutory limitations to transactions with affiliates regardless of whether the institution was a member of an S&L holding company.[118] The former holding company affiliate transaction statutes were quite broad in application and very restrictive because of the scope of the term 'affiliate' and because nearly all affiliate transactions were prohibited. FIRREA imposed the same restrictions on transactions with affiliates, including loans to insiders applicable to banks and set forth in Sections 22(h), 23A and 23B of the Federal Reserve Act,[119] to all S&Ls in the same manner and to the same extent as applicable to member banks under that Act.[120]

Notably, the extension of Sections 23A and 23B of the Federal Reserve Act to S&Ls in the same manner and to the same extent as to member banks reflects the intent to equalize treatment of banks and thrift institutions. In addition, this intent is further evidenced in FIRREA by the extension to thrift institutions of limitations on loans to bank insiders (executive officers, directors, and persons directly or indirectly controlling more than 10 per cent of a bank's voting securities)[121] in the same manner and to the same extent as they apply to member banks.[122] FIRREA authorized the OTS to impose on any S&L additional restrictions on transactions between S&Ls and affiliates and on loans or extensions of credit to insiders if it is deemed necessary to protect the safety and soundness of the institution.[123]

C. LTV Ratios and Real Estate Appraisal Standards

The Senate version of FIRREA would have required specific maximum LTV ratios that insured depository institutions, including banks and thrift institutions, would have had to follow in making residential and non-residential real

---

117 *Ibid.* at § 221(4) (codified at 12 U.S.C. § 1828(m)(2)(B)).

118 *Ibid.* at § 301. Under prior laws, there were specific statutory prohibitions on transactions between an S&L holding company's subsidiary and insured institution and the institution's affiliates. See National Housing Act, at § 408(d) (codified at 12 U.S.C. § 1730a(d)). There were also separate regulations governing transactions between an insured institution and its 'affiliated persons' to address potential conflicts of interest. See 12 C.F.R. §§ 563.40, 563.41, 563.43, 563.45, 571.7, 571.9 (1988). The holding company statutes addressed transactions between a holding company's insured institution and its affiliates other than officers, directors, and natural persons who are controlling persons, and the conflict of interest regulations applied in these respects. 12 C.F.R. §§ 563.41, 563.43 (1988).

119 See 12 U.S.C. §§ 371c, 371c-1, 375b.

120 See FIRREA, *supra* note 1, at § 301.

121 See 12 U.S.C. § 375b.

122 See FIRREA, *supra* note 1, at § 301. This necessarily included application of regulations promulgated by the Federal Reserve Board, commonly known as Regulation O, to thrift institutions. See 12 C.F.R. Part 215 (1989).

123 *Ibid.* at § 301.

estate loans.[124] The specific LTV ratios were not enacted as final legislation under FIRREA, but Congress directed the federal banking agencies to consider the standards set forth in the Senate version of FIRREA and otherwise implement such standards as consistent with safety and soundness principles.[125]

Nonetheless, Title XI of FIRREA, the *Real Estate Appraisal Reform Amendments,* directly addressed real estate transactions by requiring the use of State-certified or licensed real estate appraisers in connection with such transactions. Title XI further established a system of uniform national appraisal standards for real estate-related financial transactions engaged in, contracted for, or regulated by the federal regulatory agencies. Thus, FIRREA required the federal banking agencies and the RTC to establish real estate appraisal standards and established an Appraisal Subcommittee under the FFIEC in order to set those appraisal standards.

VI. FIRREA: IMPACT ON THE THRIFT INDUSTRY

The FIRREA legislation, representing a comprehensive and abrupt policy reversal in numerous facets, did not immediately resolve the thrift industry crisis, as thrift institutions and banks alike continued to fail and costs of the problem continued to mount. The FHLBB regulations, CEBA and FIRREA cumulatively accelerated asset value deflation in depository institution sensitive assets, particularly real estate. Although each of these actions considered separately seemed appropriate to regulators and legislators at the time, they cumulatively reinforced the reactive psychology that precipitated asset value deflation. The asset value deflation thereafter infected the capital bases of S&Ls, banks, insurance companies, pension funds and all other organizations that had invested directly or indirectly or otherwise engaged in lending activities in the real estate market.

FIRREA failed to guarantee that all insolvent institutions and claimants thereof would receive the same treatment after seizure or intervention by the FDIC or RTC, and ensured that the intended shifting of accountability from misguided, conflicting, or ill-timed government monetary, fiscal, and legislative policies to the industry itself occurred with wide ranging effects. For instance, FIRREA granted the FDIC and RTC the authority to discriminate amongst claims on failed institutions, in contrast to the traditional rule that all claims in the same class must receive the same percentage recovery.

The agencies are obligated to pay only the amount a claimant would have received if the agencies had liquidated the assets and liabilities of the institution, which is often a steep discount from full recovery. The agencies also retained discretion to select some claimants for additional payments, thus enabling the agencies to treat insiders less well than other claimants.[126]

---

124 See Norton and Whitely, *supra* note 5, at 2A-82.
125 See H. Conf. Rep. No. 222, 101st Cong., 1st Sess. 402 (1989).
126 See P. Swire, 'Bank Insolvency Law Now That It Matters Again', 42 Duke L. J. 469 (1992), at p.487.

In addition, the FDIC and RTC obtained wide-ranging enforcement powers both before and after insolvency, with no close analogues to creditor powers in bankruptcy, including the imposition of civil money penalties of up to USD1 million per day for violations of thrift and bank regulations;[127] the issuance of temporary cease and desist orders to freeze assets of institution-affiliated parties upon a mere *prima facie* showing that money penalties are appropriate;[128] and the inability to protect against these penalties by filing for bankruptcy.[129] These enforcement proceedings obviously enhanced the ability of agencies to recover for losses arising from insolvent institutions, and encouraged litigation and shifting of accountability of systematic losses from government policies to the industry itself.

Notwithstanding the enforcement superpowers set forth under FIRREA, Congress continued to focus on the notion that many egregious crimes occurred in the thrift industry during the 1980s which played a significant part in the thrift industry crisis but were not necessarily addressed under FIRREA. The concept of shifting accountability from government to industry underscored this trend, and resulted in additional legislation designed to further shift the burden away from government and on to the industry.

According to US regulatory authorities, during the late 1980s and early 1990s: 1,617 banks failed; 1,300 thrifts failed; and these failures were estimated to result in losses approximating USD300 billion over the next 40 years. The costs associated with the resolution of these failures assuredly added billions of dollars to this figure. In Texas alone, nine of the top ten banks failed, particularly beginning in 1987.

The element of criminal fraud allegedly contributed anywhere from 11 per cent to 33 per cent of the thrift institutions and banks that failed, and again, allegedly, large numbers of surviving institutions still operating today were subjected to fraudulent activities perpetrated by insiders. The US regulatory authorities estimated that insider fraud was present in approximately 25 per cent of all bank failures and in approximately 33 per cent of all thrift failures as of 1989, respectively. Finally, 64 per cent of RTC controlled thrifts allegedly had suspect criminal conduct referred to the US Department of Justice.[130]

According to the US General Accounting Office, fraud and insider abuse were major factors in a significant portion of US financial institution failures in the 1980s. Real estate lending projects were common vehicles for financial institution fraud, generally considered as the 'perfect device for fraud and insider abuse' and effectively destroyed many thrift institutions and banks alike.[131] In December 1989, the then-US Attorney General Richard Thornburg set a primary objective for the Department of Justice as bringing to justice '...

---

127 See 12 U.S.C. § 1818(i)(2).

128 See 12 U.S.C. § 1818(c).

129 See 12 U.S.C. § 1818(i)(1); *Carlton v. Firstcorp. Inc.*, 967 F.2d 942, 945 (4th Cir. 1992).

130 See generally, US General Accounting Office Report to the Chairman, Committee on the Judiciary, US Senate, 'Bank and Thrift Criminal Fraud', GAO Rep. B-245890, 8 January 1993 ('GAO Report'); including response of the US Department of Justice to the GAO Report, dated 1 October 1992.

131 *Ibid.*

all those who have sought to capitalize on the American dream ... by destroying the financial solvency of institutions designed to serve them.'[132]

VII. CONCLUDING NOTE: MOVE TO FURTHER CRIMINALIZATION – THE CRIME CONTROL ACT OF 1990

The Crime Control Act of 1990[133] responded to this political rhetoric and the notion that the failure of the thrift industry involved many other criminal activities that the FIRREA legislation did not address directly. As such, the Crime Control Act established special Department of Justice financial institution fraud units and groups; significantly enhanced the ability of the Justice Department and federal banking agencies to seize the assets of wrongdoers and reduce the use of bankruptcy to avoid civil or criminal penalties; created three new federal crimes (concealing assets from a conservator, receiver, or liquidating agent of a financial institution; obstructing the examination of a financial institution; and organizing, managing, or supervising a continuing financial crimes enterprise and receiving USD5 million or more from such an enterprise over a 24-month period). Thus, the Crime Control Act established criminal liability for knowingly concealing assets or property from the FDIC when it acts as receiver or conservator.

The FDIC was granted increased authority to nullify transfers made by 'institution affiliated parties' who have breached their duties to the bank, for up to five years prior to the inception of the receivership or conservatorship. The FDIC and RTC were further authorized to use the courts to attach or freeze assets of the institution preventing wrongful disposal, pending investigation and prosecution of civil and criminal claims and charges based on such breaches.[134]

The Crime Control Act also authorized the FDIC and the RTC the power to request a court to freeze the assets of any person involved in such civil or criminal claims.[135] The Crime Control Act also provided these agencies with new powers that preempted rules otherwise applicable in bankruptcy. In order to ensure that bank insiders did not benefit from their criminal activities, the Act declared that certain banking-related claims were no longer dischargeable in bankruptcy.[136]

---

132 *Ibid.* at 75.

133 See Pub. L. No. 100-647,(1990).

134 See 12 U.S.C. § 1821(d)(17)(A). See *FDIC v. Cafritz*, 762 F. Supp. 1503 (D.D.C. 1991).

135 See 12 U.S.C. § 1821(d)(18). The stated purpose of the provision is 'Protecting Assets From Wrongful Disposition.' See Crime Control Act 1990, Pub. L. No. 101-647, tit. XXV, subtit. B, 104 Stat. 4789, 4863 (1990). It would appear the statute should be read more narrowly than its 'all person' language would suggest. The power should arise only with respect to assets sought by the agencies acting as receiver or conservator or in their related failed-bank capacities. A similar power to seek prejudgment attachment is also given to the FDIC as an enforcement power against open banks. 12 U.S.C. § 1818(i)(4).

136 Individual debts are not dischargeable if they arise from fraud or defalcation while acting in a fiduciary capacity to an insured depository institution, or from reckless failure to fulfill any commitment by the individual to maintain the capital of the institution. 11 U.S.C. § 523(a)(11)-(12).

Finally, the Crime Control Act established new rules applicable to any entity, such as a bank holding company, that was committed to maintaining the capital of an insured bank.

If the holding company later becomes bankrupt, the FDIC is given high priority to the amount of the commitment.[137] These rules became more important following the passage of subsequent comprehensive legislation in 1991 which routinely required such commitments by BHCs to maintain the capital of undercapitalized banks.[138]

In June 1990, then-President George Bush pledged to 'put the cheats ... chiselers and ... charlatans behind bars'[139] and the newly enacted legislation under FIRREA and the Crime Control Act all but guaranteed the phasing in of a period of massive civil and criminal litigation as the FDIC, RTC, and OTS moved to prosecute individuals allegedly involved in criminal activities or grossly negligent activities and recoup costs incurred to the government in resolving such affected institutions. FIRREA was enacted in significant part to address financial institution fraud by strengthening civil and criminal penalties for defrauding or otherwise damaging financial institutions and depositors.

The Crime Control Act built upon FIRREA by providing additional tools to combat financial institution fraud, including: (1) new financial institution related offenses; (2) increased fines and prison terms; (3) expanded restitution; and (4) measures to protect assets from wrongful disposition using 'asset freezes'. Following enactment of FIRREA, the US Attorney General designated criminal fraud in financial institutions as a top enforcement priority. The Dallas Bank Fraud Task Force was established to prosecute criminal fraud in financial institutions.

The Crime Control Act authorized a doubling of resources directed to 'the enormous and unprecedented challenge,' and created a new Justice Office of Financial Institution Fraud. Using the Dallas Bank Fraud Task Force as a model, the Department of Justice planned to combine resources of financial institution regulators, the DOJ Criminal Division, the FBI, IRS, US Secret Service and other investigative agencies to create Bank Fraud Task Forces in 26 US cities where criminal bank and thrift fraud was most prevalent.[140]

Only two additional task forces were established based on the Dallas model, however. Nonetheless, nearly 3,500 defendants were charged, and

---

137 See 11 U.S.C. at §§ 365(o), 507(a)(8) (Supp. III 1991). A Chapter 11 trustee debtor is required to assume and immediately cure any deficit under any commitment by the debtor to banking agencies to maintain the capital of an insured depository institution. *Ibid.* at § 365(o). Such obligations pursuant to assumed executory contracts are administrative expense claims given first priority under the Bankruptcy Code. *Ibid.* at §§ 503(b)(1)(A), 507(a)(1). In slight contrast, the same obligations in a Chapter 7 liquidation proceeding are given new eighth priority. *Ibid.* at § 507(a)(8). No explanation is given in the legislative history for the differing treatment between reorganization and liquidation. See H.R. Rep. No. 868, 101st Cong., 2nd Sess., Pt 1, at 179-180 (1990), reprinted in 1990 in USCCAN 6472, 6585-6586.

138 'Federal Deposit Insurance Corporation Improvement Act of 1991,' Pub. L. No. 102-242, at 131, 105 Stat. 2236, 2253-67 (codified at 12 U.S.C. § 1831o).

139 *Ibid.*

140 *Ibid.*

approximately 2,600 defendants were convicted, involving losses estimated at USD11.5 billion, during the period between 1 October 1988 and 30 June 1992.

Of the 2,603 convicted, 1,700 were sentenced to prison, most for terms of less than two years, and fewer than 2 per cent of those convicted received sentences of more than ten years. The restitution and fines ordered in these cases approximated USD84.6 million. By August 1992, approximately 4.5 per cent of the total restitution ordered was collected.

For various reasons, the Department of Justice believed that the 'money had disappeared' and that there was little or nothing to recover at the conclusion of the criminal case. The GAO determined that the extent and impact of fraud was difficult to ascertain, because it was extremely difficult to determine when and if suspect activity crossed the line between poor business judgment and fraud. The GAO also found that putting a dollar value on losses caused by fraud was also exceedingly difficult.[141]

The US Department of Justice opined in October 1992 that the near collapse of the thrift industry was the result of 'a series of complex factors' and underscored that regardless of which set of numerical data was reviewed, insider fraud was not conclusively shown to be a major factor in the thrift industry crisis.[142]

In addition, the Department of Justice opined that the prevalent view that the thrift industry collapse was primarily a 'law enforcement issue' was simply incorrect, and therefore shifting accountability for the thrift industry losses to 'criminals' and 'insiders' was a politically convenient but irresponsible and inaccurate conclusion.[143]

In responding to the General Accounting Office's assessment of the Department of Justice's efforts to investigate and prosecute financial institution fraud, the Department of Justice reiterated that while fraud and real estate-related fraud in particular were certainly factors in some thrift institution failures, such fraud was simply not a major factor in all or even a majority of these failures. Instead, economic factors in the real estate markets (the 'boom' period of asset value inflation followed by the 'bust' period of asset value deflation generated by misdirected and conflicting government policy reversals in multiple arenas covered in this work) and in other financial markets played a far greater role in the thrift industry crisis than insider fraud.

The General Accounting Office, as the investigative arm of Congress, predictably concluded otherwise despite the bold assertions of the Department of Justice. Notwithstanding the unsupported findings of the GAO Report, the extent of fraud as a major factor in thrift institution failures is simply unknown at this time, and indeed may remain unknown, but the systemic existence of criminal fraud cannot be reasonably inferred without empirical and anecdotal study of the reasons for all the failures. The Department of Justice advised the General Accounting Office as follows:[144]

---

141 *Ibid.*

142 See Justice Department Response, at 1, in GAO Report, *supra* note 130.

143 See Justice Department Response, *supra* note 142, at 1-2.

144 *Ibid.* at 2.

'[P]rofessional prosecutors simply will not indict someone because they are named in a criminal referral as part of a misplaced search for scapegoats. Nor should they. The US criminal justice system must not become a tool of partisan politics or cater in any way to a lynch-mob mentality.'

10. Effect of Supervisory and Legislative Reregulation on the Thrift and Banking Industries and Real Estate Lending Markets

I. INTRODUCTION

The ongoing and cumulative effects of supervisory legislative reregulation in the mid to late 1980s were to take a fundamental toll on the structure and future operations of the US thrift and banking industries, and upon the US real estate markets. This chapter attempts to identify and to decipher these various impacts.

II. IMPACT ON THRIFT FINANCIAL OPERATIONS

CEBA, FIRREA and FHLBB reregulation not only limited the definition of regulatory capital, but also increased regulatory capital requirements. Limiting the definition of capital had the effect of reducing leverage; increasing capital requirement has the same effect. In other words, each has the effect of restricting growth or contracting assets.

The FHLBB adopted new capital regulations in 1985 which required more capital, when the aim should have been to preserve existing capital. The objectives of increasing capital and reducing leverage are each salutatory and underscore the movement to the risk-based capital adequacy framework in the late 1980s, discussed later in this chapter. These actions must be well conceived, transparent, consistent, timely, realistic; and generally achievable without rendering the institutions insolvent.

Unfortunately, none of these criteria were satisfied under FIRREA, which dramatically altered the capital requirements for thrift institutions in a series of abrupt policy reversals. For example: (1) the 'Core Capital' rules of FIRREA were confusing;[1] (2) there were different rules for banks and

[1] See, e.g., 'Comptroller Plans to Issue Rules to Ease Core Capital Confusion', Am. Banker (11 September 1989).

S&Ls;[2] and (3) there were numerous financial institutions at the time which simply could not meet the FIRREA capital requirements.[3] With the acceleration of asset value deflation and a constantly changing regulatory climate, it is inherently difficult to raise new capital, not only for existing financial institutions, but also for the institutions participating in FDIC and RTC 'bailout' acquisition arrangements.[4]

The political rhetoric about raising new capital is appropriate only if it is based on realistic, achievable goals, and new regulations supporting this rhetoric are appropriate only if they are constructive, transparent, long term and similarly achievable. The establishment of new 'reactive' capital regulations that are based on political considerations, misunderstandings of the current economic conditions, and attempts to shift accountability to less culpable parties outside of government itself only led to further losses.

FIRREA also put an end to the future creation of goodwill and required the elimination of all goodwill by December 1994. In other words, if a thrift institution had USD10,000,000 of unamortized goodwill on its books as of December 1994, it had to write off that amount and unless that amount was replaced by USD10,000,000 of new capital, the institution would be required to restrict growth or contract assets as appropriate. Of course, either action would, in turn, lead to reduced earnings potential.

Further, through CEBA, FIRREA and FHLBB reregulation, the definition of capital was limited, which effectively reduced leverage and caused restrictions on growth or contraction of assets, leading in turn to reduced earnings potential.

In addition, FHLBB reregulation eliminated the practice of loan loss deferral prospectively in 1984, and the adoption of GAAP under CEBA and FIRREA ultimately eliminated any deferred loan losses still remaining on the books of thrift institutions.

Moreover, the investment vs. loan debate pertaining to acquisition, development and construction (AD&C) loans was resolved in most cases with the AD&C loan being deemed an 'investment' instead of a 'loan', and the FHLBB required financial statements to be restated to reflect this resolution. Thus, earnings were negatively restated and investments were positively restated, leading to even further reduced earnings potential and capital adequacy. The end results were (1) loss of capital through loss of earnings; (2) loss of leverage; (3) violation of growth regulations and resulting supervisory agreements; (4) shrinkage of assets; and (5) reduced earnings potential.

Not to be forgotten, the use of 'income capital', 'net worth' and 'mutual capital' certificates as part of the regulatory forbearance processes used to

---

2 See, e.g., 'Capital Standards Interagency Differences in Bank and Thrift Capital Standards', *Banking Expansion Reporter* (3 September 1990).

3 See Charles McCoy and Paulette Thomas, 'Ongoing Fiasco. Hundreds of S&Ls Fall Hopelessly Short of New Capital Rules', *Wall Street Journal* (7 December 1989).

4 See Howard Rudnitsky, 'Where is the Bottom?', *Forbes* (17 September 1990), at p.136. See also Fred R. Bleakley, 'Banks Fund Their Sources of Capital Drying Up', *Wall Street Journal* (8 October 1990); John Evans, 'The 8% Capital Rule, Still A Year Off, Has Impact Now', Am. Banker (28 November 1990).

sustain distressed thrift institutions and banks alike became obsolete following CEBA and FIRREA, as they were inconsistent with GAAP.

Another significant impact contributing to the thrift industry problem resulted from the 'reclassification of asset' regulations adopted by the FHLBB. The salutatory effects of 'classification of assets' regulations on banks are well known and had been consistently applied for quite some time. The same has not been true for S&Ls, however, as the FHLBB did not adopt a final rule for commercial loans setting forth the asset classification categories similar to the banking system (namely substandard, doubtful and loss) until December 1985.

The new FHLBB regulation generally retained the characteristics of the national bank system that significantly enhanced the draconian effect of the regulation. Under this new FHLBB 'classification of asset' regulation, the FHLBB examiners could classify loans as 'substandard', 'doubtful' or 'loss' in much the same way as national bank examiners. The differences in application, however, were extreme. For example: (1) both bank and thrift examiners relied on appraisals, but following FHLBB reregulation, the appraisal requirements for S&Ls (themselves changed a minimum of four times until January 1986 when the FHLBB Memo #R41c was adopted) were much more stringent leading to lower valuations; and/or (2) if an asset of an S&L was classified as substandard, the asset was treated as a scheduled item, thus increasing the contingency component of the institution's minimum regulatory capital requirement by an amount equal to 20 per cent of the dollar amount of the substandard asset.

In effect, this classification required an increase to the S&L's capital. Banks, on the other hand, were simply required to book the classification as a reserve (which constituted an expense entry to the income statement, but not an immediate reduction in capital). In addition, because of the interworkings of the classification of asset regulation and the FHLBB Memo #R41c, the examiners of an S&L had broad discretion over the S&L. The examiners could disagree with the S&L's appraisals; they could order a new appraisal; they could require use of only appraisers approved by them. Ultimately, the classification of assets regulation governing S&Ls was again changed to be compatible with banks.

Nevertheless, these types of regulations gave broad discretion to the examiners and the supervisory staff. In a downward, spiraling market with little purchase and sale activity, the survival of a bank or S&L became dependent upon the subjective appraisal valuations of properties.

The reclassification of thrift institution financial assets by FHLBB examiners further contributed significantly to downward adjustments in asset values and accelerated asset value deflation. For example, if an S&L purchased a portfolio of stocks, the question arose whether the institution held the stocks as an 'investment securities' or as an inventory of 'trading securities'. If the securities were held as 'investment securities', then the securities had to be reported at the original acquisition cost until sold. However, if the securities were held as an inventory of 'tradable securities' and if these securities lost value during the holding period, the loss had to be reported at fair value, with the reported loss reducing earnings and capital. The resolution as to whether given securities should be classified as being held as investments or trading inventory was not always clear, and accounting standards inherently permitted some degree of management discretion in establishing this reporting position. If FHLBB examiners disagreed with management discretion in this respect, the resulting impact would include (1) loss of capital through loss of earnings; (2) loss of leverage; (3) violation of regulations and resulting supervisory agreements; (4) shrinkage of assets; and (5) lower earnings potential.

Finally, in June 1989 Carol T. Crawford, Assistant Attorney General of the US Department of Justice, concluded that 'it is clear that FSLIC's forbearance letters do not "foreclose" Congress from enacting legislation that would impose new capital requirements on thrift institutions.' Many investors in and acquirers of distressed S&Ls during the 1980s relied upon letters from the FHLBB and/or FSLIC granting forbearances on capital requirements and other operative regulations. To nullify those forbearances through new legislation such as FIRREA may be legal and may not technically constitute a breach of a previous FSLIC undertaking, although tiresome litigation recently resolved certain of these issues in favor of investors, which received a judgment against the Federal Government in excess of USD900 million for reliance upon such promises. Nevertheless, actions such as these created a debilitating environment of distrust of regulatory credibility and a 'chilling' of future sales and solutions.[5]

The most basic RAP accounting standards and GAAP reinterpretations by the FHLBB which prior to 1986 contributed significantly to asset value inflation were reversed by the TRA, CEBA, and FIRREA, thereby creating the opposite effect, and contributed significantly to asset value deflation.

III. IMPACT ON REAL ESTATE LENDING PRACTICES

The aforementioned reregulatory policies and legislation in TRA and FIRREA had a devastating impact on the real estate lending markets, which are critically dependent on determinations of valuation given the economic and regulatory environment existing at the time in question. As indicated in earlier chapters, one method of establishing real estate values is through the use of comparables. If a contiguous parcel of real estate sells at a certain price, this information will be an indication of value for the adjoining parcel being appraised. This comparative sales information is called a 'comparable'.

In a deflationary period, comparables reflexively indicate decreased values for all similar properties in close proximity to the parcel of real estate being appraised. Also, in a deflationary period, banks and S&Ls are dependent on appraised values or recent market value sales in determining the market value of any parcel of real estate for loan or investment purposes. Obviously, the market value of any particular parcel will fall and if sold at a lower price, will affect all values of similar property in close proximity.

---

[5] See, e.g., *U.S. v. Winstar Corporation, et al.*, 116 S.Ct. 2432 (1996).

Further, during deflationary periods, appraised values and market values reflect, and add momentum to decreasing values, as one comparable is built on one another. In the late 1980s, these factors accelerated asset value deflation in the real estate markets.

A. Thrift Industry and Texas Banks

The disastrous effect of the 'free fall' in real estate values on thrifts and Texas banks culminating in the passage of FIRREA was not an overnight phenomenon. Beginning in 1984 and 1985, as reregulation of the thrift industry commenced in earnest, the FHLBB generally overreacted to stinging criticism from Congress. Personnel in the Federal Home Loan Bank (FHLB) of Dallas were shaken up with tough regulators appointed to key positions. New appraisal standards were adopted, resulting in lower values and lower comparables and often applied on a retroactive basis. New capital regulations were adopted which required more capital when the name of the game should have been to preserve existing capital. New growth restriction and classification of asset regulations were also adopted. All of these measures treated the emerging S&L crisis as one that could be cured by simply tightening the rules, and they collectively failed to take into account their effect on the dynamics of the real estate industry and its interrelation with the value of assets held by thrifts and banks. The spiraling depression in values accelerated significantly in 1986, as an estimated 30 per cent to 50 per cent of market value simply evaporated in a manner similar to the October 1987 stock market debacle, and operating losses for thrift institutions and many banks reached monumental proportions.

The net operating losses were caused by the following factors. First, the reregulation of the thrift industry generally resulted in the curtailment of new lending activities, as the reregulation largely precluded further growth (i.e. there was no capital to support any growth). Borrowers failed to pay interest, much less principal; and income was not realized from collateral by reason of legal issues and lender liability considerations.[6] Second, the reregulation generally resulted in a systematic increase in cost of funds in spite of FDIC/FSLIC insurance (the so-called Texas premium); legal fees running up to USD500,000 per month at many thrifts; consultant fees equal to that same amount being incurred per month; property operating and management cost increasing with respect to real estate owned and non-performing assets; and hidden costs arising from constant regulator involvement, required independent reappraisals, additional accounting and personnel expense. Third, the reregulatory environment generally caused significant and often unnecessary delays in restructuring non-performing loans through lender liability litigation initiated by borrowers (sometimes successful); regulatory delays, control or scrutiny; and intercreditor disagreements on participated loans.

---

6 For instance, the author notes that one of the smaller bank holding companies was at one point a defendant in more than 350 lender liability lawsuits handled by 49 different law firms.

B. National Banks

Although the dangerous scenario described above initially developed in the thrift industry and Texas-based banking organizations, it soon spread in varying degrees to banks in other regions of the United States. The federal banking regulations required that other real estate owned (OREO) be 'marked to market' at least on an annual basis.[7] The actual practice conducted by the OCC in pervasively declining regional markets was to require that banks *anticipate future value declines* by establishing 'OREO valuation reserves', a direct charge against capital (unlike the loan loss reserve). As liquidity in regional real estate markets weakened, comparable sales became so infrequent that they were deemed meaningless by bank regulators for purposes of market appraisal. The Texas experience showed that the value of a bank's OREO portfolio was then determined by the judgment of regulators using their own discounted cash flow computer models and assumptions, even as the regulators were based elsewhere in the United States and generally lacked personal knowledge of the regional market in question. These techniques were also used to value land, an appraisal method not sanctioned by any professional appraisal body. The effect of OREO write-downs and valuation reserves on a bank's earnings and capital were simply devastating and clearly accelerated asset value deflation. As banks were subject to rapidly growing OREO portfolios, they were typically deficient in the following areas:

1. *Project Information Files*

In general, neither the bank's credit files nor its working files on a given real estate project contained complete, accurate information regarding cost, status of completion, tenancy, lease-up progress, compliance with local or national regulation, operating costs and so forth. In other words, the bank failed to have on file all relevant information necessary to analyze real properties and otherwise prepare itself to operate, enhance the value of, and ultimately to sell real estate holdings.

2. *Data Base Problems*

Although banks were quite sophisticated in monitoring loan portfolios, they were generally ill prepared to capture and manipulate the data necessary to accurately track and analyze real estate portfolios, as until asset value deflation set in, such institutions never had the need to engage in real estate portfolio analysis. A complete, accurate portfolio database is necessary to maintain the confidence of regulators, but is even more important in the marketing of real estate. A bank must be able to respond instantaneously when a bank stock analyst, regulator or potential buyer requests information on, for example, specific types of property in specified geographical areas. In addition, a complete database is critical to the grading and categorization process.

---

[7] 12 C.F.R. § 7.3025.

3. *Real Property Accounting Systems*

As the OREO portfolios accumulated through foreclosure, banks recognized that each piece of real property absorbed through default or otherwise arrived with different accounting systems (if such systems existed at all). The banks had to quickly establish standardized charts of accounts and reporting formats for use by on-site property managers to avoid ensuing chaos, as budgeting, forecasting and ability to hold on-site managers accountable for results are impossible without such standardization. In addition, property level accounting must roll up accurately to the bank's general ledger and internal controls must be established to prevent misapplication of operating income.

4. *Value Enhancement*

Most OREO properties were necessarily underperforming and reduced in value. Since future OREO portfolios were accumulated as a result of pervasive declines in real estate values and the inability of real property managers to service their debt, it is axiomatic that acquiring banks would be unable or unwilling to dispose of OREO properties quickly and at fair prices. In order to minimize the negative effect on capital adequacy during such unavoidable holding periods, banks had to establish an ongoing 'value enhancement activity', that is, a unit made up of people knowledgeable in the real estate business areas of increasing occupancy and rental income while reducing operating costs. Without this value enhancement, bank properties were either not marketable at all (exposing them to continual write-down) or marketable only at 'fire sale' prices resulting in recognized economic and accounting losses.

5. *Real Estate Marketing and Sales*

The banks were required to promptly analyze, grade and categorize each OREO property in their real estate portfolios. The majority of OREO properties had no upside market potential and had to be disposed of immediately at the then-existing market prices. As significant percentages of properties had enough potential to justify intense value enhancement efforts, however, the marketing and sale of such properties, while overseen by bank personnel, must be executed by experienced local brokers directed by bank personnel pursuant to a rational marketing plan

6. *Appraisal Systems*

Most banks were ill prepared to meet the regulatory requirements for accurate independent appraisals of OREO, especially as growth of OREO properties accelerated dramatically. The primary consequence of an inadequate appraisal system is loss of regulator confidence in real estate appraisal systems, which generally results in increasingly larger directed write downs of property values and reduced confidence in bank management.

Unfortunately, virtually no thrift institutions or banks alike established expertise in these areas in the 1980s because thrifts and banks provide banking services, not real estate services. The skillful handling of OREO property portfolios to minimize damage to the bank requires all these disciplines, however. Bank and S&L directors and officers are charged by US financial laws with maintaining the safety and soundness of their institutions, and the consequences of engaging in 'unsafe and unsound' practices through the examination process are quite severe.[8]

As rapidly deteriorating real estate markets greatly increase risk to most banks, boards of directors must consider and take action on a variety of issues arising from declining real estate values. These issues include demonstration of due diligence, knowledge of portfolio value and dynamics, balance sheet structure and preparedness to deal with deteriorating collateral values and the certain threat to capital adequacy.

IV. RECHARACTERIZATION OF REAL ESTATE LENDING TRANSACTIONS

The phase of asset value deflation and reregulation significantly affected the characterization of certain real estate transactions to the detriment of thrift institutions and banks alike. Several consequences and aspects of these characterizations are reviewed below, including (1) in substance foreclosures; (2) interest capitalization; and (3) troubled debt restructurings.

A. In Substance Foreclosures

The concept of 'in substance foreclosure' under US law[9] provides that under certain conditions, a loan secured by collateral will be deemed real estate otherwise owned by the lender, notwithstanding that the borrower still has legal title to the collateral. The lender is charged with knowledge of when these conditions exist. If the lender continues to report the loan as a 'loan' for financial regulatory purposes, the lender will in all likelihood continue to record interest on the loan as interest income. Further, the lender will also in all likelihood not have appraised the underlying collateral for purposes of 'marking to market' the value of the loan and its collateral. At best, the lender may have to establish specific reserves against losses. If, subsequent to this reporting, the lender's accountants or regulators declare that the 'loan' should have been recharacterized and reported as an 'in substance foreclosure', the interest income reported by the lender after the date of the 'in substance foreclosure' (an ISF) must be revised and, as of that date and annually thereafter, any 'marked to market' loss must be booked against the lender's capital.[10]

---

[8] 12 U.S.C. § 1818.

[9] 12 C.F.R. § 7.3025. See also FASB, 'Statement of Financial Accounting Standards' No. 15, paras. 28, 29, 34 and 84.

[10] *Ibid.*

The conditions underlying an 'in substance foreclosure' were not easily recognized, however. The general criteria for recharacterizing loans as 'in substance foreclosures' are as follows. First, the debtor has little or no equity in the collateral, considering the current fair value of the collateral. Second, the proceeds for repayment of the loan can be expected to come only from the operation or sale of the collateral. Third, the debtor has either: (i) formally or effectively abandoned control of the collateral to the creditor; *or* (ii) retained control of the collateral but, because of the current financial condition of the debtor, or the economic prospects for the debtor and/or the collateral in the foreseeable future, it is doubtful that the debtor will be able to rebuild equity in the collateral or otherwise repay the loan in the foreseeable future.[11]

The first two criteria are used to identify situations where most of the risks and rewards of ownership of the collateral have passed from the borrower to the bank. Even if the value of the collateral securing the loan has dropped so that there is little or no equity in that particular investment, the borrower or guarantor may currently have demonstrably sufficient strength or outside sources of cash to service and eventually retire the debt. In that case, the second criteria is not met and there is no in substance foreclosure. Thus, value of collateral for a secured loan may drop to zero without a finding of ISF if the borrower or guarantor has the demonstrable current wherewithal to repay the loan from other sources. Likewise, if all loans to a borrower are cross collateralized and total debt is reasonably exceeded by the value of all cross-pledged collateral, then the first criteria is not met and there is no finding of ISF.

The third criteria leaves room for subjective evaluation of the borrower's ability to rebuild equity in the collateral or otherwise repay the loan in the *foreseeable* future. This subjective evaluation should be prudently exercised by the workout officer and management. For example, when using forecasts to assess the borrower's ability to repay the loan or to assess the prospects for improvement in the value of the collateral, the longer the time projected, the less reliable the projected results. Projections should be reasonably near term and be based on independently derived supportable assumptions.

In the 1980s, lender decisions regarding whether certain real estate lending transaction were 'loans' or 'in substance foreclosures' in this respect, even if supported by the opinions of professional accountants, were frequently subject to second guessing and recharacterized by regulators, resulting in subsequent restatement of earnings and financial reports. The restatements due to such recharacterizations then subjected lenders to shareholder derivative and class action litigation under applicable US securities laws for material misrepresentations or omissions.

The ISF determination affected the thrift institution's or bank's accounting for a loan as substantially repossessed, as legal title to the asset remains in the borrower until it is passed to the bank either by consent or through foreclosure. The loan is not in default solely by being found to be an ISF. It may

---

11 See US Securities and Exchange Commission F.R.R. § 401.09(c)(F.R.R. 28)(GAAP Release 17)(1989). See also FASB, 'Statement of Financial Accounting Standards' No. 15, at paras 28-29.

be in the bank's best interest to obtain control over the price and timing of the sale of the collateral to eliminate an asset acquired for debt previously contracted as soon as possible, but action must be taken in a way to protect the bank from lender liability allegations. Therefore, the course of dealing must minimize the bank's exposure to such allegations.

B. Interest Capitalization

The accounting standards for interest capitalization involve an election as to whether interest paid on certain real estate loans is more correctly categorized as 'interest income' or as 'capital investment'. In deciding which election to make, the source of the interest payment must be analyzed. If the source of payment is borrower funds (as opposed to lender funds), the interest can be recorded as interest income. If the source of payment is an advance by the lender of its own funds under a line of credit or otherwise, however, then closer scrutiny is required.

Based upon the facts, the interest may have to be capitalized.[12] In a downward spiraling real estate market, capitalization of interest becomes more and more of a possibility, and systemic elections by thrift and bank management sustained and compounded the impact of asset value deflation. The capitalized interest on loans is defined as 'uncollected interest' which is added to the unpaid principal balance in accordance with a contractual loan agreement.[13]

In real estate development lending, it is common for the loan agreement to contain a 'line item' loan allocation for the costs of construction. One of the line items is often an 'interest reserve' out of which advances are made periodically to pay interest charges on the outstanding balance of the construction loan. When construction is complete and all line item allocations including the interest reserve are fully advanced, the loan (including the interest allocation) is repaid through permanent financing or sale of the project in the normal course of business.

Interest capitalization concerns arise primarily when the project loan is not paid at maturity through permanent financing or sale as was expected. In these cases, the 'interest reserve' has been fully advanced, the loan has matured, but the source of repayment is delayed. If the loan is renewed pending receipt of the source of repayment, the interest reserve is by definition capitalized into the loan.

Interest capitalization concerns also arise from loan origination or increasing an original loan to create a new interest reserve to carry the renewed loan pending its repayment. Depending on the source of repayment of the new loan, it too may be deemed capitalized interest on the original loan. Of course, interest capitalization for reporting purposes is appropriate only when the borrower has the ability to repay the debt in the normal course of business.[14] The preceding sentence does not mean that any construction

---

12 OCC Examining Circular 229 (May 1985). See also FASB, 'Statement of Financial Accounting Standards' No. 15, at paras 28-29.

13 See OCC Examining Circular 229 (1985).

14 *Ibid.*

loan which is not repaid at maturity must automatically be placed on non-accrual. It is not unusual in the real estate development business for permanent financings and sales to be temporarily delayed and for additional well-structured loans to be extended to pay interest on the original loan during the delay. These are circumstances under which continued accrual is appropriate.

The interest capitalization on short-term real estate loans should be based upon the borrower's ability to discharge the indebtedness in the normal course of business, based upon the surrounding circumstances and based upon prudent credit judgment (including source of repayment and value of collateral). The appropriateness of interest capitalization for accounting purposes is based primarily on the creditworthiness of the borrower and guarantors.

In addition to the general criteria for creditworthiness, the following questions should be considered in determining whether capitalization of interest is appropriate. First, was interest capitalization anticipated upon approval of the initial loan? Second, is the loan well secured by (i) collateral that has a realizable value sufficient to discharge the debt (including capitalized interest) in full; or (ii) the guaranty of a financially responsible and capable party? Third, is repayment of the loan based on a reasonably ascertainable event in the future? Fourth, can the borrower obtain funds from sources other than the bank on similar terms and rates? Finally, is there little or no doubt as to the ultimate collection of all principal and interest?

If the answers to these questions are predominantly in the affirmative, then interest capitalization may be acceptable. The primary test remains the overall credit quality of the loan. Credits of sound quality may merit interest capitalization even if some of these questions are answered negatively. However, only in very unusual circumstances will a loan classified substandard merit interest capitalization.

C. Troubled Debt Restructurings

A troubled debt restructuring (TDR) is one 'in which the bank, for economic or legal reasons related to the borrower's financial difficulties, grants a concession to the borrower that it would not otherwise consider.'[15] Basic knowledge of TDR accounting is important to workout officers in preventing 'nonaccrual status' for certain loans, and in restoring existing nonaccrual loans to 'performing' status. The determination that a given restructuring is a TDR requires that the restructuring be carried on the bank's financial statement as a non-performing asset even if the loan is current as to interest, according to SFAS No. 15,[16] which is an extremely complex undertaking. The important understanding for purposes of this work is that a given debt restructuring which makes perfect business sense may nonetheless be

---

15 OCC Banking Circular 195 (1 May 1985). See also, OCC Examining Circular 234 (30 October 1995) regarding Troubled Real Estate Loans, as supplemented by OCC Banking Circular 208, Supplement #1 (10 July 1987).

16 See 'Statement of Financial Accounting Standards' No. 15.

deemed a TDR by the bank's independent accountants, such that the objective of reducing non-accrual assets is not achieved.[17]

The touchstone of TDRs lies in the granting of concessions because of the borrower's difficulties. For example, extending a loan at an interest rate equal to that generally charged for loans with similar risk would not be a TDR even if the rate were lower than the rate on the original loan. If the new terms of the troubled debt restructuring provide for a reduction of either interest *or* principal (referred to as a modification of terms), SFAS 15 requires that the recorded amount of the loan on the bank's books (principal plus accrued interest) be compared to the total future contractual cash payments (including both principal and interest) expected to be collected.

A loss is recognized *only* if the total of such future combined payments is less than the recorded amount of the loan. Otherwise, no loss is recognized and the only additional accounting requirement is to determine the new effective interest rate for income recognition purposes. However, the restructured loan will be carried as a non-performing asset.

The new effective interest rate is often equal to the stated loan rate included in the restructured loan document. However, adjustments may be required if (a) the loan principal is reduced, (b) the new contractual rates are on a graduated basis (e.g. 8 per cent first year, 10 per cent second year, etc.), (c) due and unpaid interest is not added to principal or otherwise included in the contractual interest rate amount, or (d) the repayment terms have other unusual provisions. If an effective interest rate computation is required, it should be based upon future contractual payment terms excluding all payments which are contingently payable. This rate is calculated so as to yield a constant rate of interest over the remaining life of the loan. It is expected the rate will generally be less than the original loan rate and may be as low as zero without any requirement to recognize a loss.

In addition, subject to the rules on interest capitalization discussed *supra*, the bank or thrift may extend additional credit to a borrower at interest rates below the current market rate. Since this is a new loan to the same borrower, no special accounting rules apply. Accordingly, discounting or loss recognition is not necessary. However, if the new loan is granted in connection with the restructuring of an existing loan, it will be considered part of the restructuring and accounted for as previously described.

In all TDRs, the collectibility of future payments is potentially questionable. Therefore, a credit analysis should be performed to determine if any additional amounts should be charged to the allowance for loan losses. The analysis should include the borrower's ability to meet the new terms of the loan based upon projected cash flows, profitability and other credit factors.

---

[17] The bank should not negotiate a less favorable business deal in an attempt to merely achieve more favorable accounting treatment, however. Given the complexity of FAS 15, the advice and counsel of the bank's internal accounting staff should be sought as soon as a plan begins to take shape and before commitments are made to the borrower.

V. REAL ESTATE APPRAISALS

The use of comparables in real estate market appraisals may have both positive and negative ramifications, depending on financial market conditions and inflationary expectations. In a downward, spiraling market, such 'comparable appraisals' also spiral downward until the issue arises as to whether the market is determining appraised values or whether the appraised values are determining FMV. Unfortunately, in markets weakened by asset value deflation and the attendant 'drying up' of capital and financing, the market value of property is determined by the appraisal. The appraised valuations, instead of being market driven, become the product of subjective determination by appraisers based on assumptions, and the application of such subjectivity tends to err on the side of caution in terms of valuation (i.e. the low side of value rather than the high side of value) for several reasons.

First, is the psychology of the market, as in whether FMVs are declining and whether the natural presumption is that this trend will continue. Second, in a downward spiraling market, the 'mark to market' losses must be reserved or realized by thrift institutions and banks. Since these institutions are required to market this property for sale once foreclosed upon, market values will reflect liquidation value, not 'going concern' value, leading to lower values and by implication lower comparables. Third, is that the bank and thrift regulators, because of their presumptions and perception of market psychology, become skeptical of values, and real estate appraisers necessarily become fearful of potential liability for overstating asset values.

Thus, the appraisers quickly understood that in appraising property, for a federally insured bank or S&L (particularly when the appraisal is ordered or required by the regulators), it was a much safer practice to err on the side of caution and provide lower appraisals in arriving at determinations of FMV.

A. Effect of Tightening of Appraisal Standards

The FHLBB initially adopted formal appraisal standards on 6 June 1977 in FHLBB Memorandum R41, and from 6 June 1977 through 30 November 1990, this memorandum was revised on many occasions to impose increasingly stringent appraisal standards. For instance, in 1979, 1982, and 1986, the FHLBB issued subsequent memoranda of the R41 series which systematically revised the definition of 'market value' such that, notwithstanding identical situations, the FMV of the same property actually decreased as each new definition was adopted.[18]

Thus, new real estate appraisal standards were eventually adopted, resulting in lower values and lower comparables, and were often applied on

---

[18] FHLBB Memorandum #R41 and #R41a (definitions were the same) were both adopted in 1977; FHLBB Memorandum #R41a-I was adopted in 1979; FHLBB Memorandum #R41b was adopted in 1982; and FHLBB Memorandum #R41c was adopted in 1986.

a retroactive basis.[19] The regulations established three appraisal standards that had to be included in the appraisal policies of every banking and thrift institution. For instance, the appraisal must be based upon the definition of 'market value' as set forth in the regulation. This definition contemplates the consummation of a sale as of a specified date and the passing of title from buyer to seller under open and competitive market conditions requisite to a fair sale. In addition, the appraisal must be presented in a narrative format. The appraisal report must be sufficiently descriptive to enable a reviewer to readily ascertain the estimated value reported and the rationale for that estimate. The analysis is required to be as detailed and in depth as the complexity of the real estate requires. Further, an appraisal must contain a sales history of the real estate appraised. Generally, sales within the three previous years must be disclosed.

B. Problematic Definitions: Market Value, FMV and Fair Value

The above review makes clear that if true 'market value' is not determined by the free activities of the market place, then the determination of 'market value' is necessarily contrived and thus becomes simply a function of definition and the processing of that definition. The definitional confusion therefore arises as to whether 'market value' is the same as 'fair market value' or 'fair value'? If none of these terms are established through transactional activities, but instead reflect definitional and regulatory concepts, then the answer depends on whether the definition of each term is identical.

The inherent problematic nature of regulatory definitions as applied in market transactions is apparent.

The definition used in real estate appraisals for federally insured thrift institutions was defined in the 'R' Memorandum series and most recently in 12 C.F.R. 563.17-1a. For these appraisals, the actual terminology required 'market value'. The prefix of 'fair' was not included. Within this definition is the specific requirement that '... a reasonable time is allowed for exposure in the open market ...'. The key phrase is 'a reasonable time'. Herein lies a vast arena of subjectivity. Statistically, one can prove that 'a reasonable time' for properties like major office buildings, industrial properties, large multi-use development tracts, etc. might well be one or two years. Thus, the estimation of market value when contemplating a reasonable time period inherently accounts for a marketing period that could extend up to two years.

The banking industry, governed by FDIC regulations, has typically used the term 'fair value', a term not including the adjective of 'market'. This definition is set forth in 12 U.S.C. 29, and the terminology of 'a reasonable time, is confined to a marketing period not to exceed 12 months.

Appraisal guidelines were implemented by the FDIC for certain institutions, whereby an 'accelerated sale value' is estimated. The FDIC recognized

---

19 The real estate appraisal standards are currently located at 12 C.F.R. § 563.17.1a(c)(1) (1998). See also, OCC Banking Circular 225 (21 December 1987) containing Uniform Guidelines for Real Estate Appraisal Policies for National Banks and OCC Advisory 90.2 (8 February 1990) regarding Real Estate Project and Development Lending by All National Banks.

that a determination of a 'reasonable time' for market exposure is dependent on local market conditions. If market conditions for the property indicate an average marketing time longer than six months, the financial institution must provide an 'accelerated sale value'. In short, if the 'market value' estimate incorporates 'a reasonable time' of longer than six months to sell, further discounting is required.

Based on the preceding, there was confusion within the industry, resulting in rather wide disparities between various regulatory agencies and financial institutions in reporting real asset values. The following simple example shows the difference in 'value' that would result by simply changing the definition of the 'value' being estimated. For an example, assume that the 'market value' of a high-rise downtown office building is estimated to be USD20,000,000 and based on statistical studies and surveys of major investors and commercial brokerage firms, 'a reasonable time for exposure in the open market' is 18 months. For this example, a 12 per cent discount rate is used for the mathematical calculations. The following shows the resulting value indications:

'Estimated Market Value' (assumes 18 months is reasonable exposure)	\$20,000,000
'Estimated Fair Value' (18 months – 12 months = 6 months x 12% discount factor)	\$18,840,905
'Accelerated Sales Value' (18 months – 6 months = 12 months x 12% discount factor)	\$17,748,985

By simply changing definitions, different values are estimated – all of which are, by definition, correct. Within the Dallas, Texas, area appraisers regularly received guidelines from various S&Ls whereby one required 'market value' and another 'fair value'. From the appraiser's perspective, this is merely a technical problem. From an industry viewpoint, the potential was for inconsistent, if not misleading, reporting standards.

If the dollar value of real property is based on how 'market value' or 'fair value' or 'fair market value' is defined, then the dollar value of the property will necessarily change if the definition of any one of those terms change. Further, if regulatory concerns lead to redefining the term 'market value' such that different and more stringent appraisal standards are adopted, one must necessarily conclude that:

1. simply by reason of the definitional change, the numerical representation of 'market value' will be lower;
2. lower 'market value' will be reflected in real estate comparables;
3. the practice of 'marking to market' will reflect further losses or an increase in loan loss reserves;
4. the recognition of further losses or an increase in loan loss reserves will reduce earnings and capital;

5. reduced earnings and capital will, unless remedied by subsequent capital injections, require contraction of deposits and shrinkage of real estate and other assets;
6. the shrinkage of assets will require their sale or disposition; and
7. the sale or disposition of such assets into a downward, spiraling market will result in compounded losses.

The meaning of the term 'mark to market' must be called into question and, if not carefully administered by the regulatory authorities, definitions of such terms as 'market value' may in fact not prevent but instead cause abuses or losses, respectively. The causative relationship is insidious because it is driven more by the subjectivity of regulatory definitions and interpretations thereof rather than by freely negotiated transactions in the real estate market. The end result is that the thrift and banking institution industries become contaminated by the subjective opinions and reflexive psychology of regulatory authorities.

VI. COST OF FUNDS AND RESTRICTIONS ON GROWTH

Notwithstanding federal deposit insurance, as the financial condition of a bank or S&L deteriorated, its cost of funds for fully insured deposits (the amount of interest it paid on deposits) reasonably increased. This deterioration was either real or perceived through the media and/or evaluations of rating agencies, so regardless of whether the deterioration was real or perceived, the cost of funds increased. The increased cost of funds (referred to in 1987–1988 as the 'Texas premium' because such increases were common among Texas banking and thrift institutions) given the real estate and oil market collapses and distressed institutions, reduced profits or compounded losses, and accelerated asset value deflation.

The effects of the Texas premium did not stop at just one thrift institution, however, as the premium effectively increased the cost of funds for all banks and thrift institutions since each financial institution was required to pay higher depository interest rates to retain its deposit base. Ironically, depositors generally demanded higher depository interest rates from the failing and distressed institutions notwithstanding the availability of federal deposit insurance on their deposits. In other words, a sufficient lack of confidence translated throughout depositor bases to demand higher depository interest rates, but the lack of confidence did not cause most depositors to systematically remove deposits from the institution paying those rates, as evidenced by observations of the author while conducting transactions in Texas from 1986 through 1989.

In addition, in 1985, the Federal Home Loan Bank of Dallas placed approximately 155 Texas S&Ls under some form of supervision. Many of these S&Ls were placed under this supervision based upon a violation of a regulation adopted in March 1985 covering the growth of deposit liabilities and assets. In essence, this regulation prohibited further growth unless certain capital requirements were maintained, and unquestionably affected the leverage ratio applicable to S&Ls. The regulation was appropriate in concept, but the problem was that it was at least five years too late and totally inconsistent with the previous regulatory and administrative solution of allowing the thrift industry to grow out of the crisis.

VII. 'MARK TO MARKET' ASSET VALUE

To the extent that collateral securing a loan decreases in value below the outstanding principal balance of the loan and there is no other adequate credit or collateral source to assure repayment of the loan, the bank or S&L holding the loan must determine the current market value of the collateral securing the loan and book a reserve for the loan equal to the excess of the outstanding principal balance of the loan over the current market value of the collateral. This is required by applicable accounting and regulatory standards and is known as 'marking to market'.

Unfortunately in a declining real estate market, there is a tendency for the market to 'freeze' as new buyers refrain from entering the market until prices have 'bottomed out'. Nevertheless, the appraisal process is still required. In these circumstances, the appraisers are left to determine valuations that are necessarily influenced by market psychology, attendant reactive thinking and the growing downward pressures of asset value deflation. In the absence of comparables, appraisers often looked to the most recent 'depressed' value comparable, projected eventual sales in the distant and uncertain future, calculated cost to carry the asset for the extended period, and discounted the projected net sales proceeds to net present value.

This analysis produced, in many circumstances, a negative asset value. If this process occurs, real estate values become totally subjective and abstract with no relationship to the free market. Although there is no actual transaction that is closed or any attendant cash lost, the bank or S&L must continue booking reserves and report the reserves on its income statement as an expense. The result of this reporting is decreasing income or increasing losses.

A bank may report USD100 million in losses for a calendar quarter, *notwithstanding the absence of an actual cash loss*. The loss, although not a cash loss, certainly impacts reported earnings and therefore stock value and capital adequacy, however. Public confidence in the financial institution is eroded, subjecting the institution to systemic withdrawal by depositors of their *uninsured* deposits, and the prospects of the failure of the institution become apparent.

Of course, this is not the only impact of 'marking to market' asset value, other notable impacts include the following; for example, when the financial institution forecloses on the collateral, the institution will be required to not only report on its income statement as an operating loss the excess of the outstanding principal balance of the loan over the value of the collateral securing the loan, but also reflect this excess as a loss of capital. Moreover, a series of capital losses brought about by marking to market asset values will impact the capital structure of a bank or S&L requiring an infusion of new capital or a selling (shrinkage) of assets. The higher the leverage ratio, the greater the required asset shrinkage unless new capital is invested. Further, new capital is typically unavailable for financial institutions holding large portfolios of real estate loans in a downward spiraling market for the same reasons that liquidity becomes scarce for the investors in real property, as investors wait for market prices to 'bottom out'.

Thus, the bank or S&L must sell assets into the declining market in order to shrink, and such instances of 'dumping' or 'fire sales' of assets cause further losses and the need to repeat the cycle of reporting such losses on the income statement, reflecting the loss of capital and selling more assets to shrink even further. In addition, even if the market value of real estate subsequently increased, the bank or S&L could not reflect that increase as a gain in profits or capital. 'Marking to market' asset values under current accounting and regulatory rules work only down, not up.[20] Therefore, the application of the 'mark to market' of asset values reflected US public policy, and the damage resulting from this policy was vast and incalculable.

VIII. DECREASED LEVERAGE

As previously noted, leverage increases as capital requirements decrease. If there is a capital requirement of 5 per cent, the leverage ratio is 20 to 1; if the capital requirement is 3 per cent, the leverage ratio is 33 to 1. Similarly, leverage decreases as capital requirements increase. If the capital requirement is 8 per cent, the leverage ratio is 12.5 to 1. Thus, just as asset value inflation was enhanced by an increase in leverage brought about by a reduction in required capital, asset value deflation was enhanced by a decrease in leverage brought about by an increase in required capital. This increase in required capital was the result of FHLBB reregulation, CEBA and FIRREA.

The capital requirement for S&Ls was ultimately increased to equal the capital requirements of banks. Therefore, assuming (i) S&Ls had a 3 per cent capital requirement and a leverage ratio of 33 to 1, liabilities to capital and (ii) banks had a 5.5 per cent capital requirement and a leverage ratio of 18 to 1 assets to capital, then (iii) S&Ls would either have to increase their capital to the 5.5 per cent capital requirement or sell assets (shrink) to achieve that result. In addition, (1) the definition of 'capital' was contracted; (2) supervisory

---

[20] In Lawrence J. White, *The S&L Debacle: Public Policy Lessons for Bank and Thrift Regulation* (Oxford University Press, 1991), Professor White discusses the deficiencies of the 'historical cost' accounting principles of GAAP as applied to banks and savings and loans. His point is that all assets of a bank and savings and loan should routinely be reflected at market value instead of historical cost. Although his arguments make sense, a change at this time of the nature he suggests would be even more draconian for those financial institutions holding large investments in real estate related assets. If a change of this nature is made, it must be done gradually with ample time given to the financial institutions to cover their initial mark to market loss.

goodwill was required to be written off entirely by the end of 1994; and (3) RAP was no longer available to enhance 'capital' in the S&L industry. GAAP is now the standard for both banks and savings and loans.

If these changes in the definition of 'capital' cause a decrease in capital, then the affected institutions will clearly have to infuse new, acceptable capital or sell assets (shrink) to achieve the required capital standards. Finally, the capital requirements for banks was also increased following the implementation of the 1988 Basle Committee Capital Accord.

By the end of 1994, banks were required to satisfy an 8 per cent capital requirement. In order to satisfy this requirement, both banks and S&Ls either had to increase their capital to 8 per cent based on the current size of its asset base or sell assets (shrink) to achieve that result. The foregoing represent some examples of the 'decreased leverage' caused by reregulation, CEBA and FIRREA. These requirements have a similar impact to a 'mark to market' asset value loss. If capital cannot be raised, selling assets in a market only creates further loss. The result is further enhancement of asset value deflation.

IX. CONCLUDING NOTE: SHIFTS IN MONETARY POLICY AND POLITICAL ACCOUNTABILITY

US monetary, fiscal, and exchange rate policies fueled the asset value deflation in the mid-1980s just as they fueled asset value inflation in the early 1980s. Asset value deflation manifested itself through falling real estate values, and such values continued to decline because of various contributory elements, including the increased capital requirements for banks and thrift institutions. With capital difficult to raise in this falling market, banks and S&Ls, in order to satisfy the capital requirements, have been forced to shrink by forcing payments of loans (as opposed to renewing loans) and by selling off assets. For similar reasons, bank and S&L management refrain from making new loans into the falling market or risking capital that may be necessary to address the economic conditions that will most certainly appear if the market does not recover. As an increasing loan volume in the banking and S&L systems at large increases the money supply exponentially (unless controlled by monetary policy), a decreasing loan volume in these systems decreases the money supply exponentially (unless otherwise controlled by monetary policy).

If uncontrolled or partially controlled, the result is a reduced supply of money with an attendant 'credit crunch'. If totally controlled, the result is a stabilization of the money supply and a limitation of the reduction. If real estate lending is of concern because of falling real estate values and 'risky' conditions, the available money will seek alternatives other than real estate with the attendant credit crunch continuing.

It is perhaps presumptuous, even dangerous, to assess blame outside the judicial system. There were numerous instances of criminal activity and fraud existed in both S&Ls and bank failures, and criminal activity and wrongdoing must be punished. The systematic shifting of politically motivated 'blame' on bank and S&L management, however, should not be used as a legitimate policy tool to escape political accountability for failures to mitigate banking or thrift industry crisis.

The following actions were nonetheless taken by Congress and the Bush Administration since 1989 in an attempt to assess blame and impose retribution for the US thrift industry and banking crises – the passing of FIRREA in 1989 in the enactment of the Crime Control Act in 1990.

Most important was the support and passage of FIRREA as legislation that 'strengthened the enforcement powers of federal regulators and depository institutions' and 'the civil sanctions and criminal penalties for defrauding or otherwise damaging depository institutions and their depositors'.[21] FIRREA, in assessing blame and imposing retribution,

1. abolished the FHLBB and the position of Chairman thereof and
   a. created the office of director of the Office of Thrift Supervision (OTS) and gave it supervisory and regulatory authority over federal and State savings associations and savings and loan holding companies; and
   b. created the Federal Housing Finance Board and granted it the primary duty to oversee and supervise the activities of the federal home loan banks;
2. dissolved the FSLIC and instead charged the FDIC with the responsibility to insure the deposits of savings associations, examine them as necessary for insurance purposes and issue regulations barring associations from engaging in certain activities;
3. increased the amount of criminal and civil money penalties for legal and regulatory violations;
4. expanded the ability of the OTS to remove officers and directors of S&Ls;
5. provided the FDIC additional powers allowing termination or suspension of deposit insurance on short notice; and
6. authorized the expenditure of an additional USD75 million for the US Department of Justice to prosecute criminal activities in relation to thrifts and banks.[22]

The next most important action was the support and passage of the Crime Control Act of 1990 which in essence gave greatly expanded powers in the form of prejudgment writs to the regulators of federally insured institutions for purposes of collecting monies from those who have caused loss to federally insured institutions. The Crime Control Act of 1990 which established the following:

---

[21] See generally Joseph J. Norton, 'The Changing Face of Bank Regulation and Supervision in the United States: A Period of Supervisory Reregulation', in *Bank Regulation and Supervision in the 1990s* (J. Norton (ed.), Lloyd's of London Press Ltd, New York, 1991).

[22] See generally Norton, *supra* note 21; White, *supra* note 20, at pp.179–180. Professor White critiques FIRREA and points out the anger which Congress and the Bush Administration had acted. Professor White was one of three members of the Federal Home Loan Bank Board at the time of the passage of FIRREA.

1. financially compensated individuals that provide information leading to criminal convictions or civil penalties;
2. established minimum jail sentences for bank fraud and embezzlement with the maximum sentence increased from 20 to 30 years;
3. authorized long-term prison sentence to be imposed on 'financial kingpins' who receive over USD5 million in profits from their crimes in a 24-month period;
4. extended the statute of limitations on certain offenses for up to ten years; and
5. granted regulators with authority to freeze and seize assets of *suspected* wrongdoers of financial institutions.

11. Further Deregulation: The 1991 FDICIA Legislation

I. INTRODUCTION

Notwithstanding the thrift industry crisis and bailout organized under the 1989 FIRREA legislation, commercial bank failures across the United States, but particularly in the Southwest and New England regions, remained at high levels and imposed significant pressure on the Bank Insurance Fund (BIF). By 1990 the BIF needed to be recapitalized and given the thrift crisis and BIF issues, the Bush Administration through the Treasury Department promulgated an ambitious financial modernization plan. The plan called for reforms to the deposit insurance system; increased supervision of and intervention in undercapitalized banks; limitations on the abilities of States to authorize new banking powers; consolidation of the bank regulatory structure; authorization for nationwide interstate banking; approval of new securities and investment activities for commercial banks; and authorization of cross-ownership of institutions in the financial services industry (hereinafter the 'Treasury Financial Modernization Report' or 'Treasury Report').[1]

The majority of the provisions of the Bush Administration's Treasury Financial Modernization Report, given the S&L crisis, continued vested interests and regulatory debate on authorization of new banking powers, and failed to acquire overall Congressional support. Many of the primary issues of the Treasury Report concerning revision of the regulatory structure, expanded powers, and removal of the separation between banking and commerce were opposed by various vested interests. Banking institutions became concerned that they could lose the securities and insurance powers already granted to them by their respective banking agencies through deregulatory initiatives and validated by the courts in subsequent litigation. Moreover, the concept of deregulation was superseded by concerns over protection of the deposit insurance funds. Many of the suggested reforms for the deposit insurance funds, however, also largely failed to acquire Congressional support. Thus, the lack of consensus and the immediate need to recapitalize

[1] See generally Department of Treasury, *Modernizing the U.S. Financial System* (1991).

the BIF moved Congress to abandon structural reform of the financial services industry and instead move piecemeal to address selected priorities under the Federal Deposit Insurance Corporation Improvement Act of 1991 (FDICIA).[2]

Thus, less than 28 months after passage of FIRREA, Congress concluded that there remained significant concerns for the need to further increase regulation of US banking institutions. The FDICIA was enacted to provide for new and more restrictive uniform banking standards. The FDICIA bill started out as a vehicle for recapitalizing the FDIC insurance fund,[3] but quickly expanded into an omnibus piece of legislation, significantly expanding the enforcement and supervisory authorities of the federal banking agencies. The FDICIA legislation, although not as far encompassing in scope as FIRREA, nonetheless contained significant provisions, the most important of which for purposes of this work include the 'prompt corrective action' (PCA) provisions,[4] new industry standards in real estate lending and further restrictions on brokered deposits and insider lending activities,[5] enhanced examinations and audits of banking institutions,[6] and the implementation of foreign bank legislation on foreign bank operations in the United States.[7]

II. RATIONALE FOR FDICIA

FDICIA, similar to CEBA, began as a deliberate attempt to repeal the Glass-Steagall Act, to expand bank powers, and to restructure the banking industry framework. Similarly to FIRREA, however, the FDICIA legislation was revised to meet the limited objectives of recapitalizing the BIF and providing for banking organizations what FIRREA had provided for thrift institutions in the way of enhanced supervisory and regulatory oversight.

---

2 See Pub. L. No. 102-242, 105 Stat. 2236 (codified in sections of 12 U.S.C.).

3 See FDICIA, *supra* note 2, at Title I, 'Safety and Soundness, Subtitle A, Deposit Insurance Fund'. This subtitle provided for the recapitalization and restructuring of the FDIC Bank Insurance Fund.

4 *Ibid.* at Title I, 'Safety and Soundness, Subtitle D, Prompt Regulatory Action' (discussed *infra* in this chapter).

5 *Ibid.* at Title III, 'Federal Deposit Insurance Reform, Subtitle A, Activities' (imposing limitations on brokered deposits solicited by undercapitalized institutions; placing significant restrictions on FDIC-insured State bank activities; requiring adoption of uniform standards for extensions of credit secured by real property made for the purposes of construction or a building or other improvement to real estate; requiring banking agencies to jointly review capital standards to ascertain whether those standards are sufficient to facilitate 'prompt corrective action' to prevent or minimize loss to deposit insurance funds).

6 *Ibid.* at Title I, 'Safety and Soundness, Subtitle B, Supervisory Reforms' (instituting enhanced annual on-site examinations and comprehensive and uniform examination improvement program).

7 *Ibid.* at Title II, 'Regulatory Improvements, Subtitle A, Regulation of Foreign Banks' (implementing the Foreign Bank Supervision Enhancement Act of 1991, bringing foreign bank operations in the United States under enhanced and comprehensive federal control, supervision, and enforcement).

The resulting legislation under FDICIA mandated significant changes to the banking regulatory apparatus. FDICIA increased the FDIC's authority to borrow from the Treasury to cover deposit insurance losses from USD5 billion to USD20 billion, and any borrowing in this respect was to be repaid from deposit insurance assessments against institutions. The FDIC was authorized to borrow funds on a short-term basis for working capital, and such borrowing was to be repaid by the sale of assets acquired from failed or distressed institutions. FDICIA further provided that the BIF was to reach the reserve ratio requirement of 1.25 per cent per USD100 of deposits established under FIRREA within 15 years, and the SAIF capitalization was to be achieved within a 'reasonable' time period.

Notwithstanding the deposit insurance fund provisions, FDICIA was largely a supervisory reregulatory initiative for banking and thrift institutions. FDICIA was established in a reactive political environment defined by the S&L bailout, the ongoing commercial banking crisis, and an understanding that both crises had occurred because the supervisory structure had failed to act in a timely manner to address and anticipate problems at the outset. The 'prompt corrective action' provisions were the clearest manifestation of this perception. These provisions required the federal banking agencies to establish five separate categories of capitalization for institutions, extending from 'well capitalized' to 'critically undercapitalized'. As a particular institution's capital reserve ratio dropped down from one category to another, the banking agency regulating that institution was required to undertake increasingly severe action against the institution. These actions entailed restricting the institution from engaging in certain actions to closing institutions that remained 'critically undercapitalized'.

III. FDICIA AND CAPITAL ADEQUACY

The FDICIA legislation required that thrift and banking agencies take 'prompt corrective action' when thrift and banking institutions regulatory capital falls below certain levels. The US banking laws and the Basle Committee directives established domestic and international standards for capital adequacy, which generally provide that the minimum capital of a well-capitalized bank should not be less than 8 per cent of assets.[8] These laws and directives also provide for certain minimum standards ratios for 'risk-based' capital adequacy.[9]

8 See 12 U.S.C. § 1831o.
9 *Id.*

FDICIA amended the Federal Deposit Insurance Act of 1950[10] and introduced the concept of 'prompt corrective action' to resolve the problems of insured depository institutions.[11]

Capital levels became the mechanism for timing the 'prompt' regulatory intervention required for distressed institutions under the pre-commitment approach (PCA) scheme.[12] The four banking and thrift agencies introduced regulations separately to implement the FDICIA PCA scheme,[13] but published a joint final consolidated PCA regulation in late 1992.[14]

A. FDICIA Classifications

The banking and thrift agencies adopted uniform levels of capital for defining the statutory classifications as follows:

Well-capitalized
Well capitalized, meaning significantly in excess of regulatory capital standards.[15]

Adequately capitalized
Adequately capitalized, meaning in compliance with all applicable standards.[16]

Undercapitalized
Undercapitalized, meaning failure to comply with regulatory capital standards.[17]

---

10 See Act of 21 September 1950, ch. 967, § 2[1], 64 Stat. 873 (codified at 12 U.S.C. §§ 1811-1833c).

11 See FDICIA § 131, 105 Stat. at 2253 (codified as amended at 12 U.S.C. § 1831o).

12 The catalyst for the PCA was borne in part from a Congressional Budget Office Study. See United States Congress, House of Representatives, Staff of Congressional Budget Office Memorandum, 'The Cost of Forbearance During the Thrift Crisis' (June 1991) (on file with author).

13 See FRB, 'Membership of State Banking Institutions in the Federal Reserve System: Rules for Practice for Hearings; Prompt Corrective Action,' 57 Fed. Reg. 29,226 (codified at 12 C.F.R. Pts 208 and 263) (proposed 1 July 1992); OCC, 'Prompt Corrective Action,' 57 Fed. Reg. 29,808 (1992) (codified at 12 C.F.R. Pts 6 and 19) (proposed 7 July 1992); FDIC, 'Prompt Corrective Action,' 57 Fed. Reg. 29,662 (1992) (codified at 12 C.F.R. Pts 308 and 325) (proposed 6 July 1992); OTS, 'Regulatory Capital: Prompt Corrective Action', 57 Fed. Reg. 29,826 (1992) (codified at 12 C.F.R. Pt 565) (proposed 7 July 1992).

14 See 'Prompt Corrective Action; Rules of Practice for Hearings', 57 Fed. Reg. 44,866 (1992) (codified at 12 C.F.R. Pts 6, 19, 208, 263, 308, 325 and 565).

15 'Well capitalized' is defined as total risk-based capital ratio of at least 10.0 per cent; Tier 1 risk-based ratio of at least 6.0 per cent; leverage ratio of at least 5.0 per cent; and no outstanding regulatory directive to improve or maintain any specific capital level. *Ibid.* at 44,687.

16 'Adequately capitalized' is defined as a total risk-based capital ratio of at least 8.0 per cent; Tier 1 risk-based ratio of at least 4.0 per cent; and a leverage ratio of at least 4.0 per cent or if otherwise rated as 'composite 1' at least 3.0 per cent. *Ibid.*

17 'Undercapitalized' is defined as a total risk-based capital ratio of less than 8.0 per cent; Tier 1 risk-based ratio of less than 4.0 per cent; or a leverage ratio of less than 4.0 per cent (or 3.0 per cent). *Ibid.*

Significantly undercapitalized
Significantly undercapitalized, meaning significantly below required minimum regulatory capital levels.[18]

Critically undercapitalized
Critically undercapitalized, meaning below a tangible capital to assets level specified by the regulatory agencies which may not be less than 2 per cent of assets.[19]

B. PCA Intervention Mandates

Under FDICIA, if an institution is, after notice and opportunity for hearing, determined to be in unsound condition, or to be engaging in unsound practices,[20] it may be reclassified as undercapitalized.[21] Regulatory intervention is mandatory if an institution is at or approaching the level of undercapitalization, and attempted distributions of capital and management fees to any controlling persons are prohibited if they would result in an institution becoming undercapitalized.[22]

The undercapitalized institution, within 45 days of becoming undercapitalized, must submit a capital restoration plan[23] or else become subject to one of several regulatory enforcement actions. The methods of intervention include a forced merger, requiring other recapitalization measures, and restricting: (1) interest rate payments; (2) asset growth; (3) any activity posing excessive risks; and (4) capital distributions by the parent holding company.[24]

The federal banking agency in question may also require divestiture of: (1) a subsidiary of the institution; (2) a nondepository affiliate by the institution's parent company; and/or (3) an institution by a controlling company.[25]

The same remedies may be applied to 'significantly undercapitalized' institutions.[26] The critically undercapitalized institutions, within 90 days of becoming critically undercapitalized, may be placed into receivership, conservatorship, or other action agreed upon between the FDIC and the banking agency in question.[27]

---

18 'Significantly undercapitalized' is defined as a total risk-based capital ratio of less than 6.0 per cent; Tier 1 risk-based ratio of less than 3.0 per cent; or a leverage ratio of less than 3.0 per cent. *Ibid.*

19 'Critically undercapitalized' is defined as a ratio of tangible equity capital to total assets that is equal to or less than 2.0 per cent or otherwise fails to meet the statutory requirements under FDIA § 38(c)(3)(A), 12 U.S.C. § 1831o(c)(3)(A). *Ibid.*

20 See Federal Deposit Insurance Act, as amended by FDICA, § 39, 12 U.S.C. § 1831s. Non-complying institutions must submit plans which may be part of a capital restoration plan. *Ibid.* § 38(e), 12 U.S.C. § 1831o(e)(2).

21 *Ibid.* § 38(g), 12 U.S.C. § 1831o(g).

22 *Ibid.* § 38(d)(1) & (2), 12 U.S.C. § 1831o(d)(1)-(2).

23 *Ibid.* § 38(e)(2), 12 U.S.C. § 1831o(e)(2).

24 *Ibid.* § 38(f)(2), 12 U.S.C. § 1831o(f)(2).

25 *Ibid.* § 38(f)(2)(I), 12 U.S.C. § 1831o(f)(2)(I).

26 *Ibid.* FDIA § 38(f)(1)(A), 12 U.S.C. § 1831o(f)(1)(A).

27 *Ibid.* FDIA § 38(h)(3)(A), 12 U.S.C. § 1831o(h)(3)(A).

1. *Operation Restrictions*

The 'undercapitalized banks' are subject to increasingly restrictive and severe regulatory controls on operations which are designed to enable and to force the institution to regain an acceptable level of capitalization. The 'critically undercapitalized' banks are subjected to the most severe operating restrictions, including, but not limited to prohibition of the following activities without FDIC approval:[28]

1. any material transaction outside of the ordinary course of business;
2. extending credit for highly leveraged transactions;
3. amending the banks charter or bylaws;
4. materially changing accounting methods;
5. engaging in transactions with affiliates;
6. paying excessive compensation or bonuses;
7. paying interest on deposits significantly in excess of the banks market; and
8. generally making payments on subordinated debt.

2. *Affirmative Actions*

In addition, the federal banking agencies, if they find that a potential action be taken by a bank would involve a 'significant' (e.g. other than a minimal or nominal) dissipation of assets or that it would prejudice the interest of depositors, may require the bank, and any institution-affiliated party, to take affirmative action, through the use of a 'cease and desist order' to include the following actions:[29]

1. requiring recapitalization of the institution by the issuance of shares or obligations, or by forcing an acquisition or merger of the institution in cases where grounds exist for appointment of a conservator or receiver;
2. restricting transactions with affiliates by making the sister-bank exemption of Section 23A of the Federal Reserve Act inapplicable;
3. restricting the amount of interest paid on deposits to a level comparable to prevailing rates offered in the region where the institution is located;
4. prohibiting asset growth or requiring a reduction in assets;
5. requiring an institution to alter, reduce, or terminate any activity deemed to pose excessive risk;
6. requiring that a director or officer who held office more than 180 days immediately before the institution became undercapitalized be dismissed, or that 'qualified senior executive officers' be employed by the institution;
7. prohibiting deposits from correspondent banks, including renewals and roll-overs of prior deposits;

---

[28] See 12 U.S.C. § 1831o(h)-(i).
[29] See 12 U.S.C. § 1831o(f)(2).

8. prohibiting any bank holding company that controls an institution in question from making capital distributions without the approval of the FRB;
9. requiring the divestiture of any subsidiary or affiliate if the entity to be divested is in danger of becoming insolvent and poses significant risk to the institution, or is likely to cause a significant dissipation of the institution's earnings or assets; or
10. requiring a company controlling the institution to divest itself of the institution, if to do so would improve the institution's financial condition and future prospects.

3. *Appointment of Receiver*

The appropriate federal agency must appoint a receiver or conservator for the bank not less than 90 days after it becomes critically undercapitalized unless the agency and the FDIC determine that some other action better serves the purpose of the statute.[30] If other action is taken, that decision must be reviewed every 90 days and a receiver or conservator appointed unless a new determination is made that other action is more beneficial.[31] In any event, a receiver must be appointed within 270 days from the date the bank became critically undercapitalized unless the primary regulatory agency and the FDIC find that the bank has a positive net worth and has been in substantial compliance with an acceptable capital restoration plan, is profitable or has an upward trend in earnings and is reducing its ratio of non-performing loans to total loans, and that further, the bank is viable and is not expected to fail.[32]

C. Problematic Aspects of PCA

The PCA approach adopted under FDICIA raised serious concerns. First, Congress and the banking agencies miscalculated the costs that would be incurred as a result of the enormous holdings of assets that needed to be liquidated by RTC under FIRREA. In other words, the asset value deflation engendered as a result of FIRREA guaranteed that the 'fire sale' of assets would result in massive losses when those assets were liquidated. For instance, FDIC officials clearly indicated to Congress that assets absorbed by the RTC or otherwise would be expected to lose at least 20 per cent of their liquidation value simply by being taken over by the government.[33] The liquidation program involving billions of dollars in assets in a 'fire sale' context presented adverse consequences on values of assets held by institutions.

---

30 See 12 U.S.C. § 1831o(h)(3).

31 *Ibid.*

32 See 12 U.S.C. § 1831o(h)(3)(c). Any time the deposit insurance fund incurs a material loss, the inspector general or the primary federal regulator of the institution involved must prepare a written report reviewing the agency's supervision of the institution and make recommendations for preventing such loss in the future.

33 See generally, W. Seidman, *Full Faith and Credit: The Great S & L Debacle and Other Washington Sagas* (Times Books, 1993).

Second, the investment environment during the passage of FDICIA was certainly not conducive for most investors to purchase assets from failed institutions. The RTC was left in the undesirable position of having a limited audience of the largest institutions to purchase the assets of failed S&Ls.[34]

The real estate market became flooded with distressed real estate holdings of failed thrifts absorbed by the RTC.[35] The sales practices utilized by RTC, under a statutory mandate to liquidate such assets as quickly as possible, further added to the depressed value of the real estate on the secondary market.[36]

Third, the FDICIA interfered with efforts by investors to maintain weak or failed S&Ls and avoid shifting the burden to public bailout. Although FDICIA provides for institutions to raise capital from investors through the sale of 'shares or obligations'[37] the ability of investors to rely on the recapitalization plans agreed upon by the agencies was supplanted. Most importantly, the investors involved in recapitalization efforts under FIRREA were subject to the government refusing to honor its obligations under forbearance agreements which devastated investor positions taken in such recapitalization efforts.[38]

In addition, the FDICIA regulatory scheme offered little protection to investors. For instance, the Act, subject to certain exemptive authority granted to the FDIC, prohibits insured institutions from paying principal or interest on subordinated debt, beginning 60 days after the institution becomes critically undercapitalized, subject to narrow exceptions, even if the subordinated debt were issued prior to the effective date of FDICIA.[39]

FDICIA was subject to rigorous debate during its passage as a result of the conflicting mandates. FDICIA created a structure of capital requirements for thrifts and banks that did not facilitate investor confidence and expansion in lending. The policy of increasing capital requirements at a time when real estate asset values were sinking in the wake of massive RTC liquidations resulted in a curtailment of lending and investment activity as institutions added to their core capital holdings. The asset deflation problems are exacerbated when a program of liquidation expands the supply of real estate while credit contraction simultaneously reduces demand.

---

[34] See 'Federal Home Loan Bank Board 1988 Deals', Hearings Before the House Committee on Banking, Finance and Urban Affairs, 101st Cong., 2d Sess. (1990) (Testimony of William Seidman, Chairman, FDIC).

[35] See 'Oversight on the Condition of the Financial Services Industry', Hearings Before the Senate Committee on Banking, Housing, and Urban Affairs, 100th Cong., 2d Sess. (1988).

[36] See Seidman, *supra* note 33.

[37] See FDIA, as amended by FDICIA, § 38(f)(2)(A), 12 U.S.C. § 1831o(f)(2)(A).

[38] The ensuing mass of litigation following abrogation of such agreements traditionally resulted in the government prevailing until the US Supreme Court considered the *Winstar* decision in 1996. See 116 S.Ct. 2432 (1996).

[39] See FDIA, as amended by FDICIA, § 38(h)(2)(A) & (B), 12 U.S.C. § 1831o(h)(2)(A) & (B).

IV. BANK CAPITAL AND PROMPT CORRECTIVE ACTION

Determination of the level of a bank's capitalization is made in accordance with regulatory accounting principles, which have not always, necessarily, been the same as generally accepted accounting principles. In the United States, prior to the public manifestation of the S&L crisis, several areas of difficulty arose in determining thrift institution capital levels, and hence their 'safety and soundness' or 'solvency' for purposes of initiating enforcement action. Some of these areas included determinations of the value for accounting purposes of supervisory goodwill arising from certain acquisition, merger or other financial institution consolidation transactions; goodwill created through 'push down' accounting methods to avoid losses from marked-to-market value of loan portfolios suffering from negative interest rate spread and disintermediation in a high interest rate and inflationary environment; deferred loan losses; the value of deferred mortgage servicing rights; unidentified intangible assets; the value of investments in subsidiaries; and appraised equity capital.[40]

The determination of a bank's capital level has become an increasingly complex task. The current definitions and regulations are the result of protracted debate and rule-making development. At the end of the 19th century, the average ratio of bank capital to assets among US banks approximated 20 per cent. With a surge in bank portfolios as a result of the First World War and rapid economic expansion during the 1920s, this figure was reduced to 13 per cent. Then, through the Great Depression to the end of the Second World War, 6 per cent became the norm. In the 1950s there was an upward movement to around 10 per cent. This figure has since dropped to around 7 per cent.[41]

The decline in bank capital levels and the bank collapses endemic to the depression (and for that matter to bank failures since then) give no indication that capital levels were critical, however. In fact, it was not until 1981 that any formal bank capital adequacy regulation existed in the United States.[42] Beginning in the late 1970s, however, capital adequacy, as a concern of prudential bank supervision, became more important. As the bank regulators became more aware of the general deterioration of capital levels of US banking institutions, and as the magnitude of the LDC Debt Crisis implications for these institutions became apparent in 1982, capital adequacy went beyond the examination level and was transformed into a core regulatory banking objective to ensure the prudential supervision of

---

40 See Lawrence J. White, *The S & L Debacle: Public Policy Lessons for Bank and Thrift Regulations* (Oxford University Press, 1991), at pp.36-49.

41 See Joseph J. Norton, 'Recent Developments in the Regulation and Supervision of U.S. Financial Institutions: The Evolution of Capital Adequacy Standards and the Financial Institutions Reform, Recovery and Enforcement Act of 1989 (FIRREA)', *Institute of European Finance, Research Monographs in Banking and Finance No. 9212* ('*Norton IEF Monograph*'), at p. 14.

42 *Ibid.* at p.14.

banking institutions and the safety and soundness of the banking system itself.[43]

Despite the evolving complexity of capital adequacy standards in the United States and internationally over the past 20 years, economists and regulators have continued to observe that inadequate capital is not a verifiable major cause of bank failure in real world situations, as the primary causes are generally determined to be poor management, fraud and unanticipated external economic conditions being primary causes.[44] Further, although capital may delay the inevitable results of insolvency, this problem is more often a matter of liquidity. Normally in a poorly run institution (particularly if combined with economic conditions) capital is never adequate in a worst case situation.[45]

A fundamental paradox runs throughout recent attempts to identify and classify risks to bank capital. As more regulatory precision is given to the concept, more definitional problems arise. Instead of narrowing the gap of comprehensibility, the floodgates of ongoing complexity and incomprehensibility are opened.[46] While capital adequacy may be a legitimate regulatory concern for prudential supervision of banking activities,[47] primarily, capital adequacy standards are measurement standards. These measurement standards are only true if the represented underlying quality of the assets to which the standards relate is true.[48]

This volume has examined a few of the factors affecting the 'quality' or 'value' of the assets which comprise and underlie bank capital. A corollary to the undercapitalization of a bank as a condition to regulatory enforcement action, including the appointment of a receiver or conservator, is a determination that the bank is not operating in a 'safe and sound' manner. The safety and soundness of the banking system as a whole is dependent on the safety and soundness of the individual banks in that system. In response to the savings and loan and banking crises of the late 1980s and early 1990s, US banking law has also recently been amended to prescribe standards relating to the safety and soundness of banks in a number of areas, including: internal controls and audit systems; loan documentation; credit underwriting; interest rate risk; asset growth; compensation of management; and asset quality.[49]

Upon consideration of the variety of possible causes of bank capital impairment in the United States during the late 1980s and early 1990s, and the track record of government policies of increasing invasiveness, it is highly questionable whether congressionally mandated intervention through the prompt corrective action provisions of FDICIA served any real ongoing purpose other than as a self-serving effort to protect wounded pride of Congress at having already botched up the US banking and thrift

---

43 *Ibid.*
44 See note 41, *supra* at p.68.
45 *Ibid.*
46 See note 41, *supra* at p.81.
47 See note 41, *supra* at p.82.
48 See note 41, *supra* at p.81.
49 See § 39 of the Federal Deposit Insurance Act, as added by PL 102-242, § 132, 105 Stat. 2236.

industries.[50] In effect, Congress attempted to close the door to BIF and SAIF, after the funds have already been depleted. Perhaps it would be more appropriate for Congress to evaluate its own participation, performance, and culpability in events leading up to the American thrift and banking capital inadequacy crisis, rather than prescribing an ever greater government role in the micro-management of the US thrift and banking industries.

V. FDICIA AND BANK REREGULATION

A. Examinations

FDICIA also embodied the concept that 'on-site' examinations were critical to ensure that individual institutions engaged in 'safe and sound' banking practices. FDICIA therefore required federal banking agencies to conduct annual 'safety and soundness' examinations of all insured depository institutions. Financially sound institutions with assets under USD100 million could be examined every 18 months. Federal banking agencies could also alternate their examinations with State regulator examinations. FDICIA further required each institution holding assets in excess of USD150 million to provide its respective regulatory agency with annual financial statements audited by an independent public accounting firm.

B. Safety and Soundness Standards

The federal bank and thrift agencies were required to establish 'safety and soundness' standards in three distinct areas: (1) operations and management; (2) asset quality, earnings, and stock valuation; and (3) employee compensation. The agencies were further required to revise the risk-based capital standards to account for interest-rate risk.

---

[50] See C. Golembe, 'FDICIA: A Mean-Spirited, Special-Interest Measure Without Redeeming Features', 11 No. 21 Banking Pol'y Rep 2 (November 1992); See also, Ricki Helfer, 'Rules Versus Discretion in the Intervention of Troubled Financial Institutions: The United States Perspective,' presented at the High Level Meeting on the Reform of Latin American and Caribbean Financial Systems, Caracas, Venezuela, 27-28 October 1997. The Ms. Helfer, the then-Chairman of the FDIC, notes that, '[T]he FDIC has conducted a study of the lessons of the US financial crises of the 1980s and 1990s and has analyzed the effect of this PCA standard on decisions not to close financial institutions that got into trouble prior to the enactment of FDICIA. The study shows that as many as 143 insured financial institutions that are open and healthy today could have failed before 1991 if the PCA standard for closing troubled financial institutions had been in place. Even more significant is the question of what would have happened to the 10 largest US banks, who had 100 per cent of their capital exposed to sovereign borrowers unable to service debts denominated in foreign currencies, had the 2 per cent capital standard been in effect for determining whether to close an insured financial institution in 1983 and 1984.' See generally FDIC, *History of the Eighties, Volume 1: Lessons for the Future* (Washington D.C., 1998)

C. Uniform Standards for Real Estate Lending

FDICIA further required that uniform standards for real estate lending by insured depository institutions be established.

D. State-Chartered vs. Federally Chartered Banks

FDICIA further required that State-chartered banks could no longer engage in activities not otherwise permissible for national banks unless the bank met regulatory capital standards and the FDIC determined that the activity would not pose a risk to the deposit insurance fund.

E. Brokered Deposits

FDICIA further imposed restrictions on the use of brokered deposits. The restrictions supplemented those set forth under FIRREA but were not premised on the capital reserves of institutions. 'Undercapitalized' institutions were no longer permitted to accept brokered deposits and were subject to interest-rate limitations on deposits solicited directly from the public; 'adequately capitalized' institutions could accept brokered deposit only with FDIC permission; and 'well capitalized' institutions could accept brokered deposits without restrictions.

F. Deposit Insurance Reform

Deposit insurance reform was also a part of FDICIA. The system of risk-based premiums was required to be established by 1994. FDICIA further required the FDIC to aggregate individual interests in all IRAs and other pension-type accounts and insure only the aggregate total up to USD100,000. These provisions served to marginally reduce deposit insurance coverage.

G. 'Too Big To Fail' Policy

One of the most important provisions under FDICIA for purposes of this treatise were limitations imposed on the de facto 'too big to fail' (TBTF) policy. The FDIC was authorized to use the 'least-cost alternative' in financial institution resolutions unless it determined, and reached agreement with a two-thirds majority each of the FDIC Board of Directors and the Board of Governors of the Federal Reserve System, and the agreement of the Secretary of the Treasury in consultation with the President, that permitting the failure of the institution in question constituted 'systemic risk'. FDICIA further established linkage with a bank's level of capitalization with its access to the Federal Reserve discount window. In this respect, the Federal Reserve was required to demand that 'critically undercapitalized' institutions repay funds provided through the window not later than five days, and if this requirement was violated the Federal Reserve would be liable for any increased costs of such provision to the FDIC. Thus, the political environment of 1991 did not result in legislative stalemate, but was driven by the compelling notion that a supervisory regime with less discretion available to banking agencies was appropriate. Although the concept of deregulation was still very much on the legislative agenda, the banking crisis underscored that deregulation did not imply reduction in supervision.

VI. CONCLUDING OBSERVATIONS

In the late 1980s and continuing into the 1990s, borrowers, banks, S&Ls and examiners of banks and S&Ls have each been unwitting participants in reinforcing a deflationary spiral in real estate values fueled by the effects of monetary, fiscal and exchange rate policy reversals, reregulation, the TRA, CEBA, FIRREA, market psychology, comparables, decreased leverage and reflexive monetary policy. As previously reviewed in this chapter, in a deflationary period of decreasing values and decreasing earnings, banks and thrift institutions, *by reason of how 'banking', 'leverage', and 'capital' are defined*, wither or shrink, causing a natural deflationary momentum. Thereafter, decreasing leverage ratios and the momentum arising from comparables and the capitalistic quest for survival accelerates this deflationary process. These factors all individually and cumulatively reinforced pervasive asset value deflation.

Congress enacted FIRREA in August 1989, just nine months after the conclusion of the 1988 presidential election of George Bush. Incredibly, neither George Bush nor his Democratic opponent, Michael Dukakis, mentioned the banking crisis facing the country during the entire presidential campaign, primarily because influential politicians in both parties received enormous monetary support from the banking and thrift industries and were potentially accountable for inaction and reactive thinking with respect to the thrift and banking crises. The reregulatory impact of FIRREA was monumental in establishing the Resolution Trust Corporation and expanding the powers of the FDIC. Although FIRREA was supposed to conclusively resolve the thrift industry crisis, it did not. The years 1990 and 1991 produced the Crime Control Act of 1990 and the FDICIA of 1991,[51] but each piece of legislation was simply more of the same 'reactive' thinking that previously occurred, and generally accelerated asset value deflation.

Interestingly, the inflationary push, then deflationary slump has not been peculiar to any specific, regional real estate market. Instead, the asset value distortions examined in this book were injected into the entire US economic system through the mechanics of statutory and regulatory change and conflicting monetary, fiscal, and exchange rate policies. These distortions directly affected global financial markets through the ensuing volatility of the US dollar, the world's reserve currency. The asset value distortions first 'officially' appeared in the form of DIDMCA, Garn-St. Germain, ERTA and

---

[51] See, The Crime Control Act of 1990, is PL-101-647, 104 Stat. 4789 (1990) and Federal Deposit Insurance Corporation Improvement Act of 1991, is PL-102-242, 105 Stat. 2236 (1991); S.543, 102nd Cong., lst Sess. (1991), H. Rept. 102-407, 102nd Cong., lst Sess. (1991).

various State and federal deregulation, creating a tax-driven and finance-driven pricing, and both balance sheet leverage and momentum accelerated this process.

The inflationary push reflected real estate asset value increases through the mechanics of appraisals and comparables in turn impacted the balance sheet of every person or entity investing in or financing real estate. Borrowers reflected the increased asset values on their balance sheets, and S&Ls and banks made loans to these borrowers based upon the higher real estate values. S&Ls and banks generated retained earnings from these activities, which increased capital, which in turn allowed growth of assets and insured deposits.

Borrowers acquired new real estate assets at higher values based on comparables. Banks and S&Ls loaned money to these borrowers to allow the borrowers to purchase more real estate assets, facilitated by artful tax syndications under ERTA and Industrial Revenue Bond issuances. Speculation and inflationary expectations under the existing statutory and regulatory structures resulted, and new legislation and regulation confirmed these expectations.

The spiraling upward of values continued through leverage, momentum, comparables and reflexive action. These increased values were reflected in the balance sheets of borrowers and the same process replicated itself repeatedly. This finance driven and tax driven pricing occurred in all US real estate markets and was translated to global real estate markets and therefore other national banking industries.

This process was reversed through the dramatic reregulatory initiatives introduced through the Tax Reform Act of 1986, CEBA, FIRREA, decreased leverage and the processes of the 'marking to market' of asset values. The values built into the system were pulled out of the system. This fall in values is reflected by the value deflation. If confidence in a regional economic market remains strong, the psychology of the market maintains real estate values stable and growing, but when other economic events precipitating what would be a normal cyclical downturn occur and values begin to steadily decrease, the downward spiral of asset value deflation takes over and values abruptly reverse course.

The key to understanding the effects of pervasive asset value deflation and how it impacts regional real estate markets, one must not only understand the interrelationship of a borrower's financial statement, the lender's balance sheet and income statement, and how the regulatory agencies interact with borrower and lender, but also the effects of systemic loss of capital and FMV upon the surrounding economy. As each real estate developer, bank and S&L in a given region experience similar problems, the asset value deflation feeds upon itself and deflates the regional economy. The factors of leverage, momentum, comparables and reactive thinking complement and accelerate this process.

As real estate values continue to spiral downward, more developers, S&Ls and banks have problems. Many institutions fail and some continue to survive, but the surviving institutions generally reduce their lending activities under the aforementioned factors notwithstanding active real estate development. The over-building which resulted from the finance driven and tax driven pricing leads to a rippling effect, as tenants move from one location to the other, seeking the lowest rent. Free rent and other concessions are granted by the landlords (sometimes with funds provided by the lenders) to keep existing tenants or attract new tenants, but effective rental rates begin to fall below projections as competition drives down rental rates. Vacancies rise and debt service from real estate development loans cannot be met from net rental income alone. In some cases, expenses before debt service exceed gross income.

With rental income plummeting, commercial buildings lose their market value. The replacement cost for buildings generally exceeds market value, yet market value is the determining factor for appraisal purposes. Additional reserves and loan losses are taken by the bank or S&L that have financed the buildings.

As real estate developers lose their equity investments in given development projects, their financial statements reflect diminishing net worth. The banks and S&Ls are therefore required to (1) report such loans with indicated losses and no credit support as 'in substance' foreclosures although actual foreclosure has not yet occurred;[52] (2) defend themselves in lender liability lawsuits; (3) pursue properties in bankruptcy; and (4) incur enormous expenses in pursuit of these objectives. Of course, real estate values continue to spiral downward, and banks and S&Ls generally refrain from making more real estate loans, and instead attempt to collect on loans they have outstanding before they go into default.

Thus, the money supply available for real estate decreases and a 'credit crunch' ensues. Liquidity dries up in the region, small businesses cannot obtain credit on reasonable terms, tenants default and landlords fail, real estate service companies fail or consolidate, and law firms and accounting firms fail, shrink or consolidate. Banks and thrift institutions fail, merge, or consolidate to obtain economies of scale, and vacate excess office space. The negative effects of leverage, momentum, comparables and reflexive action continue to weave throughout this regional economy, leading to a continuing spiraling downward of values.

---

[52] An 'in substance foreclosure' is a particularly harsh result for an S&L or bank. An 'in substance foreclosure' is actually a product of accounting rather than bank or S&L regulation. The rule is applicable to situations in which neither a borrower, a guarantor nor the collateral can support the outstanding debt. It is the 'worse of all possible worlds' since, although the bank or S&L has not foreclosed on the collateral, it is deemed to have done so. The result is that as between the borrower and itself, the borrower owns legal title and is still operating and receiving the income stream form the collateral. As between the regulator and itself, the bank or S&L is deemed to own the property. The bank or S&L finds itself in the peculiar position of not owning title to the property, but having to report a loss on the loan as if it does own the property. If a bank or S&L determines that there is an indicated loss in a loan position, the bank or S&L can book a reserve for the indicated loss and offset it against income. There will be a 'hit' to capital only if income does not cover the reserve. If, on the other hand, the bank or S&L by reason of an 'in substance foreclosure' must report the property as foreclosed, the bank must report any indicated loss as a direct 'hit' to capital immediately. Nevertheless, before it can sell the property, it must in fact foreclose upon the borrower (sometimes no easy task given lender liability lawsuits, civil rights and bankruptcy procedures).

Although the total loss in any real estate portfolio cannot be identified, capital cannot be raised except for the choicest properties. Furthermore, depressed real estate values lead to a lower tax base for city, county and State. Much needed city infrastructure improvements are postponed. Much needed public programs are scraped. Tax revenues decrease. Tax rates increase. Real estate values depress further. As cities, counties, school districts, States governments and the federal government experience declining revenues due to a decreasing ad valorem and income tax base, the sole policy objective is to raise revenue by increasing taxes.

Since the mid-1980s, the spiraling downward of real estate values occurred region by region. Texas, Oklahoma, and Louisiana endured the full extent of real estate, banking and thrift industry crises, and then the crisis spread to the New England area, Washington D.C., the Midwest and California. By the early 1990s, all regions were affected, some harder than others, and the extent of the impact was generally a function of how much real estate activity occurred in the region in the 1980s and early 1990s and how the banking and S&L regulators handled their regional problems. The 'reactive' regulatory approach as exhibited in Texas and the surrounding States only made the situation worse, while the 'proactive' regulatory approach which modified the consequences of the value distortion was more appropriate but not uniformly adopted.

The resolution of bank and thrift industry crises evolved well beyond the fundamental principles of bankruptcy laws. The importance of the periods reviewed in this work is to direct emphasis on addressing crises prior to a significant number of institutions encountering insolvency. This evolution began with the increasing importance of banking systems to the social and commercial welfare of society. This evolution is most evident in the US where the very large number of banks and thrift institutions and diversity of depositors has required increasing levels of governmental regulation, supervision and enforcement in order to assure the safety and soundness of the banking system.

The evolution of deposit insurance necessarily focused the risk of loss on the FDIC by 1989 as the keeper of the BIF and SAIF, and as the receiver or conservator for virtually every troubled or insolvent bank and thrift institution. Even though the failed bank in most instances ceases to exist in receivership, the ongoing business of the failed bank is maintained by a successor of some kind.

Although the system is designed to minimize disruption in the community occasioned by a failed bank, the continuous process of deregulation and reregulation of the American banking industry, reflected in the constant stream of bailouts, acquisitions, consolidations and liquidations, has done little to inspire depositor confidence. While the more discrete, informal and direct methods of bank regulation, supervision and enforcement available in smaller and more controlled markets, such as the United Kingdom, have much to be said for them, the increasing volatility and international interconnectedness of financial markets, including but not limited to banking, appears to require even greater transparency and articulation of the processes of resolving bank insolvencies.

Today, emerging and developing economies are actively attempting to rationalize their banking systems and as a part of that effort to rationalize their deposit insurance and guaranty schemes with newly enacted regulatory schemes and processes for the resolution of bank insolvencies. When observers of the US scheme assess the efficacy of bank resolution procedures, the overwhelming attention is focused on the protection of the deposit insurance funds, the continuation of uninterrupted bank business and the mechanics of consolidation and the positioning of the successor financial institution for future success.

The failed institution's assets, however, become a source of profitability for the successor institution and the hoards of 'grave dancing' purchasers, as well as the foundation for an entire government bureaucracy. The primary purposes of recent legislation, such as CEBA, FIRREA and the Crime Control Act and FDICIA have been to protect Congress, fund the loss taking, fund the bureaucracy and provide the mechanisms to shift blame and financial responsibility onto third parties in an attempt to protect BIF and SAIF solvency.

This process largely ignores the role of government intervention in the historic process of asset value inflation and deflation. It also ignores the less than transparent government-mandated manipulation of the measurement and recordation of assets and liabilities on bank and thrift balance sheets, in an effort to delay and deflect the recognition of the consequences of those government acts of intervention. All this came to skew the related legal infrastructure underpinning the US banking and thrift systems.

Part IV
Concluding Observations

12. Concluding Observations

I. INTRODUCTION

The current influence of the US Government in establishing the framework for addressing worldwide problems of banking system distress, coupled with the ostensibly transparent responses of the US Government and industry to the US asset value inflation and deflation cycles of the 1980s, suggest some important lessons for developing and transition nations (and for that matter developed nations). Although the legislative, regulatory, monetary and fiscal policy framework in each nation presents complexity in analysis, fundamental 'lessons to be learned' from the US experience remain applicable. This concluding chapter initially reviews and elaborates upon the 'lessons to be learned' from previous chapters in this work. The chapter then considers and critiques the recent 'lessons learned' as set forth by the US regulatory agencies, principally the FDIC, in reviewing the 1980s from the regulatory perspective, and guidance set forth in the G-10 *Report of the Working Party on Financial Stability in Emerging Market Economies* of April 1997.

This work began with the proposition that a series of acts of government intervention significantly contributed to the US thrift industry and banking crises during the 1980s and early 1990s. These acts of intervention fell into a number of categories, including the obvious and well-documented policies of ill-timed financial institution deregulation and reregulation, played out against the backdrop of uncoordinated fiscal policies and initially nontransparent but favorable to industry (and (then) heavy-handed and reactive) monetary policy.

The connection of these actions with the devaluation of bank assets, precipitating the failure or distress of individual financial institutions, however, is not readily apparent. The analysis of the connections presented in this work began, not with the detailed statistical analyses employed by government agencies such as the FDIC and the GAO, but rather with an historical look at the long-standing proclivity of governments to interfere in the banking arena as a fundamental element of self-preservation, under the aegis of preserving the national sovereignty. Asset value inflation and asset devaluation have been characterized, not as the result of calculated programs of government action, but euphemistically, as a result of uncontrollable and mysterious forces such as 'external shocks' and 'exogenous events', and the financial losses have been characterized as the result of fraud or criminal activity, requiring a corresponding program of retribution and a crackdown on inept business and bank management.

Widespread financial distress does indeed provide a fertile field for excess risk-taking in the absence of 'moral hazard', and also for fraud and misconduct, and the distress does indeed seem mysterious when the prevailing expert opinion of dominant Keynesian economists and responsible government authorities during the pertinent periods, has been that the calculated programs of government action are without long term costs or consequences.

From a legal perspective, the need to better coordinate and to mesh a range of governmental policies (banking, monetary, fiscal, exchange rate, and broader economic) so that the resulting legal infrastructure is coherent and constructive becomes glaringly apparent, but is (as of yet) still lacking.

II. LESSONS TO BE LEARNED FROM THE US THRIFT INDUSTRY AND BANKING CRISES OF THE 1980s

A. Monetary and Fiscal Policies and Exchange Rate Neutrality

The US thrift and banking crises and experiences with monetary and fiscal policy in the 1980s and the more recent banking and currency crises in Latin America, East Asia and Russia underscore that artificially 'fixed' exchange rate systems are inherently unsustainable in the modern global economy. Developing and transition nations cannot afford to maintain artificially fixed exchange rate systems that do not reflect the underlying monetary and fiscal policies.

On the one hand, the artificial schemes generally lead to fundamentally inflated or deflated currency values perpetrated through sustained opportunities for speculative 'arbitrage', domestic and global institutional and political influence on governments to maintain the system for enhanced profit opportunities through foreign currency borrowing, currency trading, and financial asset purchases to maintain the artificial exchange rate relationships (generating asset value inflation). On the other hand, the trading arms of more aggressive banks, securities firms, and insurance companies and private investment companies such as 'hedge funds' establish 'targets' or 'objectives' to shoot for in currency trading to 'knock' the currency in question out of its artificial peg or fixed exchange rate regime (generating asset value deflation).

These actions generally lead to the dismantling of fixed or pegged exchange rate regimes, which occurred most visibly in East Asian nations such as Thailand and Indonesia in 1997–1998, respectively. The current trend towards exchange rate stability is evidenced in the United States by Congressional efforts to balance the budget and eliminate deficit finance, combined with the current monetary policies of the Fed, and evidenced globally by adoption of EMU, the call for a common currency in the MERCOSUR nations of South America, and by resort to currency pegs and currency boards in developing and transition nations. These schemes represent a tacit recognition of the fundamental undesirability of floating exchange rates. Unfortunately, these developments fail to address the underlying exposure of the global financial system to changes in monetary and fiscal policies.

In examining the US and global phenomena of distressed banking systems, the value of currency is necessarily dependent on the reliability and transparency of the government's commitment to maintaining sound macroeconomic policies. During the period leading up to the US thrift industry and banking crises, the US Government largely subordinated this commitment to defeating inflation. The key issue is the relativity of currency value as affecting asset values which support banking activities, as such values are altered or manipulated through continued acts of government intervention.

In the United States during the 1980s, the monetary and fiscal policies conducted by the independent central bank and Executive branch conflicted and significantly worsened the asset value inflation (boom cycle generating asset price bubbles) and deflation (bust cycle or bursting of asset price bubbles) cycles and volatile exchange rates. Developing and transition nations must accept that floating exchange rate schemes are the global norm, for better or worse, and that conducting sound monetary and fiscal policies is perhaps the most important step towards generating exchange rate neutrality. The concept of exchange rate neutrality is the most critical objective in striving for asset value neutrality and avoidance of 'boom-bust' cycles of asset value inflation and deflation.

B. The Coordination and Sequencing of Legislative, Regulatory, Monetary and Fiscal Policies

The US thrift and banking crises and experiences with legislative, regulatory, monetary and fiscal policies in the 1980s evidence many instances where policy coordination and sequencing failures significantly worsened the situation for distressed institutions and borrowers, and unfavorably facilitated asset value inflation. The bodies responsible for conducting legislative, regulatory, monetary, and fiscal policies generally failed to pursue coordinated agendas in reasonable and appropriate sequences.

These failures resulted in competition of priorities, regulatory capture, and destabilizing consequences for the US thrift and banking industries. The special interests involved in guiding or pressuring those bodies responsible for enacting legislation, promulgating regulations, or conducting monetary and fiscal policy necessarily facilitated the competition of priorities in order to promote their own interests.

The failures of relevant US authorities to bring order and stability to these priorities enhanced the asset value inflation and asset value deflation ('boom-bust') cycles and stages of distress and crisis during the 1980s. Thus, developing and transition nations should generally recognize the importance of reasonable and appropriate policy coordination and sequencing from the US experience of the 1980s.

C. 'Special Relationship' Between Government and Banking Systems and 'Political Goodwill'

The 'special relationship' between government and banking has set the stage for recurring periodic crises in the global economy. Government utilization of banking institutions as the fabric for transmission of policy and connection of domestic and international financial markets through credit, intermediary, and proprietary functions establishes this 'special relationship' and essentially incorporates the banking system as an implied part of government. This observation certainly holds in a number of nations. In so-called 'command economies' the special relationship is quite clear. In the US, the indicia of the special relationship are somewhat obscured in monetary and fiscal policies interwoven into a vast complexity of legislation and regulations generally not cognizable to the common citizen, and many legislators and professionals.

In the United States during the 1980s, the 'special relationship' between Congress, regulatory agencies, and their constituent institutions resulted in a series of government interventions which resulted in loans underwritten by assets whose fair values were generally established by 'measured value' more attributable to inflation and regulatory manipulation of definitions of value than market fundamentals. This valuation inflation phenomenon may be conceptually defined as 'political goodwill', and was particularly evident in the United States through real estate value inflation and thrift industry regulatory intervention and permissiveness during the 1980s. The nature of deficit finance and government interventions in the 1980s altered the dynamics of the special relationship and shifted the consequences of these dynamics to the thrift and banking industries holding the loans and underlying assets supporting loan repayment, the values of which included a substantial component of 'political goodwill'.

This phenomenon is also evident in real estate, oil and gas, and highly leveraged transactions in Japan, Russia, China, and East Asian nations, respectively. The abrupt reversal of dynamics in this special relationship, when the industry crisis simply became systemic in nature and had to be recognized and addressed definitively from the political arena, removed the political goodwill from asset values and facilitated asset value deflation in real estate in a volatile and short time period. Thus, developing and transition nations must take care to limit the amount of 'political goodwill' introduced into the banking system and asset classes because such goodwill essentially generates inflationary expectations, a false sense of security in asset values underwritten by bank lending operations, and eventual deflationary spirals and bank system distress.

D. Legislation, Deregulation and Asset Value Inflation

The capital requirements for the US thrift industry and banking institutions during the 1980s were managed by legislators and regulatory agencies to maximize benefits to these government-subsidized industries without regard to the prevailing inflationary environment, except to anticipate and promote their continuance by reducing capital requirements, encouraging increased leverage, manipulating underlying asset values, and the measurement and accounting for these values. The balance sheets of thrift and banking institutions reflected these policy changes.

This course of government conduct represented a deliberate series of interventions in market processes in an attempt to deflect and defer the day of reckoning for the effects of deficit finance, and asset value inflation and deflation. In order to understand any crises involving bank capital impairment, the actual composition of institution balance sheets and income statements must be clearly understood, from the perspectives of (1) the methods of measuring and communicating capital and the valuation of underlying assets which support bank capital; and (2) the policy decisions, laws, regulations, and market practices which support these methods.

The US experience in the early 1980s suggests that legislative and regulatory policy incentives to generate growth in banking systems should be phased in gradually over time in order to give immature institutions time to adjust to and take advantage of new opportunities without jeopardizing the system. In the United States, various instances of legislation and regulatory policy (in the form of systematic 'deregulation') introduced the thrift industry in particular to a plethora of new opportunities for growth in the form of new activities, reduced capital requirements, elimination of interest rate ceilings, and increased deposit insurance over a very short period of time, during a volatile financial environment and with relatively few controls on such growth.

The thrift industry vigorously engaged in these new activities and otherwise attempted to grow quickly in attempting to remove itself from the 'interest-rate dilemma' quagmire. Many of the new activities in particular were already subject to intense competition among larger banking institutions, ensuring that the thrift industry would remain at a competitive disadvantage relative to these firms. The absence of controls on growth and expansion coupled with the absence of phasing-in these new opportunities over time in a controlled manner significantly worsened the thrift industry crisis.

Thrift institutions essentially had every incentive to speculate in new riskier activities beyond the mortgage lending arena, with the full understanding that deposit insurance and policy support from their regulatory agency, the FHLBB, would likely protect them from failure. The regulatory, supervisory, and examination authorities were generally not expanded to effectively monitor these expanded powers arising from the 1980 DIDMCA and the 1982 Garn-St. Germain Act, even as the amount of deposit insurance exposure increased by over 250 per cent under DIDMCA.

E. Legislative, Regulatory and Exchange Rate Forbearance, Permissiveness and Nontransparency

In the mid-1980s, both Congress and the regulatory agencies were quite slow to respond to or otherwise resolve the systemic crises in the thrift and banking industries, respectively. With respect to the thrift industry in particular, the regulatory agency practices of the FHLBB were characterized by forbearance and permissiveness that went far beyond facilitating growth and expansion. The practices of forbearance and permissiveness resulted in the promulgation of regulations that deliberately masked the condition of the industry and regulatory interpretations of accounting principles that completely deviated from even aggressive interpretations of GAAP. These practices merely served to obscure the true condition of the industry to all but the 'insiders' and exacerbated the thrift industry crisis to the extent that in 1989 the FHLBB was abolished under FIRREA.

The concept of regulatory forbearance and permissiveness is becoming endemic in developing and transition nation banking crises. In addition, such practices are well-endowed in developed nations, particularly Japan (Ministry of Finance) and the United Kingdom (Bank of England), wherein banking system or banking institution crises resulted in public retaliation against the respective agencies and jeopardized or terminated their mission in bank regulation and supervision.

Thus, developing and transition nations should derive from the US experience through the FHLBB the lesson that regulatory forbearance and permissiveness, while temporarily favorable in periods of financial distress and widespread panic, should be utilized on a fully transparent and temporary basis or the industry concerned will be trapped in quagmire until the agency formally recognizes and addresses the crisis.

In addition, the themes of forbearance and permissiveness were evident in monetary and exchange rate policies with respect to the value of the dollar. The years of anti-inflationary monetary policy and expansive fiscal policy substantially pressured the value of the dollar to increase dramatically over the mid-1980s. The Executive Branch, although possessing the legal authority to address the exchange rate and force the Fed to implement monetary policy in support of desired exchange rates, pursued a dollar policy of benign neglect during the era of deregulation.

F. Legislation, Reregulation, Reactive Policy Reversals and Asset Value Deflation

In the US experience of the mid-1980s and continuing into the early 1990s, the US Congress and regulatory agencies reinforced a deflationary spiral in real estate and other asset values fueled by the implementation of abrupt policy reversals in a series of legislative, regulatory and fiscal policies to end the period of forbearance and permissiveness and conclusively address the thrift industry and banking crises. By 1987 the US trade and balance of payments deficits reached the greatest levels in modern history, and underscored the beginnings of dramatic reductions in the value of the dollar until the Louvre Accord of February 1987 and the public recognition of a 'politically unsustainable' trade deficit by April 1987, respectively.

The US was due for a 'sudden change in macroeconomic policy' and accumulated 'unsustainable fiscal and current account imbalances', and 'heavy reliance on short-term external financing'. The US engaged in defending an exchange rate that was far out of line with fundamentals leading to 'sudden corrections in asset prices and boom-bust cycles'.

These are precisely the conditions leading to systemic financial crises in developing and transition nations later recognized by the G-10 Working Party on Financial Stability in Emerging Market Economies in 1997. The effects of the abrupt policy reversals caused an abrupt vaporization of asset value attributable to 'political goodwill', a general spiral of collapsing comparable asset values reported by real estate appraisers, decreasing leverage, and reactive and reflexive monetary and exchange rate policies.

With respect to the thrift industry crisis, the US Congress abruptly ended years of regulatory forbearance and permissiveness with dramatic legislation that abruptly reversed years of policymaking with CEBA in 1987 and most importantly FIRREA in 1989. The FIRREA legislation represented the most dramatic policy reversal by Congress during this period. FIRREA abruptly terminated the FHLBB (replacing it with the Office of Thrift Supervision (OTS)) and eliminated the forbearance practices and permissive policies set into force by the FHLBB, which essentially placed the thrift industry into insolvency. Notably, FIRREA was enacted just nine months after the 1988 election of President George Bush, and neither the Bush Administration nor his opponent addressed the massive thrift industry and banking crises during the entire presidential campaign.

In order to compensate for the abrupt policy reversals, FIRREA provided for the transfer and sale of assets from failed institutions through the RTC, and further provided and expanded an arsenal of 'superpowers' to the FDIC and other agencies in order to hold thrift management 'accountable' for the 'fraud' and 'negligence' they had purportedly committed against their own institutions, shareholders, and the US Government in requiring deposit insurance payouts.

The passage of FIRREA thereby forced distressed institutions into insolvency and erased billions of dollars of credible institutional net worth in the process; established a system of disposing of assets of such institutions that guaranteed disposition in a 'fire sale' manner that did not recognize market value on such assets; and established the distinct political impression that the thrift industry failures were primarily generated through systemic fraud and negligence of management and directors when this was simply not the case.

FIRREA was followed by the Crime Control Act of 1990 and the FDICIA of 1991, respectively, each of which represented reactive legislation and abrupt policy reversals in various respects. The Crime Control Act augmented policy reversals set forth in FIRREA in order to hold thrift management 'accountable' for the increasingly emphasized 'fraud' and 'negligence' they had purportedly committed against their own institutions, shareholders, and the US Government in requiring deposit insurance payouts.

FDICIA addressed many banking industry issues, but most importantly for purposes of this work, FDICIA vastly reduced the ability of banking and thrift regulatory agencies to employ discretion in dealing with distressed thrift and banking institutions. The PCA structure under FDICIA essentially required such agencies to directly intervene into a distressed institution's affairs based on declining levels of capital (directly caused by the US Government's acts of intervention during the US crisis), eliminating forbearance practices and permissive policies employed during the 1980s.

Thus, developing and transition nations should recognize through the US experience that abrupt policy reversals may be counterproductive and significantly exacerbate banking crises. The US Congress and regulatory agencies following in step abruptly reversed previously relied upon policies instead of gradually easing many institutions in the thrift industry from insolvency, and addressing clearly insolvent institutions and the few institutions, engaged in fraud and negligent practices on an individual basis.

The bottom line is that the abrupt policy reversals forced many institutions, that might otherwise have survived, into insolvency and deposit insurance payouts, which reduced the political burden of dealing with the crisis but significantly increased carnage in the US real estate and banking and thrift industries, as well as the ultimate cost to US taxpayers in bailing out the banking and thrift industries. Therefore, just as the incentives were introduced far too quickly, and the forbearance and permissiveness occurred over an excessive period of time, the necessary policy reversals occurred too abruptly under the US crises experience during the 1980s.

G. Government Accountability and Loss Allocation

The asset value inflation and deflation fueled by US Government policies of intervention and resultant thrift industry and banking crises were exacerbated far beyond the effects of market forces. In the US experience of the 1980s, the abrupt policy reversals generally resulted in an expressed or implied campaign to shift political accountability for the failures of thrift institutions to those persons in charge of managing and directing them.

In the eyes of the authorities, the primary purposes of recent legislation, such as CEBA in 1987, FIRREA in 1989, the Crime Control Act in 1990 and FDICIA in 1991, were arguably to protect Congress from accountability, enhance deposit insurance funds to finance loss absorption and the resulting government bureaucracy, and to provide mechanisms to shift blame and responsibility for the crises to third parties in an attempt to protect the solvency of deposit insurance funds and the government officials responsible for policy failures. For instance, the granting and expanding of RTC and FDIC superpowers under FIRREA to pursue thrift industry managers and directors and institution-affiliated parties that had purportedly engaged in fraud or negligent practices to reimburse deposit insurance funds used to deal with insolvent institutions, inherently shifted accountability for the crises to those persons.

This process almost entirely ignored the dominant role of government intervention in the asset value inflation and deflation cycle, and further ignored the nontransparent government mandates on measuring and recording assets and liabilities on thrift and bank balance sheets and income statements. The effect was implied systematic delay and deflection of the recognition of the consequences of government intervention. The US Congress and regulatory agencies, along with the monetary, exchange rate, and fiscal policies in force over the 1980s, were simply not considered as culpable parties in the policy reversal mix. These policies did not recognize and take into account the effect of government intervention on the crisis itself, which generally resulted in misdirected remedies and compounded unnecessary losses and economic trauma in a design to obscure government accountability.

In addition, the policy reversals clearly treated the larger banking institutions regulated and supervised by the Fed and OCC, in a far different light than regional and smaller banks and the thrift industry. The LDC Debt Crisis and numerous instances of actual insolvency or near-insolvency in the commercial banking community were not subject to the same degree of accountability which occurred under FIRREA and the thrift industry. In fact, the opposite occurred, as special legislation and extreme regulatory forbearance and permissiveness were employed to ensure that the larger commercial banks would emerge from the 1980s.[1]

The differential treatment in political accountability, while perhaps arguably more necessary for the larger commercial banks, reflected a competition of priorities and a failure to accommodate similar policies for similar financial institutions, both of which were political in nature and resulted in nontransparent policymaking designed to obscure that elements of government were equally as culpable in facilitating the thrift industry crisis as the industry itself.

The US thrift industry and banking crises were not caused by systemic fraud or criminal activities. Although these crises did serve as venues to explore the nexus between opportunities and incentives for bank fraud and related criminal activity, the actual sources of capital losses on bank and thrift balance sheets were not found within systemic wrongdoing, but rather in the ongoing acts of government intervention. The process of 'criminalizing' the crises through legislation and litigation against borrowers, bank and thrift management, and 'institution-affiliated parties' for purported fraud and criminal activities constituted, in significant part, a policy of misdirection and avoidance of responsibility and accountability by the government.

Developing and transition nations should recognize that a systemic banking crisis is generally drawn from diverse causes, not all of which emanate from the fraudulent or negligent practices of institutions themselves, but many of which derive from the misdirected and volatile policies of government itself. The shifting of responsibility and accountability to the institutions themselves for banking crises in a volatile monetary and exchange rate environment may be deserved in part for a given crisis but certainly does not tell the entire story. The role of excessive government intervention must be recognized as an inherent component of contemporary banking and currency crises.

The lack of transparency in the 'special relationship' between government and banks provides the government with little incentive to recognize and effectively address the origins of banking and currency crises or to take responsibility in part for those origins. Although government intervention is generally a culpable function of banking and currency crises per se, the losses involved are not borne by government officials, who may seek to avoid accountability for their own actions and retain power and office by providing

---

1 See, S. Solomon, *The Confidence Game: How Unelected Central Bankers Are Governing the Changed World Economy* (Simon & Schuster, 1995), at 466–468.

an illusion of responsibility through reactive and repressive legislation and regulation, and monetary, exchange rate, and fiscal policies.

H. The Recognition of Linkages Between Government Intervention, Asset Valuation and Bank Capital

The US experience of the 1980s makes clear that one of the more appropriate responses to banking crises and widespread bank insolvency is to promote greater transparency of the linkages between asset valuation and bank capitalization and, on the one had, banking legislation, regulation, and supervision, and, on the other hand, monetary, exchange rate, and fiscal policy. The causes and linkages inherent in any given banking crisis remain obscure and diffuse, of course, and sometimes generate more questions instead of answers. These linkages, while somewhat more difficult to articulate with certainty in a given modern context, however, were nonetheless clearly demonstrated in the US experience of the 1980s, as reviewed in this work.

A critical point for developing and transition nations to draw from this work is that the failure to understand and reconcile these linkages will likely result in sustained periods of asset value inflation and asset value deflation and periodic banking and currency crises over time. The ideals of asset value and exchange rate neutrality, or at least mitigation of volatility in such values, will otherwise continue to elude policymakers.

Bank regulation, deregulation, reregulation, and loss allocation policies that do not recognize the foregoing context of government intervention through legislative, regulatory, monetary, and fiscal policy will lead to misdirected remedies and compound unnecessary losses and economic trauma and obscure government accountability. Unless these linkages are observed, those persons and officials responsible for drafting, implementing, and enforcing legislation, regulation, and monetary policy cannot be held accountable for their actions.

The citizens subject to periods of asset value inflation and asset value deflation and bank distress will continuously remit payment of their own funds to the government in the form of increased taxes or an 'inflation tax' which ultimately, as a result of market pressures, results in episodic periods of deflation, recession, impaired asset values, and banking system crises. The payment of defense, full employment, social programs, and other instances of 'government intervention' such as banking system solvency should be borne by the citizens generally in a transparent manner through tax legislation, and fiscal and budgetary discipline, not through obscure and diffuse processes rooted in problematic government policies that encourage economic behavior which destabilizes the banking system.

The linkages are evident in both the US experience of the 1980s and further in China and Russia, where years of financing social and political objectives have resulted in State-owned or State-directed bank loans to State-owned enterprises (SOEs) in the context of no prior assumption of existing or future underlying asset values in a capitalist structure or of debt repayment supported by such 'assets'. The SOE lending operations represent 'political goodwill' in its purest form.

III. CRITIQUE OF EXTERNAL EVALUATIONS

A. FDIC Report on the US Banking Crisis of the 1980s and 1990s

In December, 1997, the FDIC produced a two volume examination of the American banking crisis of the late 1980s and early 1990s.[2] While recognizing the effects of 'moral-hazard' and excessive risk-taking encouraged by the deposit insurance system, the FDIC cited as the chief example of this risk-taking the high concentration of high risk commercial real estate lending. As we have seen in this study, however, there are a number of policy factors which contributed to the high concentration of commercial real estate lending, other than the moral-hazard of deposit insurance, which facilitated the implementation of those policies.

The FDIC did acknowledge, however, that 'poorly conceived deregulation and disruptive tax-law changes'[3] contributed to the outcome. In answer to the question, 'how did the American bank regulatory and deposit system function during the crisis', the FDIC concluded that:

> 'Despite bank and thrift failures in numbers not seen since the Great Depression, the government's promise to protect insured depositors was fully honored: no depositor lost a penny on federally insured deposits, there was no significant disruption of the financial intermediation process, and a high degree of financial stability was maintained. These results did not come cheap, but the financial cost for the banking industry was borne by the banks themselves and by their customers, rather than by taxpayers, who ended up bearing most of the much greater cost of the S&L debacle.'

While accurate insofar as they go, the FDIC's conclusions seriously understate the damage and losses suffered during the thrift industry and banking crises. If the role of the FDIC as the primary federal bank regulatory authority is so limited in scope as to measure its success in the terms expressed above, one might conclude that its success is that of a transfer agent which simply applied deposit insurance and taxpayer money to solve current problems of collection of debts supported by 'political goodwill.' In that case, its success is limited only by the amount of current funds at its disposal. This observation is supported by the lessons drawn by the FDIC from the crisis, as expressed in the Report.

A first lesson drawn by the FDIC is that, 'Problems in the operations of depository institutions must be identified at an early stage if serious deterioration in the institution's condition is to be prevented, and early identification requires continuous and sometimes burdensome monitoring of the institutions' activities.'[4] It is axiomatic that early problem identification will

---

2 See FDIC, *History of the Eighties, Volumes 1 & 2: Lessons for the Future* (Washington D.C., 1997); References are to Vol. I; see also the video recording of the 'History of the Eighties - Lessons For the Future Symposium', held by the FDIC on 16 January 1997, produced by the FDIC, portions of which are reproduced in Volume II of the FDIC publication.

3 *Ibid.* at p.81.

4 *Ibid.*

contribute to early and effective problem resolution. The FDIC proposal, then, is to increase burdensome monitoring of banks' financial conditions, rather than to identify and deal with the fundamental underlying causes of the crisis. Predictably, the FDIC lesson learned is that the agency needs greater resources and increased funding.

Naturally, a second lesson drawn by the FDIC from the crisis is that, 'Adequate funding of the deposit insurance agency is essential to effective regulatory control of risk-taking by insured institutions.'[5] Without greater funding, the FDIC feels that it could not close insolvent institutions, thereby 'controlling bank risk and moral-hazard problems'[6] and reducing 'losses to the insurance fund when failure did occur.'[7] Notwithstanding this serious constraint, the FDIC apparently concludes that its response to the crisis constituted a job well done.

The third conclusion in the FDIC Report is that, 'The treatment of large-bank failures had undesirable side effects, but it is unclear whether alternative resolution methods would have been successful in the environment of the 1980s.'[8] In these cases, most notably in the case of *Citicorp and Citibank*, the 'special relationship' between government and money center banking was so entwined that the consequences of market discipline on those institutions was simply unthinkable: the bank was 'too big to fail.'[9] This did not prove to be the case with a significant number of large regional banks, which were eventually permitted to fail. In some cases, the FDIC admits, the delay in closure contributed to increases in resolution costs.[10] The FDIC does not mention that in some cases, the banks were closed, merged and consolidated with no loss to the deposit insurance funds whatsoever. In any case, the FDIC concludes that since the banks that were 'too big to fail' were not allowed to fail, '... the experience of the 1980s provides little guidance on whether their actions would have led to runs on other large banks and to more general financial market instability.'[11]

---

5 See note 2, *supra* at p.82.

6 *Ibid.*

7 *Ibid.*

8 *Ibid.*

9 See *The Confidence Game, supra* note 1, at pp.466-468. On the day before Thanksgiving, 1990, Citibank and fed officials met in New York. 'Citibank, and with it the entire banking system, the central bankers informed them (Citibank officials), was headed for big problems unless they took drastic and immediate steps to add USD5 billion to Citi's capital base. Corrigan and Taylor said that they were worried that Citibank, which had one of the lowest capital-to-asset ratios and highest non-performing loan ratios among big banks, didn't have sufficient capital to survive the huge losses that were coming on its USD30 billion commercial real estate portfolio. Loan losses in regions of the country where the real estate bubble had burst were running fifteen to twenty times the amount Citi was anticipating.' At conferences in England during November and December, the author presented Citibank as an example of the depth of the American crises, based on public information regarding Citibank's commercial real estate portfolio and the author's experience with loan losses then being experienced by American banks, illustrating then Citicorp's insolvency. This example was viewed at the time with incredulity and disbelief.

10 See, *History of the Eighties, Volume 1, supra* note 2, at pp.82-83.

11 *Ibid.* at p.83.

A fourth lesson drawn by the FDIC from the crisis appears to be more an observation than a lesson. The FDIC observes that, 'Statutory rules limiting regulatory discretion may help prevent a repetition of the regulatory lapses that occurred in the 1980s, but it remains to be seen whether such rules will be maintained in a future period of widespread banking distress.'[12] This is, in fact, an important lesson. The FDICIA, which limited regulatory discretion, was simply a congressional attempt to display rigor in its response to the crisis. For so long as the 'special relationship' between American Government and banking continues, the resolution of banking crises will continue to be political and as such, political discretion will continue to dominate the resolution process.

A fifth lesson drawn by the FDIC from the crises reflects the fundamental misdirection of regulatory focus in this respect. The FDIC concludes that, 'Bank regulation can limit the scope and cost of bank failures, but is unlikely to prevent failures that have systemic causes.'[13] The FDIC restates the obvious generalities regarding systemic causes of the banking crisis, such as 'broad economic and financial market changes, ill-considered government policy actions, and structural weaknesses that inhibited geographic diversification and made many banks vulnerable to regional and sectoral recessions.'[14] The FDIC makes no real attempt to explicate the changes, actions and weaknesses which directly contributed to the circumstances which have drawn the agency into the morass of 'bank and thrift failures in numbers not seen since the Great Depression.'[15]

A sixth lesson drawn by the FDIC is essentially a corollary of the fifth. That is, 'That the ability of regulators to curb excessive risk-taking on the part of currently healthy banks was (and continues to be) limited by the problem of identifying risky activities before they produce serious losses and by competing public policy objectives.'[16] This lesson drives at the heart of the American banking crises, but the FDIC fails to attack an analysis of why activities become risky and what the relationship of that risk bears to the competing policy objectives.

A final lesson drawn by the FDIC from the crisis is that, 'Differences in perspective among federal bank regulators may have delayed recognition of the nature of the problems of the 1980s.'[17] The FDIC description of the differences in primary responsibilities of the various regulatory agencies, and the need for checks and balances among them as a source of delay in problem resolution, fails also to make the point that the parochial focus of these separate agencies inhibits the abilities of those agencies arguably most well placed to come to grips with the fundamental systemic causes of the American crisis and the ongoing global crises. Unfortunately, the collective analytical powers of the agencies have been largely wasted on self-congratulatory turf protection.

---

12 *Ibid.*
13 *Ibid.*
14 See note 10, *supra* at p.84.
15 *Ibid.*
16 *Ibid.*
17 See note 10, *supra* at p.85.

The entire effort of the FDIC in its exhaustive Report appears to have been to validate its own role, seek an expanded role and additional resources, and to then observe that the fundamental systemic issues are outside its mandate, and that if new systemic problems 'are allowed to develop in the future, bank regulation alone will not be able to prevent a major increase in the number of bank failures.'[18]

B. G-10 Report of the Working Party on Financial Stability

In contrast to the FDIC Report, the G10 Report of the Working Party on Financial Stability in Emerging Market Economies, entitled Financial Stability in Emerging Market Economies, published in April 1997, in response to an initiative at the Lyon summit of the Group of Ten in June 1996, focused directly on the effects of 'an unstable macroeconomic environment, in the wake of major structural transformations, or as a result of important distortions in the real economy ...', as the context in which 'microeconomic and institutional failings' give way to systemic crises. Despite, however, the overall acceptance by the working party of the macroeconomic sources of vulnerability of the domestic banking systems to crises, its report also maintains that the root causes of financial crises are generally to be found in microeconomic and institutional failings, and the report goes on to analyze in some detail the key features of a robust financial system, as well as a strategy for promoting robust financial systems. The analysis and strategy focuses on the development and maintenance of institutional and financial market infrastructure, market functioning, regulation, and supervision as the building blocks for a robust financial system.

The strategy pursued by the Working Party is sound and comprehensive insofar as it goes. The strategy is clearly delineated in the Core Principles for Effective Banking Supervision, a Consultative Paper Issued by the Basle Committee On Banking Supervision in April 1997, and appended to the report as an Exhibit thereto.

The aspect of the Working Party Report, which leaps out from the page, however, does focus on the fundamental issue. 'The vulnerability of the financial sector is inherent to the function it performs, namely to transform risk and liquidity. Financial sector crises are thus closely associated with a breakdown of these functions.' The Working Party notes that these breakdowns are reflected in the 'areas of corporate governance and management, the incentive structure provided by the financial and institutional frameworks, market discipline and regulatory and supervisory structures.' The Report primarily addresses these frameworks and structures because it is able to do so. Nonetheless, the foregoing observation by the Working Party is immediately followed by the following observation, which is, interestingly enough, not further conclusively addressed in the Report:

'Macroeconomic instability – high and variable inflation rates, booms and busts in economic activity, and unsustainable fiscal and external positions – is the most obvious and direct source of vulnerability faced by banks and the financial sectors on

---

[18] See note 10, *supra* at p.84.

account of its adverse effect on asset price volatility and the allocation of financial resources. Although financial institutions, in principle, can hedge against volatility in their own portfolios, macroeconomic risks or volatility cannot be hedged away in the aggregate. Thus, in economic downswings banks cannot protect against a deterioration in the quality of loan portfolios, which erodes their capital and reserve positions. While economic booms or loose financial policies may improve bank profitability in the short term, they are likely to destabilize banks in the medium term, if they result in asset price bubbles and inflation.'

'Macroeconomic instability does not only reflect the structure of the economy, however. Weaknesses in macroeconomic management have often been the primary source of episodes of macroeconomic instability. *Sudden changes in macroeconomic policies, the accumulation of unsustainable fiscal and current account balances, heavy reliance on volatile short-term external financing, or the defense of an exchange rate that is out of line with fundamentals generally lead to sudden corrections in asset prices and boom-bust cycles.'* (Emphasis added).

The macroeconomic instability contemplated by the Working Party follows from inflation, particularly when combined with non-neutral tax systems or incomplete markets, distorting incentives for borrowers and lenders, making the financial system even more fragile. Some of these distortions include banks adjusting to inflation by indexing interest rates and shifting portfolio into assets, the prices of which lead inflation, such as real estate, commodities and foreign exchange; shifting to a larger share of income derived from float on payments, inflation tax on unremunerated deposits and foreign exchange dealings, which dry up in a deflationary environment; inflation induced erosion of the information base for business planning and credit appraisal, contributing to higher portfolio risk; shifting to investments with short term maturities, hampering the development of longer-term debt instrument markets; and in the presence of non-neutral tax systems, a distortion of financial incentives toward over-borrowing.

The recognition that '[A] significant reduction in the rate of inflation appears to have been a factor in a number of financial crises since 1980,' as close as the Working Party comes to proposing a solution to what is essentially a problem of currency instability following a complex program of government intervention in and manipulation of currency, is a disappointing suggestion of a 'careful mix' of anti-inflationary policies to preserve bank soundness. Once again, although the Working Party gets close to the heart of the matter, it stops short of attacking directly the retained sovereign prerogative of government intervention in economic matters through currency manipulation and the exercise of related fiscal and monetary discretion to facilitate short term political objectives in a non-transparent manner.

IV. A FINAL REFLECTION: FUTURE CHANGE IS POSSIBLE AND CRITICAL IN DEVELOPING AND TRANSITION ECONOMIES

The decisions already made and implemented cannot be reversed. We can however recognize the historic context for the ongoing phenomenon of bank distress. We can also identify the purposes for which payment has been made through the 'inflation tax' of deflated asset values resulting in bank capital inadequacy and bank distress or failure. The payment of the costs of war, full employment, social programs and widespread 'big government intervention' should be borne by the citizenry generally. The citizens, through their elected representatives, can accomplish this transparently, in an appropriate and properly sanctioned manner, through tax legislation and corresponding fiscal and budgetary discipline. It should not be accomplished by an obscure process, wiping out the reputations and capital of those who have acted consistently with, and in implementation of government policies, including borrowers and banks, as well as their service providers and insurance carriers.

These lessons are starkly apparent in emerging economies such as Russia and China, where years of financing social and political objectives have resulted in State bank loans to State-owned enterprises where there existed no prior assumption of existing or future underlying 'asset' values in a capitalist sense or of debt repayment supported by such 'assets'. Those loans truly represent 'political goodwill'. Now that the countries are attempting to convert socialist systems to more market-oriented systems, it is a drastic mistake to assume that such pre-existing debts should simply be subjected to Western market-based processes of creditors' rights, borrower bankruptcy and bank insolvency resolution. The social and political costs represented by the existing debts of 'political goodwill' must be assumed by the State on some basis that affords a sustainable method and time for amortized repayment or write-off of such debts or some combination thereof. Market-based banking and financial arrangements, including methods for debt collateralization, enforcement and insolvency must be separated from the arrangements for the payment or financing of 'social and political costs'.

The lessons starkly apparent in the emerging economies are obscured in the US and other so-called 'market-based' economies by the mistaken assumption that the function of their banking systems has been purely mercantile in nature, when, in fact, enormous segments of bank financing have been utilized to further government 'social' policy and political objectives by enabling and implementing vast programs of government incentives, subsidies, guarantees and transfer payments. The US thrift industry is a prime example of such programs. The losses arising from changes in the government's fiscal, monetary and regulatory policies should be allocated on a transparent basis which recognizes the origin of the expenditures and the equitable identification both of those who have benefited from the expenditure and of those responsible for bearing the loss which occurred because the expenditure was based not on commercial value, but on social or political value. The existing laws and procedures for allocation of losses in a purely mercantile environment do not fit the magnitude of losses of 'political goodwill' translated through the banking systems which have their origins in social policy, politics and the 'special relationship' between government and banking.

Although the use of the banking system in mercantile societies to finance war and social policy has always occurred on a greater or lesser basis, never in the history of the United States has it occurred on such a scale with so little transparency, responsibility or accountability. Because of the enormous productive capability of the US economy, with a little congressional and regulatory misdirection, budget restructure, monetary policy stabilization and time, the US has avoided addressing the fundamental issues which must be addressed in the developing and transition economies.

The traditional Western-capitalist legal and economic ideology does not apply to the resolution of 'political goodwill' debt-overhang problems in emerging economies, just as they do not apply to the same 'political goodwill' debt problems in the United States and other so-called 'developed economies'. The Western nations, including the United States, however, can learn, from efforts in the developing and transition economies, to accommodate the financing of both social and mercantile objectives on a transparent and responsible basis, separating the risk of loss or cost, consistent with the purpose and beneficiaries of the risk or cost.

Selected Bibliography
(including Statutes, Regulations and Cases)

BOOKS

ADAMS, J., *The Big Fix: Inside the S&L Scandal: How an Unholy Alliance of Politics and Money Destroyed America's Banking System* (1990)

BALDERSON, F., *Thrifts in Crisis: Structural Transformation of the Savings and Loan Industry* (1985)

BARTH, J., *The Great Savings and Loan Debacle* (1991)

BARTH, BRUMBAUGH AND LITAN, *The Banking Industry in Turmoil: A Report on the Condition of the U.S. Banking Industry and the Bank Insurance Fund* (1990)

BARTH, BRUMBAUGH AND LITAN, *The Future of American Banking* (1992)

BARBANEL AND MAILLET, *Business in the Soviet Union: Primer and Overview* 152 (1991)

BAUMOL AND BLINDER, *Macroeconomics, Principles and Policies* (7th edn, 1998)

BENSTON, G., *An Analysis of the Causes of Savings and Loan Failures* (1985)

BERGSTEN, C., *Economic Imbalances and World Politics* (Spring 1987)

BERNSTEIN, E., *The Soviet Union and Bretton Woods, in a Retrospect on the Bretton Woods System* (1993)

BERNSTEIN, P., *Capital Ideas: The Improbable Origins of Modern Wall Street* (1992)

BERDYAEV, N., *The Russian Idea* (1992)

BHALA, R., *Foreign Bank Regulation After BCCI* (1994)

BLACK, W., *Examination/Supervision/Enforcement of S&Ls: 1979–1992* (1993)

BLACK, W., *The Southwest Plan and the 1988 'Resolutions'* (1993)

BOGLE J., *Bogle on Mutual Funds* (1994)

BORDO AND EICHENGREEN, (EDS), *Retrospective on the Bretton Woods System* (1991)

BROOKHEISER, R., *The Outside Story: How Democrats and Republicans Reelected Reagan* (1986)

BRUMBAUGH, R., JR., *The Collapse of Federally Insured Depositories: The Savings and Loans as Precursor* (1993)

BRUMBAUGH, R., JR., *Thrifts Under Siege: Restoring Order to American Banking* (1988)

CALOMIRIS AND CORTON, *The Origin of Banking Panics: Models, Facts and Bank Regulation in Financial Markets and Financial Crises* (1991)

CARRON, A., *The Plight of the Thrift Institutions* (1982)
CASTRO, CUTLER, KILDOYLE AND LAPIDUS, *Public Policy Toward Mutual Savings Banks in New York State: Proposals for Change* (1974)
CLIFFORD, A., *The Independence of the Federal Reserve System* (1965)
CLINE, W., *International Debt and the Stability of the World Economy* (1983)
CLINE, W., *International Debt Reexamined* (1995)
COHEN AND FRIER, *The Federal Home Loan Bank System* (1980)
COOPER, R., *The International Monetary System: Essays in World Economics* (1987)
CRANSTON, R., (ED.), *Banks and Remedies* (1992) (2nd edn, 1995)
CRANSTON, R., *Principles of Banking Law* (Oxford, 1998)
DAVIDSON AND REES-MOGG, *The Great Reckoning* (1993)
DAVIS, E., *Debt, Financial Fragility and Systemic Risk* (1992)
DALE, R., *International Banking Deregulation: The Great Banking Experiment* (1992)
DALE, R., *The Regulation of International Banking* (1984)
DAY, K., *S&L Hell: The People and the Politics Behind the $1 Trillion Savings and Loan Scandal* (1993)
DELAMAIDE, D., *Debt Shock: The Full Story of the World Credit Crisis* (1984)
DESTER AND HENNING, *Dollar Politics: Exchange Rate Policymaking in the United States* (1989)
DESTLER AND RANDALL, *Dollar Politics* (1989)
DEVLIN, R., *Debt and Crisis in Latin America: The Supply-Side of the Story* (1989)
DEWATRIPONT AND TIROLE, *The Prudential Regulation of Banks* (1994)
DOMINGUEZ AND FRANKEL, *Does Foreign Exchange Intervention Work* (1993)
DUNLOP, B., *The Rise of Russia and the Fall of the Soviet Empire* (1993)
EDITORS OF THE INSTITUTIONAL INVESTOR, *The Way It Was: An Oral History of Finance 1967–1987* (1988)
EDSALL, T., *The New Politics of Inequality* (1984)
EICHENGREEN, B., *Toward a New International Financial Architecture: A Practical Post-Asia Agenda* (1999)
EICHENGREEN AND PORTES, *The Anatomy of Financial Crises* (1987)
EICHENGREEN AND PORTES, *et al.*, *Crisis? What Crises? Orderly Workouts for Sovereign Debtors* (1995)
EICHLER, N., *The Thrift Debacle* (1989)
EISENBEIS AND HORVITZ, *The Role of Forbearance and its Costs in Handling Troubled and Failed Depository Institutions in Reforming Financial Institutions in the United States* (1993)
ELY, BERT AND VANDERHOFF, *Lessons Learned From the S&L Debacle: The Price of Failed Public Policy* (1991)
EVANS AND NOVAK, *The Reagan Revolution* (1981)
FAY, S., *Far Beyond Greed* (1982)
FELDSTEIN, M, (ED.), *The Risk of Economic Crisis* (1991)
FREIBERT, G., *The Regulatory Examination: Preparing, Managing and Responding* (1991)
FRIEDMAN AND ROOSA, *The Balance of Payments: Free Versus Fixed Exchange Rates* (1967)
FRIEDMAN AND SCHWARTZ, *A Monetary History of the United States: 1867–1960* (1963)

FUNABASHI, Y., *Managing the Dollar: From the Plaza to the Louvre* (1989)
GARDENER, E.P.M., *Banking Supervision: Evolution Practice & Issues* (1986)
GARTEN, H., *Why Bank Regulation Failed* (1991)
GILDER, G., *Microcosm* (1989)
GILPIN, R., *The Political Economy of International Relations* (1987)
GLASNER, D., *Free Banking and Monetary Reform* (1989)
GOLDSTEIN AND TURNER, *Banking Crises in Emerging Economies: Origins and Policy Options* (1996)
GOLEMBE AND HENGREN, *Federal Regulation of Banking* (1975)
GOLEMBE AND HOLLAND, *Federal Regulation of Banking, 1986–1987* (1986)
GOODHART, C., *The Evolution of Central Banks* (1988)
GRAY, J., *Financial Deregulation and the Savings and Loan Crisis* (1988)
GREIDER, W., *Secrets of the Temple: How the Federal Reserve Runs the Country* (1987)
GUP, B., *Bank Fraud: Exposing the Hidden Threat to Financial Institutions* (1990)
GYOHTEN, T., *Changing Fortunes* (1992)
HADJIEMMANUIL, C., *Banking Regulation and The Bank of England* (1996)
HADJIMICHALAKIS, M., *The Federal Reserve, Money and Interest Rates: The Volcker Years and Beyond* (1984)
HECTOR, G., *Breaking the Bank: The Decline of Bank of America* (1988)
HENDERSON, C., *Asia Falling* (1998)
HUTCHINSON, H., *Money, Banking and the United States Economy* (6th edn, 1983)
JONES, D., *Fed Watching and Interest Rate Projections* (2nd edn, 1989)
JONES, D., *The Politics of Money* (1991)
KANE, E., *The Gathering Crisis in Federal Deposit Insurance* (1985)
KANE, E., *The S&L Insurance Mess: How Did it Happen?* (1989)
KAROGLAN AND LUBRANO, *Mexico's Banks After the December 1994 Devaluation – A Chronology of the Government's Response* (1995)
KAUFMAN, G., *Restructuring the American Financial System* (1990)
KAUFMAN, H., *Interest Rates, the Markets and the New Financial World* (1986)
KAUFMAN AND KORMENDI (EDS), *Deregulating Financial Services, Public Policy in Flux* (1986)
KELLER, P., *Thrift Industry Regulation After FIRREA, PLI Order No. G4-3862* (1991)
KENEN, P., *Managing Exchange Rates* (1988)
KENNEDY, P., *The Rise and Fall of the Great Powers* (1987)
KEYNES, J., *A Treatise on Money* (1930)
KINDLEBERGER, C., *A Financial History of Western Europe* (1993)
KINDLEBERGER, C., *The International Economic Order* (1988)
KINDLEBERGER, C., *Manias, Panics and Crashes: A History of Financial Crises* (1989)
KORMENDI, R., *Crisis Resolution in the Thrift Industry: A Mid-America Institute Report* (1989)
KRIEGER, A., *The Money Bazaar: Inside the Trillion-Dollar World of Currency Trading* (1992)
KRUGMAN, P., *What Happened to Asia?* (January 1998)
KURTZMAN, J., *The Death of Money* (1993)

LASTRA R. AND SHIFFMAN, H., *Bank Failures and Bank Insolvency Law in Economics in Transition* (Kluwer 1999)
LAWRENCE, R., *Origin and Development of the Examination Council* (1992)
LEEDS AND GALE, *The 1982 Mexico Debt Negotiations* (1987)
LENZ, A., *A Sectoral Assessment of the U.S. Current Account Deficit: Performance and Prospects in International Adjustment and Financing: The Lessons of 1985–1991* (1991)
LESSARD, D., *Finance and Global Competition, Exploiting Financial Scope and Coping with Volatile Exchange Rates in New Developments in International Finance* (1988)
LINTNER, J., *Mutual Savings Banks in the Savings and Mortgage Markets* (1948)
LOCKWOOD, P., *A Guide to the Federal Home Loan Bank System* (5th edn, 1987)
LOWY, M., *High Rollers: Inside the Savings and Loan Debacle* (1991)
MACEY AND MILLER, *Banking Law and Regulation* (1993)
MADSEN AND MOESCHBERGER, *Statistical Concepts With Applications to Business and Economics* (1986)
MAKIN, J., *The Global Debt Crisis* (1984)
MALKIN, L., *The National Debt* (1987)
MARRIS, S., *Deficits and the Dollar: The World Economy at Risk* (1985)
MAYER, M., *The Bankers* (1974)
MAYER, M., *The Bankers: The Next Generation* (1997)
MAYER, M., *The Fate of the Dollar* (1980)
MAYER, M., *The Greatest-Ever Bank Robbery: The Collapse of the Savings and Loan Industry* (1990)
MAYER, M., *The Money Bazaars* (1984)
MCCOLLUM, J., *The Continental Affair: The Rise and Fall of the Continental Illinois Bank* (1987)
MELTON, W., *Inside the Fed: Making Monetary Policy* (1985)
MILLMAN, G., *The Vandals Crown* (1995)
MISKIN, F., *Preventing Financial Crises: An International Perspective* (1994)
MOFFITT, M., *The World's Money: International Banking from Bretton Woods to the Brink of Insolvency* (1983)
NORTON, J.J., *Devising International Banking Supervisory Standards* (Graham & Trotman/Martinus Nijhoff, London, 1995)
NORTON, J.J., *Prospects for International Lending and Reschedulings* (1988)
NORTON, J.J. AND WHITLEY, S.C., *Banking Law Manual* (N.Y., 1984, as suppl. annually, particularly 1985–92 suppls.)
NORTON, J.J. ET AL (EDS), *Commercial Finance Guide* (Matthew Bender N.Y. 1991, as annual suppl.)
ODELL, J., *U.S. International Monetary Policy: Markets, Power and Ideas as Sources of Change* (1982)
ODELL, J., *The U.S. International Monetary System* (1984)
OLSON, M., *The Rise and Decline of Nations* (1982)
ORNSTEIN, F., *Savings Banking: An Industry in Change* (1985)
PAPADIMITRIOU, E. (ED.), *Stability in the Financial System* (1996)
PECHMAN, J., *Federal Tax Policy* (5th edn, 1987)
PETERS, E., *Chaos and Order in the Capital Markets* (1991)
PIERCE & LEONE, *The Future of Banking* (6th edn, 1993)
PILZER, P., *Other People's Money: The Inside Story of the S&L Mess* (1989)

PIZZO, S., *Inside Job: The Looting of America's Savings and Loans* (1989)
PIZZO, FRICKER AND MUOLO, *Inside Job: The Looting of America's Savings and Loans* (1989)
PRIOGOGINE AND STENGERS, *Order Out of Chaos* (1984)
PUGH, E., *Building IBM: Shaping an Industry and Its Technology* (1995)
REID, M., *The Secondary Bank Crisis 1973–75* (1982)
REINICKE, W., *Banking, Politics and Global Finance: American Commercial Banks and Regulatory Change, 1980–1990* (1994)
ROBBINS AND ROBBINS, *How Tax Policy Compounded the S&L Crisis* (1991)
ROBERTS, P., *The Supply-Side Revolution: An Insider's Account of Policymaking in Washington* (1984)
ROBERTSON, R., *The Comptroller and Bank Supervision* (1995)
ROHWER, J., *Asia Rising* (1995)
SALSMAN, R., *Gold and Liberty* (1995)
SCOTT, H.S., AND WILLONS, P.A., *International Finance* (5th ed., Foundation Press N.Y., 1998)
SEIDMAN, W., *Full Faith and Credit: The Great S&L Debacle and Other Washington Sagas* (1993)
SHELTON, J., *Money Meltdown* (1994)
SHENG, A (ED.), *Bank Restructuring* (1996)
SHORT AND ROBINSON, *The Texas Thrift Situation: Implications for the Texas Financial Industry* (1988)
SIEGEL AND SIEGEL, *Accounting and Financial Disclosure* (1983)
SINKEY JR., *Problem and Failed Institutions in the Commercial Banking Industry* (1979)
SOLOMON, A., *The Dollar, Debt and the Trade Deficit* (1987)
SOLOMON, R., *The International Monetary System: 1945–1981* (1982)
SOLOMON, S., *The Confidence Game: How Unelected Central Bankers Are Governing the Changed World Economy* (Simon & Schuster, 1995)
SOROS, G., *The Alchemy of Finance* (1987)
SOROS, G., *The Crisis of Global Capitalism* (1998)
SPRAGUE, I., *Bailout: An Insider's Account of Bank Failures and Rescues* (1986)
SRI INTERNATIONAL, *Understanding Changes in the Southern California Economy* (1991)
STEIN, H., *Presidential Economics* (1984, 1985)
STILLER, J., *OCC Bank Examination: A Historical Overview* (1995)
STOCKMAN, D., *The Triumph of Politics* (1986, 1987)
STRUNK AND CASE, *Where Deregulation Went Wrong: A Look at the Causes Behind the Savings and Loan Failures in the 1980s* (1988)
SYMONS AND WHITE, *Banking Law* (2nd ed., 1984) (latest edition is 1998)
TECK, A., *Mutual Savings Banks and Savings and Loan Associations: Aspects of Growth* (1968)
TIMBERLAKE, R., *The Origins of Central Banking in the United States* (1978)
TRIFFIN, R., *Gold and the Dollar Crisis: The Future of Convertibility* (1961)
TUFTE, E., *Political Control of the Economy* (1978)
U.S. LEAGUE OF SAVINGS INSTITUTIONS, *Savings and Loan Sourcebook* (1981–1983)
VITTAS, D., *Financial Regulation: Changing the Rules of the Game* (1992)
VOJTA, G., *Bank Capital Adequacy* (1973)

VOLCKER, P., AND GYOHTEN T., *Changing Fortunes: The World's Money and the Threat to American Leadership* (1992)
WALMSEY, J., *The Foreign Exchange and Money Markets Guide* (1992)
WARREN, C., *Bankruptcy in United States History* (1935)
WELFLING, W., *Mutual Savings Banks: The Evolution of a Financial Intermediary* (1968)
WELLONS, P., *Passing the Buck: Banks Government and Third World Debt* (1987)
WHITE, E., *The Comptroller and the Transformation of American Banking, 1960–1990* (1992)
WHITE, L., *Competition and Currency: Essays on Free Banking and Money* (1989)
WHITE, L., (ED.), *The Crisis in American Banking* (1993)
WHITE, L., *The S&L Debacle: Public Policy Lessons for Bank and Thrift Regulation* (1991)
WILLIAMSON, J., *The Exchange Rate System, Policy Analyses in International Economics* (1985)
WILLIAMSON, J., *Targets and Indicators: A Blueprint for the International Coordination of Economic Policy* (1985)
WOELFEL, C., *Encyclopedia of Banking and Finance* (10th ed., 1991)
WOLFSON, M., *Financial Crises: Understanding the Postwar U.S. Experience* (1986)
WOOD, P., *Law and Practice of International Finance Series* (6 vols., Sweet & Maxwell Ltd, 1995–96)
WOOLLEY, J., *Monetary Politics: The Federal Reserve and the Politics of Monetary Policy* (1984)
ZISMAN, B., *Banks and Thrifts: Government Enforcement and Receivership* (1992)
ZWEIG, P., *Belly Up: The Collapse of the Penn Square Bank* (1985)

ARTICLES AND BOOK CHAPTERS

ADAMS, PECK AND SPENCER, 'FIRREA and the New Federal Home Loan Bank System', 32 Santa Clara Law Review 17 (1992)
ALTMAN, E., 'Predicting Performance in the Savings and Loan Association Industry', *Journal of Monetary Economics* 3 (October 1977)
ANNUAL SURVEY ISSUE, 'Financial Institutions and Regulations, the S&L Crisis: Death and Transfiguration', 59 *Fordham Law Review* S1 (1991)
ARROW, K., 'Risk Perception and Psychology in Economics', *Economic Inquiry* 20 (1982)
ASHMEAD, J., In Re Colonial Realty Co., 'The Second Circuit Harmonizes Bankruptcy and Bank Insolvency Law (Rejecting Established Bankruptcy Case Law in the Process)', 60 Brook. L. Rev. 517 (1994)
BARDOS, J., 'The Risk-Based Capital Agreement: A Further Step Toward Policy Convergence', *Federal Reserve Bank of New York Quarterly* (Winter 1987–1988)
BEHRENS, E., 'Classification of Loan Participants Following the Insolvency of a Lead Bank', 62 Tex. L. Rev. 1115 (1984)
BENSTON AND MARLIN, 'Bank Examiners' Evaluation of Credit: An Analysis of the Usefulness of Substandard Loan Data', *Journal of Money, Credit and Banking* 6, No. 1 (1974)

BERGER, HERRING AND SZEGO, 'The Role of Capital in Financial Institutions', *Journal of Banking and Finance*, Volume 19 (1995)

BERGER, KING AND O'BRIEN, 'The Limitations of Market Value Accounting and a More Realistic Alternative', *Journal of Banking and Finance* 15 (1991)

BERNANKE, 'Non Monetary Effects of the Financial Crisis in the Propagation of the Great Depression', 73 Am. Econ. Rev. 257 (1983)

BLACK, W., 'Ending Our Forbearers' Forbearance: FIRREA and Supervisory Goodwill', *Stanford Law and Policy Review* 102 (Spring 1990)

BLALOCK, CURRY AND ELMER, 'Resolution Costs of Thrift Failures', *FDIC Banking Review* 4, No. 1 (1991)

BLANCHARD AND TOUAANOVA, 'Comments on Doing Business in the Russian Federation', 6 U.S.F. aac. L.J. 519 (1994)

BLOCK, C., 'Overt and Covert Bailouts: Developing a Public Bailout Policy', 67 Ind. L.J. 951

BLOOM, D., 'Tax Planning for an Acquisition of a Troubled Thrift Institution', 16 *Journal of Corporate Taxation* 313 (1990)

BLUM AND HELLWIG, 'The Macroeconomic Implications of Capital Adequacy Requirements for Banks', 39 *European Economic Review* (1995)

BONSER-NEAL, C., 'Does Central Bank Intervention Stabilize Foreign Exchange Rates?', Fed. Res. Bank of Kansas City Econ. Rev., 1st Quar. (1996)

BOOT AND THAKOR, 'Self-Interested Bank Regulation', 83 *American Economic Review Papers and Proceedings*, 206 212 (1993)

BOSTON UNIVERSITY SCHOOL OF LAW, *Annual Review of Banking Law* (1982–1995)

BOVENZI, MARINO AND MCFADDEN, 'Commercial Bank Failure Prediction Models', *Federal Reserve Bank of Atlanta Economic Review* 68 (November 1983)

BREEDAN, R., 'The S&L Crisis: Death and Transfiguration', 59 Fordham Law Rev., No. 6 (May 1991)

BREEDEN, R., 'Thumbs on the Scale: The Role That Accounting Practices Played in the Savings and Loan Crisis', 59 *Fordham Law Review* S7-S931 (1991)

BRIMMER, A., 'Monetary Policy and Economic Activity: Benefits and Costs of Monetarism', *American Economic Review* (May 1983)

BRINKMANN AND HORVITZ, 'Risk Based Capital Standards and the Credit Crunch', 27 *Journal of Money, Credit and Banking* (August 1995)

BRINKMANN, HORVITZ AND HUANG, 'Forbearance: An Empirical Analysis', *Journal of Financial Services Research* 10 (1996)

BROOME, L., 'Private Market Solutions to the Savings and Loan Crisis: Bank Holding Company Acquisitions of Savings Associations', 59 *Fordham Law Review* S111 (1991)

BRYAN, L., 'Bank Failure: The Politization of a Social Problem', 45 *Stanford Law Review* 289

CALOMIRIS AND GORTON, 'The Origin of Banking Panics: Models, Facts and Bank Regulation', *Financial Markets and Financial Crises* (1991)

CAMPBELL AND GLENN, 'Deposit Insurance in a Deregulated Environment', 39 J. Fin. 775 (1984)

CANOVA, T., 'The Transformation of U.S. Banking and Finance: From Regulated Competition to Free-Market Receivership, 60 Brooklyn L. Rev. 1295 (Winter 1995)

CARGILL, T., 'CAMEL Ratings and the CD Market', *Journal of Financial Services Research* 3, No. 4 (September 1989)

CB COMMERCIAL TORTO/WHEATON RESEARCH, 1 *The Industrial Outlook*, (Spring 1997)

CIERI, 'An Introduction to Legal and Practical Considerations in the Restructuring of Troubled Leveraged Buyouts', 45 Bus. Law 333 (November 1989)

CLARK, P., *ET. AL*, 'Regulation of Savings Associations Under the Financial Institutions Reform, Recovery and Enforcement Act of 1989, 45 *Business Law Review* 1013 (1990)

CLEARMAN, D., 'FDIC and FSLIC Pursuit of Claims Against Officers, Directors and Others Involved with Failed Lenders', 58 Miss L.J. 89 (1988)

CLARK, R., 'The Duties of the Corporate Debtor to Its Auditors', 90 Harv. L. Rev. 505 (1977)

COCHEO, S., 'Is It a Bank? Is It a Thrift? It's a Colossal Flanking Maneuver', *ABA Banking Journal* 87, No. 5 (1995)

COLE AND GUNTHUER, 'Separating the Likelihood and Timing of Bank Failure', 19 *Journal of Banking and Finance* (September 1995)

COMMENT, the Banking Act of 1933 in Operation and the Contemplated Modifications, 8 St. John's L. Rev. 434 (1934)

COOKE, A., 'Note, Shareholders' Rights of Recovery When Banks Fail: Why the FDIC Should Not Receive Priority', 11 Ann. Rev. Banking L. 449 (1992)

CORRIGAN, MATTINGLY AND TAYLOR, 'The Federal Reserves' Views on BCCI', 26 Int'l Law. 936 (1992)

COURTNEY, M., 'The Great Loss: Analyzing the Northeast Banking Crisis', *Business Credit* 93, No. 6 (June 1991)

CRANE, D., 'Double Dipping: Congressional Tax Policy and the Savings and Loan Crisis, 13 Virginia Tax Rev. 101 (Spring 1993)

CURRY, BLALOCK AND COLE, 'The Relative Efficiency of Public Versus Private Management of Distressed Real Estate', *Journal of the American Real Estate and Urban Economics Association* 19, No. 4 (Winter 1991)

CURRY AND ROSE, 'Thrift Strategies after FIRREA: A Cluster Analysis of High Performance Institutions', *Journal of Business* 49, No. 3 (1997)

DEVITO, M., 'Slower Growth Forecasted for New England Financial Institutions', 10 January 1989

DIAZ-ALEJANDRO, C., 'Goodbye Financial Repression, Hello Financial Crash', *Journal of Development Economics* 19 (1983)

DIMSDALE, N., 'Banks, Capital Markets and the Monetary Transmission Mechanism', 10 *Oxford Review of Economic Policy* (Winter 1994)

DRISCOLL, L., 'For New CEO, A Year of Living Dangerously', *New England Business* 11, No. 9 (September 1989)

ECCARD AND GROSSHANDLER, 'Qualified Financial Contracts with FDIC-Insured Banks and Thrifts', 7 Rev. of Banking & Finan. Services 49 (1991)

EISENBEIS AND HORVITZ, 'The Role of Forbearance and Its Costs in Handline Troubled and Failed Depository Institutions', *Reforming Financial Institutions in the United States* (1993)

ENGLAND, C., 'Agency Costs and Unregulated Banks: Could Depositors Protect Themselves', 7 Cato J. 770 (1988)

ENGLERT, 'Bank Supervision in Historical Perspective', 34 Bus. Law 1659 (1979)

EPSTEIN, G., 'The Triple Debt Crisis', *World Policy Journal* (Commentary) (Winter 1986)

EPSTEIN AND FERGUSON, 'Monetary Policy, Loan Liquidation and Industrial Conflict: The Federal Reserve and the Open Market Operations of 1932', *Journal of Economic History* (December 1984)

FELSENFELD, C., 'The Savings and Loan Crisis', in Annual Survey Issue, *Financial Institutions and Regulations, The S&L Crisis: Death and Transfiguration* (May 1991)

FEIN, M., 'Emerging Banking System is Unique but Changes to Law May Adopt Western Standards', Russia & Commonwealth Bus. L. Rep., 11 January 1993, Lexis, Nexis Lib. Int'l File.

FELDSTEIN, M., 'A Self-Help Guide for Emerging Markets', *Foreign Affairs*, Vol. 78, No. 2 (March–April 1999)

FELDSTEIN, M., 'Refocusing the IMF', *Foreign Affairs* (March–April 1998)

FISCHEL, D., 'Regulation of Banks and Bank Holding Companies', 73 Va. L. Rev. 301 (1987)

FLANNERY AND SORESCU, 'Evidence of Bank Market Discipline in Subordinated Debenture Yields: 1983–1991', *Journal of Finance* 51, No. 4 (September 1996)

FLINT, R., 'Why D'Oench Duhme? An Economic Legal and Philosophical Critique of a Failed Bank Policy', 26 Val. U.L. Rev. 465 (1992)

FRENCH, G., 'Early Corrective Action for Troubled Banks', *FDIC Banking Review* 4, No. 2 (1991)

FREUND AND SEELIG, 'Commercial Real-Estate Problems: A Note on Changes in Collateral Values Backing Real-Estate Loans Being Managed by the Federal Deposit Insurance Corporation', *FDIC Banking Review* 6, No. 1 (Spring/Summer 1993)

GAIL, D., AND NORTON, J., 'A Decade's Journey from 'Deregulation' to 'Supervisory Reregulation': The Financial Institutions Reform, Recovery and Enforcement Act of 1989', *Business Lawyer* 45, No. 3 (1990)

GAIL, D., NORTON, J., AND O'NEAL, M., 'The Foreign Bank Supervision Act of 1991: Expanding the Umbrella of 'Supervisory Deregulation',' 26 Int'l Law 993 (1992)

GALVES, F., 'FDIC and RTC Special Powers in Failed Bank Litigation', 22 Colo. Law 473 (1993)

GALVES, F., 'Might Does Not Make Right: The Call for Reform of the Federal Government's D'Oench Duhme and 12 USC sec. 1823(e), Superpowers in Failed Bank Litigation', 80 Minn. L. Rev. 1323 (1996)

GARASON, R., 'Comptroller Plans to Issue Rules to Ease Core Capital Confusion', 11 September 1989

GARCIA, G., 'The FSLIC Is "Broke" in More Ways Than One', *Cato Journal* 7, No. 3 (1988)

GARTEN, 'A Political Analysis of Bank Failure Resolution', 74 B.U.L. Rev. 429 (1994)

GARTEN, H., 'Symposium: Scholarship in Banking Law – What Price Failure?', 50 Ohio L.J. (1989)

GARTEN, H., 'Lessons for the Next Financial Crisis', Foreign Affairs, Vol. 78, No. 2 (March/April 1999)

Garten, H., 'Universal Banking and Financial Stability', 19 Brook J. Int'l L. 159 (1993)

GARTEN, H., 'Whatever Happened to Market Discipline of Banker?', 1991 Ann. Surv. Am. L. 749 (1992)

GASTON AND STOUCK, 'OTS Argument That FIRREA Relieves Regulators of Binding Contractual commitments is Bad Policy', 55 BNA Banking Rep. 861 (1990)

GATTO, J., 'Branches, Subsidiaries and Foreign Bank Insolvencies', 7 Comp. Bus. & Cap. Mkt. L. 173 (1985)

GAY, TIMME AND YUNG, 'Bank Failure and Contagion Effects: Evidence from Hong Kong', *Journal of Financial Research* 14 (Summer 1991)

GOLD, J., 'Public International Law in the International Monetary System', 38 Southwest Law J. 799 (1984)

GOLD, J., 'Strengthening the Soft International Law of Exchange Arrangements', 77 Amer. J. Int'l Law 443 (1983)

GOLEMBE, C., 'Commentary: A Little Moral Hazard', 8 Banking Expansion Rep. p. 4, 5 (1989)

GOLEMBE, C., 'FDICIA: A Mean-Spirited, Special-Interest Measure Without Redeeming Features, 11 No. 21 Banking Pol'y Rep 2 (November 1992)

GOODE, R., 'Insolvency Implications for Banks', Chapter 7, of *The Single Market & Law of Banking 1992* (R. Cranston (ed.), 1992) (2nd edn, 1995)

GORTON, G., 'Cleaning Houses and the Original Central Banking in the United States', 1985 J. Econ. Hist. 277

GORTON AND ROSEN, 'Corporate Control, Portfolio Choice and the Decline of Banking', *Journal of Finance* 50, No. 5 (December 1995)

GRAHAM AND HUMPHREY, 'Bank Examination Data as Predictors of Bank Net Loan Losses', *Journal of Money, Credit and Banking* 10, No. 4 (1978)

GROSSMAN AND MILLER, 'Liquidity and Market Structure', 43 J. Fin. 617 (1988)

GUTTENTAG AND HERRING, 'Disaster Myopia in International Banking', Princeton Essays in Int'l Fin. No. 164 (1986)

HALL, H., 'Developments in Banking Law: 1992', 12 Ann. Rev. Banking L. 189 (1993)

HANISCH, H., 'Cross Border Insolvency: Comparative Dimensions', *Survey of Some Laws on Cross Border Effects of Foreign Insolvency Procedures on the European Continent* (I.F. Fletcher (ed.), 1990)

HARAF, W., 'Toward a Sound Financial System', 7 Cato J. 677 (1988)

HENDERSHOTT AND KANE, 'Causes and Consequences of the 1980s Commercial Construction Boom', *Journal of Applied Corporate Finance* (Spring 1992)

HESTER, D., 'Special Interests: The FINE Situation', *Journal of Money, Credit and Banking* 9 (November 1977)

HIRSCHHORN AND ZERVOS, 'Policies to Change the Priority of Claimants: The Case of Depositor Preference Laws', *Journal of Financial Services Research* 4 (1990)

HORVITZ, P., 'Book Review: Fear of Failing', 4 Yale J. on Reg. 503 (1987)

HUBER, S., 'The Competitive Equality Banking Act of 1987: An Analysis and Critical Commentary', *Banking Law Journal* 105, No. 4 (1988)

HUTNYAN, J., 'Congressional Support Seems to Grow for Crisis Mergers', Am. Banker, 1 October 1981

HUTNYAN, J., 'Desertions on Rescue Bill Question Validity of Thrift Crisis', Am. Banker, 5 June 1981

HUTNYAN, J., 'Two "Thrift" Bills Likely to Dominate Washington', Am. Banker, 28 August 1981

HYMANSON, M., 'Borrower Beware: D'Oench, Duhme and Section 1823 Overprotect the Insurer When Banks Fail', 62 S. Cal. L. Rev. 253 (1988)

ISAAC, W., 'The Role of Deposit Insurance in The Emerging Financial Services Industry', 1 Yale J. on Reg. 195 (1984)

JACKSON, H., 'Losses From National Bank Failure During the Great Depression: A Response to Professors Macey and Miller', 28 Wake Forest L. Rev. 919 (1993)

JAKUBIK, M., 'FDIC Claims of Priority in the Case of the Failed Bank', 36 Vill. L. Rev. 1151 (1991)

JAMES, C., 'Some Evidence on the Uniqueness of Bank Loans', J. of Fin. Econ. (1987)

JAMES, C., 'The Losses Realized in Bank Failures', 46 J. Fin. 1223 (1991)

JONES AND KING, 'The Implementation of Prompt Corrective Action: An Assessment', *Journal of Banking and Finance* 19 (June 1995)

JOURDAN AND ENTREKEN, 'Appraisal Management in Today's Regulatory Environment', *The Appraisal Journal* (January 1993)

KANE, E., 'Corporate Capital and Government Guarantees', 5 J. of Fin. Services Res. 357 (1992)

KANE, E., 'De Jure Interstate Banking: Why Only Now?', *Journal of Money, Credit and Banking* 28, No. 2 (1996)

KANE, E., 'Difficulties of Transferring Risk-Based Capital Requirements to Developing Countries', *Pacific-Basin Finance Journal* 3

KANE AND YU, 'Opportunity Cost of Capital Forbearance During the Final Years of the FSLIC Mess', *Quarterly Review of Economics and Finance* 36, No. 3 (Fall 1996)

KAUFMAN, G., 'Are Some Banks Too Large to Fail? Myth and Reality', *Contemporary Policy Issues*, Vol. 8 (October 1990)

KAUFMAN, G., 'Bank Runs: Causes, Benefits and Costs', 7 Cato J. 559 (1988)

KAUFMAN, G., 'Bank Contagion: A Review of the Theory and Evidence', *Journal of Financial Services Research* 8, No. 2 (April 1994)

KAUFMAN AND MOTE, 'Glass-Steagall: Repeal by Regulatory and Judicial Reinterpretation', *Banking Law Journal* 107, No. 5 (1990)

KEELEY, M., 'Deposit Insurance, Risk and Market Power in Banking', 80 Am. Econ. Rev. (December 1990)

KIMBALL AND JAMES, 'Regulation and the Determination of Bank Capital Changes: A Note', *Journal of Finance* 38, No. 5 (1983)

LANE, LOONEY AND WANSLEY, 'An Application of the Cox Proportional Hazards Model to Bank Failure', *Journal of Banking and Finance* 10 (1986)

LANGBEIN, S., 'The Thrift Crisis and the Constitution', 53 Washington & Lee L. Rev. 159 (1996)

LARR AND RIEBE, 'Real Estate Appraisals: Recommendations to Reduce Risk', *The Journal of Commercial Bank Lending* (May 1966)

LEVINE, R., 'Legal Environment, Banks and Long-Run Economic Growth: Comparative Financial Systems', 30 *Journal of Money, Credit and Banking*, No. 3 (August 1998)

LEVINTHAL, 'The Early History of Bankruptcy Law', 66 U. Pa. L. Rev.

LICHTENSTEIN, C., 'The U.S. Response to the International Debt Crisis: The International Lending Supervision Act of 1983', 25 Va. J. of Intnl. Law (1985)

MACEY, J., 'The Political Science of Regulating Bank Risk', 49 Oh St. L.J. 1277, 1284 (1989)

MACEY AND MILLER, 'Bank Failures, Risk Monitoring and The Market for Bank Control', 88 Colum. L. Rev. 1153 (1988)

MACEY AND MILLER, 'Double Liability of Bank Shareholders: History and Implications', 27 Wake Forest L. Rev. 31 (1992)

MANTRIPRAGADA, K., 'Depositors as a Source of Market Discipline', 9 Yale J. on Reg. 549 (1992)

MARKUS AND SHAKED, 'The Valuation of FDIC Deposit Insurance Using Option-Pricing Estimates', *Journal of Money, Credit and Banking* 20 (November 1984)

MARTIN, D., 'Early Warning of Bank Failure: A Logit Approach', *Journal of Banking and Finance* 1 (November 1977)

MARTIN, V., 'Appraising the Profession', *Mortgage Banking* (May 1991)

MCCORD, T., 'The Depository Institutions Deregulation and Monetary Control Act of 1980', *Issues in Bank Regulation* 3, No. 4, (1980)

MCMILLAN, H., 'What SAIF Crisis?', *ABA Banking Journal* 81 (June 1995)

MOYER AND LAMY, ''Too Big To Fail': Rationale, Consequences and Alternatives', *Business Economics* 27, No. 3 (1992)

MUSSA, M., 'Competition, Efficiency and Fairness in the Financial Services Industry', in *Deregulating Financial Services: Public Policy in Flux* 121 (1986)

NORTON, J., 'The 1982 Banking Act and the Deregulation Scheme', 38 Bus. Law. 1627 (1983)

NORTON, J., 'Bank Regulation and Supervision in the 1990s, The Changing Face of Bank Regulation and Supervision in the United States', Chapter 3 (J. Norton (ed.), Lloyd's of London Press Ltd., 1991)

NORTON, J., 'Capital Adequacy Standards: A Legitimate Concern for Prudential Supervision of Banking Activities?', 49 Ohio St. Law J. 1300, 1320 (1989)

NORTON, J., 'The Changing Face of Bank Regulation and Supervision in the United States: A Period of Supervisory Reregulation' in *Bank Regulation and Supervision in the 1990s* (J. Norton (ed.),1991)

NORTON, J., 'The Work of the Basle Supervisors Committee on Bank Capital Adequacy and the July 1988 Report on "International Convergence of Capital Measurement and Capital Standards"', 23 Int'l Law 245 (1989)

NORTON, J., 'Up Against the 'Wall': Glass-Steagall and the Dilemma of a Deregulated ('Reregulated') Banking Environment', 42 Bus. Law 327 (1987)

NORTON, J., AND OLIVE, C., 'The Ongoing Process of International Bank Regulatory and Supervisory Convergence: A New Regulatory-Market 'Partnership'', 16 Annual Rev. of Banking Law 227 (1997)

O'KEEFE, J., 'Risk-Based Capital Standards for Commercial Banks: Improved Capital Adequacy Standards?', FDIC Banking Review 6, No. 1 (1993)

OSAKWE, C., 'International Symposium 1992; Modern Russian Law of Banking and Security Transactions: A Biopsy of Post-Soviet Russian Commercial Law', 14 Whittier L. Rev. 301 (1993)

PEEK AND ROSENGREN, 'Bank Real Estate Lending and the New England Capital Crunch', *Journal of the American Real Estate and Urban Economics Association* 22 (Spring 1994)

PEEK AND ROSENGREN, 'Bank Regulatory Agreements and Real Estate Lending', *Real Estate Economics* 24 (1996)

PETTIWAY AND SINKEY, 'Establishing On-Site Bank Examination Priorities: An Early Warning System Using Accounting and Market Information', *Journal of Finance* 35 (March 1980)

PIERCE, J., 'The FINE Study', *Journal of Money, Credit and Banking* 9 (November 1977)

PRATT, R., 'No S&L Liquidity Crisis', Am. Banker, 20 May 1981

RASMUS, J., 'Capital Forbearance for Commercial Banks', *Journal of Agricultural Lending* 1, No. 4 (1988)

REISMAN, K., 'The World Bank and the IMF: At the Forefront of World Transformation', 60 *Fordham Law Review* S 349 (1992)

RILEY, J., 'Inside the Bailout: Continental Leaves a Wide Wake', *National Law Journal* (22 October 1984)

RODKEY, R., 'Banking Reform by Statute', 32 Mich. L. Rev. 881–895 (1934)

ROLLINGER, M., 'Interstate Banking and Branching Under the Riegle-Neal Act of 1994', *Harvard Journal on Legislation* 33, No. 1 (1996)

RONN AND VERMA, 'Pricing Risk Adjusted Deposit Insurance: An Option Based Model', *Journal of Finance* 41 (September 1986)

ROOT, S., 'Bank Capital, Asset Liquidation and the Credit Crunch', *Columbia Business Law Review* 169 (1993)

ROSE AND KOLARI, 'Early Warning Systems as a Monitoring Device for Bank Condition', *Quarterly Journal of Business and Economics* 24 (Winter 1985)

ROSENGREN AND PEEK, 'The Use of Capital Ratios to Trigger Intervention in Problem Banks: Too Little, Too Late', *New England Economic Review Federal Reserve Bank of Boston* (September/October 1996)

SALOMON, B., 'Savings and Loans, on the Run, Searching for a Way to Survive', *National Journal* (15 June 1985)

SAULSBURY, V., 'State Banking Powers: Where Are We Now?', *FDIC Regulatory Review* (April/March 1987)

SCHWARTZ, A., 'From Obscurity to Notoriety: A Biography of the Exchange Stabilization Fund', 29 *Journal of Money, Credit and Banking*, No. 2 (May 1997)

SCHWARTZ, A., 'Real and Pseudo-Financial Crises', *Financial Crises and the World Banking System* (Capie and Wood (eds), 1986)

SCHWEITZER, SZEWCZYK AND VARMA, 'Bond Rating Agencies and Their Role in Bank Market Discipline', *Journal of Financial Services Research* 6 (1992)

SCOTT, H., 'Supervision of International Banking Post-BCCI', 8 Ga. St. U.L. Rev. 487 (1992)

SCOTT, K., 'The Dual Banking System: A Model of Competition in Regulation', *Stanford Law Review* 30, No. 1 (1977)

SEGAL, D., 'A Note to Congress and The FDIC: After FIRREA, Where is the BIF?', 59 *Fordham Law Review* S 411 (1991)

SHARPE, W., 'Bank Capital Adequacy, Deposit Insurance and Security Values', *Journal of Financial and Quantitative Analysis* 13 (November 1978)

SHULL, B., 'Interstate Banking and Antitrust Laws: History of Public Policies to Promote Banking Competition', *Contemporary Policy Issues* 6, No. 2 (1988)

SIMPSON, M., 'Note: Scaling Back: FIRREA Federal Judges Begin to Place Limits on RTCs Conservatorship/Receiverships & Creditors of Failed Banks: Its Not a Wonderful Life', 4 Harv. L. Rev. 1052 (1991)

SINKEY, J., 'A Multivariate Statistical Analysis of the Characteristics of Problem Banks', *Journal of Finance* 30 (March 1975)

SINKEY, J., 'Identifying Large Problems! Failed Banks: The Case of Franklin National Bank of New York', 12 J. Fin. & Quantitative Analysis 779 (1977)

SLATER, K., 'U.S. Savings League Threatens to Sue Over Deregulation Actions; Charges Decisions Exceeded Congressional Mandate', Am. Banker, 29 June 1981

SMITH, T., 'Hungary Irons Out Insolvency Wrinkles', *International Corporate Law* (September, 1993)

SMITH, W., 'The General Instruments of Monetary Control', *Readings in Money, National Income and Stabilization Policy* (1965)

SOVERN, M., 'Section 4 of the Bankruptcy Act: The Excluded Corporation', 42 Minn. L. Rev. 171 (1957)

STIGLITZ, J., 'Symposium on Bubbles', *Journal of Economic Perspectives* 4, No. 2 (Spring 1990)

SUNDARARAJAN, V., 'Central Banking Reforms in Formerly Planned Economies', Fin. & Dev., March 1992, at pp. 10, 11

SWIRE, P., 'Good Old Ways Disappear in Banking Regulation', 16 Va. L. Sch. Rep. (Summer 1991)

SWIRE, P., 'Bank Insolvency Law Now That It Matters Again', 42 Duke L.J. 469 (1992)

THOMSON, J., 'Modeling the Bank Regulator's Closure Option: A Two-Step Logit Regression Approach', *Journal of Financial Services Research* 6 (1992)

TODD, F., 'Disorderly Markets: The Law, History and Economics of the Exchange Stabilization Fund and U.S. Foreign Exchange Market Intervention', *Research in Financial Services Public and Private Policy*, Vol. 4 (1992)

TUUME, D., 'Proceedings and Papers of the Symposium on Banking Law Held at NYU School of Law – April 10, 1992, Bank Regulation, Bank Accounting and Bank Failures', 1991 Ann. Surv. Am. L. 823 (1992)

TYBOUT, J., 'A Firm-level Chronicle of Financial Crises in the Southern Cone', *Journal of Development Economics* 24

VINCENS, J., 'On the Demise of Double Liability of Bank Shareholders', 75 Banking L.J. 213 (1958)
VYSMAN, I., 'Note: The New Banking Legislation in Russia: Theoretical Adequacy, Practical Difficulties and Potential Solutions', 62 *Fordham Law Review* 265 (1993)
WADE, A., 'Bank of New England's Woes', *United States Banker* 98, No. 7 (July 1989)
WARREN, E., 'Bankruptcy Policy', 54 Univ. of Chicago L. Rev. 775 (1987)
WERDT, 'The Role of Foreign Banks in International Banking', in Michael P. Malloy, *The Regulation of Banking Cases and Materials, Depository Institutions and Their Regulators* 821 (1992)
WILMARTH, A. JR., 'The Expansion of State Bank Powers, the Federal Response and the Case for Preserving the Dual Banking System', 58 *Fordham Law Review*, No. 6 (1990)
WILMARTH, A. JR., 'Too Big to Fail; Too Few to Serve? The Potential Risks of Nationwide Banks', 77 Iowa L. Rev. 957 and 1159 (1989)
WINER, 'Repudiation of Contracts Under FIRREA', 8 Rev. of Banking & Finan. Services 31 (1992)
ZISMAN AND SPEARS, 'FDIC/RTC Powers: Effect on Creditors and Shareholders', 7 Rev. of Banking & Fin. Serv. 41 (1991)
'The Aftermath of Penn Square Bank: Protecting Loan Participants from Setoffs' (Essay), 18 Tulsa L.J. 261 (1982)
'Bank Destructuring in Central and Eastern Europe: Issues and Strategies', Fin. Market Trends, February 1992, at p. 15
'Changes to Law May Adopt Western Standards', Russia & Commonwealth Bus. L. Rep., 11 January 1993, Lexis, Nexis Lib. Int'l File
'Current Legislation Affecting the Reorganization and Regulation of Banks' (Legislation), 34 Colum. L. Rev. 152 (1934)
'Legal Devices for the Rehabilitation of Banks' (Legislation), 32 Colum. L. Rev. 1395 (1932)
Note, 109 Banking L.J. 373 (1992)
'Symposium on FINE Study', *Journal of Money, Credit and Banking* 9, No. 4 (1977)

NEWSPAPERS, PRESS RELEASES AND NEWS SERVICES, MAGAZINE ARTICLES, CONFERENCES, UNPUBLISHED AND MISCELLANEOUS AND INTERNET MATERIALS

A. Newspapers

Barron's
MAHAR, M., 'The Great Collapse, Commercial Real Estate is on the Skids Across the Nation', 22 July 1991

Drysdale Securities
WELLES, C., 'Drysdale: What Really Happened, Institutional Investor', September 1982

Financial Times
RIDDELL & LASCELLES, 'JMB Rescue Revealed Weaknesses: Lawson Orders Full Review of Britain's Banking Supervision', 18 December 1984

Financial World
WILLOUGHBY, J., 'Playing Doctor', 31 May 1992

Houston Post
ELLIS, H., 'Families in Middle of Profit Scramble by Oil Firms, OPEC', 28 February 1979
O'GRADY, E., 'Soft East-Estate Market Bad News for Banks', 23 April 1984
PEACOCK, D., 'Price Boosts Will Hasten Exploration', 21 October 1973
'Real Estate's Upturn to Lag, Parley Hears', 21 January 1983

Metro Business
KORZENIOWSKI, P., 'Distress for Success', Danvers, MA, October 1990

New Orleans Business
SWARTZ AND SLUDER, 'LA. Banks Battle Tough Times for Profits, Equity', 3 February 1986

New York Times
BENNETT, R., 'Continental Fighting Rumors', 11 May 1984
GREENHOUSE, L., 'High Court Finds Rule Shift by U.S. Did Harm to S&Ls', 2 July 1996
LABATON., S. 'U.S. Bailout Hurt by Weakness of Insurance Fund', 25 November 1991
LOHR, S. 'U.N. Study Assails the Way BCCI Was Shut Down by Western Central Banks', 5 February 1992
MARTIN, D., 'Penn Square's Oil Connection', 19 July 1982
QUINT, M., 'Northeast Banks Face Heavy Losses on Problem Loans', 15 December 1989
QUINT, M., 'A Crystal Ball for Banking's Ills', 12 January 1991
REINHOLD, R., 'Desperation Descends on Oklahoma', 11 May 1986
'"Smart Money Bank": What Went Wrong', 18 May 1984

The Record
LOWRY, T., 'Howard Savings Bank Fails; First Fidelity Buys Its Assets', 3 October 1992

Tulsa World
MCUSIC, T., 'Bank Closings to Continue', 26 February 1988

UPI
TAHMINCIOGLU, E., 'Dollar Dry Dock Bank Placed in Receivership', 21 February 1992

USA Today
FETTERMAN, M., 'NCNB Chairman Hugh McColl Touts His High-Rise's Success, Despite Banking's Towering Real-Estate Woes', 28 May 1991

Wall Street Journal
BAILEY AND ZASLOW, 'Continental Illinois Securities Plummet Amid Rumors Firm's Plight is Worsening', 11 May 1984

BARRETT, J., 'High Court Backs S&Ls on Accounting, Declines to Hear Affirmative-Action Case', 2 July 1996
BARTLEY, R., 'Nixon's Worst Weekend', 15 August 1991
BLEAKLEY, F., 'Banks Fund Their Sources of Capital Drying Up', 8 October 1990
HARDY, QUENTIN, 'Yen Gains Acceptance for Global Use', 18 May 1993
KING, R., 'Another Houston: Real-Estate Developers See the Next Disaster in Central Los Angeles', 27 August 1991
KING, R., JR., 'New Bank Behemoth Has Big Burdens, Rich Potential', 23 April 1992
MACEY, J., 'Needless Nationalization of the FDIC', 14 February 1992
MCCOY AND SUSKIND, 'FDIC's Expected Losses Reflect Slump in Northeast: Increase in Reserves Stems from the Agency's Fear of Major Bank Failures', 20 December 1990
MCCOY AND THOMAS, 'Ongoing Fiasco. Hundreds of S&Ls Fall Hopelessly Short of New Capital Rules', 7 December 1989
MEISELMAN, D., 'The Political Monetary Cycle', 10 January 1984
ROSETT, C. 'Obstacle to Reform: Rooted in Soviet Past, Russia's Central Bank Lacks Grasp Basics', 23 September 1993
Schmitt, R., 'Judge Orders U.S. to Pay $908.9 Million To California Thrift Glendale Federal', 12 April 1999
SORENSON, L., 'In the Highflying Field of Energy Finance, Continental Illinois Bank is Striking It Rich', 18 September 1981
STEIN, H., 'My Price Control Days with Nixon', 16 August 1991
THOMAS, P., 'Commercial Building, In a Huge Oversupply, May Hobble Recovery', 17 May 1991
TORRES, C., 'Credit Crunch, the Banking Disaster in Mexico Whipsaws an Ailing Economy', 25 January 1996
'Howard Savings Bank: Net Losses in Fourth Period Narrowed to $6.3 Million', 28 January 1992
'On the Offensive', 15 October 1981

Washington Post
BEHR AND ROWEN, 'Fall in Price of Oil Hurts U.S. Fields; Drop in Drilling, Permanent Loss of Production Apparent', 9 March 1986
KNIGHT, J., 'FDIC's 'Hospital' Plan a Bitter Pill for Some; Government Takeover of Ailing CrossLand Savings Bank Called Unfair, Uneconomical', 1 March 1992
MARANISS, D., 'Oil Slump's Damage Spreading; Academic, Social, Cultural Advances Threatened in Three Energy States; Recovery May Take Years', 9 April 1986

B. Press Releases and News Services

FDIC Press Release 8-92, 24 January 1992
FDIC Press Release, 9 September 1988
FDIC Press Release, 6 January 1991
US Newswire: 'CrossLand Savings, Brooklyn, Placed in Receivership; Depositors Protected', 24 January 1992

C. Magazine Articles

ABA Banking Journal
'"Thrifty" Jersey Bank Sticks to Home Loans', September 1991

American Banker
ALBERT, A., 'Comptroller's Office Throws a Bash', 4 November 1983
ALBERT, A., 'Securities Industry Sues to Void Broker Rules', 13 April 1984
ALBERT AND NORTON, 'Out-of-State Buyers Eyed for Midland: Regulators Set to Deal if Texas Banks Cool', 14 October 1983
ALBERT AND RINGER, 'Dallas County Housing Glut Hurts Local Lenders; Empire Savings Cited as One of Several S&Ls that Financed "Real Estate Monster"', 20 March 1984
BASCH, 'Seigman Takes a Conciliatory Stance on Brokered Deposits, But Plans Curbs', 6 November 1985
BENNETT, A., 'Diversity, Caution Help Texas Weather Farm Crisis in Good Shape', 18 November 1985
BRENNER, L., 'Chicago Giant's Top Holder Isn't Fazed: Battermarch Financial Management Still Owns 2 Million Shares', 23 May 1984
COPE, D., 'Did Pratt's Piloting Sink S&L Industry?', 1 October 1990
COPE D., 'FDIC Pays Its Biggest Bank-Failure Tab', 2 January 1991
EASTON, N., *ET AL.*, 'Shaky Real Estate Loans Hitting Banks', 4 June 1987
EASTON AND NAYLOR, 'At Last, Relief is in Sight for the Nation's S&L Fund', 27 May 1986
EASTON AND NAYLOR, 'Thrift Group Attacks FSLIC Bailout: But US League Opposition to Treasury Plan Faces Uphill Battle', 15 December 1986
EVANS, J., 'The 8% Capital Rule, Still a Year Off, Has Impact Now', 28 November 1990
FOCER, A., 'Savings Banks Get FDIC Protection', 27 October1986
FORDE, J., '"New" Bank of New England's Rosy Prospects', 19 December 1985
GARSSON, R., '100th Congress Preps for Financial Service Struggle: FSLIC Aid Still Dominates Hill Agenda, While Industry's Divisions Remain Keen', 5 January 1987
GARSSON, R., 'Japanese Banks are Raised on a Precipice', 27 July 1992
GOODWIN, W., 'Troubled Assets Soared by 20% Last Year at the 25 Biggest Banks', 8 February 1991
GROSS AND MATTHEWS, 'FDIC Assures on Greenwich; Tells Depositors Funds Are Safe; Seeks Buyers', 30 October 1981
HAWKE, J., 'Fed Needs New Approach to Real Estate', 16 August 1989
HECTOR, G., 'Keefe Warns on State of Savings Bank Industry; Urges Federal Assistance Now', 9 December 1980
HORN, C., 'Early Intervention, Monster Needs Training', 24 December 1991
HOROWITZ, J., 'Grapevine: That Connolly "Chute"', 31 January 1990
HOROWITZ, J., 'How the Acquisition by Fleet Will Work', 24 April 1991
HUTNYAN, J., 'Rescue the Thrifts and You Question Reaganomics', 26 February 1982
HUTNYAN, J., 'Thrift Rescue Plans Getting Serious', 12 February 1982
KLAMAN, S., 'The Changing World of the Savings Bank Industry', 23 October 1978

KLEEGE, S., 'Fate of Banking in the 1990s Hinges on Real Estate Loans', 15 October 1990
LAVINE, A., 'Bank of New England Corp. Takes Its Name Seriously with Ambitious Acquisition Strategy in Four States', 2 September 1986
LEANDER, T., 'New England Graveyard Tour: Here Lie Nonperforming Loans', 12 September 1990
LUKE, R., 'Japanese Banks Tackle California Middle Market', 10 September 1988
MATTHEWS, G., 'FDIC Chase Used Threats, Coercion on Penn Square', 17 October 1983
MATTHEWS, G., 'New Jersey Banks Won't Rebound Anytime Soon, Rating Agency Says', 16 November 1990
MCCARTHY, J., 'In Moscow, A Banking Revolution', 8 November 1991
MCCORMICK, L., 'Comptroller Begins Major Revamp', 29 April 1982
MCCORMICK, L., 'Reagan Council Endorses Aids to Thrifts But Bars Direct Bailout', 27 April 1982
MCCORMICK, L., 'Volcker Says No to Thrift Bailout', 2 March 1982
MCCUE, L., 'Agencies Propose Broker Limits', 17 January 1984
MORRIS, J., 'Banks of Mid-America Treads Water, Waits for Cheap-Oil Flood to Subside', 30 April 1986
NEUSTADT D., 'Bank of Boston Acts to Stem Losses: Team Moves Fast to Spot and Work Out Sour Loans', 5 December 1989
NEUSTADT, D., 'Jersey Braces for Lending Slowdown; Vacancy Rates Drop, But So Does Demand for Space', 21 November 1989
REHM, B., 'Banks Binging Despite Realty Hangover', 8 March 1990
REHM, B., 'Fed Policy for Frequency and Scope of Examinations of State Member Banks and Inspections of Bank Holding Companies', 10 October 1985
REHM, B., 'Fed Weighs Restrictions on Real Estate', 3 November 1987
REHM, B., *ET AL.*, 'For FDIC, Bolstering the Economy Was Key', 8 January 1991
REHM, B., 'House Measure May Foil Fed Efforts to Gain Control of State Bank Limits', 10 April 1989
RINGER, R., 'Drop in Oil Prices Worries Banks in Texas and Oklahoma: Biggest Energy Lenders Construct Damage Scenarios While Waiting for Volatile Market to Stabilize', 18 February 1986
RINGER, R., 'NY Bank Profit Disappointing as Loans Falter', 8 February 1991
RINGER, R., 'States Rush to Deregulate', 9 May 1983
RINGER, R., 'Volcker Urges Care on Deregulation', 10 May 1983
ROOSEVELT P., 'Dollar Dry Dock Seeking to Raise $50 Million in Capital, Shed Assets', 10 October 1991
ROOSEVELT, P., 'Home Loan Defaults Rise in Northeast: Region Shows Foreclosure Gains as US Figure Decreases', 22 June 1989
ROOSEVELT AND REHM, 'CrossLand Seized as Regulators Reject Bids', 27 January 1992
ROSE, S., 'A Well-Heeled Gambler's Half-Hearted Reformation', 18 August 1981
ROSEY, S., 'Time to Acknowledge Truth About Bank Fund', 31 January 1992
ROTHSTEIN, J. 'Comptroller May Tighten Chartering Process', 12 October 1983

ROTHSTEIN, J., 'Garn Tells Commercial Banks to Quit Griping About Thrifts', 21 October 1981
ROTHSTEIN, J. 'House Committee Delays Vote on Thrift Emergency Bill, Skeptical Members Say Regulators Have Yet to Make Their Case For It', 3 October 1981
ROTHSTEIN, J., 'Move is on to Revive Bank and Thrift Aid', 3 August 1981
ROTHSTEIN, J., 'Regulators Revise Crisis Merger Legislation, 27 May 1981
ROTHSTEIN, J., 'Volcker Presses for Interstate, Interindustry Acquisitions; Warns Congress That Authority is Needed to Act on Troubled Thrifts', 2 October 1981
SLATER, K., 'Mutuals Ask for Capital Aid; FDIC Resisting Action', 14 August 1981
SNYDER, C. JR., 'Let's Not Compel Commercial Lenders to Mark to Market', 14 August 1991
SUDO, P., 'Small Banks Add to Chorus Against Glass-Steagall Reform', 2 March 1987
TRIGAUX, R., 'Congressional Study Calls Thrift Insurance Fund Fragile: Future Health Remains Closely Tied to Continued Low Level of Interest Rates, GAO Says', 7 December 1983
WEINER AND FORDE, 'Oil Price Drop Having Little Effect on Banks: Industry Well Insulated Against Price Changes, Analysts Say', 12 December 1985
WEINER AND RINGER, 'Falling Oil Prices Could Bleed Portfolios of Energy Banks', 22 January 1986
WEINSTEIN, M., 'New England Banks Finance a Healthy Real Estate Market', 4 June 1987
WEINSTEIN, M., 'Real Estate Joins Energy in Harrying Texas Banks; As Energy Chargeoffs Diminish Real Estate Problems Grow', 2 May 1986
ZWEIG, P., '37 Bank Openings in Texas This Month to Set Record', 4 January 1983
ZWEIG, P., 'Brokered Penn Square Funds Soared Just Before Collapse', 19 November 1982
'As Oil Prices Continue to Slide, Texas Banks Confront a Grim '86: Further Deterioration Expected in Energy and Real Estate Lending', 11 February 1986
'Farm Banks in Texas Beginning to Feel Lending Sting All Too Familiar to Their Midwestern Counterparts', 1 May 1986
'A New Wave of Fear Washes Over Midland: Business Community Afraid the FDIC Will Foreclose on Many Loans', 9 November 1983
'Will Success Spoil Continental Illinois?', 25 August 1981

Bankers' Magazine
1980–1991

Bankers' Monthly
ARVAN, A., 'The Regionals That Roar', May 1988

Banking Expansion Reporter
1982–1991

Banking Frontier
PRICE, D., 'A Mission to Moscow', 29 July 1992

Barron's
LISCIO, J., 'Star-Crossed CrossLand: But a Recap Plan Could Revive the Thrift's Prospects', 30 April 1990
'All Debits, No Credits: A Hard Look at the Government's Takeover of Continental Illinois', 30 July 1984

BNA's Banking Report
1987–1996

Bottomline
WOLFF, M., 'CrossLand Savings, Before and After', March 1989

Business Week
JERESKI, L., 'A Stomachache for the Bank that Ate New England', 5 February 1990
KERWIN, SCHINE AND BUELL, 'Golden State Worriers', 14 May 1990
LIGHT AND MEEHAN, 'The Walls Keep Closing in on New York Developers', 2 July 1990
MEEHAN, J., *ET AL.*, 'For Banks, the Panic is Coming to an End', 17 June 1991
SMITH, G., 'Lawrence Fish's Best May Not Be Good Enough', 22 October 1990
WALLACE, G., 'The 'Wild Bunch' at Penn Square; Funny Money', 27 May 1985
'Continental Ilinois' Most Embarrassing Year', 11 October 1982
'Continental Illinois Sails into a Calm', 14 May 1979
'The Stain from Penn Square Keeps Spreading', 2 August 1982

Credit Union Management
RADLOFF, K., 'Putting the Brakes on Drive-by Appraisals', October 1990

Dun's Review
'Here Comes Continental', 112, No. 6, 1978

Economist
'Bank of New England: Here We Go?', 12 January 1991
'Chain Letter from Penn Pal In Oklahoma City', 10 July 1982
'International Banking: America the Laboratory', 26 March 1988
'Oklahoma Oil and Gas; This Time the Hurting Won't Heal', 21 August 1982

Euromoney
'Banker of the Year', October 1981
'Bank Restructuring in Central & Eastern Europe: Issues and Strategies', February 1992
Financial Market Trends

Forbes
RUDNITSKY, H., 'Where is the Bottom?', 17 September 1990

Foreign Affairs
DRUCKER, P., 'The Changed World Economy', Spring 1986
FELDSTEIN, M., 'Refocusing the IMF', March–April 1998
KUCZYNSKI, P., 'Latin American Debt', Winter 1982–1983

Fortune
EHRBAR, A., 'Toil and Trouble and Continental Illinois', 7 February 1983
FROMSON, B., 'The Screwiest S&L Bailout Ever', 19 June 1989

McCOMAS, M., 'More Capital Won't Cure What Ails Banks', 7 January 1985
ROWE, F., 'Texas Has a Lesson for the Rest of Us', 1 August 1988
SHEELINE, W., 'The Big Names in S&L Bailouts', 26 September 1988
WELCH, J., 'Jack Welch's Lessons For Success', 15 January 1995

Institutional Investor
LEWIS, J., 'The War for California', July 1990
MILLIGAN, J., 'KKR, Member FDIC', 25, No. 7, June 1991
OSBORN, N., 'Continental Illinois Shakes Up the Competition', 14, No. 10, 1980
SENDER, H., 'Japan's California Comeuppance', July 1990
TANGMAN, M., 'The Once, and Future, Banking Crisis?', November 1995
WELLES, C., 'Drysdale: What Really Happened', September 1982

Journal of Agricultural Lending
RASMUS, J., 'Capital Forbearance for Commercial Banks', No. 4

Money
SCHOENBERG, E., 'The S&L Black Hole: How It Will Suck You In', July 1990

Newsday
BENKELMAN AND O'BRIEN, 'CrossLand Bailed Out; Seized Thrift Gets $1.2B from FDIC', 25 January 1992
DUGAS, C., 'Federal Regulators to Close American Savings Bank', 12 June 1992

Newsweek
DENTZER, IPSEN & LAMPERT, 'Forgetting the Rules', 2 August 1982

Oil and Gas Investor
TOAL, B., 'Credit Where Credit Is Due', (April 1988)

People
'A Dream Dies in Texas; Once a Land of Unlimited Promise, the Lone Star State Has Lost Its Shine and Now Has a Barrel of Troubles', 10 November 1986

Savings Institutions
MORRALL, K., 'Weakening Northeast Real Estate Market Raises Concerns', 111, No. 4, April 1990
'Texas Marketers Battle High Rates and Bad Publicity', September 1988

The Atlantic
FALLOWS, J., 'A Permanent Boomtown, Houston', July 1985

The National Journal
BELLUCK, P., 'Continental Illinois Rescue May Doom FDIC Plan to Share the Insurance Risk', 11 August 1984

Thrift Advisor
August 1989 issue

Time
GREENWALD, J., 'No End In Sight', 13 August 1990
'Burying Mother; Oil Woes Break a Texas Bank', 24 October 1983

United States Banker
DODGE, R., 'The Long Road Back in Texas', July 1985
U.S. News & World Report
WALLACE, *ET AL.*, 'The Great S&L Fire Sale Bailouts', 9 January 1989

Washington Financial Reports (BNA)
1980–1991

D. Conference Materials

ABA, NATIONAL INSTITUTE, 'Multinational Commercial Insolvency'(ABA, 1993)

BARTH, BARTHOLOMEW AND LABICH, 'Moral Hazard and the Thrift Crisis: An Analysis of 1988 Resolutions', in *Proceedings of the Conference on Bank Structure and Competition*, Federal Reserve Bank of Chicago (May 1989)

BARTH, BRUMBAUGH, SAUERHAFT AND WANGE, 'Thrift Institution Failures: Causes and Policy Issues', in *Proceedings of the Conference on Bank Structure and Competition*, Federal Reserve Bank of Chicago (May 1985)

CAPRIO AND KLINGEBIEL, 'Bank Insolvency: Bad Luck, Bad Policy or Bad Banking?', paper presented at the World Bank Annual Bank Conference on Development Economics, Washington (25–26 April 1996)

DAHL, HANWECK AND O'KEEFE, 'The Influence of Auditors and Examiners on Accounting Discretion in the Banking Industry', paper presented at Academy of Financial Services Conference (October 1995)

DEGENNARO AND THOMPSON, 'Capital Forbearance and Thrifts: An Ex Post Examination of Regulatory Gambling', in *Proceedings of the Conference on Bank Structure and Competition*, Federal Reserve Bank of Chicago (May 1993)

DE JUAN, A., 'The Roots of Banking Crises: Micro economic Issues and Issues of Supervision and Regulation', Presented to the AIDB/G-30 Conference on Banking Crises in Latin America, Washington, DC (6–7 October 1995)

FISCHER AND GUEYIE, 'Financial Liberalization and Bank Solvency', paper presented at the symposium on Business Finance in Emerging Markets, held at the University of Laval, Québec (31 August–1 September 1995)

GARBER, P., 'Managing Risks to Financial Markets from Volatile Capital Flows: The Role of Prudential Regulation', Conference Paper (1995)

GAVIN AND HAUSMAN, 'The Roots of Banking Crises: The Macroeconomic Context', presented at the Conference on Banking Crises in Latin America, Washington, DC, October 1995 (1995)

HANWECK, FISSEL AND O'KEEFE, 'A Comparative Analysis of Modeling Methodologies of Financially Distressed Banking Firms', paper presented at the Financial Management Association Meetings (October 1995)

HELFER, R., 'Rules Versus Discretion in the Intervention of Troubled Financial Institutions – The United States Perspective', paper presented at the High Level Meeting on the Reform of Latin American and Caribbean Financial Systems, Caracas, Venezuela (27–28 October, 1997)

ISAAC, W., 'Depository Institutions – The Challenge of Today's Problems and Tomorrow's Opportunities', Address to the 52nd annual convention of the Independent Bankers' Association of America (16 March 1982)

McLEAN, K., 'Legislative Background of the Depository Institutions Deregulation and Monetary Control Act of 1980', in Federal Home Loan Bank Board of San Francisco, Saving and Loan Asset Management Under Deregulation: Proceedings of the Sixth Annual Conference in San Francisco, California (8–9 December 1980)
O'KEEFE AND DAHL, 'The Scheduling and Reliability of Bank Examinations: The Effects of FDICIA', paper presented at the Financial Management Association Conference (October 1995)
'Lessons From Bank Failures Worldwide', paper presented at the conference on Regulating Depository Institutions, held at Koç University, Istanbul (3 November 1995)

E. Unpublished Materials

BILLET, GARFINKEL AND O'NEILL, 'Insured Deposits, Market Discipline and the Price of Risk in Banking', unpublished paper (November 1995)
DAHL, HANWECK AND O'KEEFE, 'Audits, Exams and Accounting Integrity in Banking', unpublished paper (February 1995)
FOLKERTS-LANDAU AND GARBER, 'The New Financial Architecture: A Threat to the Markets?', Deutsche Bank Research (April 1999), on file with author
HAISTEN, W., 'The Leverage or the Last Straw in Deciding the Savings Association Industry's Future?', Financial Institutions-Banking Law Paper (1996), on file with author
PADOA-SCHIOPPA, T., 'Address to the 9th International Conference of Banking Supervisors', Stockholm (1996)
WINSTAR, 'The Leverage or the Last Straw in Deciding the Savings Industry's Future', (Fall 1996) (on file with the author)
'Blueprint for Reform: The Report of the Task Group on Regulation of Financial Services' (1984) (on file with author)

F. Miscellaneous and Internet Materials

BANK OF AMERICA, 'The California Economy in 1990: Surmounting the Challenges', *Economic and Business Outlook* (January 1990)
BENSTON, G., 'An Analysis of the Causes of Savings and Loan Failures', Monograph Series in Finance and Economics No. 1985-4/5 (New York, Salomon Brothers Center for the Study of Financial Institutions, 1985)
BERGER AND DAVIES, 'The Information Content of Bank Examinations', Working Paper 94-24, the Wharton Financial Institutions Center (1994)
BERGER, KING AND O'BRIEN, 'The Transformation of the U.S. Banking Industry: What a Long, Strange Trip It's Been', *Brookings Papers on Economic Activity* 2 (1995)
BLANCHARD AND SUMMERS, 'Perspectives on High World Real Interest Rates', *Brookings Papers on Economic Activity* 2 (1984)
BORDO, M., 'The Gold Standard, Bretton Woods and Other Monetary Regimes: An Historical Approach', National Bureau of Economic Research Working Paper No. 4310 (Cambridge, Mass., April 1993)

BORDO, SIMARD AND WHITE, 'France and the Bretton Woods International Monetary System: 1960–1968', National Bureau of Economic Research, Working Paper No. 4642 (Cambridge, Mass., February 1994)

CARRON, A., 'The Plight of the Thrift Institutions' (Washington D.C., Brookings Institution, 1982)

CB COMMERCIAL TORTO/WHEATON RESEARCH, *The Office Outlook*, Vols. 1 and 2 (Fall 1995)

CORRIGAN, E., 'How Central Banks Manage Financial Crises', An Address by E. Gerald Corrigan, Chairman, International Advisors, Goldman, Sachs & Co., Shanghai, China (October 25, 1995) (available at <http://www.gsco.com/about/speeches/shanghai.html>)

ELY, B., 'The Role of Accounting in the S&L Crisis'(Washington D.C., National Commission on Financial Institution Reform, Recovery and Enforcement, 1993)

E&Y KENNETH LEVENTHAL REAL ESTATE GROUP, '1993 Japanese Disinvestment in U.S. Real Estate', unpublished paper (1994)

FELDSTEIN, M., 'Self-Protection for Emerging Market Economies', NBER Working Paper No. 6907 (National Bureau of Economic Research: 1999)

GORTON, G., 'Banking Panics and Business Cycles', Oxford Economic Papers, No. 40 (December 1988)

HALSTEN, M., 'Winstar: The Leverage of the Last Straw in Deciding the Savings Association Industry's Future?', Financial Institutions – Banking Law Paper (1996) (on file with author)

HENSLEY, D., 'Where Concerns Mount, Growth Continues', UCLA Business Forecasting Project (March 1990)

KPMG PEAT MARWICK, Financial Institutions Reform, Recovery and Enforcement Act of 1989: Implications for the Industry (1989)

KRUGMAN, P., 'What Happened to Asia?', available on PK home page at <http://web.mit.edu/krugman/www/DISINTER.html>

MAYER, M., 'Risk Reduction in the New Financial Architecture: Realities, Fallacies, and Proposals', Working Paper No. 268, Jerome Levy Economics Institute, Bard College (1999) (available at <http://www.levy.org/docs/workpap/papers/268.html>)

NATIONAL ASSOCIATION OF MUTUAL SAVINGS BANKS, *Mutual Savings Banking: Basic Characteristics and Role in the National Economy* (1962)

NATIONAL COUNCIL OF REAL ESTATE INVESTMENT FIDUCIARIES AND THE FRANK RUSSELL COMPANY, The Russell-NCREIF Real Estate Performance Report (Fourth Quarter, 1994)

NATIONAL COUNCIL OF SAVINGS INSTITUTIONS, 1986 National Fact Book of Savings Institutions (1986)

NORTON, J., 'Recent Developments in the Regulation and Supervision of U.S. Financial Institutions: The Evolution of Capital Adequacy Standards and the Financial Institutions Reform, Recovery and Enforcement Act of 1989 (FIRREA)', Institute of European Finance, Research Monographs in Banking and Finance No. 92/12, Norton IEF Monograph

PACIFIC GAS AND ELECTRIC, *Economic Outlook* (May 1993)

POZDENA, R., 'Why Home Prices Don't Fall (Much)', FRBSF (4 January 1991)

SALEM AND WANG, 'California Banking: Industry Outlook', Prudential-Bache Securities (15 October 1990)

SMITH, BARNEY, California Banking Report (18 October 1990)
WELLS FARGO, Annual Report (1980–1994)
WOJNILOWER, A., 'The Central Role of Credit Crunches in Recent Financial History', *Brookings Economic Papers*, 2: 1980 (Brookings Institution, 1980)
'Banking Agencies Adopt Uniform Interagency Bank Soundness Rating System', 1978–1979 Transfer Binder, Fed. Banking L. Rep. (CCH) (11 May 1978)
'Capital Standards Interagency Differences in Bank and Thrift Capital Standards', *Banking Expansion Reporter* (3 September 1990)
'Memorandum re: Depositor Preference, Insurance Costs and the Cost of Supervision', *The Golembe Reports* 2 (1994)
The NCREIF Real Estate Performance Report, Third Quarter, 1996
National Fact Book of Mutual Savings Banking (1980–1981)
National Real Estate Index, Market History Reports, 1985–1993 (1994)
Notice to Practitioners, Certain Real Estate Lending Activities of Financial Institutions (November 1983)
Notice to Practitioners, 'ADC Loans' (November 1984)
Notice to Practitioners, 'ADC Arrangements' (November 1986)
The Russell-NCREIF Real Estate Performance Report, Third Quarter, 1992

US STATUTES, REGULATIONS AND CASES

A. Statutes

Banking Act of 1933, Pub. L. No. 73-66, 48 Stat. 168 (1933)
Banking Act of 1935, 49 Stat. 684 (1935)
Competitive Equality Banking Act of 1987 (CEBA), Pub. L. No. 100-86, 100 Stat. 552 (1987)
Crime Control Act 1990, Pub. L. No. 101-647, tit. XXV, subtit. B, 104 Stat. 4789, 4863 (1990)
Depository Institutions Deregulation and Monetary Control Act of 1980 (DIDMCA), Pub. L. No. 96-221, 94 Stat. 132 (1980)
Emergency Tax Recovery Act of 1981 (ETRA), Pub. L. No. 97-34, 95 Stat. 172 (1981)
Federal Deposit Insurance Act (FDIA), 45 Stat. 873 (1950)
Federal Deposit Insurance Cooperation Improvement Act of 1991 (FDICIA), Pub. L. No. 102-242, 105 Stat. 2236 (codified in scattered sections of 12 U.S.C.)
Financial Institutions Regulatory and Interest Control Act of 1978 (FIRICA), Pub. L. No. 97-320, 92 Stat. 3641 (1978) (codified in scattered sections of 12 U.S.C.)
FLA.STAT.ANN §§ 658.20–21 (1991)
Garn-St. Germain Act, at § 111, 96 Stat. at 1469 (codified as amended at 12 U.S.C. § 1823(c)(1))
Home Owners Loan Act (HOLA), 48 Stat. 128,12 U.S.C. §1421 et seq.
International Loan Supervision Act of 1983 (ILSA), Pub. L. No. 98-191, 97 Stat. 1278

Internal Revenue Code (IRC), 26 U.S.C. § 1 et seq.
National Housing Act, Pub. L. No. 73-479, 48 Stat. 1246 (1934)
National Bank Act, June 3, 1864, 13 Stat. 99 (1864), as amended,12 U.S.C. § 1 et seq.
Riegle-Neal Interstate Banking and Branching Efficiency Act of 1994, Pub. L. No. 103-328, 108 Stat. 2338 (1994)
Tax Reform Act of 1986, Pub. L. No. 99-514, 100 Stat. 2085 (1986) (TRA)
TEX.REV.STAT.ANN Banks and Banking §§ 342 et seq. (1991); CAL. Financial Code § 361 (1992)

B. Regulations

Code of Federal Regulations (C.F.R.), Parts 12, 18, and 24
Federal Register (1980–1992)

C. US Cases

Anderson v. Hershey, 127 F.2d 884 (6th Cir. 1942)
Atherton v. FDIC, 57 F.3d 1231 (3rd Cir, 1996), 117 S. Ct. 666 (1996).
Bayshore Executive Plaza Partnership v. FDIC, 750 F Supp. 507 (S.D. Fla. 1990)
Bellaire v. Comptroller of the Currency, 697 F.2d 674 (5th Cir. 1983)
Board of Governors of the Federal Reserve System v. Dimension Financial Corp., 474 U.S. 361 (1986)
Carlton v. Firstcorp. Inc., 967 F.2d 942, 945 (4th Cir. 1992)
Chase Manhattan Bank, N.A. v. FDIC, 554 F.Supp. 251 (W.D.Okla. 1983)
City of Newport v. Fact Concerts Inc., 453 U.S. 247 (1981)
D'Oench, Duhme & Co. v. FDIC, 315 U.S. 447 (1942)
FAIC Securities, Inc. v. United States, 595 F. Supp. 73 (D.D.C. 1984)
FDIC v. Cafritz, 762 F. Supp. 1503 (D.D.C. 1991)
FDIC v. Cremona Co., 832 F.2d 959 (6th Cir. 1987)
FDIC v. Ritchie, 646 F. Supp. 1581 (D. Neb. 1986)
FDIC v. Wood, 758 F.2d 156 (6th Cir. 1985)
Fidelity Sav. & Loan Ass'n v. FHLBB, 540 F.Supp. 1374 (N.D.Cal.), rev'd, 689 F.2d 803 (9th Cir. 1982), cert. denied, 461 U.S. 914 (1983)
Gunter v. Hutcheson, 674 F.2d 862 (11th Cir. 1982)
Investment Company Institute v. Camp, 401 U.S. 617 (1971)
Irving Indep. Sch. Dist. v. Packard Properties, 741 F. Supp. 120 (N.D. Tex. 1990)
Lane v. Schilling, 279 P. 267 (Or. 1929)
Manufacturers Hanover Trust Co. v. Drysdale Securities Corp., et al., 801 F.2d 13 (2d Cir. 1986)
Northeast Bancorp v. Board of Governors of the Federal Reserve System, 472 U.S. 159 (1985)
Professional Asset Management v. Penn Square Bank, 566 F. Supp. 134 (W.D. Okla. 1983)
SEC v. Drysdale Securities Corp., et al., 785 F.2d 38 (2d Cir. 1986)
Seattle-First Nat'l Bank v. FDIC, 619 F.Supp. 1351 (W.D. Okla. 1985)
Securities Indus. Ass'n v. Board of Governors of the Federal Reserve System, 450 U.S. 46 (1981)

Securities Indus. Ass'n v. Board of Governors of the Federal Reserve System, 468 U.S. 137 (1984)
Securities Indus. Ass'n v. Board of Governors of the Federal Reserve System, 468 U.S. 207 (1984)
Securities Indus. Ass'n v. Board of Governors of the Federal Reserve System, 839 F.2d 47 (2d Cir.), cert. denied, 486 U.S. 1059 (1988)
Sparkman, 703 F.2d 1097 (9th Cir. 1983)
Transohio Savings Bank v. Director, OTS, 967 F.2d 598, 604 (DC 1992)
U.S. v. Winstar, 116 S. Ct. 2432 (1996)

OFFICIAL DOCUMENTS

A. US Documents

1. *Committee on Agriculture, Nutrition and Forestry (House)*

'Report of the Commodity Futures Trading Commission on Recent Developments in the Silver Future Markets' (Washington, DC, May 1980)

2. *Committee on Banking, Housing/Finance and Urban Affairs (House)*

Bank Supervision, Prompt and Forceful Regulatory Actions Needed, Report to the Chairman, House Committee on Banking, Finance and Urban Affairs, Subcommittee on Financial Institutions Supervision, Regulation and Insurance (April 1995)
Condition of the Savings Association Insurance Fund, The (SAIF), 104th Cong., 1st sess. (1995)
Continental Illinois National Bank: Report of an Inquiry into its Federal Supervision and Assistance, Subcommittee on Financial Institutions Supervision, Regulation and Insurance, Staff Report, 99th Cong., 1st sess. (1985)
D'ARISTA, J., 'Federal Reserve Structure and the Development of Monetary Policy, 1915–1935 (House Banking Committee, 1971)
Deposit Interest Rate Ceilings and Housing Credit: The Report of the President's Inter-Agency Task Force on Regulation Q, 96th Cong., 1st sess., (1979)
Financial Institutions and the Nation's Economy (FINE) Discussion Principles, 94th Cong., 1st sess. (1975)
Majority Staff Study on Chartering of National Banks: 1970–1977, 96th Cong. 2d sess. (1980)

3. *Committee on Government Operations (House)*

Federal Regulation of Brokered Deposits in Problem Banks and Savings Institutions, Report, 98th Cong., 2d Sess (1984)
HANCOCK AND WILCOX, 'Appraisal Reform: Implementation Status and Unresolved Issues', Report to the U.S. House Committee on Government Operations (1992)

'Silver Prices and the Adequacy of Federal Actions in the Marketplace: 1979–1980' (Washington, DC, October 1982)

4. *Congressional Budget Office*

'Economic Effects of the Savings and Loan Crisis: A CBO Study' (Washington, DC, 1992)
'Reforming Federal Deposit Insurance' (September 1990)
'Resolving the Thrift Crisis: A CBO Study' (Washington, DC, 1993)

5. *Congressional Hearings and Other Reports, Statements, Records (House and Senate)*

Adequacy of Federal Home Loan Bank Board Supervision of Empire Savings and Loan Association, Hearing Before the Committee on Government Operations, U.S. House of Representatives 98th Cong., 2nd Sess. (1984)
Agency Actions to Reduce the Negative Impact of Regulations on Credit Availability, Subcommittee on Financial Institutions, Supervision, Regulation and Deposit Insurance, Hearing, 103d Cong., 1st Sess. (1994)
Bank and Thrift Criminal Fraud, U.S. General Accounting Office Report to the Chairman, Committee on the Judiciary, U.S. Senate, GAO Rep. B-245890, 8 January 1993; including response of the U.S. Department of Justice to the GAO Report, dated 1 October 1992
Capital Requirements For Thrifts As They Apply to Supervisory Goodwill, Hearing Before the House Committee on Banking, Finance and Urban Affairs, Subcommittee on General Oversight and Investigations, 102d Cong., 1st Sess. (1991)
Condition of Deposit Insurance Funds and the Impact of the Proposed Deposit Insurance Premium Reduction on the Bank and Thrift Industries, Subcommittee on Financial Institutions and Consumer Credit, Hearing, 104th Cong., 1st Sess. (1995)
Congressional Quarterly Almanac (1990–1996)
Congressional Record (1979–1991)
Cost of Forbearance During the Thrift Crisis, Memorandum, The, United States Congress, House of Representatives, Staff of Congressional Budget Office (June 1991) (on file with author)
Credit Availability: The Availability of Credit in Our Economy and to Try to Determine Whether or Not There is Currently a Credit Crunch, 101st Cong., 2d Sess. (1990)
Credit Crunch, U.S. House Committee on Banking, The, Finance and Urban Affairs, Subcommittee on Domestic Monetary Policy, Hearing, 102d Cong., 1st Sess. (1991)
Credit Crunch and Regulatory Burdens in Bank Lending, The, Subcommittee on Commerce, Consumer and Monetary Affairs, Hearing, 103rd Cong., 1st Sess (1993)
Deposit Insurance Reform and Related Supervisory Issues, Hearing, 99th Cong., 1st Sess (1984)
Depository Institutions Amendments of 1982, The, Subcommittee on Financial Institutions Supervision, Regulation and Insurance, 97th Cong., 2d Sess. (1982)

Depository Institutions Deregulation Act of 1979, The, Hearings on S. 1347 Before the Subcommittee on Financial Institutions on the Senate Committee on Banking, Housing and Urban Affairs, 96th Cong., 1st Sess (1979)

Discussion Principles, U.S. House Committee on Banking, Currency, and Housing, Subcommittee on Financial Institutions in the Nation's Economy (FINE Study), Hearings, 94th Cong., 1st Sess. (1975)

Economic Impact of the Oil Price Collapse, The, U.S. Congress, Joint Economic Committee, 99th Cong., 2d Sess. (12 March 1986)

Economic Implications of the 'Too Big to Fail' Policy, Hearing, Statement of John P. LaWare, U.S. House Committee on Banking, Finance and Urban Affairs, Subcommittee on Economic Stabilization, 102d Cong., 1st Sess. (1991)

Equity for the Small Saver, Hearings Before the Subcommittee on Financial Institutions of the Senate Committee on Banking, Housing and Urban Affairs, 96th Cong., 1st Sess., (11 April 1979) (testimony of FHLBB Chairman McKinney)

Failure of Independent CPAs to Identify Fraud, Waste and Midmanagement and Assure Accurate Financial Position of Troubled S&Ls, Hearing Before the House Committee on Banking, Finance and Urban Affairs, 101st Cong., 1st Sess. (Washington D.C., 1989)

Failure of the Bank of New England, Hearing, U.S. House Committee on Banking, Finance and Urban Affairs, 102d Cong., 1st Sess. (9 January 1991)

Federal Home Loan Bank Board 1988 Deals, Hearings Before the House Committee on Banking, Finance and Urban Affairs, 101st Cong., 2nd Sess. (Washington D.C., 1990)

Federal Home Loan Bank Board's Supervision and Failure of Empire Savings and Loan Association of Mesquite, Texas, Hearing Before the House Committee on Government Operations, H.R. Rep. No. 953, 98th Cong., 2nd Sess. (Washington D.C., 1984)

Federal Regulations of Brokered Deposits in Problem Banks and Savings Institutions, U.S. House Committee on Government Operations, Report, 98th Cong., 2d Sess. (1984)

Financial Condition of BIF and SAIF and Proposals to Merge the Banking and Thrift Industries, Subcommittee on Financial Institutions and Consumer Credit, Hearing, 104th Cong., 1st Sess. (1995)

Financial Institutions in the Nation's Economy (FINE), 'Discussion Principles', U.S. House Committee on Banking, Currency and Housing, Subcommittee on Financial Institutions Supervision, Regulation and Insurance, Hearing, 94th Cong., 1st Sess. (1975)

Financial Institutions Reform, Recovery and Enforcement Act of 1989, Hearings Before the Subcommittee on Financial Institutions Supervision, Regulation and Insurance of the House Committee on Banking, Finance and Urban Affairs, 101st Cong., 1st Sess. (1990) (testimony of FHLBB Board Member)

Full Faith and Credit for FSLIC Notes, Hearings Before the House Committee on Banking, Finance and Urban Affairs, 100th Cong., 2d Sess. (1988)

General Accounting Office, 'International Monetary Fund: Lending Policies', Testimony before the Subcommittee on Domestic and International Monetary Policy, Committee on Banking and Financial Services, U.S. House of Representatives (22 June 1999), on file with author

Hearings Before the Subcommittee on Financial Institutions of the Senate Committee on Banking, Housing and Urban Affairs, 96th Cong., 1st Sess., 35–36, April 11, 1979)

Hearings on Deposit Insurance Reform and Related Supervisory Issues, Before the U.S. Senate Committee on Banking, Housing and Urban Affairs, 99th Cong., 1st Sess. (1984)

Hearing on International Monetary Arrangements for the 21st Century, Committee on Banking and Financial Services, U.S. House of Representatives (21 May 1999) (testimony available at <http://www.house.gov/banking>)

Hearings on Oversight on the Supervision and Regulation of Money Market Mutual Funds and the Effects of the Funds in Financial Markets, Before the Subcommittee on Financial Institutions of the Senate Committee on Banking, Housing and Urban Affairs, 96th Cong., 2d Sess. (1980)

Hearing on Proposals for a New International Financial Architecture, Committee on Banking and Financial Services, U.S. House of Representatives (20 May 1999) (testimony available at <http://www.house.gov/banking>)

H.R. 962, The Economic Growth and Financial Institutions Regulatory Paperwork Reduction Act of 1993, Subcommittee on Financial Institutions Supervision, Regulation and Deposit Insurance, Hearing, 103d Cong., 1st Sess. (1994)

Impact of Faulty and Fraudulent Real Estate Appraisals on Federally Insured Financial Institutions and Regulated Agencies of the Federal Government, Hearings, U.S. House Committee on Government Operations, 99th Cong., 1st Sess. (1985)

Impact of Appraisal Problems on Real Estate Lending, The, Mortgage Insurance and Investment in the Secondary Market, Hearings, 99th Cong. 2d Sess. (1986)

Insured Brokered Deposits and Federal Depository Institutions, Subcommittee on General Oversight and Investigations, 101st Cong., 1st Sess. (1989)

Inquiry into Continental Illinois Corp. and Continental Illinois National Bank, Hearings Before the Subcommittee on Financial Institutions Supervision, Regulation and Insurance, U.S. House Committee on Banking Finance and Urban Affairs, 98th Cong. 2d. Sess. (1984)

Majority Staff Study on Chartering of National Banks: 1970–1977, Senate Committee on Banking, Housing and Urban Affairs, 96th Cong., 2d Sess. (1980)

Oversight Hearing on the Condition of the Financial Services Industry, Hearings Before the Committee on Banking, Housing and Urban Affairs, 100th Cong., 2d Sess. (1988)

Oversight Hearing to Examine the Impact of FIRREA on the Federal Home Loan Bank System, Hearings Before the Subcommittee on General

Oversight and Investigation, House Committee on Banking, Finance and Urban Affairs, 101st Cong., 1st Sess. (Washington D.C., 1989)
Oversight on the Condition of the Financial Services Industry, Hearings Before the Senate Committee on Banking, Housing and Urban Affairs, 100th Cong., 2d Sess. (1988)
Proposed Restrictions on Money Brokers, U.S. House Committee on Government Operations, Hearing, 98th Cong., 2d Sess. (1984)
Reform of the Nation's Banking and Financial Systems, Subcommittee on Financial Institutions Supervision, Regulation and Insurance, Hearing, 100th Cong., 1st Sess. (1987)
Regulation Q and Related Matters, Hearings Before the U.S. House Committee on Banking, Finance and Urban Affairs, Subcommittee on Financial Institutions Supervision, Regulation and Insurance, 96th Cong., 2d Sess. (1980)
Report of the President's Commission on Financial Structure and Regulation, The (1971) (Hunt Commission Report), U.S. House Committee on Banking, Currency and Housing, Subcommittee on Financial Institutions in the Nation's Economy (FINE), 'Discussion Principles', Hearings, 94th Cong., 1st Sess. (1975) ('FINE Study')
Savings and Loan Policies in the Late 1970s and 1980s, Hearings Before the House Committee on Banking, Finance and Urban Affairs, 101st Cong., 2d Sess., No. 101-176 (1990)
Senate Committee on Agriculture, Nutrition and Forestry, Report of the Commodity Futures Trading Commission on Recent Developments in the Silver Futures Markets (May 1980) (on file with author); Securities and Exchange Commission, The Silver Crisis (October 1982)
Silver Prices and the Adequacy of Federal Action in the Marketplace, 1979–1980, Hearing Before the Subcommittee on Government Operations, Before the U.S. House of Representatives (31 March–22 May 1980)
Statement of Chairman McKinney, Equity for the Small Saver, Hearings Before the Subcommittee on Financial Institutions of the Senate Committee on Banking, Housing and Urban Affairs, 96th Cong., 1st Sess., 42 (1979)
Statement of Federal Home Loan Bank Board to Senate Committee on Banking, Currency and Housing, Serial No. 97-37, on S. 1720
Statement for the Record by the Comptroller General of the United States Concerning the Federal Rescue of Continental Illinois National Bank, submitted to the House Committee on Banking, Finance and Urban Affairs (Washington D.C., 14 December 1984)
Status on the Implementation of Title XI, The Appraisal Reform Amendments of the Financial Institutions Reform, Recovery and Enforcement Act of 1989 (FIRREA), 101st Cong., 2d Sess., 17 May 1990
Tax Aspects of Government-Assisted Savings and Loan Acquisitions, Hearings on H.R. 1135, H.R. 1338, H.R. 1326 and H.R. 561 Before the Committee on Ways and Means, 102nd Cong., 2d Sess. (1992)
Testimony of Richard Pratt, Chairman, FHLBB, Before the House Committee on Banking, Finance and Urban Affairs, 101st Cong., 2d Sess. (1990)
Testimony of B. Weinstein, Director, Center for Economic Development and Research, Professor of Applied Economics, University of North Texas,

Before the Senate Committee on Banking, Housing and Urban Affairs, U.S. Congress, 24 May 1995

Testimony of C. Whalen, Chief Financial Officer, Legal Research International, Inc., Before the Senate Committee on Banking, Housing and Urban Affairs, U.S. Congress, 24 May 1995

To Authorize a National Usury Ceiling, Hearing Before the Subcommittee on Domestic Monetary Policy of the House Committee on Banking, Finance and Urban Affairs, 97th Cong., 2d Sess. (1982)

Transactions to Resolve Failed Depository Institutions, 1990, Hearing Before The House Comm. on Banking, Finance and Urban Affairs 101 St. Cong. 2d. Sess. 620 (1990)

Unintended Effects of FIRREA on the Home Building Industry and Other Related Matters, The, Hearing Before the Subcommittee on General Oversight and Investigations of the House Committee on Banking, Finance and Urban Affairs, 101st Cong., 2d Sess. (1990)

6. *Department of Commerce*

National Data Book and Guide to Sources: Statistical Abstract of the United States 1988 (108th edn, 1988)

Survey of Current Business, Bureau of Economic Analysis (1982–1987)

7. *Department of the Treasury*

'Hedge Funds, Leverage and the Lessons of Long-Term Capital Management', Report of the President's Working Group on Financial Markets (April 1999) (joint report of the Treasury Department, Federal Reserve, SEC and CFTC, respectively)

'Modernizing the U.S. Financial System: Recommendations for Safer, More Competitive Banks' (Washington, DC, U.S. Government Printing Office, 1991)

8. *Federal Deposit Insurance Corporation*

CARNS, F., 'Economic Conditions in Louisiana, Oklahoma and Texas', FDIC Banking and Economic Review (April 1986)

COBOS, D., 'Forbearance: Practices and Proposed Standards', *FDIC Banking Review* 2, No. 1 (1989)

CURRY, GOLDBERG AND HUDGINS, 'Characteristics of Failure and the Cost of Resolution in the Thrift Industry', unpublished paper, FDIC (February 1997)

DAVISON, L., 'Bank Examination and Supervision', unpublished paper, FDIC (February 1996)

ECCLES AND O'KEEFE, 'Understanding the Experience of Converted New England Savings Banks', *FDIC Banking Review* 8, No. 1 (Winter 1995)

FREUND, J., 'Howard Savings Bank: Observations of Regulator/Banker Differences in Evaluating Commercial Real Estate Risks', unpublished paper (FDIC, 1996)

HOLLAND, INSCOE, WALDROP AND KUTA, 'Interstate Banking – The Past, the Present and Future', *FDIC Banking Review* 9, No. 1 (1996)

HORNE, D., 'Bank Dividend Patterns', *FDIC Banking Review* 4, No. 2 (1991)
ISAAC, W., Address Before the Management Conference of the National Council of Savings Institutions, FDIC PR-92-83 (December 6, 1983)
ISAAC, W., 'Statement on Federal Assistance to Continental Illinois Corporation and Continental Illinois National Bank', Statement of the Chairman of the Federal Deposit Insurance Corporation before the House Committee on Banking, Finance and Urban Affairs (4 October 1984)
MURTON, A., 'Bank Intermediation, Bank Runs and Deposit Insurance', *FDIC Banking Review* 2, No. 1 (1989)
O'KEEFE, J., 'The Texas Banking Crisis: Causes and Consequences: 1980–1989', *FDIC Banking Review* 3, No. 2 (Washington, DC, Winter 1990)
SEIDMAN, W., Address to the Conference of State Bank Supervisors, Washington, DC (9 December 1985)
SILVERBERG, S., 'A Case for Depositor Preference', FDIC Banking and Economic Review (May 1986)
VOESAR, D., 'Economic Conditions in Oklahoma', FDIC Banking and Economic Review 4, No. 8 (November/December 1986)
Capital Maintenance, 49 Red. Reg. 29,399 (1984) (codified at 12 C.F.R. Pt 325) (proposed 20 July 1984)
Capital Maintenance, 50 Fed. Reg. 11,128 (1985) (codified at 12 C.F.R., Pt 325)
Capital Maintenance, 50 Fed. Reg. 11,128, 11,130 (1985) (final rule)
Capital Maintenance; Supplemented Adjusted Capital Proposal, 51 Fed. Reg. 6,126 (1986) (to be codified at 12 C.F.R., Pt 325)
Deposit Insurance for the Nineties: Meeting the Challenge, 1989
FDIC, *The First Fifty Years: A History of the FDIC 1933–1983* (1984)
FDIC Annual Report (1934)
FDIC Annual Report (1950)
FDIC Annual Report (1979–1990)
FDIC Annual Report (1982)
FDIC Annual Report (1985)
FDIC Annual Report (1984)
FDIC Annual Report (1985)
FDIC Annual Report (1987)
FDIC Annual Report (1990)
FDIC Division of Finance, 'Failed Bank Cost Analysis, 1986–1996', (1995)
FDIC Division of Finance, 'Failed Bank Cost Analysis, 1986–1995', (1996)
FDIC, 'An Examination of the Banking Crises of the 1980s and Early 1990s', *History of the Eighties: Lessons for the Future, Volumes 1 and 2* (1998)
'FDIC Establishes Three New Banks to Assume Deposits of Bank of New England, N.A., Boston, Massachusetts, Connecticut Bank & Trust Company, N.A., Hartford, Connecticut and Main National Bank, Portland, Maine', FDIC News Release, PR-3-91 (6 January 1991)
FDIC Policy Statement 55 Fed. Reg. 21, 934 (1990)
FDIC, 'State Powers Bank Study' (1991) (on file with author)
FDIC Statement of Policy on Assistance to Operating Insured Depository Institutions, 57 FR 60203 (18 December 1992)
FDIC Statement of Policy on Capital Adequacy, 46 Red. Reg. 62.693 (17 December 1981)

'FDIC to Sell Bank of New England Franchise to Fleet/Norstar', FDIC News Release, PR-61-91 (22 April 1991)
Federal Deposit Insurance Corporation, *Historical Statistics on Banking: A Statistical History of the United States Banking Industry 1934–1992* (1993)
Federal Deposit Insurance Corporation Office of Inspector General, '1994 Failed Banks Trend Analysis', 1995
Federal Deposit Insurance Corporation, Statement of Policy (31 March 1980 and 28 May 1987)
Mandate for Change: Restructuring the Banking Industry (1987)
Permanent Assistance Program for Continental Illinois National Bank and Trust Company, PR-87-84 (26 July 1984)
'Report on Continental Illinois', unpublished Paper (1985)
Statement of Policy on Qualified Financial Contracts, 2 FDIC, Law, Regulation, Related Acts 5901
Statistics on Banking: A Statistical History of the United States Banking Industry, 1934–1994, Vol. 2 (1995)
'A Study of the Desirability and Feasibility of a Risk-Based Deposit Insurance System', 1990
'Systemic Risk ('Too Big to Fail')', unpublished Paper (1995)
Video Recording of the 'History of the Eighties – Lessons For the Future Symposium', held by the FDIC on 16 January 1997, produced by the FDIC, portions of which are reproduced in Volume II of the FDIC publication

9. *Federal Home Loan Bank Board*

Adjustable Rate Mortgage Loan Instruments, 46 Fed. Reg. 24148 (1981)
Amendments to Net Worth and Statutory Reserve Requirements, 47 Fed. Reg. 52,961 (1982)
Bank Holding Companies and Change in Bank Control; Capital Maintenance; Supplemental Adjusted Capital Measure, 51 Fed. Reg. 3,976 (1986 (to be codified at 12 C.F.R., Pt 225) (proposed 31 January 1986)
FHLBB Memorandum No. R41, R41a and R41c
FHLBB Memorandum No. R41C; Fed. Banking L. Rep. (CCH), § 40.185.176
FHLBB Memorandum No. R-64
Federal Home Loan Bank Board, Annual Report, (1979)
HEMEL, E., 'Deregulation and Supervision Go Together', Outlook of the Federal Home Loan Bank System (November/December 1985)
Insurance of Accounts, Amendments Relating to Acquisition Credit Subject to Deferral, 44 Fed. Reg. 76,567 (1979)
Maturity of Time Deposits, 45 Fed. Reg. 76103 (1980)
Memorandum R-31a (March 8, 1974)
Mutual Fund Investments, 46 Fed. Reg. 18686 (1981)
Negotiable Order of Withdrawal Accounts, 45 Fed. Reg. 76103 (1980)
Net Worth Amendments, 45 Fed. Reg. 76111 (1980)
Net Worth Amendments, 47 Fed. Reg. 3,543 (1982)
Net Worth Requirements of Insured Institutions, 50 Fed. Reg. 6891 (1985) (to be codified at 12 C.F.R., Pts 561, 563, 570, 571 and 584)
Prompt Corrective Action, 57 Fed. Reg. 29,662 (1992) (codified at 12 C.F.R., Pts 308 and 325) (proposed 6 July 1992)

Prompt Corrective Action; Rules of Practice for Hearings, 57 Fed. Reg. 44,866 (1992) (codified at 12 C.F.R., Pts 6, 19, 308, 325 and 565)

Regulatory Capital (Net Worth) Requirements of Insured Institutions, 51 Fed. Reg. 33,565 (1986) (to be codified at 12 C.F.R., Ch. V and Pts 561 and 563)

Regulatory Capital Requirements of Insured Institutions, 51 Fed. Reg. 16,550 (proposed May 5, 1986) (to be codified at 12 CFR, pts. 561, 563 and Ch. V)

Reserve Requirements and Policies Relating to Insurance of Accounts of de Novo Institutions, 48 Fed. Reg. 54,320 (1983)

Revision of Real Estate Lending Provisions, 45 Fed. Reg. 76095 (1980)

Service Corporation Activities, 46 Fed. Reg. 24526 (1981)

Service Corporation Investment Authority, 45 Fed. Reg. 56029 (1980)

Statement of Policy, Accounting for Acquisition, Development and Construction Loans, 50 Fed. Reg. 18,233 (1985)

Treatment of Gains and Losses on the Sale or Other Disposition of Mortgage Assets, Mortgage-Related Securities and Debt Securities: Republication of Reserve Requirements, 46 Fed. Reg. 50,048 (1981)

Treatment of Goodwill Acquired in Mergers, 46 Fed. Reg. 42,274 (1981)

Trust Powers, 45 Fed. Reg. 76111 (1980)

10. Federal Reserve

AKHTAR, M., 'Causes and Consequences of the 1989–92 Credit Slowdown: Overview and Perspective', *Federal Reserve Bank of New York Quarterly Review*, Vol. 18 (Winter 1993–94)

AVERY AND HANWECK, 'A Dynamic Analysis of Bank Failures', in *Proceedings of the Conference on Bank Structure and Competition* (Federal Reserve Bank of Chicago, May 1985)

BARKER AND HOLDSWORTH, 'The Causes of Bank Failures in the 1980s', Federal Reserve Bank of New York, Research Paper No. 93-25, August 1993

BENSTON AND CARHILL, 'FSLIC Forbearance and the Thrift Debacle in Credit Markets in Transition', *Proceedings of the Conference on Bank Structure and Competition* (Federal Reserve Bank of Chicago, May 1992)

BOYD AND GERTLER, 'Are Banks Dead? Or, Are the Reports Greatly Exaggerated?', in the *Proceedings of the Conference on Bank Structure and Competition* (Federal Reserve Bank of Chicago, May 1994)

BRAUER AND FLAHERTY, 'The New York City Recession', *Federal Reserve Bank of New York Quarterly Review* 17, No. 1 (Spring 1992)

BROADDUS AND GOODFRIEND, 'Foreign Exchange Operations and the Federal Reserve', *Federal Reserve Bank of Richmond Annual Report* (1996)

BROWNE, L., 'Why New England Went the Way of Texas Rather Than California', *Federal Reserve Bank of Boston New England Economic Review* (January/February 1992)

BROWNE AND ROSENGREN, 'Real Estate and the Credit Crunch: An Overview', *Federal Reserve Bank of Boston New England Economic Review* (November/December 1992)

CALOMIRIS AND MASON, 'Contagion and Bank Failures During the Great Depression: The June 1932 Chicago Banking Panic', in *Proceedings of the*

Conference on Bank Structure and Competition (Federal Reserve Bank of Chicago, May 1995)

CASE, K., 'The Real Estate Cycle and the Economy: Consequences of the Massachusetts Boom of 1984–87', *Federal Reserve Bank of Boston New England Economic Review* (September/October 1991)

COLE, CORNYN AND GUNTHER, 'FIMS: A New Monitoring System for Banking Institutions', Federal Reserve Bulletin 81 (January 1995)

COLE AND GUNTHER, 'A CAMEL Rating's Shelf Life', Federal Reserve Bank of Dallas Financial Industry Studies (December 1995)

COLE, MCKENZIE AND WHITE, 'The Causes and Costs of Thrift Institution Failures: A Structure-Behavior-Outcomes Approach' (Federal Reserve Bank of Dallas Working Paper, 1990)

CORRIGAN, E., 'A Perspective on Recent Financial Disruptions', Federal Reserve Bank of *New York Quarterly Review* 14, No. 4 (Winter 1989–1990)

CORRIGAN, E., 'Are Banks Special?', *Federal Reserve Bank of Minneapolis Annual Report* (1982)

DEGENNARO AND THOMPSON, 'Capital Forbearance and Thrifts: An Ex Post Examination of Regulatory Gambling', *Proceedings of the Conference on Bank Structure and Competition* (Federal Reserve Bank of Chicago, May 1993)

DEMIRGÜC-KUNT, A., 'Deposit-Institution Failures: A Review of Empirical Literature', *Economic Review*, Federal Reserve Bank of Cleveland, Vol. 25 (Fourth Quarter 1989)

DEMSETZ, SAIDENBERG AND STRAHAN, 'Agency Problems and Risk Taking at Banks', *Federal Reserve Bank of New York Staff Report* 29 (September 1997)

DUWE AND HARVEY, 'Problem Banks: Their Characteristics and Possible Causes of Deterioration' (Federal Reserve Bank of Kansas City Banking Studies, Kansas City, 1988)

EDWARDS, C., 'Open Market Operations in the 1990s', *Federal Reserve Bulletin* (November 1977)

EDWARDS AND MISHKIN, 'The Decline of Traditional Banking: Implications for Financial Stability and Regulatory Policy', *Federal Reserve Bank of New York Economic Policy Review* (July 1995)

EHLEN, J., 'A Review of Bank Capital and Its Adequacy', *Federal Reserve Bank of Atlanta Economic Review* 68, No. 11 (1983)

Federal Reserve Board, Annual Report of 1986 (reviewing credit expansion data of 1984)

Federal Reserve Board, 'Capital Maintenance', 49 Fed. Reg. 30,317 (1984) (codified at 12 C.F.R. Pts 208, 225 and 263) (proposed 30 July 1984)

Federal Reserve Board, 'Capital Maintenance', 50 Fed. Reg. 13,067 (1985) (codified at 12 C.F.R. Pts 208, 225 and 263) (proposed 30 July 1984)

Federal Reserve Board, 'Capital Maintenance', 50 Fed. Reg. 16,057, 16,063 (1985) (final rule)

Federal Reserve Board, 'Financial Developments of Bank Holding Companies in 1984' *Federal Reserve Bulletin* (December 1985) (reviewing 1981 capital adequacy data)

Federal Reserve Board, 'Monetary Policy and Open Market Operations in 1982', *New York Federal Reserve Quarterly* (Spring 1983)

Federal Reserve Board, 'Monetary Policy Report to Congress', Annual Report, February 19, 1980 (describing 1980 targets for M-1 and other aggregates)

Federal Reserve Board, 'Monetary Policy Report to Congress', Annual Report (Washington, DC, 1981)

Federal Reserve Board, 'Profitability of Insured Commercial Banks in 1984' *Federal Reserve Bulletin* (November 1985)

Federal Reserve Board, 'Rating Systems – Bank Holding Companies' (Fed. Reserve Reg. Serv., Vol. 1, 1978)

Federal Reserve Board of Governors, Federal Reserve System: Purposes and Functions, (6th edn, Washington D.C., September 1974)

Federal Reserve System, Board of Governors of, Annual Report (1980–1994)

Federal Reserve System, Board of Governors of, Annual Report (1981)

Federal Reserve System, Board of Governors of, Federal Deposit Insurance Corporation; Office of the Comptroller of the Currency; and Office of Thrift Supervision, Joint Report: Streamlining of Regulatory Requirements (23 September 1996)

Federal Reserve System: Purposes and Functions (Washington, DC, Board of Governors of the Federal Reserve System, 1984, as periodically updated)

FLOOD, M., 'The Great Deposit Insurance Debate', Fed. Reserve Bank of St. Louis Economic Rev., July/Aug. 1992

GAJEWSKI, G., 'Assessing the Risk of Bank Failure', *Proceedings of the Conference on Bank Structure and Competition*, Federal Reserve Bank of Chicago (May 1989)

GARCIA, G., *ET AL.*, 'The Garn-St. Germain Depository Institutions Act of 1982', *Federal Reserve Bank of Chicago Economic Perspectives* 7, No. 3 (1983)

GILBERT, R., 'The Effects of Legislating Prompt Corrective Action on the Bank Insurance Fund', *Federal Reserve Bank of St. Louis Economic Review* 74, No. 4 (July/August 1992)

GILBERT, R. 'Implications of Annual Examinations for the Bank Insurance Fund', *Federal Reserve Bank of St. Louis Economic Review* 75, No. 1 (January/February 1993)

GILBERT, R., 'Requiem for Regulation Q: What It Did and Why It Passed Away', *Federal Reserve Bank of St. Louis Economic Review* 67, No. 2 (1986)

GILBERT, R., 'Supervision of Undercapitalized Banks: Is There a Case for Change?', *Federal Reserve Bank of St. Louis Economic Review* 73, No. 3 (1991)

GILBERT, STONE AND TREBLING, 'The New Capital Adequacy Standards', *Federal Reserve Bank of St. Louis Economic Review* 67, No. 5 (1985)

GREENSPAN, A., 'Optimal Bank Supervision in a Changing World', *Proceedings of the Conference on Bank Structure and Competition*, Federal Reserve Bank of Chicago (May 1994)

GUNTHER, J., 'Financial Strategies and Performance of Newly Established Texas Banks', *Federal Reserve Bank of Dallas Financial Industry Studies* (December 1990)

GUNTHER AND ROBINSON, 'Moral Hazard and Texas Banking in the 1980s', Federal Reserve Bank of Dallas Financial Industry Studies (Dallas, Texas, December 1990)

GUNTHER AND ROBINSON, 'The Texas Credit Crunch', Federal Reserve Bank of Dallas (1991)

HALL, MEYER AND VAUGHAN, 'Do Markets and Regulators View Bank Risk Similarly?', Federal Reserve Bank of St. Louis, Supervisory Policy Analysis Working Paper No. 1-97 (February 1997)

HARLESS, C., 'Brokered Deposits: Issues and Alternatives', *Federal Reserve Bank of Atlanta Economic Review* 69, No. 3 (1984)

HEGGESTAD AND KINIG, 'Regulation of Bank Capital: An Evaluation', *Federal Reserve Bank of Atlanta Economic Review* 67, No. 3 (1982)

HETZEL, R., 'Too Big to Fail: Origins, Consequences and Outlook', *Federal Reserve Bank of Richmond Economic Review* 77, No. 6 (November/December 1991)

HUMPAGE, O., 'Institutional Aspects of U.S. Intervention, Fed. Res. Bank of Cleveland Econ. Rev., 1st Quar. (1994)

HUNTER AND SRINIVASAN, 'Determinants of De Novo Bank Performance', *Federal Reserve Bank of Atlanta Economic Review* (March/April 1990)

JENKS, M., *ET AL.*, 'New England Economic Summary, First Quarter 1990', Federal Reserve Bank of Boston New England Economic Indicators (August 1990)

JOHNSON, R., 'Anticipated Fiscal Contraction: The Economic Consequences of the Gramm-Rudman-Hollings Bill for the U.S. Economy (Federal Reserve Board, February 1986)

JOHNSON, R., 'Historical Beginnings ... The Federal Reserve' (Federal Reserve Bank of Boston, 1977)

KAEN AND MICHALSEN, 'The Effects of the Norwegian Banking Crisis on Norwegian Bank and Nonbank Stocks', *Proceedings of the Conference on Bank Structure and Competition*, Federal Reserve Bank of Chicago (May 1995)

KAMINSKY AND REINHART, 'The Twin Crises: The Causes of Banking and Balance-of-Payments Problems', International Finance Discussion Paper No. 544 (Washington: Board of Governors of the Federal Reserve Systems, March 1996)

KAUFMAN, G., 'The Savings and Loan Rescue of 1989: Causes and Perspective', Working Paper Series on Regional Economic Issues No. WP-89-23 (Federal Reserve Bank of Chicago, 1989)

KEETON, W., 'The New Risk-Based Capital Plan for Commercial Banks', *Federal Reserve Bank of Kansas City Economic Review* 74, No. 10 (1989)

KOROBOW AND STUHR, 'A Nationwide Test of Early Warning Research in Banking', *Federal Reserve Bank of New York Quarterly Review* 2 (Autumn 1977)

KOROBOW AND STUHR, 'The Relevance of Peer Groups in Early Warning Analysis', *Federal Reserve Bank of Atlanta Economic Review* 68 (November 1983)

MCNEILL, C., 'The Depository Institutions Deregulation and Monetary Control Act of 1980', Fed. Res. Bull. 66, No. 6 (June 1980)

MELTZER, A., 'U.S. Policy in the Bretton Woods Era', 5th Annual Homer Jones Memorial Lecture of Washington University on 8 April 1991, reprinted in *Federal Reserve Bank of St. Louis Review* (May/June 1991)

Membership of State Banking Institutions in the Federal Reserve System: Rules for Practice for Hearings; Prompt Corrective Action, 57 Fed. Reg. 29,226 (codified at 12 C.F.R., Pts 208 and 263) (proposed 1 July 1992)

MENGLE, D., 'The Case for Interstate Branch Banking', *Federal Reserve Bank of Richmond Economic Review* 76, No. 6 (1990)

MEULENDYKE, A., 'U.S. Monetary Policy and Financial Markets', in M.A. Akhtar, *Understanding Open Market Operations*, Federal Reserve Bank of New York (1997)

MULLINEAUX, D., 'Monetary Rules and Contracts: Why Theory loses to Practice', *Business Review* (Federal Reserve Bank of Philadelphia, March–April 1985)

PEEK AND ROSENGREN, 'The Capital Crunch in New England', *Federal Reserve Bank of Boston New England Economic Review* (May/June 1992)

PEEK AND ROSENGREN, 'Will Legislated Early Intervention Prevent the Next Banking Crisis?', Working Paper Series, No. 96-5, Federal Reserve Bank of Boston (1996)

Permanent Assistance Program for Continental Illinois National Bank and Trust Company, PR-87-84 (26 July 1984)

PETERSEN, YUCEL AND PHILLIPS, 'The Texas Construction Sector: The Tail That Wagged The Dog', *Federal Reserve Bank of Dallas Economic Review* (Second Quarter 1994)

PUTNAM, B., 'Early-Warning Systems and Financial Analysis in Bank Monitoring', *Federal Reserve Bank of Atlanta Economic Review* 68 (November 1983)

RANDALL, R., 'Can the Market Evaluate Asset Quality Exposure in Banks', Federal Reserve Bank of Boston New England Economic Review (July/August 1989)

REIFSCHNEIDER, TETLOW AND WILLIAMS, 'Aggregate Disturbances, Monetary Policy and the Macroeconomy: The FRB/US Perspective', *Federal Reserve Bulletin* (January 1999)

ROSENBERG AND GIVEN, 'Financially Troubled Banks: Private Solutions and Regulatory Alternatives', 104 Banking L.J. 284 (1987)

SCHMIDT, R., 'The Effect of Price Expectations on Drilling Activity', *Federal Reserve Bank of Dallas Economic Review* (November 1984)

SHAFFER, S., 'Inferring Viability of the U.S. Banking Industry from Shifts in Conduct and Excess Capacity', *Proceedings of the Conference on Bank Structure and Competition*, Federal Reserve Bank of Chicago (May 1994)

SHAFFER AND PICHÉ, 'Brokered Deposits and Bank Soundness: Evidence and Regulatory Implications', Federal Reserve Bank of New York Research Paper, No. 8405 (1984)

SHORT, E., 'FDIC Settlement Practices and the Size of Failed Banks', *Federal Reserve Bank of Dallas Economic Review* (March 1985)

SHORT AND ROBINSON, 'Deposit Insurance Reform in the Post-FIRREA Environment: Lessons from the Texas Deposit Market', Federal Reserve Bank of Dallas Financial Industries Working Paper (December 1990)

SIEGMAN, C., 'The Bank for International Settlements and the Federal Reserve', *Federal Reserve Bulletin* (October 1984)

SIMONS AND CROSS, 'Do Capital Markets Predict Problems in Large Commercial Banks?', *Federal Reserve Bank of Boston New England Economic Review* (May/June 1991)

THOMPSON. J., 'Using Market Incentives to Reform Bank Regulation and Federal Deposit Insurance', Econ. Rev., Fed. Reserve Bank of Cleveland, First Quarter 1990
TODD, W., 'An Insider's View of the Political Economy of the Too Big to Fail Doctrine', Working Paper 9017, Federal Reserve Bank of Cleveland (1990)
TRUMAN, E., 'The Mexican Peso Crisis: Implications for International Finance', 82 Fed. Res. Bull. 199 (March 1996)
VOLCKER, P., 'The Political Economy of the Dollar, *Federal Reserve Bank of New York Quarterly Review* (Winter 1978 1979)
WALL, L., 'Too Big to Fail After FDICIA', Fed. Reserve Bank of Atlanta Econ. Rev. 78, No. 1 (January/February 1993)
WHALEN AND THOMSON, 'Using Financial Data to Identify Changes in Bank Conditions', *Federal Reserve Bank of Cleveland Economic Review* 24 (Quarter 2, 1988)
ZIMMERMAN, G., 'Factors Influencing Community Bank Performance in California', *Federal Reserve Bank of San Francisco Economic Review*, No. 1 (1996)
'Principal-Agent Problems in Commercial Bank Failure Decisions', Working Paper 9106, Federal Reserve Bank of Cleveland (April 1991)
'The (Declining?) Role of Banking', *Proceedings of the Conference on Bank Structure and Competition* (May 1994)
'An Examination of Bank Failure Misclassifications Using the Cox Model', *Proceedings of the Conference on Bank Structure and Competition* (Federal Reserve Bank of Chicago, May 1987)
Comment Letter from William W. Wiles, Secretary of the Board of Governors of the Federal Reserve System (26 February 1985)
'Citicorp', 68 *Federal Reserve Bulletin* 656 (1982)
'Deposit-Institution Failures: A Review of the Empirical Literature', *Federal Reserve Bank of Cleveland Economic Review* 27 (March 1991)
'Silver Prices and the Adequacy of Federal Action in the Marketplace: 1979–1980', Hearing Before the House Subcommittee on Government Operations (31 March–22 May 1980) (reports to the Federal Reserve and SEC)

11. FFEIC

Annual Reports (1979–1991)
Country Exposure Report (December 1982)
'Capital Trends in Federally Regulated Financial Institutions', 1980
'FFIEC Notice of June 17, 1981', 46 Fed. Reg. 32,948, 23 June 1981

12. Financial Accounting Standards Board

Accounting Principles Board Opinion No. 17 (1970)
Accounting Standards, 'Original Pronouncements' (July 1973–1 June 1989)
FASB, Statement of Financial Accounting Standards No. 15
SFAS No. 72, Statement of Concepts No. 72, 'Accounting for Certain Acquisitions of Banking or Thrift Institutions' (February 1983)
Statement of Accounting Standards No. 5, 'Accounting for Contingencies'

13. *FRBSF Weekly Letter*

KEELEY AND ZIMMERMAN, 'The Big Switch' (14 June 1985)

NEUBERGER AND ZIMMERMAN, 'The California Deposit Rate Mystery' (27 January 1989)

POZDENA, R., 'Why Home Prices Don't Fall (Much)' (4 January 1991)

SCHMIDT AND SHERWOOD-CALL, 'California's Recent Performance' (17 August 1990)

SHERWOOD, CALL, C., 'The Silicon Valley Economy' (29 May 1992)

ZIMMERMAN, G., 'The Growing Presence of Japanese Banks' (28 October 1988)

ZIMMERMAN, G., 'California's Community Banks in the 1990s' (26 January 1996)

'Economic Impacts of Military Base Closings and Realignments?' (8 August 1993)

'Geographic Deposit Competition' (6 September 1985)

'Small California Banks Hold Their Own' (26 January 1990)

'What's Happening to Southern California?' (21 August 1992)

'Whither California?' (8 August 1993)

14. *General Accounting Office*

'Bank and Thrift Criminal Fraud: The Federal Commitment Could Be Broadened', GAO/GGD-93-48 (1993)

'Bank and Thrift Regulation: Implementation of FDICIA's Prompt Regulatory Action Provisions', GAO/GGD-97-18 (November 1996)

'Bank and Thrift Regulation: Improvements Needed in Examination Quality and Regulatory Structure', GAO/AFMD-93-15 (Washington, DC, February 1993)

'Bank Insider Activities: Insider Problems and Violations Indicate Broader Management Deficiencies', GAO/GGD-94-88 (1994)

'Bank Supervision: OCC's Supervision of the Bank of New England Was Not Timely or Forceful', GAO/GGD-91-128 (September 1991)

'Bank Supervision: Prompt and Forceful Regulatory Actions Needed', GAO/GGD-91-69 (Washington, DC, April 1991)

'Deposit Insurance: A Strategy for Reform', GAO/GGD-91-26 (Washington, DC, March 1991)

'Deposit Insurance: Overview of Six Foreign Systems', GAO/NS1AD-91-104 31 (1991)

'Deposit Insurance Funds: Analysis of Insurance Premium Disparity Between Banks and Thrifts', GAO/AIMD-95-94 (1995)

'Examination of the Federal Savings and Loan Insurance Corporation's Financial Statements For the Years Ended December 31, 1984 and 1983' (1985)

'Failed Banks: Accounting and Auditing Reforms Urgently Needed', GAO/AFMD-91-43 (1991)

'Failed Banks: FDIC Documentation of CrossLand Savings FSB, Decision was Inadequate', GAO/GGD-92-92 (1992)

'Failed Thrifts: Bank Board's 1988 Texas Resolutions', GAO-GGD-89-59 (1989)

'Failed Thrifts: Internal Control Weaknesses Create an Environment Conducive to Fraud, Insider Abuse and Related Unsafe Practices', GAO/T-AFMD-89-46 (22 March 1989)
'FDIC Oversight of 1988 Deals Needs Improvement', GAO/T-GGD-90-93 (1990)
'Financial Crisis Management, GAO Staff Study', GAO/GGD-97-96 (1997)
'Financial Audit: Resolution Trust Corporation's 1995 and 1994 Financial Statements', GAO/GGD-96-123 (July 1996)
'Financial Crisis Management: Four Financial Crises in the 1980s', GAO/GGD-97-96 (May 1997)
'GAO Report to the Chairman', Committee on the Judiciary, U.S. Senate, Bank and Thrift Criminal Fraud B-245890, 8 January 1993
'GAO's Analysis of Bank Board's 1988 Deals', GAO/T-GGD-89-11 (1989)
Government-Sponsored Enterprises: The Government's Exposure to Risk, GAO/GGD-9097 (1990)
'International Financial Crises: Efforts to Anticipate, Avoid, and Resolve Sovereign Crises', GAO/GGD/NSIAD-97-168 (July 1997)
'Mexico's Financial Crisis: Origins, Awareness, Assistance and Initial Efforts to Recover', GAO/GGD-96-56 (February 1996)
'The Need to Improve Auditing in the Savings and Loan Industry', GAO/T-AFMD-89-4 (June 1989)
'The Net Worth Certificate Program and the Condition of the Thrift Industry' (Washington, General Accounting Office, 1985)
'Net Worth Certificate Programs: Their Design, Major Differences and Early Implementation', GAO/GGGD-85-8 (5 November 1984)
'Regulatory Burden: Recent Studies, Industry Issues and Agency Initiatives', GAO/GGD-94-28 (1993)
'Response of the U.S. Department of Justice to the GAO Report', 1 October 1993
'Thrift Failures: Costly Failures Resulted From Regulatory Violations and Unsafe Practices', GAO/AFMC-89-62 (June 1989)
'Thrift Industry: Cost to FSLIC of Delaying Action on Insolvent Savings Associations' (1986)
'Thrift Industry: Forbearance for Troubled Institutions, 1982–1986', Briefing Report to the Chairman, Committee on Banking, Housing and Urban Affairs, United States Senate, GAO/GGD-87-78BR (Washington, May 1987)
'Thrift Industry: Net Worth and Income Capital Certificates' (1986)
'Thrift Resolutions: RTC Policies and Practices Did Not Fully Comply with Least-Cost Provisions', GAO/GGD-94-110 (June 1994)
'Thrifts and Houston Finance: Implications of a Stricter Qualified Thrift Lender Test' (1991)
'Troubled Financial Institutions: Solutions to the Thrift Industry Problem', GAO/GGD-89-47 (1989)

15. *Joint Committee on Taxation*

'Current Tax Rules Relating to Financially Troubled Savings and Loan Associations (JCS 3-89) (16 February 1989)

16. *National Commission on Financial Institution Reform, Recovery and Enforcement*

Black, W., ADC Lending, Staff Report No. 2 (1993)
Black, W., Examination/Supervision/Enforcement of S&Ls, 1979–1992, Staff Report No. 4 (1993)
Institute for Strategy Development, The Role of Congress and the Executive Branch in the S&L Crisis: System, Structure and Signals Unremarked, Consultant Study No. 4 (1992)
Origins and Causes of the S&L Debacle: A Blueprint for Reform, A Report to the President and Congress of the United States' (Washington, DC, July 1993)
'Cash Cow', Examples, Staff Report No. 6 (1993)

17. *Office of the Comptroller of the Currency*

Bank Failure: An Evaluation of the Factors Contributing to the Failure of National Banks (1988)
Bank Letters BL-12-86 (March 27, 1986), BL-15-86 (April 11, 1986) and BL-24-87 (9 July 1987)
Bulletin BB-89-39 (13 December 1989)
Comment Letter from H. Joe Selby, Acting Comptroller of the Currency (22 July 1985)
Haskins and Sells Study: 1974–1975 (1975)
'Joint News Release of the Comptroller of the Currency and Federal Reserve Board', reprinted in 1 Fed. Banking L. Rep. (CCH) P5554A (17 December 1981)
'Joint Press Release of the Comptroller of the Currency and Federal Reserve Board', reprinted in 1 Fed. Banking L. Rep. (CCH) P5461 (13 June 1983)
Major Issues Affecting the Financial Services Industry (1988 and 1989)
Minimum Capital Ratios, 49 Fed. Reg. 34,838 (1984) (codified at 12 C.F.R., Pt 3) (proposed 3 September 1984)
Minimum Capital Ratios, 50 Fed. Reg. 10,207 (1985) (codified at 12 C.F.R., Pts 3 and 7)
Minimum Capital Ratios: Risk-Based Capital Standards for National Banks, 51 Fed. Reg. 10,602 (1986) (to be codified at 12 C.F.R., Pt 3)
OCC Banking Circular 195 (1 May 1985)
OCC Banking Circular 225 (21 December 1987)
OCC Banking Circular 229 (May 1985)
OCC Examining Circular 234 (30 October 1995)
OCC Quarterly Journal (1981–1999)
Office of the Comptroller of the Currency, Board of Governors of the Federal Reserve System and FDIC, Joint News Release (17 May 1984)
Permanent Assistance Program for Continental Illinois National Bank and Trust Company, PR-87-84 (26 July 1984)
Prompt Corrective Action, 57 Fed. Reg. 29,808 (1992) (codified at 12 C.F.R., Pts 6 and 19) (proposed 7 July 1992)
Stiller, J., 'OCC Bank Examination: A Historical Overview' (1995)
Uniform Guidelines for Real Estate Appraisal Policies for National Banks and OCC Advisory 90.2 (8 February 1990) regarding Real Estate Project and Development Lending by all national banks

18. Office of Thrift Supervision

'Capital Adequacy: Guidance on the Status of Capital and Accounting Forbearances and Capital Instruments Held by a Deposit Insurance Fund, Thrift Bulletin No. 38-2, 9 January 1990

Financial Institutions Reform, Recovery and Enforcement Act of 1989: Bibliography (1993)

Regulatory Capital: Prompt Corrective Action, 57 Fed. Reg. 29,826 (1992) (codified at 12 C.F.R., Pt 565) (proposed 7 July 1992)

Thrift Bulletin 35 (26 October 1989)

19. President's Economic Council

Economic Report of the President: 1984 (1984)

20. Securities and Exchange Commission

The Silver Crisis (Washington, DC, October 1982)

21. US President

Blueprint for Reform: The Report of the Task Group on Regulation of Financial Services (1984)

The Report of the President's Commission on Financial Structure and Regulation, Hunt Commission Report (1971)

The Report of the President's Inter-Agency Task Force on Regulation Q (1979) (on file with author)

22. Miscellaneous

Cohen, Henry, 'Federal Deposit Insurance Corporation Assistance to an Insured Bank on the Ground That the Bank is Essential in Its Community', Congressional Research Service, Library of Congress (1984)

Conference of State Bank Supervisors, A Profile of State-Chartered Banking (1977–1994)

Havens and Prakash, 'Real Estate – A California Perspective', California Department of Banking Working Paper (May 2, 1990)

Resolution Trust Corporation, Annual Report (1991)

Resolution Trust Corporation, Open Bank Assistance: A Study of Government Assistance to Troubled Banks from the RFC to the Present, Working Paper (May 1990)

Resolution Trust Corporation, Statistical Abstract (August 1989/September 1995)

U.S. League of Savings Institutions, S&L Fact Book 1976 (1976)

U.S. League of Saving Institutions, Annual Report (1980–1994)

B. Non US and International

1. The Bank Of England

Cork, Sir Kenneth, GBE, Chairman, Report of the Review Committee, Insolvency Law and Practice, (London: HMSO, 1990)

'A Method of Quantifying Companies Relative Financial Strength', D.A.J. Marais, Bank of England Discussion Paper No. 4 (1979)

'Secondary Banking Crisis and the Bank of England's Support', 18 Bank of England Q. Bull No. 2, 230 (June 1978)

'The Supervision of the UK Banking System', 15 Bank of England Q. Bull No. 2, 190 (June 1975)

2. *Bank for International Settlements*

Annual Reports (1966–91)

Recent Innovations in International Banking (Cross Report) (1986) (for G-10)

Reports on the International Financial Architecture (October 1998) (available at <http://www/bis.org/publ/othp01.html>) (Reports of the Working Groups on 'Transparency and Accountability, Strengthening Financial Systems;' and 'International Financial Crises', respectively)

3. *The Basle Committee on Banking Supervision*

Core Principle for Effective Banking Supervision (1997)

Final Report on International Convergence of Capital Measurement and Capital Standards (15 July 1988)

The Implementation of the Basle Concordat, Practical Aspects of International Collaboration between Banking Supervisory Authorities (with Offshore Group of Banking Supervisors) (Aug. 1987)

Joint Press Statement of the Basle Committee and IOSCO Technical Committee (27 July 1994), with accompanying Basle Committee, Risk Management Guidelines for Derivatives (July 1994)

Management of Banks' Off-Balance-Sheet Exposures, The: A Supervisory Perspective (1986), Deposit protection schemes in the Group of Ten countries (including Luxembourg and Switzerland)

Minimum Standards for the Supervision of International Banking Groups and their Cross-border Establishments (June 1992)

Prudential Supervision of Netting, Market Risks and Interest Rate Risk, The Consultative Proposal (April 1993)

Report on International Development in Banking Supervision, Report No. 9 (Sept. 1994), Basle Committee on Banking Supervision Supervisory Cooperation in Crisis Situations and Co-ordination of National Measure for the Liquidation of an EU Banking Group by the Contact Group of EU Banking Supervisory Authorities 1992–1993

Supplement to the Concordat – The Ensuring of Adequate Information Flows between Banking Supervisory Authorities (April 1990)

4. *European Communities/European Union*

Commission Recommendation of 22, 12, 86 (87/63/EEC) Concerning the Introductory of Deposit Guaranty Schemes in the Community (OJ L33 4,2,87, p. 16)

EEC Second Council Directive of 15 December 1989 on the coordination of laws, regulations and administrative provisions relating to the taking up and pursuit of the business of credit institutions and amending Directive 77/780/EEC, OJ L. 386/1, 1989

EEC Council Directive of 17 April 1989 on the own funds of credit institutions, OJ L 142/16, 1989; modified by Directive 91/633/EEC, OJ L 339/33, 1991; modified by Directive 92/16 EEC, OJ L 75/48, 1992.
EEC Council Directive of 18 December 1989 on a solvency ration for credit institutions, OJ L 386/14, 1989. Commission Directive of 19 December 1990 adapting the technical definition of 'multilateral development banks' in Council Directive 89/647/EEC of 18 December 1989 on a solvency ration for credit institutions, OJ L 17/20, 1991.
EEC Council Second Directive of 6 April 1992 on the supervision of credit institutions on a consolidated basis, OJ L 110/52, 1992.

5. *Group of Ten*

'Financial Stability in Emerging Market Countries: A Strategy for the Formulation, Adoption and Implementation of Sound Principles and Practices to Strengthen Financial Systems' (April 1997)
'International Capital Movements and Foreign Exchange Markets: A Report to the Ministers and Governors by the Group of Deputies' (April 1993)
'The Resolution of Sovereign Liquidity Crises' (Basle, Switzerland) (May 1996)

6. *Group of Seven*

Report of G7 Finance Ministers to the Koln Economic Summit, Cologne, Germany (18–20 June 1999) (available at <http://www/library.utoronto.ca/g7/finance/fm061999.html>).

7. *Group of Thirty*

CORRIGAN, E., 'The Financial Disruptions of the 1980s: A Central Banker Looks Back' (Washington, DC, 1993)
DEANE AND PRINGLE, 'Economic Cooperation from the Inside' (1984)
KENEN AND PACK, 'Exchange Rates, Domestic Prices and the Adjustment Process' (Occasional Paper No. 1, New York, 1980)
KRAFT, J., 'The Mexican Rescue' (New York, June 1984)
ROOSA, R., 'The United States and Japan in the International Monetary System: 1946–1985' (New York, 1986)
ROOSA, R., *ET AL.*, 'Reserve Currencies in Transition' (New York, 1982)
'The Problem of Exchange Rates', A Policy Statement (1982)

8. *IMF/World Bank*

ALEXANDER, TOMAS AND ENOCH (EDS), The Adoption of Indirect Instruments of Monetary Policy, IMF Occasional Paper, No. 126 (Washington: International Monetary Fund, 1995)
ALEXANDER AND CARAMAZZA, 'Money Versus Credit: The Role of Banks in the Monetary Transmission Process', in Frameworks for Monetary Stability (Washington: International Monetary Fund, 1994)
BENNATHAN AND THOMPSON, 'Privatization Problems at the Industry Level' (World Bank Discussion Paper 182, 1992)

BERG, J., 'The Nordic Bank Crisis – Lessons to Be Learned' (unpublished, Washington: International Monetary Fund (July 1995)

BORISH, LONG AND NOEL, 'Restructuring Banks and Enterprises: Recent Lessons from Transition Countries' (World Bank Discussion Paper 279, Washington, DC, 1995)

CAPRIO, FOLKERTS-LANDAU AND LANE, EDS, 'Building Sound Finance In Emerging Market Economies' (Washington, IMF and World Bank, 1994)

CAPRIO AND KLINGEBIEL, 'Bank Insolvency: Bad Luck, Bad Policy or Bad Banking?' (Presented to the World Bank Annual Conference on Development Economics, 1996)

CHAMLEY AND HONOHAN, 'Taxation of Financial Intermediation: Measurement Principles and Application to Five African Countries' (World Bank Policy Research Working Paper 421 1990)

CLAESSENS, S., 'Banking Reform in Transition Countries' (Background Paper for the 1996 World Development Report, mimeo, 1996)

DE JUAN, A., 'Does Bank Insolvency Matter? And What to Do About It?', Economic Development Institute of the World Bank Working Paper (Washington: Economic Development Institute of the World Bank, 1991)

DREES AND PAZARBASIOGLU, 'The Nordic Banking Crises: Pitfalls in Financial Liberalization', IMF Working Paper 95/61 (Washington, International Monetary Fund, June 1995)

FISCHER, S., 'On the Need For An International Lender of Last Resort' (IMF: January 1999) (available at <http://www.imf.org/external/np/speeches/1999/010399.html>).

GOLD, J., Exchange Rates in International Law and Organization, IMF (1988)

GOLDSTEIN AND OTHERS (1993a), 'International Capital Markets: Part I: Exchange Rate Management and International Capital Flows', World Economic and Financial Surveys (Washington: International Monetary Fund, 1993)

GRAY AND ASSOCIATES, 'Evolving Legal Frameworks for Private Sector Development in Central and Eastern Europe' (World Bank Discussion Paper 1993)

GRAY, C., 'Summary of Research Proposal: Bankruptcy Law and Enterprise Restructuring in Hungary' (Internal Proposal at World Bank, 30 September 1993)

HONOHAN AND VITTAS, 'Bank Regulation and the Network Paradigm: Policy Implications for Developing and Transition Economies' (World Bank Policy Research Paper 1996)

JOHNSTON AND PAZARBASIOGLU, 'Linkages Between Financial Variables, Financial Sector Reform and Economic Growth and Efficiency', (IMF WP/95/103, 1995)

LEE AND NELLIS, 'Enterprise Reform and Privatization in Socialist Economies' (World Bank Discussion Paper 104, 1990)

LINDGREN, GARCIA AND SAAL, 'Bank Soundness and Macroeconomic Policy' (International Monetary Fund, 1997)

MASSON AND MUSSA, 'The Role of the IMF: Financing and Its Interactions with Adjustment and Surveillance' (Washington, DC, 1995)

MATHIESON AND HAAS, 'Establishing Monetary Control in Financial Systems with Insolvent Institutions', Staff Papers, International Monetary Fund, Vol. 42 (March 1995)
NELLIS, J., 'Improving the Performance of Soviet Enterprises' (World Bank Discussion Paper 1990)
ROJAS-SUAREZ AND WEISBROD, 'Financial Fragilities in Latin America' (IMF Occasional Paper, 1995)
SAK AND SCHIFFMAN, 'Bankruptcy Law Reform In Eastern Europe' (Private Paper in the Legal Department of the IMF, 1994)
SHENG, A. (ED.), 'Bank Restructuring: Lessons from the 1980s' (World Bank, Washington, DC, 1996)
TANZI, V., Transition to Market (International Monetary Fund, 1993)
TENCONI, R., 'Restructuring of the Banking System in Guinea', World Bank, mimeo (1988)
WALLICH, C., 'Russian and the Challenge of Fiscal Federalism' (World Bank Discussion Paper 1990)
WIJNBERGEN, S., 'On the Role of Banks in Enterprise Restructuring: The Polish Example' (Private Paper prepared with the support of The World Bank, 4 October 1993)
'Aspects of the International Banking Safety Net', Occasional Paper No. 23, William *et al.* (1983)
Bank Failure: An Evaluation of the Factors Contributing to the Failure of National Banks (Washington, June 1988)
'Capital Requirements for Commercial Banks: A Survey of the Issues', Staff Paper by Short (1978)
'Deposit Insurance: Theory and Practice', Staff Paper by McCarthy (1980)
'The Economy of the USSR', published by The World Bank, International Monetary Fund, Organisation for Economic Co-Operation and Development and the European Bank for Reconstruction and Development (1990)
'The Financial Crisis in Emerging Markets: Lessons for Eastern Europe and Asia', Stanley Fischer, First Deputy Managing Director of the International Monetary Fund, Comments at East/West Institute, New York (23 April 1999) (available at <http://www.imf.org/external/np/speeches/1999/042399.html>)
'Russia, The Banking System during Transition'(World Bank Country Study, 1993)

9. OECD/United Nation

2 UNTS 30. 60 Stat. 1401 (27 December 1945)
Banks Under Stress (1992)
PECCHIOLI, R., Internationalization of Banking: The Policy Issues (OECD) 1983 and Prudential Supervision in Banking (OECD, 1987)
Report of the Task Force of the Executive Committee on Economic and Social Affairs of the United Nations, 'Towards a New International Financial Architecture' (United Nations, 21 January 1999) (available at http://www.un.org/esa/coordination/ifa.html)
United Nations Executive Committee on Economic and Social Affairs, 'Towards a New International Financial Architecture' (January 1999) (available at <http://www.un.org/esa/coordination/ifa.html>)

Index

AD & C loans
  thrift industry, and 91–92
Amortization
  goodwill, and 86
Appraised equity capital
  thrift industry, and 82–83
Asset-value deflation
  'credit crunch', and 255
  effects 254–255
  reregulation, and 172–173
  Tax Reform Act 1986, and 176

Bank capital
  prompt corrective action
    FDICIA, and 249–251
Bank capital requirements 107–109
  evolution 107–109
  'subordinated debt' 108
Bank powers, expansion of 103–107
  jurisdictional debate 105–107
  motivation behind 104–106
Bank regulation
  FDICIA, and 251–253
Banking agency deregulation and
    forbearance 99–119
  bank entry 99–101
  brokered deposits as sources of
    funding, and 101–103
  capital requirements 107–109
  see also Bank capital requirements
  chartering process 99–101
  differences in bank-thrift capital
    requirements 117–118
  expansion of bank powers,
    and 103–107
  see also Bank powers, expansion of
  LDC debt crisis 109–115
  see also LDC debt crisis
  off-balance sheet activities,
    and 115–116
  Penn Square Bank failure 101–103
  risk-based capital
    requirements 115–117
  state banking agency
    deregulation 118–119
Banking crisis 164
  legislation 6–7
  roots of 3–4
Bretton Woods system
  breakdown of 3
Brokered deposits
  Bush Administration 189–190
  Penn Square Bank failure,
    and 101–103

Capital adequacy
  FDICIA, and 243–248
Capital credits
  thrift industry, and 87
Carter Administration
  'benign neglect' 8
Commercial real estate 121–141
  aggressive loans 122
  boom 121–123
  'boom-bust' scenario 122
  cyclical nature of industry 121
  demand for 121
  non-recourse financing 131
  policy risk 122
  real estate appraisals 127–131
  see also Real estate appraisals
  risks 121–122
  values 123–127
  see also US real estate values
Comparables
  real estate appraisal, and 128
Competitive Equality Banking Act
  1987 176–182
  background 176–178
  continuing thrift crisis,
    and 181–182
  distressed and failed banking organi-
    zations and thrift institutions 181

FSLIC recapitalization, and 178–181
Thrift Industry Recovery Act 180
Continental Illinois National Bank 47–48,150–154
actions of banking agencies, and 153
bailout 152
growth strategy 150–151
liquidity crisis 47
non-preparing loans 151
policy implications 152
Cracks in the banking and financial system 37–50
abandonment of monetarist operating technique 46–47
FHLBB 49–50
Crime Control Act 1990 215–218
additional tools to combat fraud 216–217
effect 215
freezing of assets 215
General Accounting Office, and 217–218
Criminalization
move to 215–218
Critique of external evaluations 271–275
future change 275–277

Decreased leverage 236–237
Deposit disintermediation
Regulation Q, and 4–5
Deposit insurance coverage
DIDMCA, and 15–16
DIDMCA 11–21
background to 11–12
deposit insurance coverage, and 15–16
effect on monetary policy operations 20–21
effects 63–67
expansion of permissible activities 16–17
expansion of thrift powers 16–17
impact on balance sheet of thrift institution 66–67
key provisions 12
monetary conditions following 28–29
NOW accounts 15–16
removal of Regulation Q interest rate ceilings 13–15
reserve requirements 12–13
state usury laws, pre-emption of 17–20
thrift industry, and 73–74
Dollar
appreciation 136–137, 148–149, 150, 156–157, 158–159
decline 140–141
exchange rate policies, and 149
Drysdale Securities (May 1982) 42–43

Emergency acquisitions
Garn-St Germain Act 55–57
ERTA 28–36
effects 63–67
impact of 30–31
monetary and exchange rate conditions following 31–36
provisions affecting real estate 29–30
superdollar, beginnings of 32–33
Exchange rate and monetary policy in 1985 158–159
Exchange rates
Reagan Administration, and 136–138

Fair value
definition 232–234
FDIC
Penn Square Bank, and 44–46
powers to assist distressed institutions 54–58
FDIC Report on US banking crisis 271–274
adequate funding 272
alternative resolution methods 272
early problem identification 271–272
effect of conclusions 271
effect of statutory rules 273
regulatory agencies 273
regulatory forms 273
FDICIA 241–257
background 241–242
bank capital and prompt corrective action 249–251
bank regulation, and 251–253
examinations 251
safety and soundness standards 251
brokered deposits 252
capital adequacy, and 243–248
classifications 244–245
adequately capitalized 244

critically undercapitalized 245
significantly undercapitalized 245
undercapitalized 244
well-capitalized 244
deposit insurance reform 252
PCA intervention mandates 245–247
affirmative actions 246–247
appointment of receiver 247
operation restrictions 246
problematic aspects 247–248
'prompt corrective action' 243–244
rationale 242–243
state-chartered vs. federally chartered banks 25
'too big to fail' policy 252–253
uniform standards for real estate lending 252
Federal Home Loan Bank Board (FHLBB)
support for emergency acquisition provisions 49–50
FHLBB Memorandum R-49 79–81
FHLBB reregulation 170–173
asset value deflation, and 172–173
calendar year 1985 170–171
calendar year 1986 171
calendar year 1987 172
FHLBB Southwest Plan 182–190
consolidation of insolvent thrifts 185
effects 187–190
goodwill, and 183
implications 187–190
initial FSLIC Note 186
insolvency of FSLIC, and 188
'loss coverage' 186–187
political parties, and 189
rationale for transactions 183–184
structure of transactions 184–185
tax-free basis of arrangements 188
unassumed Obligations 185–186
FIRREA 191–218
accounting compliance 194–199
affirmative corrective actions 205
capital requirements 194–199
cease and desire orders 205
burden of proof 205–206
civil money penalties 207–208
concept of institution-affiliated party 204–205
core capital requirement 197
culmination of legislative reregulation in 1980s 191–218
deposit insurance reorganization 200–201
enforcement superpowers 204–209
FDIC enforcement provisions 208–209
Federal Housing Finance Board 193
FHLBB treatment of goodwill 198–199
fraud, and 214–215
genesis 192
goodwill, and 194
impact of capital requirements 197–198
impact on thrift industry 213–215
legislation 1989 191–218
LTV ratios 212–213
material policy deficiencies 198
new capital standards for thrift industry 193–194
objectives in disposition of assets 202
personal liability of director and officers 208
primary objectives 192–193
principal purposes 192
prohibition orders 206–207
qualified thrift lender test 199–200
real estate appraisal standards 212–213
removal orders 206–207
Resolution Trust Corporation (RTC) 193, 201–204
restrictions 209–213
restrictions on thrift activities 209–211
restrictions on thrift subsidiaries, affiliates and insiders 211–212
review of objectives 192–201
subsidiaries of thrift institutions 196
supervision orders 206–207
three separate capital standards 195–196
Fiscal policy
conflict with monetary policy 145–147
FMV
definition 232–234
FOMC meeting May 1982 43
FOMC meeting June 1982 46
FSLIC

powers to assist distressed institutions 54–58
Fraud
FIRREA, and 214–215

G-10 Report of the Working Party on Financial Stability 274–275
Garn-St. Germain Act 1982 51–67
aim 8
backdrop 51–52
diversification of asset holdings 53–54
effects 52, 63–67
emergency acquisitions 55–57
enactment without serious debate 52
FDIC powers to assist distressed institutions 54–58
FSLIC powers to assist distressed institutions 54–58
immediate objective 51–52
impact on balance sheet of thrift institution 66–67
key failure of 52
net worth certificates 57–58
open bank assistance 55
real estate lending provisions 59–63
see also Real estate lending provisions
thrift industry crisis, and 64–65
General Accounting Office
Crime Control Act 1990, and 217–218
Goodwill
accounting interpretations 83–85
amortization, and 86
FIRREA, and 194
supervisory. *See* Supervisory goodwill

Home improvement loan
meaning 62
Home loan
meaning 61–62

ILSA 112–115
aim 113
LDC debt crisis, and 112–115
requirements 113–114
In substance foreclosures 226–228
concept 226
conditions underlying 227
criteria 226–228
Inflation
LDC debt crisis, and 39, 40
Initial FSLIC Note 186
Institution-affiliated party
meaning 204–205
Interest capitalization 228–229
appropriateness 229
concerns arising 228
Interest rates 147–148
discount rate 1983 147–149

LDC debt crisis (February 1982) 37–42, 109–115
capital adequacy requirements, and 114
capital requirements, and 39–40
Fed, and 38–39
ILSA 112–115
Mexico 41
origins 37–38, 110
reduction of inflation, and 39, 40
regulatory forbearance, and 111–112
Legislative deregulation 1980–1982 11–36
DIDMCA. *See* DIDMCA
impact on balance sheet of thrift institution 66–67
Reagan Administration 22–25
see also Reagan Administration
US economy, and 65
Lesser developed nations. *See* LDC debt crisis
Lessons to be learned from crises of 1980s 262–270
coordination and sequencing of legislative, regulatory, monetary and fiscal policies 263
exchange rate neutrality 262–263
government accountability and loss allocation 268–270
legislation, deregulation and asset value inflation 264–265
legislation, reregulation, reactive policy reversals and asset value deflation 266–268
legislative, regulatory and exchange rate forbearance, permissiveness and non-transparency 265–266
monetary and fiscal policies 262–263
political goodwill 264
recognition of linkages between government intervention, asset valuation and bank capital 270

'special relationship' between government and banking systems 264
Leverage
decreased 236–237
Loan origination fees
thrift industry, and 81–82

Mark to market asset value 235–236
Market value
definition 232–234
Mexico
debt crisis 1982 41
default on dollar denominated borrowings 48–50
financial receivership 48
Monetary discipline
1979–1982 143–145
Monetary policy
conflict with fiscal policy 145–147
shifts in 237–239
Monetary policy operations
effect of DIDMCA on 20–21

National banks
real estate lending provisions 59
NCREIF Property Index 124
Net worth certificates
Garn-St Germain Act 57–58
Non-recourse financing
commercial real estate, and 131
NOW accounts
DIDMCA, and 15–16

Open bank assistance
Garn-St Germain Act 55

Penn Square Bank (June 1982) 44–46, 101–103
brokered deposits, and 101–103
emergency funds 44
FDIC solution 44–46
insolvency 44
Plaza Accord 1985 138–139, 140
Political accountability
shifts in 237–239
Post-deregulatory matters 143–168
appreciation of dollar 156–157
banking crises 164
banking priorities 164–166
economic fragility 154–158
end of deregulation era 159–168
government forbearance 154–158
hidden consequences of financial deregulation 156
legislative gridlock 166
monetary priorities 164–166
regulatory capture 164–166
short-term interest rates 155
thrift industry crisis 160–164
Prompt corrective action
FDICIA, and 243–244
Purchase and goodwill
accounting 83–85
FHLBB guidance 83–85

Reagan Administration 22–25
bond market, and 26–27
'deregulation' 8
ERTA. *See* ERTA
Fed monetary policy errors 34–36
floating exchange rates 136–138
legislative deregulation, and 22–25
monetarism 25–27
monetary conditions following DIDMCA 28–29
policy conflicts with Fed 25–27
recession, and 33–34
regulators' bill 23–24
'supply side economics' 8, 22
tax cuts 22–23
Real estate
ERTA provisions affecting 29–30
Real estate appraisals 127–131, 231–234
application of standards on retroactive basis 231–232
appraisals affecting 130–131
comparable values 128
effect of tightening of standards 231–232
fair value
definition 232–234
FMV
definition 232–234
leverage ratio 129
'mark to market' 234
market value
definition 232–234
methods 130
problematic definitions 232–234
psychology of market, and 231
regulation 127–128
standards 130
Real estate lending provisions 59–63
Garn-St Germain Act 59–63
national banks 59

thrift institutions 60–63
aggregate lending limits 60–61
appraisals 61
combination loans 63
home improvement loans 62
home loans 61–62
loan charges 61
loans to acquire or improve real estate 62–63
LTV ratios 60–61
repayment 61
Recession
Reagan Administration, and 33–34
Recharacterization of real estate lending transactions 226–230
in substance foreclosures 226–228
see also In substance foreclosures
interest capitalization 228–229
troubled debt restructurings 229–230
Regulation Q
limitations 4
removal of interest rate ceilings 13–15
Regulatory accounting principles (RAP) 77–79
FHLBB deviations 78–79
inflation of reported capital, and 79–83
thrift industry, and 77–79
Reregulation 135, 167–168, 169–190
AD & C loans, and 220
asset values, and 221–222
background 169–170
beginnings 167–168
Competitive Equality Banking Act 1987 176–182.
see also Competitive Equality Banking Act 1987
cost of funds 234–235
decreased leverage 236–237
effect 219–239
FHLBB. *See* FHLBB reregulation
FHLBB initiatives 167–168
impact on real estate lending practices 222–226
appraisal systems 225–226
data base problems 224
national banks 224–226
project information files 224
real estate marketing and sales 225
real property accounting systems 225
Texas banks 223
thrift industry 223
value enhancement 225
impact on thrift financial operations 219–222
legislative 169–190
mark to market asset value 235–236
monetary policy, shifts in 237–239
political accountability, shifts in 237–239
raising new capital, and 219–220
reclassification of asset regulations 221
restrictions on growth 234–235
supervisory 169–190
Tax Reform Act 1986 173–176
Residential property
meaning 19
Resolution Trust Corporation 201–204
effects 203
General Operating Policies 203
objectives 201–202
responsibilities 201

SFAS No. 72 89–90
State banking agency deregulation 118–119
State usury laws
DIDMCA, and 17–20
Subordinated debt
bank capital requirements 108
Superdollar
beginnings of 32–33
Supervisory goodwill 85–89

Tax Reform Act 1986 173–176
asset value deflation, and 176
effect 174–176
real estate pricing, and 174–175
Texas
collapse in real estate prices 135
Thrift industry 73–97
accounting interpretations 83–90
accounting standards 77–83
AD & C loans 91–92
amortization 86
appraised equity capital 82–83
capital credits 87
capital requirements 75–77
reduction 76–77
deferral of losses on sale of assets 79–81

DIDMCA, and 73–74
differences in bank-thrift
capital requirements 117–118
effects of accounting deviations 89
FHLBB deregulation 73–97
Calendar Year 1981 93–94
Calendar Year 1982 94–95
Calendar Year 1983 95–96
May-December 1980 92–93
FHLBB deregulatory permissiveness 1980–1983 92–96
FHLBB-industry agreements 88–89
FHLBB Memorandum R-49 79–81
five-year averaging
provisions 76–77
FSLIC acquisitions
programs 85–89
inflation of reported capital 79–83
legislation 6–7
legislative proposals 6
loan origination fees 81–82
purchase and goodwill
accounting 83–85
regulatory accounting
principles 77–79
regulatory structure 74–75
roots of crisis 3–4
SFAS No.72 interpretations 89–90
short-term interest rates,
and 96–97
supervisory environment 74–75
supervisory goodwill 85–89

Thrift industry crisis 160–164
consensus points on 161–162
onset of policy reversal 162–164
trigger points of
insolvency 162–164
Thrift Industry Recovery Act 180
Thrift institutions
diversifiction of asset
holdings 53–54
real estate lending provisions.
see Real estate lending provisions
Troubled debt restructurings 229–230
meaning 229
touchstone of 230

US real estate values 123–127
NCREIF Property Index 124–126
rolling 4-quarter returns 125, 126
inflation, and 126

International Banking, Finance and Economic Law

1. J.J. Norton, Chia-Jui Cheng and I. Fletcher (eds): *International Banking Regulation and Supervision: Change and Transformation in the 1990s*. 1994
ISBN 1-85333-998-9

2. J.J. Norton, Chia-Jui Cheng and I. Fletcher (eds): *International Banking Operations and Practices: Current Developments*. 1994
ISBN 1-85333-997-0

3. J.J. Norton: *Devising International Bank Supervisory Standards*. 1995
ISBN 1-85966-1858

4. Sir Joseph Gold: *Interpretation: The IMF and International Law*. 1996
ISBN 90-411-0887-4

5. R. Smits: *The European Central Bank: Institutional Aspects*. 1997
ISBN 90-411-0686-3

6. M. Andenas, L. Gormley, C. Hadjiemmanuil and I. Harden (eds): *European Economic and Monetary Union: The Institutional Framework*. 1997
ISBN 90-411-0687-1

7. T. Wan: *Development of Banking Law in the Greater China Area: PRC and Taiwan*. 1999
ISBN 90-411-0948-X

8. R.P. Buckley: *Emerging Markets Debt: An Analysis of the Secondary Market*. 1999
ISBN 90-411-9716-8

9. P. Cartwright (ed.): *Consumer Protection in Financial Services*. 1999
ISBN 90-411-9717-6

10. T. Traisorat: *Thailand: Financial Sector Reform and the East Asian Crises*. 1999
ISBN 90-411-9734-6

11. M.I. Steinberg: *International Securities Law: A Contemporary Analysis.* 1999
ISBN 90-411-9738-9

12. M. Giovanoli and G. Heinrich (eds.): *International Bank Insolvencies: A Central Bank Perspective.* 1999
ISBN 90-411-9728-1

13. K.N. Schefer, *International Trade in Financial Services: The NAFTA Provisions.* 1999
ISBN 90-411-9754-0

14. J.J. Norton and Y. Huang (eds), *Financial Regulation in the Greater China Area: PRC, Taiwan and Hong Kong SAR.* 2000
ISBN 90-411-9763-X

15. Y. Shim, *Korean Bank Regulation and Supervision: Crisis and Reform.* 2000
ISBN 90-411-9778-8

16. A. Hudson (ed.), *Modern Financial Techniques, Derivatives and Law.* 2000
ISBN 90-411-9781-8